SUN FATHER'S WAY

Five things alone
are necessary
to the sustenance
and comfort
of the dark ones, the Indians,
among the
children of earth:

The sun, who is the Father of all.
The earth, who is the Mother of men.
The water, who is the Grandfather.
The fire, who is the Grandmother.
Our brothers and sisters the Corn,
*and seeds of growing things.**

*Recorded by Cushing, 1920:19. Mr. Cushing went from the East to Zuñi in 1879 and lived there four and one-half years, becoming a member of the group, dressing, eating, and living as an Indian. He learned to speak Zuñi within a year, and attained an important position in the council. He was adopted into the Pitchikwe clan; and in 1881 was initiated into the Bow priesthood, where he held high offices. He was at Zuñi for the last time in 1888, and he died in 1900.

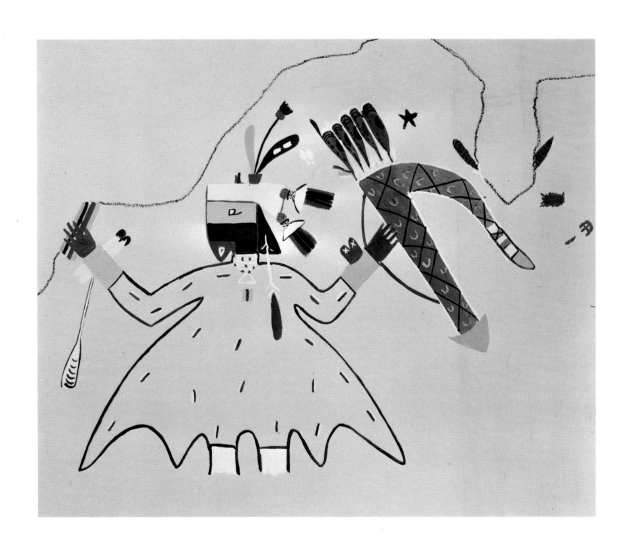

UNIVERSAL DEITY.
Figure 54. *Layer H-31.*

SUN FATHER'S WAY

THE KIVA MURALS OF KUAUA

A PUEBLO RUIN
CORONADO STATE MONUMENT
NEW MEXICO

BERTHA P. DUTTON

THE UNIVERSITY OF NEW MEXICO PRESS   ALBUQUERQUE

THE SCHOOL OF AMERICAN RESEARCH   SANTA FE

MUSEUM OF NEW MEXICO PRESS   SANTA FE

To the People
who have dwelt in this land
from the long distant past unto this day
believing that
man should so live as to be in harmony with nature
this book is respectfully dedicated

FOREWORD

THE WORD *ARCHAEOLOGY* has in the minds of many, perhaps most people, something of a magical connotation. The archaeologist himself labors long and hard, frequently under difficult or dangerous circumstances, in the hope of making some truly important discovery. More often than not the work, although always making some aspects of a bygone culture more meaningful and supplying a few more chapters of the story of mankind through the ages, results in nothing of breathtaking significance.

During the excavations at the ruin site known as Kuaua, on the west bank of the Rio Grande near Bernalillo, New Mexico, routine digging was under way in the south plaza, preparatory to bringing a phase of the work to its conclusion. Suddenly, dull toil shifted to alert interest. With the dirt thrown onto a wheelbarrow, there appeared fragments of plaster covered with flecks of color. The archaeologist in charge began careful investigation with a small trowel, soon revealing the outstretched fingers of an upraised hand painted on the wall of a subterranean chamber. Interest changed to excitement. Then a grotesquely masked head was brought to view, and finally an entire figure. This proved to be one of many depictions painted on the wall of a square room. There was not one decorated surface only, but evidence of many similar ones.

This was all very provocative, and it was soon realized that the archaeologists working at Kuaua had unearthed materials of great cultural value. In an attempt to present these mural paintings in their proper perspective, the following chapters will review briefly the history of the region and of the excavations conducted, will treat of the Kuaua paintings themselves, and will indicate something of how they may be ethnologically interpreted.

ACKNOWLEDGMENTS

In the first place, this book owes much to the interest and coordinated research provided by Hulda R. Hobbs (Mrs. Finis L. Heidel) and by Agnes C. Sims, respectively. Their part in the work is elaborated upon in the pages which follow.

Secondly, when the manuscript was brought to its initial completion, copies were distributed to a number of my colleagues and associates, seeking their criticisms and suggestions. These good people were so kind as to add this task to their full schedules, and each provided certain ideas for further clarity or improvement of the presentation. It is with sincere appreciation that I acknowledge assistance from these formal critics:

Erik K. Reed, Regional Chief of History and Archaeology, Southwest Region, National Park Service, Santa Fe, New Mexico. His familiarity with Southwestern history and extensive knowledge of all aspects of archaeology made him, as the first reader of the manuscript, a most effective critic.

Edmund J. Ladd, Archaeologist, City of Refuge, Hawaii, rendered valuable aid with the Zuñi data, as will be seen later.

Watson Smith, archaeologist, who was in charge of the kiva paintings for the Peabody Museum Awatovi expedition, and was author of the definitive publication thereon (see bibliography), and who now is in charge of Peabody Museum West of the Pecos, Tucson, Arizona. He was highly qualified to pass on my work and to suggest certain alterations.

Gordon Vivian, Supervisory Archaeologist, Southwest Archaeological Center, Gila Pueblo, Globe, Arizona, the original supervisor on the Kuaua project, whose knowledge of Southwestern archaeology—particularly of the Anasazi—is almost incomparable, helped clarify certain points.

J. Charles Kelley, Professor of Anthropology and Director of the Museum, Southern Illinois University, Carbondale, Illinois, supervised the excavation of a certain sector at Kuaua. After devoting a number of years to Southwestern archaeology, he has more recently expanded his work to include excavations and research in the states of Durango and Zacatecas, Mexico. He questioned some statements and aided in their resolution.

Loraine (Mrs. George) Lavender, Santa Fe, New Mexico, business woman and civic leader, served as "guinea pig" to determine whether or not a layman might read this work attentively. The fact that she did so with sustained interest, and without benefit of illustrations, was encouraging.

Paul Horgan, author, director of the Center for Advanced Studies at Wesleyan University, and member of the Board of Managers, School of American Research, served as a committee of one for that institution. His skillful pen and fluency with words made him a most helpful reader of this work.

The late Tyler Dingee, master photographer, made painstaking black and white reproductions of the murals portrayed in this publication, and duplicated the color work with great exactness.

In addition to these, the manuscript was also read by Carroll L. Riley, Assistant Professor of Anthropology, Southern Illinois University, Carbondale, Illinois. His specialization is that of ethnology of the Southwest and of northern Mexico, which thus made him particularly alert to statements concerning cultural influences.

Lastly, I gratefully acknowledge the aid and information which I have received from several of my fellow staff members at the Museum of New Mexico.

BERTHA P. DUTTON

TABLE OF CONTENTS

ILLUSTRATIONS

Layer H-31. Fig. 54. Universal Deity. *In color.*　　　　*Frontis*

SUN FATHER'S WAY

BOOK ONE

I. THE SPANIARDS ENTER THE INDIAN WORLD

HISTORICAL BACKGROUND

It is difficult to think of New Mexico, today, without a city of Albuquerque spreading ever more widely from its original plaza near the Rio Grande. But Albuquerque is a modern town,[1] situated in the heart of what was formerly known as the Tiguex province, a region inhabited by sedentary groups of (Tigua or) Tiwa-speaking Indians.[2]

Doubtless, Indian traders and adventure seekers wandered back and forth over the entire Southwestern region and into the areas to

the south, as well as elsewhere, for centuries. Verbal accounts concerning the Indians of the unexplored lands lying to the north found their way into central Mexico and reached the ears of the Spanish conquerors about the third decade of the sixteenth century.[3] By 1535, the Spaniards in Mexico began to hear of the many-storied houses built of stone and adobe, in which the Indians to the north dwelt.

In the spring of 1540, with knowledge gained from Alvar Núñez Cabeza de Vaca[4] and from Friar Marcos de Niza,[5] Francisco Vásquez de Coronado assembled an expeditionary

NOTE: Throughout this work non-English words when first used will show such accents and orthographic signs as may apply. Thereafter, words will appear in usual type, unless appearing otherwise in direct quotations. Use of the Spanish phonetic system will approximate proper pronunciation of Indian words. Since the sound of "n-y" is common in words herein, the character "ñ" is employed, thus Zuñi rather than Zun-yi.

1. It celebrated its 250th anniversary in 1956.
2. The pueblo-dwelling Indians of the Southwest do not constitute tribal groups. Rather, each village functions as an entity, each an aggregate of farming, house-building people, alike in some ways and unalike in others. They speak several languages. Presently, dialects of the Tiwa (Tigua) tongue are spoken at Taos and Picurís, northernmost of the pueblos, and at Sandía and Isleta, near Albuquerque. The Tewa language is used by the people of San Juan, Santa Clara, San Ildefonso, Pojoaque, Nambé, and Tesuque, all to the north of Santa Fe. Jémez, northwest of Albuquerque on Jemez creek, is the only group which speaks Towa, but the same tongue was spoken by the Pecos Indians. Tiwa, Tewa, and Towa are related languages which derive from a common family, the TANOAN. Piro also belonged in this family and was spoken by Indians living down-valley from the southern Tiwa.

The language of Zuñi, used by the Indians located on the Zuñi reservation, southwest of Gallup, New Mexico,

belongs to the ZUÑIAN family. Tanoan and Zuñian appear to have originated in the same parent stock, that known as AZTECO-TANOAN, but the relationship has not been established definitely.

A language known as Keres is spoken with dialectic differences in the other pueblos of New Mexico: Cochití, Santo Domingo, and San Felipe along the Rio Grande, between Albuquerque and Santa Fe; Santa Ana and Zía on Jemez creek; and in Laguna and Acoma, some fifty miles west of Albuquerque. In general, linguists believe that the KERESAN language is quite distinct from any of the more inclusive families of North America.

The Hopi Indians of northeastern Arizona, with exception of those at Hano (whose original tongue was Tano, or southern Tewa, and who now speak both of these Indian tongues), speak a Shoshonean language belonging to the UTO-AZTECAN family of the AZTECO-TANOAN stock.

The location of these linguistic groups in late prehistoric times was probably not very different from the present positions. See Dutton, 1963.

3. See Sauer, 1937:270-273.
4. A member of the ill-fated Narváez expedition, who with three other survivors made his way from the Florida coast to Mexico City, arriving there in 1536. See Hammond and Rey, 1940: 3 ff.
5. Who is commonly credited with having reached the Zuñi region in 1539, and coming within sight of Hawikuh, then the major pueblo.

army at Compostela on the Pacific coast of New Spain, as Mexico was designated. Some 230 well outfitted horsemen, 62 foot soldiers, a company of Indians, and missionaries,[6] started the march on 22 February to conquer the "Seven Cities" of the north. Their destination, the Zuñi villages as we know them, was reached on 7 July of the same year, and Hawikuh was the first occupied by the Spaniards. With Coronado was Pedro de Castañeda de Náxera, most famous of the chroniclers of this expedition, who twenty years later recorded his reminiscences of this area and of the Indians dwelling here.

We frequently fail to comprehend how rapidly news travels among aboriginal peoples, but signals of various sorts, runners, traders, and visitors carry the word of events and gossip with surprising alacrity. There seems to be no doubt that Indians of different provinces watched the progress of the Spanish expeditions into their territories, and passed on the word to neighboring groups. While Coronado was at Zuñi, a party of Indians came there from Pecos (Cicuyé) to offer themselves as friends. They brought gifts of "tanned hides and shields and head pieces." In return, the general gave them "some glass dishes and a number of pearls and little bells which they prized highly." The Pecos Indians told the Spaniards about the bison and "described some cows which, from a picture that one of them had painted on his skin, seemed to be cows. . . ."[7] Resulting from this information, Coronado dispatched Don Hernando de Alvarado from Hawikuh with Fray Juan de Padilla and twenty men toward the east, with the Pecos Indians. The party traveled by way of Acoma and, after ten days, "reached the village and river of Tiguex"—the Rio Grande, on 7 September.[8] They visited the Indian settlements situated along the stream, and Alvarado reported these to be the best villages that had been observed. He advised that winter quarters for the entire force be established here. His suggestion was followed, and García López de Cárdenas, the army master, came on from Hawikuh to make the arrangements. Coronado, himself, after an inspection of the villages along the river further south, arrived in Tiguex, at the pueblo of Coofor,[9] which Lopez de Cardenas called *Alcánfor*. Two other pueblos, Moho (Mohi) and Arenal, are also mentioned as being close to Alcanfor.[10] Mohi is the pueblo which Castañeda called Tiguex.

The Indians met the white men with friendliness, and Lopez de Cardenas secured comfortable quarters for all, in the terraced houses which the Tiwas left plentifully supplied with food. Castañeda says that, in order to accommodate so many, it was necessary for all of the Indians to abandon their pueblo[11] and go to others belonging to their friends. They took nothing with them but the clothes they were wearing.[12] Such friendliness and hospitality could only have been offered by an aboriginal people, unaffected as were the Pueblo Indians at that time.

By late autumn, however, the displaced Tiwas became hostile toward the intruders,

---

6. With some 1500 animals also (Hammond and Rey, 1940:7).

7. Winship, 1896: 490.

8. Winship, 1896:390. *See* Hammond and Rey, 1940:19, 22-23, 219, 253, 331.

9. Hammond and Rey, 1940:326, footnote 9, state, "This pueblo served as the headquarters for the expedition during the two years it remained on the Rio Grande. Tello recorded the name as Coofer and Coofort (*Crónica*, pp. 414-415, 436-437), and Mota Padilla, as Coofer (*Historia*, p. 160):" 347.

10. Hammond and Rey, 1940:220, 333, testimony of Coronado.

11. The Spaniards applied the term *pueblo,* or village, to the multi-house and ceremonial structures in which the aborigines lived; the people themselves they designated as *Pueblo Indians. See* Hammond and Rey, 1940:219, 223, 329.

12. Winship, 1896:492. *Cf.* Hammond and Rey, 1940: 329.

who, one may well believe, became increasingly less welcome. During the severe winter, they demanded more food, warm garments and blankets; they ravished the Indian women;[13] and otherwise abused the gentle acceptance and social practices of the pueblo dwellers. After so much of this, the Indians assumed an aggressive attitude. They killed a number of the army horses and mules, and drove off others to Arenal, which the Spaniards reported was inclosed by a stockade.[14] The whole province was up in arms. The Indians assembled, then, in Arenal and Mohi (Tiguex), two of the strongest villages, where the Spaniards attacked them. Besides open attack the Spaniards used smudge fires to drive out the Indians. At Arenal, a few of the Spaniards, climbing atop the houses, persuaded the Indian warriors to surrender, promising them protection and safety. This promise, however, was unknown to Captain Cardenas and he, under orders that no prisoners were to be taken alive, directed that the captives be burned as a warning to the neighboring villages. Some twenty-five to thirty were burned at the stake. At Mohi, the Indians defied the soldiers of Coronado until thirst forced them to abandon their stronghold. They tried to slip away unnoticed, but Spanish sentries saw them and summoned the soldiers. Many of the Indians were killed, and others drowned in the icy water of the Rio Grande as they tried to flee. The siege lasted fifty days.[15] Other clashes followed these conflicts.

Castañeda relates that as soon as the soldiers had completed reduction of the "refractory natives, and the whole country had been overawed by the terrible punishment, the general undertook to re-establish peaceful relations and confident intercourse between his camp and the surrounding villages."[16] Zia (Chia) was visited by one of Coronado's captains (and given four bronze cannons, in poor condition). There were said to be seven pueblos in the Keres province, though Zia apparently was not recognized as being Keres-speaking. These were visited by other members of the expedition. Another captain with several men went into the Jemez province and noted seven villages; they, too, crossed to Yunque-yungue, which was later to become the seat of Spanish government in New Mexico. There were then two "very fine villages," one on each side of the river (Rio Grande—site of the pueblo of San Juan), and four in the rough mountainous country. The explorers got as far north as Taos. All these Pueblo peoples were at peace. But, Castañeda says that the twelve villages of Tiguex were not repopulated at all during the time the army was there, "in spite of every promise of security that could possibly be given to them."[17] Pecos, at first so friendly toward the Spaniards, became warlike and was "unwilling to make advances toward peace or to give any food to the army."[18]

In April of 1541, Coronado and his full army left the Tiwa region, marching northeastward through the Tano (southern Tewa) pueblos of the Galisteo basin to Pecos and thence to the great plains in search of the fabled Quivira. The withdrawal of the Spanish invaders must have been cause for much relief among the Tiwas; some of their pueblos were reoccupied. But the alleviation of their burden and domination was short lived. The corn which the soldiers had taken from the Tiwas was nearly gone, and their horses were tired and weakened. After weeks of futile searching for the anticipated riches of Quivira,

13. Winship, 1896:495-497. See Hammond and Rey, 1940:23.

14. Hammond and Rey, 1940:24.

15. Winship, 1896:497-501, and Hammond and Rey, 1940:24-25, 225, 227-231, 333, 334, 347-349, 352-363.

16. Winship, 1896:383; see also Hammond and Rey, 1940:353.

17. Winship, 1896:503.

18. Winship, 1896:510.

Coronado held council, with result that all but some thirty select companions were sent back to Tiguex, where they arrived in mid-July. The Tiwas were frightened and left their pueblos again. Before the end of October, Coronado and his party were also at Tiguex, for the second winter. The severe illness of Coronado, hardships without reward for his soldiers, and lack of high adventure or serious conflicts led to the decision to abandon the Pueblo country and to the return of the expedition to Mexico. Early spring of 1542 found the Tiwa villages freed of the soldiers.

Castañeda, in summing up his impression of the Tiguex and surrounding Indian groups, gives us this information:

> In general, these villages all have the same habits and customs, although some have some things in particular which the others have not. They are governed by the opinions of the elders. They all work together to build the villages, the women being engaged in making the mixture and the walls, while the men bring the wood and put it in place. They have no lime, but they make a mixture of ashes, coals, and dirt which is almost as good as mortar, for when the house is to have four stories, they do not make the walls more than half a yard thick. They gather a great pile of twigs of thyme and sedge grass and set it afire, and when it is half coals and ashes they throw a quantity of dirt and water on it and mix it all together. They make round balls of this, which they use instead of stones after they are dry, fixing them with the same mixture, which comes to be like a stiff clay. Before they are married the young men serve the whole village in general, and fetch the wood that is needed for use, putting it in a pile in the courtyard of the villages, from which the women take it to carry to their houses.
>
> The young men live in the estufas [ceremonial rooms or kivas],[19] which are in the yards of the village. They are underground, square or round, with pine pillars. Some were seen with twelve pillars and with four in the center as large as two men could stretch around. They usually had three or four pillars. The floor was made of large, smooth stones, like the baths which they have in Europe. They have a hearth made like the binnacle or compass box of a ship, in which they burn a handful of thyme at a time to keep up the heat, and they can stay in there just as in a bath. The top was on a level with the ground. Some that were seen were large enough for a game of ball. . . . The houses belong to the women, the estufas to the men. . . .
>
> The country is so fertile that they do not have to break up the ground the year round, but only have to sow the seed, which is presently covered by the fall of snow, and the ears come up under the snow . . . . There are a great many native fowl in these provinces, and cocks with great hanging chins [turkeys] . . . .
>
> The villages are free from nuisances, because they go outside to excrete, and they pass their water into clay vessels, which they empty at a distance from the village. They keep the separate houses where they prepare the food for eating and where they grind the meal, very clean. This is a separate room or closet, where they have a trough with three stones fixed in stiff clay. Three women go in here, each one having a stone, with which one of them breaks the corn, the next grinds it, and the third grinds it again. They take off their shoes, do up their hair, shake their clothes, and cover their heads before they enter the door. A man sits at the door playing on a fife while they grind, moving the stones to the music and singing together . . . . They have their preachers. Sodomy is not found among them. They do not eat human flesh nor make sacrifices of it. The people are not cruel . . . . The men here wear little shirts of tanned deerskin and their long robes over this. In

---

19. *Kiva*, the Hopi Indian name of the sacred assembly and lounging chamber; now in general usage by the Pueblo peoples.

all these provinces they have earthenware glazed with antimony and jars of extraordinary labor and workmanship, which were worth seeing.[20]

Captain Juan Jaramillo, another member of the Coronado expedition, adds other information of value. In speaking of the Indians of the same region, he tells us:

[They] have corn and beans and melons, skins, and some long robes of feathers which they braid, joining the feathers with a sort of thread; and they also make them of a sort of plain weaving with which they make the cloaks with which they protect themselves. They all have hot rooms underground, which, although not very clean, are very warm. They raise and have a very little cotton of which they make the cloaks which I have spoken of above.[21]

Coronado, writing to Viceroy Mendoza, makes the statement: "So far as I can find out, the water is what these Indians worship, because they say that it makes the corn grow and sustains their life, and that the only other reason they know is because their ancestors did so."[22]

The Coronado *entrada,* it should be recognized, left an indelible imprint on the Tiwas and other of the Indian peoples in the north. Certain of the friars and lay brothers remained behind,[23] carrying on their missionary work; and many of the Mexican Indians [Tlaxcaltecans?] stayed in the Pueblo country. Several of the latter were noted by Antonio de Espejo

among the Zuñi, in 1583; and it may be expected that they introduced Mexican traits which influenced the Zuñi organizations. It is likewise clear that, henceforth, the endemic cultures of the greater Southwest must have been influenced to varying degrees and increasing intensity by the introductions of European origin, which reached their height during the period 1598-1680, and included: sheep, horses and all the gear pertaining to them; armor, weapons, forms of clothing and ornaments; the ritual and paraphernalia of Christianity—which doubtless called for modified Indian productions such as pottery vessels, vestments, paintings and other decorative devices; perhaps new foods, or at least new food uses and preparations; and numerous non-material features. There were also Negroes and persons of unknown ancestry to add new traits to the Indian cultures, and to bloodstreams.

Doubtless, relatively normal procedures were resumed during the years which followed and gave birth to new generations. By 1581, when Fray Agustín Rodríguez and Captain Francisco Sánchez Chamuscado brought the second Spanish expedition into the north country, such innovations as had persisted from the earlier entrada must have merged with the aboriginal traits so as to then appear "traditional." To this second expedition goes the credit of having connected the name "New Mexico" with that portion of the northland which was occupied by the Pueblo Indians,[24]

20. Winship, 1896:520-522; *see also* Hammond and Rey, 1940:254-256.

21. Winship, 1896:587.

22. Letter, 3 August 1540 (Winship, 1896:552-563).

23. Winship, 1896:400-401: Fray Juan de Padilla was determined to return to the Quivira country, which he first visited with Coronado. "He was accompanied by Andres Docampo [del Campo], a Portuguese . . . besides five Indians, negroes or half-bloods, two 'donados' or lay brethren, Indians engaged in the church service, who came from Michoacan and were named Lucas and Sebastian, a

mestizo or half-blood boy and two other servants from Mexico.

"The friar was successful in his labors until he endeavored to enlarge the sphere of his influence, when the jealousy, or possibly the cupidity, of the Indians led them to kill him, rather than permit the transference to some other tribe of the blessings which he had brought to them."

Docampo and other companions of the friar took the news to Mexico, apparently previous to 1552.

Coronado also left Fray Juan de la Cruz at Tiguex, where he likewise was killed. The friar Luis Descalona [de Escalona] remained at Pecos; his fate is unknown.

24. Bloom, 1940:107.

and of having led directly to the permanent occupation of the Rio Grande country by the Spaniards.[25]

It is known that Chamuscado and his party,[26] coming up the Rio Grande, passed through the Piro country. Although the explorers did not realize it, the Piro tongue was but dialectically different from the Tiwa. Espejo, later, reported that the Tano and the Piro governed themselves in similar manner, and that "like the rest have idols which they worship."[27] Inasmuch as Tano, Piro, and Tiwa all belonged to the Tanoan language family, it appears probable that cultural differences were not very pronounced. Therefore, what is said of the Piro, from the vicinity of modern San Marcial up river to the territory which they recognized as Tiwa, should give a fair description of the whole region. Hernán Gallegos, scribe of the Chamuscado-Rodriguez expedition, records that their party spent a night in a large ruin which seemed to have been long abandoned: a walled-in pueblo, built of adobe, three stories high. Two leagues further upstream, they came to a pueblo of many houses, three stories high, from which the Indians had fled as the Spaniards approached. There, he says:

> . . . We found in the houses many turkeys and much cotton and corn . . . . In this valley of the said pueblo we found many fields of corn like that of Mexico, and also fields planted to beans, calabashes, and cotton . . . . We found the houses very well planned, square and built of mud-walls, whitewashed in the interior and decorated with many monsters and other animals and pictures of persons . . . . They have much crockery, such as pots, large earthen jars and flat *comales*

[griddles], all painted and of better quality than that of New Spain.

Continuing on in the Piro country, Gallegos states:

> . . . We came to a pueblo of many large houses three and four stories high, plastered on the inside and with very square windows. All the houses were painted in many designs and colors. We marched through this nation for four days, constantly passing many pueblos, for there were days when we passed two of them . . . .[28]

The party, then entering the Tiguex region, listed pueblos on each side of the river, noting four to the south of Isleta. Near Albuquerque, Alameda may be identified; still further north, they recorded the native name, Puaray, for the first time.

Speaking of one of these Tiwa pueblos, Gallegos says:

> We entered this pueblo and they gave us much corn. They showed us many pots and other earthenware containers very well painted . . . . The way they build their houses, which are square, is as follows. They bake [?] the clay; they build the walls narrow; they make adobes for the doorways. The lumber used is pine and willow. They use many timbers ten and twelve feet long. They provide them with movable ladders by means of which they climb to their quarters. They are movable wooden ladders, for when they retire at night they lift them up since they wage war with one another.
>
> These people are clothed like the others. I wish to describe here their garments, because, for a barbarous people, it is the best attire that has been found among them. It is as follows. The men have caps, I mean on the crown of their heads, a sort of skull cap formed by their own hair. Others wear their hair long, to the shoulders, as the Indians of New Spain formerly did. Some adorn themselves with painted cotton pieces of cloth

25. Hammond and Rey, 1927:2.

26. Three friars, nine soldiers-traders, and nineteen Indian servants, with 600 head of stock, 90 horses, coats of mail for horse and rider, provisions, and articles of merchandise for barter.

27. Bolton, 1916:180.

28. Hammond and Rey, 1927:24-26.

three spans long and two thirds wide, with which they cover their privy parts. Over this they wear, fastened at the shoulders, a blanket of the same material, painted with many figures and colors. It reaches to their knees like the clothes of the Mexicans. Some, in fact most of them, wear cotton shirts, hand painted and embroidered, that are very charming. They wear shoes. Below the waist the women wear cotton skirts, colored and embroidered, and above, a blanket of the same material, painted and worked like those used by the men. They wear it after the fashion of the Jewish women. They girt themselves over it with cotton sashes adorned with tassels. They comb their hair, which is long.

* * *

The women part their hair like the Spanish people. Some have light hair, which is surprising.... The women are the ones who spin, weave, decorate and paint. Some do it as well as the men.[29]

The Chamuscado-Rodriguez expedition visited Keres and Tewa pueblos along the Rio Grande, the northern Tiwa settlements, the Tano or southern Tewa in the Galisteo basin, and some of the pueblos around the salt lakes east of the Manzano range. They journeyed into the Pecos and Canadian drainages —the bison country—and made contact with Indians of the western plains.[30] Early in September, Fray Juan de Santa María left the party, without permission, to return to New Spain with view to reporting to his superiors. This disturbed the Indians, and as a result they followed him for two or three days, and then killed him.[31]

The expedition also entered the Jemez province, and traveled westward to Acoma and the Zuñi villages. Assembled again at Puaray, Chamuscado and his soldiers decided to with-

draw from the northland. Rodriguez and Francisco López, the friars, elected to remain "for the conversion of the natives," though the soldiers begged them not to do so, in light of what happened to Fray Juan de Santa Maria. The soldiers left Puaray on 31 January 1582, going down the Rio Grande as they had come.

In 1583, Antonio Espejo came into the same territory with a small party (which included women and children) for the purpose of rescuing the missionaries and exploring mining possibilities. Near the junction of the Rio Conchos with the Rio Grande, a friendly Indian called Juan Cantor, who had served as interpreter and servant to Rodriguez, joined the group; and he, certainly, would have been able to identify places which he had previously seen.

Espejo recorded very good information concerning the Piro villages. He says:

... from each pueblo the people came out to receive us, taking us to their pueblos and giving us a great quantity of turkeys, maize, beans, tortillas, and other kinds of bread.... They grind on very large stones. Five or six women together grind raw corn ... and from this flour they make many different kinds of bread. They have houses of two, three, and four stories, with many rooms in each house. In many of their houses they have their estufas for winter, and in each plaza of the towns they have two estufas, which are houses built underground, very well sheltered and closed, with seats of stone against the walls to sit on. Likewise, they have at the door of each estufa a ladder on which to descend, and a great quantity of community wood, so that strangers may gather there.

In this province some of the natives wear cotton, cow hides, and dressed deerskin. The mantas they wear after the fashion of the Mexicans, except that over their private parts they wear cloths of colored cotton. Some of them wear shirts. The women wear cotton skirts, many of them being embroidered with

29. Hammond and Rey, 1927:26-28.
30. Hammond and Rey, 1927:9.
31. Benavides, 1945:54, reports that the friar preached at San Pedro [or Paako], where "these Tioas [Tiwas] killed him and burned his body."

colored thread, and on top a manta like those worn by the Mexican Indians, tied around the waist with a cloth like an embroidered towel with a tassel. The skirts, lying next to the skin, serve as flaps of the shirts. . . . and all, men as well as women, dress their feet in shoes and boots, the soles being of cowhide and the uppers of dressed deerskin. The women wear their hair carefully combed and nicely kept in place by the moulds that they wear on their heads, one on each side, on which the hair is arranged very neatly, though they wear no headdress. In each pueblo they have their caciques . . . . These caciques have under them . . . *tequitatos*,[32] who are like *alguaciles*, and who execute in the pueblo the cacique's orders . . . . And when the Spaniards ask the caciques of the pueblos for anything, they call the *tequitatos*, who cry it through the pueblo in a loud voice . . . .

The painting of their houses, and the things which they have for balls and dancing, both as regards the music and the rest, are all very much like those of the Mexicans . . . .

. . . In each one of these pueblos they have a house to which they carry food for the devil, and they have small stone idols [fetishes] which they worship. Just as the Spaniards have crosses along the roads, they have between the pueblos, in the middle of the road, small caves or grottoes, like shrines, built of stones, where they place painted sticks and feathers, saying that the devil goes there to rest and speak with them.[33]

They have fields of maize, beans, gourds, and *piciete* [tobacco] in large quantities . . . . Some of the fields are under irrigation, possessing very good diverting ditches, while others are dependent upon the weather . . . . Their arms consist of bows and arrows, *macanas* and *chimales;* the arrows have fire-hardened shafts, the heads being of pointed flint, with which they easily pass through a coat of mail. The *chimales* are made of cowhide, like leather shields; and the *macanas* consist of rods half a vara long, with very thick heads. With them they defend themselves within their houses . . . .[34]

While they were among the Piros, the expedition received word that the friars had been murdered.[35] There was some discussion as to whether or not the party should continue on into the Tiwa territory, but it was decided to do so. Arriving there, they are said to have found thirteen large settlements,[36] the names of which they recorded thus: Poguana (or Puaguana), Comisse (or Comise), Achine, Guagua, Gagosse (or Gagose), Simassa, Suyte, Nocoche, Hacala, Tiara, Tayçios, Cassa (or Casa) , and Puala "where the friars had been killed."[37] In the narrative of Diego Pérez de Luxán, who accompanied Espejo, it is stated:

We stopped by the said river [Rio Grande] close to the pueblo of Puala [which was the Puaray of Coronado] where they had mur-

32. Dozier, 1954:269, points out that this official is possibly the "Outside Chief," who, he says "is an intermediary for the cacique—one for each moiety chief among the Rio Grande Tewa—in all secular affairs and meetings with nonvillagers. The position exists in virtually all the Rio Grande pueblos." Benavides, 1945:44, says that among the pueblo officials "the most honored is he who fills the office of town crier."

33. These were, indeed, pueblo shrines where feathered prayersticks were deposited.

34. Bolton, 1916:177-179.

35. Benavides, 1945:55-56, relates that Lopez was killed when he approached a group of Indians in their fields, whereas Rodriguez was warned by friendly Tiwas. He brought the body of Lopez in and buried him in the Puaray plaza, after which Rodriguez moved to another pueblo, a league distant, to continue his preaching. There, however, he met a similar fate and his body was thrown into the Rio Grande, "which flows along the edge of this pueblo." Benavides learned of Lopez' place of burial through Christianized Indians, and removed the body to Sandia, then said to be the principal pueblo of the Tiwa province.

36. Espejo, 1916:179, says "sixteen pueblos, one of which is called Pualas," where they found that the two friars, three Indian boys, and a half-breed had been killed.

37. Hammond and Rey, 1929:115.

dered Fray Agustín and his companion and the servants who had remained with him. For this reason we named it Puala de los Mártires. The pueblo of Puala has four hundred houses, most of them two stories high, not counting the ground floor, which makes them three stories. The inhabitants of all these settlements had taken to the sierra because all had taken part in killing the friars. Some Indians soon came to find out what we wanted to do and we sent them to bring the others in peace. There was one among them playing an instrument resembling a flageolet. Seeing that they did not want to come we decided to seek them in the sierra [this was evidently Sandia mountain to the east of the river], and we found them there about a league from Puala . . . . When the Indians saw us they began climbing higher up the sierra where we saw seven or eight thousand Indians [Espejo and his men were given to exaggeration]. We appealed to them in a friendly way and dismounted from our horses. Then some came down and treated for peace by means of signs and agreed to return to their pueblos because they said their women and children were suffering greatly from cold [it was during February].

After this we returned to our camp where we awaited them for three days . . . .

During this time there came Indians [probably Keres] from eight or ten leagues up the river with presents of turkeys. They told us they were friendly and begged us to go to their pueblos and they would serve us there. We were informed in this locality that ten or twelve days farther on was a very rich province and the people Mexican; and that thirty days still farther on was the province called Maxosa and another called Suny [Maxosa refers to the present Hopi pueblos, and Suny to Zuñi]. In view of this we decided to set out the next morning. Our Lord permitting, I shall give an account of what may befall us. I merely say that this province of the Tiguas [Tiwas], from this pueblo of Puala onward, contains neat and clean peo-

ple, for so they are in eating and sleeping. They sleep in estufas and have their houses whitewashed, and they use very good crockery.[38]

We left this place . . . and marched four leagues up the river, persuaded by some Indians of the Quites [Queres or Keres] nation belonging to another settlement who had been present at the death of the friars. We stopped at a place an harquebus shot from the pueblo of these natives. This pueblo was called Çachiti [Cochiti]. The people are very peaceful. They gave us maize, tortillas, turkeys, and pinole. We bartered very fine buffalo-skins for sleigh-bells and small iron articles.[39]

From Cochiti, the Espejo party went on to Zia,[40] thence westward across the Rio San José valley to Acoma[41] and then to Zuñi; a small group also visited several of the Hopi pueblos. Once back at Zuñi, the soldiers and missionaries parted company. The latter with their following returned to Mexico; Espejo, Luxan, seven others, and their servants, returned to the Tiwa country, reaching the Rio

38. With the Piro Indians who occupied villages to the south of the Tiwas, at Acoma, with the Zuñi and Hopi, the Espejo party makes mention of kivas, painted figures, ceremonial dancing and singing, but concerning the Tiwas they are provokingly mum.

39. Hammond and Rey, 1929:80-82.

40. Described as having five large plazas and many smaller ones, with houses three and four stories high. Luxan says: "The dress of the men consists of some blankets, a small cloth for covering their privy parts, and other cloaks, shawls, and leather shoes in the shape of boots. The women wear a blanket over their shoulders tied with a sash at the waist, their hair cut in front, and the rest plaited so that it forms two braids, and above a blanket of turkey feathers" (Hammond and Rey, 1929: 84-85).

41. Where the women were then wearing "Mexican" blankets as part of their dance costumes; they were "very elegant with paintings, feathers, and other trappings" (Hammond and Rey, 1929:87). Espejo, 1916:183, says that here, the people "performed a very ceremonious mitote [Indian ceremony] and dance, the people coming out in fine array. They performed many juggling feats, some of them very clever, with live snakes."

Grande at Puaguana, south of Puala, on 19 June. The next day they made camp near Puala. Everywhere the Indians were hostile. Efforts were made to induce the residents of Puala to return to their village, but they remained in the mountains mocking the Spaniards.[42] The party went on to Puala, where Luxan records that there were some thirty Indians on top of their houses. The Spaniards requested food, but the Indians mocked them like the others. Consequently, says Luxan:

> . . . the corners of the pueblo were taken by four men and four others with two servants began to seize those they could lay hands on. We put them in an estufa. And as the pueblo was large and some had hidden themselves there we set fire to the big pueblo of Puala where we thought some were burned to death because of the cries they uttered. We at once took out the prisoners two at a time and lined them up against some poplars close to the pueblo of Puala and they were garroted and shot many times until they died. Sixteen were executed, not counting those who burned to death. Some who did not seem to belong to Puala were set free. This was a strange deed for so few people in the midst of so many enemies. [43]

At Puala, the Spaniards had learned "that two captains of Coronado were in this pueblo two years."[44]

Other expeditions from Mexico into the Tiwa province came after Espejo, some of them unauthorized. Gaspar Castaño de Sosa entered the Pueblo country from the east, via the Pecos river, in 1590, bringing men, women, and children, and wagons. He covered the area from Taos to Isleta, spending a short time in Tiguex, probably at Isleta, where he

learned that a number of Spaniards, not of his own company, had recently passed through the village.[45] These, a few days later, arrested Castaño as an illegal entrant, which charge was eventually proven to be wrong.[46] Leyva de Bonilla and Antonio Gutierrez de Humaña, about 1593, spent a year among the Pueblos, making headquarters at San Ildefonso, before being killed along with most of their followers on a trip to the bison plains.

In 1598, Juan de Oñate brought colonists[47] up the Rio Grande. He is reported to have seen the "portraits" of Rodriguez and Lopez on the walls of a room at Puaray (Puala). Oñate was accompanied by Captain Gaspar Pérez de Villagrá, whose graphic account of the colonization enterprise was published in 1610, as *La Historia de la Nueva México*. In this he states, of the first pueblo[48] in which they were received:

> On the walls of the room where we were quartered were many paintings of the demons they worship as gods. Fierce and terrible were their features. It was easy to understand the meaning of these, for the god of water was near the water, the god of the mountains was near the mountains and in

---

42. *See* footnote 50, page 13.

43. Hammond and Rey, 1929:116.

44. Hammond and Rey, 1929:91.

45. Hull, 1916:330.

46. Hodge, Hammond and Rey (Benavides), 1945, note 33, give credit to Castaño for instituting a republican form of government among the Pueblo Indians for civil purposes, inasmuch as previous negotiations had failed completely. *See* Hull, 1916:324.

47. Bolton, 1916:202. At the beginning of the march, "the colony now consisted of four hundred men, of whom one hundred and thirty had their families. For carrying baggage there were eighty-three wagons and carts, and a herd of more than seven thousand head of stock was driven on foot." Among them were ten friars (Lynch, 1954:xviii, introduction of *Benavides' Memorial of 1630*, notes that by 1600 there were about fifteen Franciscans in New Mexico, with missions at Jemez, San Ildefonso, Santo Domingo, Picuris, and Pecos).

48. The southernmost Piro village on the west bank of the Rio Grande was Trenaquel, near San Marcial; on the opposite side of the stream, Qualacú was the southernmost (Espinosa, 1933:145, note 3).

like manner all those deities they adore, their gods of the hunt, crops and other things they have. [49]

Since unmarried men of the pueblos slept in the kivas, it is likely that the expeditioners were quartered in these chambers. Villagra, then, is referring to mural paintings which depicted some ceremonial of the Pueblo Indians. He says further:

We halted at the pueblo of Puarai, where we were well received. The Indians took the priests to the quarters which had been prepared for them. The walls of their rooms had been recently whitewashed, and the rooms were cleanly swept. The next day, however, when the whitewash had dried, we were able clearly to see, through the whitewash, paintings of scenes which made our blood run cold . . . . There, pictured upon the wall, we saw the details of the martyrdom of those saintly men, Fray Agustín, Fray Juan, and Fray Francisco. The paintings showed us exactly how they had met their death, stoned and beaten by the savage Indians.[50]

The Spaniards did not allow the Indians to suspect that they had seen these paintings. They were sorely afraid that they might meet with a similar fate, and so they stole from Puaray in the dead of night, to another pueblo, Santo Domingo. There, they found two Christian Indians, called Cristóbal and Tomás—who "knew the language of all the Indian tribes, and [were] well acquainted with the lay of the land."[51] They had come from New Spain with Castaño de Sosa, in 1590. They had remained of their own accord, had married into the pueblo, and "were content with their lot."[52] Through these two, the Spaniards were able to speak with the inhabitants of these regions, which certainly permitted of their getting more accurate information than had most of their predecessors. Villagra records:

We visited a good many of these pueblos. They are all well built with straight, well-squared walls. Their towns have no defined streets. Their houses are three, five, six and even seven stories high, with many windows

---

49. Villagra in Espinosa, 1933:140.
50. Villagra in Espinosa, 1933:132.

Inasmuch as none of the mural paintings at Kuaua, Awatovi, or Pottery Mound, are of such style of portraiture as to show features identifiable with any particular human being, it seems unlikely that an Indian artist would have portrayed Rodriguez and Lopez in such a manner, if at all — which is indeed doubtful, especially in a ceremonial chamber.

On the other hand, if a kiva painting had been plastered over with a coat of plaster — as might have been done following the painting of symbolic representations which accompanied any important ceremonial that the Indians would have held in the kiva — a considerable amount of the color of the underlying painting must have been obscured, as well as significant details. I suggest, therefore, the possibility that, instead of having seen a representation of the "stoned and beaten" death of the friars, the Spaniards saw a painted-over depiction of an Indian ceremonial, such as that illustrated in the *New Mexico Magazine* (LeVinness, March, 1959:22-23, 52), and which pertains to a myth centering around fertility rites, in which the twin War gods are the primary characters,

serving the supreme deity of the Indians, their father, the Sun.

It should be noted also that the Villagra account is inaccurate in its mention of three priests having been killed at Puaray. He includes Fray Juan, who is Fray Juan de Santa Maria, and who had left the Chamuscado-Rodriguez expedition and had been killed at Paako in 1581. The fact that more than two representations appear to have been observed by the Oñate-Villagra party on the kiva walls at Puaray lends support to the belief that it was a painting of an Indian ceremonial which they saw through a covering coat of plaster.

Furthermore, Espejo was at Puaray on or about 21 June 1581, and Oñate was there on 21 June 1598, which would have been precisely at the time that the Indians were celebrating the Summer solstice. The most elaborate of all the Sun cult rites are carried out during the Summer solstice, and these are fraught with symbolism and ceremonial "killings." Part of these ceremonies are held off in the timbered mountains, at some distance from the pueblos. One can scarcely imagine a time when the Spaniards would have been any less welcome!

51. Villagra in Espinosa, 1933:204.
52. Villagra in Espinosa, 1933:143.

and terraces . . . . The men spin and weave and the women cook, build the houses, and keep them in repair. They dress in garments of cotton cloth, and the women wear beautiful shawls of many colors. They are quiet, peaceful people of good appearance and excellent physique, alert and intelligent. They are not known to drink, a good omen, indeed.[53] We saw no maimed or deformed persons among them. The men and women alike are excellent swimmers. They are also expert in the art of painting, and are great fishermen. . . . The rivers abound with many fish such as bagre, mojarra, armadillos, corbina, shrimp, perch, needle-fish, turtles, eels, trout, and sardines.[54] These exist in such quantities that a single Spaniard in one day, with a bare hook, was able to catch more than six arrobas weight of fish.[55]

Oñate settled his colony near the Tewa site of Yugewinge [Yunque-yungue], on the east side of the Rio Grande, at the present San Juan (Ohké), on 11 July 1598. This first capital of the Spaniards in New Mexico was called San Juan de los Caballeros. The following year, a location on the west side of the stream, near its junction with the Rio Chama, was selected and named San Gabriel.[56] Diffi-

cult years followed; additional friars and military reinforcements brought in by the succeeding governor, Pedro de Peralta, in 1609, made the Spanish foothold more secure. During the winter of 1609-1610, the capital of the colony was moved to a new and permanent site, La Villa Real de Santa Fe. A violent breach of relations between the church and state occurred during the administration of Peralta, and began a rivalry and controversy which troubled New Mexico throughout the Spanish domination. This made life increasingly difficult for the Indians. Missionary work was extended; by 1616, some twenty friars were ministering to approximately 10,000 Indians baptized as Christian Catholics. Fray Alonso de Benavides was appointed *custos* of the Franciscan missions in New Mexico in 1623, and was formally received by the governor at Santa Fe on 24 January 1626.

Benavides gives brief accounts—often confused and commonly exaggerated—of the Indian peoples. Describing the Tiguex province, he states:

> The first and principal city of this province is also called Tihues [Tiguex]. . . . This city lies in a plain on the banks of a very pleasant river; it is surrounded with walls of stone and gypsum . . .

Again, he says that the Tiwa were "a nation of many settlements and houses, clothed people and excellent farmers, but very savage and great sorcerers." He mentions fifteen or sixteen pueblos in the province, to which he attributes "some 7,000 souls in a district of twelve or thirteen leagues," through which the Rio Grande ran centrally—then described as very swift, subject to bad floods, and the

---

53. To Fathers Arteaga and Zúñiga are attributed the planting of the first vines and the manufacture of wine at Senecú mission of the Piro in 1626.

54. Benavides (Ayer, 1916:36-37) wrote of the Rio Grande and smaller streams as being "very abundant in catfish [bagres], trout, silvery chubs [sardinas], eels, shovel-noses [agujas], matalotas, suckers [boquinetes], gar-pikes [cassones], and many others." A note accompanying the Luxan narrative (Hammond and Rey, 1929:126) says, "Matalote means some hard, bony, sharp-backed fish." According to Lummis, "it might be the sunfish or 'punkinseed', of which there are half a dozen species in the lower Rio Grande; or the buffalo fish, *corcobado* (hunchback), which is common as far up as Chama; or possibly the *gaspregou* or sheepshead (Aplodinotus granniens), a big lean, tough, bony fish common in Texas rivers, but mostly below El Paso."

55. *In* Espinosa, 1933:143-144.

56. Upon completion of the church at San Juan, in

1598, the Spaniards performed *Los Moros;* and the *Matachin* was introduced to the Indians. Dozier (1957:33) notes that such pageants "were undoubtedly intended to substitute and replace native ceremonies, but instead they became an added series . . . ."

cause of much hardship to the friars in crossing back and forth. [57]

During the three years that Benavides spent in New Mexico, his efforts were extended to the Keres, Tiwa, Piro, and Tano pueblos[58] and to the Apaches roaming over southern New Mexico. Benavides was replaced in 1629, but the missionary activities steadily increased, and their effect upon the Indians must have been profound. It is recorded that: "An essential part of every mission was the school where the natives were taught reading, writing, music [of the Church] and citizenship. Christian doctrine . . . was given the first place, but the friars . . . also set up workshops where the new Christians were taught the trades, arts and crafts."[59]

In 1638, Fray Juan de Prada reported that in the area from Senecu to Taos, and from the Salinas to Hopiland, the Pueblo Indians—who lived in adobe pueblos of two or three stories, in an organized state subject to their captains and chiefs—totaled 40,000 or a little less. He stated: "although there must have been more than sixty thousand baptized, to-day those conversions are diminished to that extent on account of the very active prevalence during these last years of smallpox and the sickness which the Mexicans called *cocolitzli*." He recorded that the "Indians are notably poor and live a wretched life, for their entire property is limited to the raising of a little cotton, from which they weave the blankets with which they clothe themselves and which they sometimes exchange for buffalo and deer skins which the unconverted Indians are accustomed to bring, who live adjacent to our people and with whom they maintain peace, although always insecure, because these people do not keep their word." Prada recorded also that: "In the most important of these pueblos thirty convents have been built in addition to many other churches in the smaller villages," and, "where there were nothing other than the ceremonial chambers of barbarous idolatries to-day temples may be seen that are frequented by Christians, who acquaint themselves with the Christian faith and good customs."[60]

Mission development reached its height by 1639, after which decline resulted from conflicts between the Spanish religious and military authorities. The Indians resented the changes wrought by both in their way of life, the tribute exacted of them, forced labor, and general loss of freedom, and sought means of ridding themselves of the Spanish domination.[61] Between 1639 and 1641, political strife became so acute that civil war was barely averted.[62]

In the areas outside of Santa Fe—the single Spanish settlement—the office of local administrator (*alcalde mayor*) came to be eagerly sought by prominent citizens, "partly because of the prestige involved, partly because it afforded an opportunity to control Indian affairs, especially the recruiting of Indian labor."[63] Both the Church and the civil officers increased their influence[64] and authority over the Indians. Certain individuals were particularly oppressive. Something of the enormity of the demands made upon the Indians is

---

57. Benavides, 1945:47, 54, 64-65.

58. Of whom he says, "All these nations were divided, at the time of their paganism, into two factions: warriors and sorcerers"—thus indicating the dual importance of the warrior society and of the priesthood (*see* Benavides, 1945:42).

59. Lynch 1954:xx; *see also* Benavides, 1954:18.

60. *In* Hackett, 1937:108-109.

61. *See* Benavides, 1945, Appendix XVI:168-177.

62. *See* Scholes, 1935:195.

63. Scholes, 1937b:386.

64. In a material way, the fact that a shipment of goods from New Mexico to Parral, Mexico, in 1660, included among other things woolen stockings, leather jackets, shirts, and breeches, indicates that the attire of the Indians had been influenced thereby, to a greater or lesser degree (*see* Scholes, 1937b:391). If they were making these items, the Indians were doubtless wearing them also in increasing numbers.

shown in the accounts concerning Governor Bernardo López de Mendizábal. It is said that:

> . . . even before his formal reception as governor in the Villa of Santa Fé, his agents were busy rounding up Indians to serve as day laborers or to manufacture goods for export, and during his two-year term of office he entered into some form of business relationship with hundreds of natives in the pueblos of the central Río Grande-Jémez-Salinas area. During the *residencia* of López in 1660 numerous petitions and complaints were presented in the name of Indians alleging that the governor had failed to pay them for services rendered or for goods supplied . . . . the petitions provide an excellent example of the manner in which Indian labor was used to advance the governor's business schemes.

The Indians of the central and southern pueblos were employed to gather piñon and salt and transport the accumulated supplies to convenient places for shipment. The following items are taken from the claims presented in 1661: (1) fifty Indians from Senecú, thirty-six from Socorro, and ten from Alamillo, and a number of pack mules and horses from each pueblo were employed for about two weeks transporting piñon to a warehouse in Senecú; (2) sixty-three Indians from Socorro worked for three days carrying salt from the east bank of the Río Grande to the pueblo of Socorro; (3) sixty laborers from Cuarac [Quarai] were forced to go to the pueblo of the Jumanos and from there to the Río Grande with loads of piñon, and were engaged in this labor for seventeen days; (4) nineteen Indians from Abó worked for six days carrying maize from Tabirá and the Jumano pueblo to the house of Capt. Nicolás de Aguilar, the *alcalde mayor* of the Salinas district; (5) as many as forty Indians from Jémez were employed at one time taking piñon to depots in San Felipe, Cochití, or Santa Fé; (6) twenty-two Indians from Galisteo were sent to the house of Capt. Aguilar in

the Salinas area for maize to be transported to Santa Fé; (7) Indians from Tabirá loaded salt at the salt marsh and took it to the house of Sargento Mayor Francisco Gómez who had an estancia called Las Barrancas on the Middle Río Grande; (8) the claim presented in the name of the Jumano pueblo listed three items of labor, *viz.*, twenty-three Indians for five days, fifty-one for three days, and twelve for six days.

The manufacture of stockings for the governor's account was carried on in a number of villages. The petitions presented in 1661 included the following claims: Senecú, 100 pairs; Socorro, 30 pairs; San Ildefonso, 262 pairs; San Juan, Santa Clara, Jacona, Pojuaque, Nambé, and Cuyamungué, a total of 280 pairs; Alamillo, 46 pairs; Santo Domingo, 156 pairs; Jémez, 360 pairs; Tano pueblos, 165 pairs. Several claims were also made in behalf of individual Indians.

The washing of hides, tanning leather, painting leather door-hangings, and the manufacture of shoes and leather doublets were other forms of service performed by the Indians. An Indian named Francisco Cuaxin presented a claim for the balance due on account of making 38 doublets, 10 leather jackets, and 49 pairs of shoes. The Indians of Pecos asked payment for 100 *pergaminos* [parchments] and seven tents made of hides, as well as an assessment of half a *fanega* [or about a half-bushel] of piñon furnished by each household in the pueblo. The pueblo of Santa Ana claimed payment for washing 80 hides, or a total of 160 days of labor, and the Indians of Jémez presented a bill for washing 500 hides at one *real* each.

Most of the wagons made for the governor to be used in the transportation of accumulated supplies were built near Puaray by carpenters from the Tiwa villages, Sia, Santa Ana, and Jémez. More than thirty wagons were said to have been built, the average price being ten pesos each. The Indians of the Tewa towns also made claim for labor in cutting and hauling timber for wagon parts.[65]

From the few facts stated above, it will be seen that within one hundred years of the entrada of Coronado and in less than a half-century of colonization, the culture of the Indians of the Rio Grande had been pitilessly altered. Their highly developed society—wherein complex religious and secular organizations coordinated all activities to the end that the people were industrious and devout, that they dwelt in large, well built and well kept pueblos, produced an abundance of foodstuffs and other necessities and assembled stores for less favorable times, and were in harmony with their environment—was ill prepared to contest the new régime. First was the impact of a new religion which they did not comprehend, and which made little effort to understand their basic concepts. They were forced to meet increasing demands of both church and state, with result that many became virtual slaves, or poverty stricken. Their fields were neglected and their dwellings unkept. Families were displaced, new diseases and armed conflicts took a great toll of lives, and among the Indians general remissness prevailed.

Frequent changes among the governmental officials and agents of the church, with alternating policies, added to the confusion. For instance, after preceding administrations had rigidly suppressed the Indian religious practices, Governor Lopez, so oppressive in other ways, not only gave permission for the dancing of katsina [*catzina*][66] but he commanded the Indians to dance them. Thus from about 1660 on, these formerly forbidden ceremonies were enacted in the Tiwa, Tewa, and Keres villages, and even in the plaza of Santa Fe.

The Indians did not understand these fluc-

tuating policies, and they became increasingly discontented with the plight in which they found themselves; and their hostility against the Spaniards mounted. Among the Spaniards, the bitterness between church and state grew to such intensity, during the years 1659-1664, that the New Mexico colony never recovered. A general decline was in evidence by 1680. It is held that there were then about 2,800 Spaniards in New Mexico. And it was in this situation that the Pueblo Rebellion was fomented.

On 11 August 1680, the greatest unification which the Southwestern Indians ever achieved saw the initiation of a well planned revolt.[67] It is known that the Indians of Tiguex figured prominently in the revolt. At that time, of the twelve pueblos named by Rodriguez, only four remained inhabited: Isleta, Alameda, Sandia, and Puaray.[68] A year later, Governor Antonio de Otermín burned the villages of this province—the four named and four others; three more were sacked—in an attempt to overcome the rebellion and reconquer the land. The inhabitants of Nafiat—the pueblo which the Spaniards called Sandia—rebuilt their pueblo, but, when the Spaniards reappeared in 1692, they fled to the Hopi country where, aided by the people of Mishongnovi, they built a pueblo on Second Mesa. In 1748, nearly 350 Tigua (Tiwa) returned to the Rio Grande and reestablished Sandia in its present location. They brought back ceremonies, practices, and many traits learned from the Hopi. After Isleta—called Shiehwíbbak in Tiwa—was overcome by Otermin in 1681, he conducted 385 captives from that pueblo to El Paso, where they built a village called Isleta del Sur. The original Isleta was reoccupied, about 1706, when scattered groups of Indians were gathered there and a

---

65. Scholes, 1937b:393-395.
66. *In* Hackett, 1937-III:131 ff.

67. *See* Chavez, 1959:85 and 89, for an interesting suggestion in regard to the instigator of the Rebellion.

68. Hackett, 1911:127, quoting *Auttos tocantes*, 28, gives the population as: Isleta 2,000; Sandia 3,000; Puaray 200; and Alameda about 300.

mission built.[69] The remains of the other pueblos gradually eroded, and were practically forgotten.

Two and a half centuries passed. Then archaeologists began investigating the ruins of old Tiguex. Sites on the flood plain of the Rio Grande had all but disappeared, having weathered down and blown full of sand, or having been plowed under and planted over in the process of agriculture in the valley. On the adjoining terraces, however, numerous mounds gave testimony of former pueblos and small settlements.

It is difficult to identify these with certainty, but the historical accounts, as we have seen, leave no doubt that Coronado wintered his troops in one of these Tiwa villages (Mohi) during 1540 and 1541, that these were the communities described by Villagra in 1598, and that here were the pueblos which Governor Otermin and his soldiers burned and otherwise plundered in the attempt to hold the province of New Mexico in the uprising of 1680-1691.

The Indians were free from Spanish domination until 1692, when General Diego de

Vargas effected his "bloodless" reconquest of the north country. A number of the pueblos were inhabited once more; some of the Indians joined with their kinsmen; and others shifted to new locations.

In the modern period, as noted previously, only two Tiwa-speaking villages remain in the former Tiguex province: Isleta, about thirteen miles south of Albuquerque, and Sandia, approximately that distance to the north of the metropolis. Far to the north, Picuris and Taos speak Tiwa. To the north and northwest of the southern Tiwa pueblos are the five Keres villages of the east; about fifty miles to the west, on the Rio San Jose, are two other Keres pueblos, Acoma and Laguna. North of Santa Fe, five of the Tewa villages persisted, Pojoaque having become extinct as a pueblo. Jemez, to the west on Jemez creek, completes the surviving groups.

Within this more and more restricted region, and with gradually increasing pressures from the outside, the Pueblo Indians continued on with their concepts of life, maintaining their principles insofar as that was possible, selecting that which would fit into their cultures, and rejecting that which would not.

---

69. *See* Lynch, 1954:18, and references cited therein.

II. MODERN RESEARCH REVEALS THE RECORDS

THE ARCHAEOLOGICAL HISTORY
OF PUARAY AND KUAUA

Various identifications of the places and peoples mentioned by the chroniclers of the Spanish expeditions have been made by modern historians and scientists, and there has been considerable disagreement.

Across the Rio Grande from Bernalillo, New Mexico, about a quarter-mile west of the stream, one of the most conspicuous of the terrace ruins was thought by Adolf Bandelier and Charles F. Lummis to be Puaray of the conquest period. This site is approximately one mile south from state highway number 44. A short distance to the north from the same highway, also on the river terrace west of Bernalillo, is another extensive ruin called Kuaua,[70] which gave evidence of having been an important center. Bandelier and Lummis felt that the site which they identified as Puaray was the Tiwa pueblo in which the army of Oñate was quartered in 1598 and, therefore, the location of the mural paintings which were said to depict the murder of the Franciscan friars, Rodriguez and Lopez.

Some authorities have held that Kuaua was the Puaray of Villagra; and others have made different identifications. Gordon Vivian notes that Bandelier, in 1886, believed that the Puaray here discussed was the "Puaray" referred to in all of the Spanish accounts, but it is his opinion that at least two of the Tiguex

towns were mistakenly referred to by various chroniclers as being a single "Puaray."[71] He, himself, favored another site[72] as the location of Puaray (of Villagra). Wesley L. Bliss[73] concluded that still another site[74] was the most likely, though he felt that the ruin favored by Vivian, as well as another nearby,[75] should be examined further. These men agree that historical Puaray was on the *east* side of the Rio Grande, several miles southward from the Puaray of Bandelier.

Hoping to shed new light on this problem, studies were initiated by the School of American Research, the Museum of New Mexico, and the University of New Mexico. On 29 March 1934, students engaged in archaeological studies at the university—including the author—made a visit to Puaray of Bandelier,[76] and closely examined the site. Professor Edgar L. Hewett, then head of the department of archaeology and anthropology at the university in Albuquerque, and director of the other

---

70. Sinclair, 1951:3, gives the Tiwa meaning as "Evergreen."

71. Vivian, 1934:154; Bandelier, 1892, pt. II:220.
72. No. 13 of the Fisher survey, 1931.
73. Bliss, 1948:218-219.
74. No. 11 of the Fisher survey.
75. No. 10 of the Fisher survey. Hackett, 1915:381-391, postulated this as being Puaray. He says, "the records of Otermín . . . show conclusively that Alameda was about eight leagues above Isleta and on the same or west side of the stream, that Puaray was one league above Alameda but on the east bank of the river and that Sandia was one league above Puaray and on the same side of the stream." *See* Scholes, 1937a:57-59.
76. Sandoval county, fractional school section No. 36, Township 13N., Range 3W., New Mexico principal meridian, and an additional small area in the Alameda Grant. The elevation is about 5,000 feet.

two agencies in Santa Fe, led the party, assisted by Paul A. F. Walter, Jr., and Marjorie Ferguson Tichy (Mrs. E. V. Lambert).

Surface collections of potsherds and rock specimens were obtained; test pits were sunk into the debris, the visible limits of the ruin determined, a base line established for mapping purposes, and plots indicated by stakes. On 3 April, work was resumed and excavation got under way, producing satisfactory results from the beginning. On 4 May, funds supplied by the New Mexico Relief Administration (FERA) permitted of a labor crew of seventeen men, under the direct supervision of Mr. Vivian[77] and Mrs. Tichy, with advanced students in archaeology overseeing the actual excavating and removing the materials found.

Work at Puaray (of Bandelier) continued through 1934. Over 375 rooms were excavated, laying clear the entire west and south house groups, where all the rooms were of adobe construction; nearly 500 burials were removed, and several hundred pottery pieces, and bone and stone artifacts. In the central plaza, about which the rooms were built in rectangular blocks, a large circular kiva was unearthed, 33 feet in diameter and subterranean to a depth of eight feet. This had an entrance-way through the west wall, opening into a small ladder-way which extended upward to the ground surface. Neither here nor elsewhere was any evidence of mural paintings discovered.

The excavation of this pueblo ruin, then, failed to identify it as the "Puaray" wherein Espejo and Oñate reported depictions of the martyred friars on the walls of their quarters.[78]

Some black-on-white sherd areas were found away from the ruin, but not in association with it. There were a very few Glaze I, II, and III sherds[79]—too few to have significance; the predominant decorated type was Glaze IV, which was followed by wares extending into historic times. The site, which was probably abandoned before the Rebellion of 1680, is thus essentially a historic pueblo.[80] Bliss identifies it as Culiacan of the Gallegos record, agreeing with Mecham.[81] Bits of porcelain of Spanish introduction, metal tools, and a small piece of Spanish armor were found, indicating that this pueblo had known Spanish contact and influence.

Archaeological attention was also directed toward the ruin of Kuaua, which name certainly equates with the *Guagua* of the Espejo expedition of 1583. It has been identified as La Palma of the Chamuscado-Rodriguez expedition.[82] Again the excavations were a joint undertaking of the three institutions above-mentioned. With the assistance of the FERA, this project, initiated on 26 June 1934, likewise, was under the direction of Professor Hewett, and, initially, under the immediate supervision of Mr. Vivian.

The excavation of Kuaua[83] was a major undertaking. It continued for five years, utilizing the training and abilities of a long list of individuals. The results were important. But at present we shall consider mainly those facts germane to this study.

Like Puaray (of Bandelier), Kuaua was built of adobe. It covered an area of approximately one-fourth mile along the river, or

77. In connection with his investigations in this area, Mr. Vivian prepared a thesis, "A Restudy of the Province of Tiguex," for the M.A. degree (1932) at the University of New Mexico. His choice as supervisor of the project was thus logical and opportune.

78. Hackett, 1937:355, records the statement of Juan Domínguez de Mendoza that Otermin burned Alameda, Puaray, and Sandia, in which were great stores of maize, beans, wool, hides, and other necessities.

79. Pecos classification. *See* Kidder and Shepard, 1936; *see also* Mera, 1933. Inasmuch as pottery types are the material documentation of cultural phenomena, they are signally important. The reader is referred to the small book, *Potsherds* (Colton, 1953), for information as to how potsherds are dated and used chronologically.

80. Mrs. Lambert, personal conversation.

81. Bliss, 1948:219.

82. Mecham, 1926:268.

83. Long. 106-36, Lat. 35-20; Township 13N., Range 4 E., Sec. 30, Sandoval county.

PLATE I. The ruin of Kuaua on the west bank of the Rio Grande. A portion of Sandia Mountain is seen at the upper right. The north plaza appears at the left with its two-period rectangular kiva. Between this and the river, the small east plaza shows its rectangular chamber (Kiva VI). At the right, Kiva III (restored) may be noted in the south plaza; next is the large circular kiva; and then the small circular chamber which contained the earliest cultural remains. At the far right, the Lummis section is seen. *New Mexico State Tourist Division photo.*

north-south, and about one-eighth mile east-west. The common soil of the area, when mixed with water, becomes an adhesive material. The Indians packed the mixture into large balls, allowed them to dry, then placed them firmly with adobe mortar for walls of their structures. This corroborates the statement made by Castañeda concerning the building methods of the Tiwa Indians (see pages 6, 8). After a course about twelve inches in height was put in place this was allowed to dry, then the procedure was carried on until the desired wall height was achieved—sufficient to clear a man's head by several inches. Beams and cross poles, covered with reeds, bark and earth, supported chamber roofs, and served as floors for rooms which were built above, or for out-of-door living, which was so much a part of Pueblo life.

Kuaua had two large plazas—of which the south one gives evidence of having been the older—and a smaller east plaza. The site showed clearly that the inhabitants had dwelt in one section, and then another, there being no very large population at any given time. Some of the rooms fell into ruin, while chambers were added at other locations. The older, south portion, referred to as the Lummis section,[84] was burned during the period of Glaze I, or about the middle of the 14th century. Below several floors, there was fill of fallen roofing and burned corn—in some cases several inches deep, over which other floors were directly placed. Later, this part of the pueblo was allowed to fall into disuse as new dwellings were built elsewhere.

Within the two main plazas, five subterranean kivas were excavated, these being of both circular and rectangular form.[85] Within the house blocks, certain rooms were found equipped with features like those of the kivas: rectangular altar-deflectors, fire pits, loom holes, etc.[86]

The earliest cultural remains were discovered in a small, circular kiva (15′5″ diameter) located in the southwest part of the ruin. After its abandonment, the kiva had been completely filled with debris. As evidenced by the predominance of pottery of Glaze I type, this may be dated to the early 14th century.

In the northeast sector of the same plaza, a square kiva (roughly 23′ each way) contained well defined strata, in five natural levels. Here, too, Glaze I pottery was most plentiful, with Glaze II nearly as abundant, thus indicating that the filling had commenced in the 1300's and continued to about 1400; later types were negligible in number. This kiva had been abandoned because of its burning; the outline of the burned and rotted roof was found resting on the floor.

A large, circular kiva (slightly over 30′ diameter),[87] also in the south plaza, revealed no long continued deposition. There was a steady record of Glaze I in small amounts; a paucity

---

84. J. Charles Kelley was assigned as supervisor of this section. By the first of September, 1934, forty rooms had been excavated, including two ceremonial rooms arranged within the house block.

85. See Tichy, 1938:72-76.

86. In the ceremonial rooms in the south house block, each approximately 17 feet long, were floor features comparable in every essential to the kivas: Room 26 or Kiva 2 (the earlier one) and Room 18 or Kiva 1—both of which had been built after fire ravaged that section of the pueblo. They had been made usable as ceremonial rooms by the removal of walls between dwelling rooms of ordinary size, and by providing entrances into them. In the surrounding forty-room section there were twenty doorways; of these only six had not been sealed with adobe and stones. Of the latter, three gave direct access to the ceremonial rooms in the house block; one led to the antechamber of Kiva 1; one gave onto the plaza; leaving but one doorway between secular rooms.

In one chamber, the rectangular altar and fire pit were oriented toward the east; the other, at the junction of the south and east house blocks, had these features on the south side. Both chambers had sets of loom holes in the floor.

In the north house block, a ceremonial room very much like the two in the south section was identified. In it the altar and fire pit orientation was toward the south.

87. See Hawley, 1950:286-300, for discussion of big and little kivas.

PL. II. Ceramic specimens from Puaray (of Bandelier) and Kuaua. a, b, d, e) Early glaze-paint decorated pottery, Kuaua; crosses on "d" indicate War god significance; c) Early glaze-paint decorated bowl, Puaray, with dragon fly design, crosses indicating War god, probably the elder, right-handed twin. f) Bandelier black-on-grey, Puaray.

c　　a　d　　e　b　　f

of Glaze II-III (1400-1475)—as occurred in many other parts of the ruin; a greater percentage of Glaze IV or D (1475-1500) than anything else; and a fair representation of Glaze V or E[88] (1500-1680 or, here, until abandonment of the site). The presence of Abiquiu and Bandelier black-on-grey wares in small numbers attests to association with the north while deposition in this kiva was active.

A smaller kiva (III) —18′ square—located a short distance to the southwest from the above-mentioned rectangular chamber contained 16th century fill. On its walls were ceremonial paintings. This will be discussed more fully, further on.

In the north plaza, a rectangular kiva (31′ long) was cleared, showing that it had been built within a greater rectangular chamber. From the ceramic deposition, most of which occurred in a three-foot accumulation of refuse which rested on the kiva floor—for above this there was wind-blown sand—it was obvious that the fill was predominantly late: Glaze V, IV, and VI or F,[89] in that order, thus indicating the heaviest concentration from about 1500 until abandonment. The Glaze

IV, however, shows that the kiva was receiving refuse during the 1475-1500 period; and the small quantity of Glaze VI material suggests that there were perhaps a few hangers-on at Kuaua after its general depopulation, or perhaps that the site was sporadically occupied.

In the east plaza, another rectangular kiva (VI) was unearthed, the latest of those excavated.

In noting that Kuaua was established in the 1300's, it is important that we recall something of the population movements which were going on at that time. Especially severe droughts had plagued portions of the Southwest during the 1200's, with the most prolonged of all extending from 1276 to 1299.[90] This drought was not so severe in the Rio Grande area as in that of Mesa Verde and of Flagstaff. It was relatively dry from 1251 to 1299, with the worst years in the 1250's in the Rio Grande. Tree growths were slight from 1445-1464, 1469-1483, and 1560-1594.[91] Drought and other

88. Glaze D of Mera equates with Glazes III-IV of Kidder and Shepard, and Glaze E equates with their Late Glaze IV-Glaze V. At Kuaua there was some representation of all the types included in Mera's Glaze V series.

89. Glaze F of Mera equates with Glaze VI of Kidder and Shepard.

90. Douglass, 1935:49.

91. Smiley, Stubbs and Bannister, 1953:53. Also, in 1661, it was recorded that the area had just been through "so serious a famine that the Indians had to sustain themselves on seeds of grasses, *tierra blanca,* and herbs of very injurious character; and most of the Spaniards on "bran, *quilites* [a water plant], green barley, and other herbs . . ." (Declaration of Capt. Andrés Hurtado, Santa Fe, September, 1661 [Folio 169] in Hackett, 1937-II:187). The latter source records the period of 1573-1593 as a very bad drought.

disturbances undoubtedly accounted for the shifting of sedentary peoples from some locations to more favorable ones, from time to time. The great settlements of the Chaco Canyon had been mainly deserted by the mid-12th century; and the exodus from pueblos of the Kayenta and Mesa Verde regions was generally completed by the end of the 13th.[92] During these centuries, the Indian peoples were evidently moving to places with more adequate water supplies, such as the Little Colorado and Rio Grande drainages, or where they had increased security of one kind or another.[93] Since some of those who peopled the Tiguex province apparently came into the area during the 1300's, it seems reasonable to assume that they represent these re-settling groups.[94]

Prior to 1300, and for a short time thereafter, the dominant characteristic of non-culinary pottery in the Rio Grande area was its black-on-white decoration, regardless of type or provenience. This was a trait attributable to the Anasazi peoples of the north—the Four Corners region. Some of the old Pueblo groups used a mineral paint for achieving the black designs; this was particularly favored by the *Chaqueños*. Others, such as the Kayenta and Mesa Verde peoples, preferred an organic carbon paint which they derived from plants. About 1300, and probably concurrent with these incoming migrants to the valley, a new kind of pottery predominated, red ware ornamented with glaze-paint embellishments skillfully controlled.[95]

Seeking the source of glaze-paint decoration, it is found that pueblo-dwelling Indians in the White Mountain area of Arizona (in the vicinity of modern Pinedale and Showlow—which then was thickly populated)[96] came to possess such a medium—paint of which the chief constituents are lead and copper—probably around 1250. It was the first true innovation concerned with pottery decoration that had appeared in centuries.[97] It would seem to have become a favorite almost instantly. Many peoples were on the move throughout the Southwest. They carried pieces of the colorful and attractive wares with them into new areas; and they began to produce pottery with glaze-paint decoration in their new locations. The earliest examples in the Albuquerque, or ancient Tiguex, region would appear to have been imported, for they are of excellent quality. By 1325 to 1350, however, the production of glaze-paint decorated wares was local. It spread up and down the Rio Grande and its tributaries, to Pecos and the Saline pueblos east of the mountain ranges paralleling the Rio Grande. Mineral deposits in those mountains provided the necessary components for glaze-paints.

At Kuaua, the circular kivas would expectedly denote an occupancy by people of Anasazi origin, that is, from the Four Corners area where the tradition of circular kivas prevailed. This is not unlikely in light of general archaeological knowledge of the regions to the north, and it is in keeping with the folk history of those Pueblo peoples who came to be known in our day as the Acoma and Zuñi, in particular. There is also the possibility that

92. The latest construction date in the old Pueblo domain (the so-called Basket Maker-Pueblo, or *Anasazi* ["the ancient ones"], region centering around the Four Corners area of Arizona, New Mexico, Colorado, and Utah, is 1284 at Mummy Cave in Canyon del Muerto; the latest at Mesa Verde is 1274. Chaco Canyon showed the longest occupation, primarily from 919 to 1130, with a date of 1178 derived from the pueblo ruin known as Yellow House.

93. Dittert, 1959:73, observes that following long drought moist conditions reappear in the Acoma region after 1300.

94. Wendorf and Reed, 1955:133, call attention to the fact that it was only after the abandonment of the San Juan drainage, between 1250 and 1300, and the movement of a considerable number of the western Anasazi to the Rio Grande, that this area became a leading Pueblo center.

95. *See* Shepard, 1942, for a discussion of the glaze-paint wares.

96. *See* Reed, 1950:120.

97. *Cf.* Martin, 1959:84.

they might have been Tiwa-speaking people of the Tanoan stock.[98]

Thus it may have been that an immigrating Anasazi group, which made black-on-white pottery, established itself, in the early 1300's, in the fertile Rio Grande valley, where its well developed horticultural practices and integrated religious rites brought forth the small pueblo which we know as the Lummis section of Kuaua.

If this were the case, it would seem that scarcely was the settlement founded before other people began coming into the region and into its very midst. Presumably these were people from the west or southwest—the so-called Mogollon province—for it appears that square kivas were a trait of that area. We have a square kiva not far distant from the original, circular one at Kuaua; and the two show partial contemporaneity, on sherd evidence. These newcomers were probably those who brought the idea of glaze-paint decoration into this area. It was exceedingly popular from the start, and soon dominated the scene.

The pueblo apparently thrived for a time, under favorable conditions, as attested by the accumulations of corn which were found during the excavations. This may have contributed to its ill fortune, for we have evidence of a conflagration which swept through the pueblo, indicating that some enemy group may have attacked the well supplied village, plundered it, and wrought its destruction. The small rectangular kiva was likewise burned. It has been noted that there was a paucity of sherd material representing the period from about 1400 to around 1475, which suggests that the site may have been abandoned, or greatly reduced in population for a time. The

dry years mentioned above probably were responsible for this situation.

Significant occupation is indicated from the latter part of the 15th century onward. A house block several rooms in width was built along the north side of the pueblo, extending east from the unit which continued northward, considerably widened, from the Lummis section. Rooms were also constructed along the east side, and these ultimately were joined across the north, forming the large north plaza. Farther toward the east other dwellings were projected, about Kiva VI.[99]

During this period rectangular ceremonial structures prevailed. Kiva III in the south plaza, the large kiva in the north plaza, and Kiva VI in the east plaza, which was also decorated with symbolic paintings, bespeak intensified ceremonial activities, in turn reflecting a period of relative peace and plenty.

One of the prerequisites for the development of a powerful priesthood and elaborate ritualistic display is economic affluence. There must be an adequate supply of laborers and successful hunters who provide ample quantities of food, and those who attend to the other necessities of life (produce pottery, basketry, spin, weave, tan leather, etc.); if there be need for protection, there must be those who serve as guards and warriors. Members of a priestly hierarchy are concerned with the socio-political organizations which pertain to the religious life and general well-being of the community. They are too occupied with sacerdotal practices to have time for profane pursuits. Consequently, those who carry on the secular activities must provide not only enough for their own requirements, but must make certain that there is sufficient for the priesthood as well. That such a state existed at Kuaua for a period before and after the turn of the 15th century is beyond doubt.

---

98. Today, Indians at Sandia, the only remaining Tiwa-speaking pueblo in the close vicinity of Kuaua, claim that their old people used to live at Kuaua, and that its survivors joined their kinsmen at Sandia. Likewise, Santa Ana Indians say that the pueblo of Kuaua was one of their old towns, which would indicate Keresan affiliation.

99. This, likely, was the condition of Kuaua at the time the Spaniards arrived in the Tiguex province.

During the excavations, some 1200 rooms were uncovered. Over 600 skeletons were unearthed—reflecting a high mortality—and large quantities of pottery, bone and stone artifacts, milling stones, pieces of textiles, fragments of coiled and wickerwork baskets, various kinds of seeds, corn, etc. But the thing which brought Kuaua to international attention was the discovery of a kiva with paintings remaining on its walls and upon its altar.

One day, in February, 1935, in a shovel full of dirt that was thrown onto a wheelbarrow from a test trench in the south plaza, Mr. Vivian saw that there were fragments of plaster covered with flecks of color. He took over the laborer's tools and began a careful investigation. While the portion of wall then uncovered was without decoration, indications were found of underlying pigments. Removing a small section of this sterile outer layer, he made certain that beneath it were paintings of figures. First to be revealed were the outstretched fingers of an upraised hand. Further inspection disclosed a masked figure, painted white and outlined in part by black lines (*see* Pl. VI, center). Other details came to light, as will be discussed below (Layer A-8, fig. 4).

Slowly, as the fill was removed, it became obvious that this figure occupied the westernmost limit of the north wall of a rectangular

PL. III. Murals *in situ,* west and north walls, Kiva III; niche toward left; cleared for jacketing, with Layer A-8 exposed.

chamber. Here, then, in this subterranean room, it appeared that an important discovery had been made. From that time on, the excavation of Kuaua centered around this feature. That it was a ceremonial chamber became certain as more of the walls were uncovered and additional depictions came to light: costumed beings wearing sacred masks, accompanied by ritualistic paraphernalia; altar designs; and many symbolic elements of Pueblo life, shown in black, white, red, yellow, and green colors.[100] The chamber, too, had all the regular features of a Rio Grande kiva: ventilator shaft, altar, fire pit, loom holes, etc.

As the chamber was excavated, three different periods of construction were determined. First, there had been a large, rectangular room. Then, new walls and floor had inclosed a second structure, 18 feet square and eight feet deep. It was on the walls of this construction that the murals occurred. Lastly, a secondary wall had been built across the east end of this room to serve as a reenforcement. It was built directly *over* the wall which bore the paintings, and was devoid of both plaster and decoration. It was found that the north, west, and south walls were adorned with relatively well preserved murals. In contrast, the east wall was largely destroyed. Generally, the plaster—an adobe and silt mixture—had fallen or been knocked from the uppermost portions of the walls, after the chamber's abandonment and before the fill had risen high enough to cover the paintings. The west wall was best preserved, with plaster extending to a height of five feet in the middle, and seven to seven and a half feet at the corners. The walls were about 16 inches thick.

Progress was made slowly. The plastering was not in a single layer only, but in numerous layers one on top of another, forming an aggregate nearly two inches thick. Several of the sheer layers, averaging approximately one-thirtieth of an inch, showed decoration. As this was the first time that such a promising discovery had been made, techniques had to be devised as the excavation proceeded. Mr. Bliss, who had gained technical experience from palaeontological expeditions, was mainly responsible for adapting suitable procedures and carrying out this phase of the project.[101]

MURAL PRESERVATION

At first, a plaster layer was uncovered and allowed to dry naturally. Then the upper part was treated heavily with white shellac to hold the layers against the wall and to prevent their separating from each other. Exposed bits of painting, where the outer plaster coatings had fallen away, were sprayed with liquid celluloid to hold the pigments and to waterproof them. With the plaster thus temporarily secured, the murals were fully exposed on portions of the north and west walls. To uncover the most recent paintings, several undecorated layers of plaster were first removed. As soon as the paintings were disclosed, photographs and scale drawings in matching colors were made.

Due to dampness in the chamber, constant treatment of the plaster layers with shellac and celluloid was necessary. One of the very important features of the Kuaua murals is the fact that these fragile records of the past were preserved.

It became evident that some form of permanent preservation must be devised, which could not be given in the field. No further paintings were exposed, therefore. The remainder of the wall faces was left with the protecting, barren layers of plaster intact. Scaled drawings were made of the walls, and the position of each detail noted, so that the chamber could be rebuilt or shown by model. After this, preparation was made to remove the plaster

---

100. *See* Bliss, 1936:81-86.

101. *See* Bliss, 1935 and 1948, for details.

PL. IV. Original plaster Layer N-41 showing Fig. 93, Paiyatuma, with rabbit stick
(Fig. 90) , under his wing.

layers in their entirety. This, it was readily recognized, would necessitate expenditure of more funds than were available from the agencies participating in this enterprise. Consequently, Frank C. Hibben of the university staff, who had been present when the first pieces of painted plaster were discovered in the test trench, and again when it was ascertained that this was a kiva with its walls painted, led a successful campaign for funds to carry on the preservation work.

Over the plaster and exposed murals, a thick layer of wet tissue paper was first applied. On top of this, layers of plaster-of-paris, and plaster-of-paris with burlap strips, were built up and reenforced with lath. This interior jacket was made in removable sections, averaging three feet in width and extending from

Pl. V. Walls of Kiva III jacketed and being removed by block and tackle for transportation to the laboratory at the University of New Mexico.

top to bottom of the wall. They were inter-locked by means of special joints which could be sawed in two without injuring the murals beneath. After the jacket was completed on the interior of each wall, it was strengthened by a framework of timbers to hold the entire wall immobile.

On the exterior of the chamber, the earth was dug away from the walls, and the latter cut down to the level of the jacket on the interior. Then a horizontal layer of the wall, a foot in depth, was removed from the back of the wall plaster. This strip—the back side of the basal layer of wall plaster—was given a heavy coating of shellac. When this had dried, it was covered with the first layer of the permanent jacket of plaster-of-paris and burlap strips, extending the full length of the wall. Work continued in this manner, a horizontal, one-foot section at a time, until the back of the wall was completely jacketed. Each one-foot section was extended to cover and tie in with the layer above it, to insure rigidity. When this first layer had completely covered the outside walls, a heavy timber framework was built in with the final lath-strengthened layers of jacketing. Then the wall plaster, not otherwise wholly inclosed, was undercut at the bottom, and a heavy strip of jacket carried under the wall, binding the interior and exterior frameworks together.

At the southwest and northwest corners, the great jackets were sawed from top to bottom. The exposed ends were covered with a light layer of plaster-of-paris. There were, then, three large sections, the smaller east section, and an entire altar to be removed by block and tackle from the excavation to trucks, for transportation to the laboratory. As the jacketed segments weighed from 2,080 to 4,000

PL. VI. Original kiva walls propped at an angle in the laboratory for removal, layer by layer. Above left, canvas copy of Layer A-8; in center, copies of Figs. 4, 10, and, above, 16.

pounds, this was no little chore. Nevertheless, they were taken to a room assigned to this project at the university in Albuquerque.

Originally, the subterranean chamber, which was designated as Kiva III in the excavation records, had had no means of access except through a hatchway in the roof. Complete clearing showed, at the east side of the room, a small opening at floor level, leading to a vertical shaft which ascended to the surface on the exterior of the wall. In front of this horizontal opening, leaving walking space between it and the wall, was a rectangular altar; before the altar a rectangular fire pit with rounded corners was sunk into the floor; and in front of the fire pit evidence of ladder bases indicated that this feature rose diagonally, over the pit and altar, to extend out through the hatchway. There were also small holes regularly placed in the floor, which served as anchors of the basal supports for looms, the

upper bars of which were secured to the ceiling beams.

In the laboratory, in Albuquerque, the exterior framework which held the kiva walls was placed next to the laboratory wall, tilted slightly backward. Then the interior framework was removed and the jacket sections sawed apart and lifted free of the painted layers. Sand had filtered between some of the layers and, had the walls been kept fully erect, large pieces of plaster would have fallen off. The humidity of the laboratory had to be maintained at a high degree in order to keep the kiva walls from drying too much.

At this point, the extremely delicate work of uncovering the paintings was begun. This was done, primarily, with flexible palette knives. A careful check was made of each layer, barren or decorated; and it required considerable skill to remove a sterile layer of plaster which had been applied directly over paint-

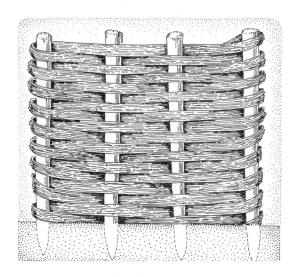

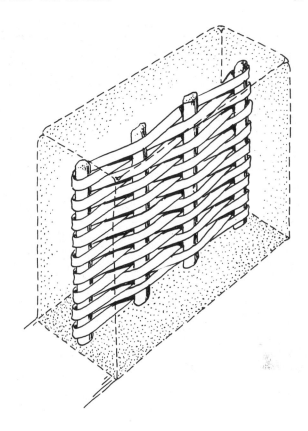

PL. VII. Altar in Kiva III. *Above:* Showing method of construction. *Right:* Perspective view. *Drawings by Dorothy Luhrs.*

ings. As the work progressed, it was found that there were many more plaster layers than field examination had disclosed. Consecutive *numbers* were assigned to each layer of plaster, and *letters*, alphabetically, to each painted layer; individual units were indicated as *figures* and numbered in order as revealed.

As each painted layer was exposed, the depictions were photographed; scaled drawings were made and the colors indicated. The drawings and laboratory notes were prepared by Mr. and Mrs. Frank Palmer. Full-size copies of the murals were painted on canvas by Indian artists, largely, although some of the painting was done by non-Indians. Some restoration was made on these copies, but only where there was evidence as to the original design and coloring. Later, one-quarter size reproductions were made to facilitate studies of the paintings. None of the portrayals bore any resemblance to the descriptions of the chron-

iclers regarding Rodriguez or Lopez. They show no elements which are not purely Indian, and none which are secular in any manner.

Finally, came the preservation of the kiva paintings, themselves. Commercial pressboard was employed as the base material. This was painted with a mixture of adobe with sizing, to provide a natural background color. To the paintings, a hardening solution was applied; this also had a tensile strength. After a second application, a cheap grade of muslin sheeting was placed over the paintings, and more of the solution added to make the contact complete. When almost dry, the muslin was rolled away from the wall and the painted layer of plaster adhered to the cloth. This was then treated and mounted on the permanent base. A solvent was next applied to the cloth, which was rolled off, leaving each original painting on the mount, as it had appeared in the kiva. Layer after layer, this procedure was repeated, through many months, until every possible figure and motif was recorded and preserved. The laboratory phase of the project lasted for more than two years.

Like the walls, the altar was covered with numerous plaster layers. Its height was $32\frac{1}{4}$ inches, its thickness 12, and its width $41\frac{1}{8}$. Here, too, painted layers were interspersed with unpainted layers. Most of the decorations were indeterminable, simply showing patches of color: red, black, green, yellow, and indefinite hues.[102] Eventually, the altar was torn apart and examined. It was found to have been built around four posts embedded in the ground. Around these, flat reed-like fibers were woven, in and out (see Pl. VII). This supporting framework was then covered with adobe, in which potsherds, corn, charcoal, ash, and bits of wood were mixed throughout.[103] The corners were slightly rounded. The potsherds from the altar were identifiable as being of Glaze V and VI types, which would suggest 16th century construction for this feature.

The paintings which had decorated the walls of Kiva VI, in the east plaza, fared less well than those of Kiva III. One section of painted plaster had slid in toto down onto the floor of the chamber. There, water had stood on it for a period of time, so that the paintings were marred by mud cracks. It was impossible to preserve these, though reproductions were made (see Pls. XXVI-XXX).

ASSESSING THE EVIDENCE

The latest cultural remains at Kuaua relate to the Glaze VI (or Glaze F) period, when a decadent type of glaze-paint decoration with simplified designs prevailed. With the Indian wares, were found some examples of glazed pottery from Mexico and a few pieces of majolica ware which was brought in by the Spanish explorers and early colonists; but, all in all, there was very little evidence of Spanish contact at this site, and none whatsoever in the kivas.

Even though paintings were unearthed at Kuaua—paintings of considerable importance in extending our knowledge of ceremonial art and practices of centuries past—the lack of depictions of events or personalities pertaining to the Spaniards, together with the paucity of items which they introduced into the northland, and which certainly would appear at the site where Coronado and his army spent two winters, make it evident that Kuaua could not have been the village which was then identified as Tiguex.[104]

Thus, the archaeological evidence produced at both Puaray (of Bandelier) and Kuaua was of a negative character insofar as the primary objective of the projects was concerned.

As we have observed, the excavations at Kuaua revealed extensive burning. Since Otermin is known to have sacked many towns in this region in 1681-1682, when he attempted to put down the Pueblo uprisings, it had been generally supposed that the end of Kuaua might have been attributable to his destruction.[105]

However, it is to be noted that when Castaño de Sosa was in the Pueblo region, in late 1590 and early 1591, he found many villages deserted, and in some there was evidence of recent warfare inasmuch as many bodies of dead Indians were lying about. Castaño visited the Tiguex province, and it was then recorded: "From one of these deserted pueblos on the east side of the river [Rio Grande] there were

---

102. One was an indeterminable brownish stain which, from its use, was thought to have been green originally (Bliss, 1948:221).

103. Cf. with Castañeda's description, pages 6, 8, herein.

104. The historical data provided by Hammond and Rey, 1940, were unknown at the time of these excavations.

105. Gunn, 1904:309, attributes kiva burning to Governor Trevino, prior to the Rebellion of 1680.

in sight fourteen pueblos, some of which were only one-quarter of a league apart. A number of these pueblos were visited although from most of them the inhabitants had fled, in fear lest the lieutenant [Castaño] had come to avenge the death of the missionaries."[106] Castaño went on to a large and prosperous pueblo, "the last one to be visited on the west side of the river," which Hackett identified as Isleta, but no mention is made of Kuaua.

Then, when Otermin was in the region, he spent considerable time in the Tiguex province, where many of the pueblos were referred to by name, but not Kuaua. This would indicate that it was, then, either a place of no importance or one already abandoned. That the three prominent Tiwa pueblos at that time were Sandia, Puaray (on the same, or east, side of the Rio Grande), and Alameda (on the opposite side of the stream) is adequately recorded. A member of the Otermin expedition, Juan Dominguez de Mendoza, recommended that they unite their forces in a place in the vicinity of these pueblos, which he described as "almost in a triangle, two leagues across."

No mention of Kuaua is found in the accounts of the Rebellion of 1680.

Therefore, it appears likely that the burning of Kuaua—which pertained to the original, south section—occurred at an earlier date, as suggested above. Some time thereafter, the site was occupied more extensively, and by a people with highly developed socio-religious organization which embraced a strong priesthood and interrelated societies of an esoteric nature—as evidenced by the painted kivas. This way of life prevailed during the last half of the 15th century and into the 16th. It has been noted above that a particularly severe drought occurred between the years of 1573 and 1593.

This could have incited internecine warfare and been responsible for the many abandoned pueblos which Castaño noted, and it would seem to explain the depopulation of Kuaua at that time. The archaeological evidence would lend support to this conclusion.

THE MURALS AS MUSEUM DISPLAYS

During the course of subsequent archaeological work and related undertakings at Kuaua, the so-called Painted Kiva (Kiva III) was rebuilt, chiefly under the supervision of Albert G. Ely, following the prepared records. With knowledge gleaned from this and other kivas at the site and from other ruins in the Rio Grande valley, it was possible to restore it to its original state, complete with roof and entry ladder. Then, Indian artists and non-Indian supervisors were again employed, and replicas of the original murals were frescoed on the kiva walls. In 1940, Kuaua was set aside as the Coronado State Monument, where the site and a museum exhibiting the archaeological and historical features of the Tiguex province were dedicated as part of the Cuatro-Centennial observance of the entrada of Francisco Vasquez de Coronado into New Mexico (*see* Pl. VIII).

Today, one may visit the Coronado State Monument, view the museum, the partially restored dwelling units and the five other kivas which have been excavated, stabilized and restored in part, and enter the Painted Kiva which now appears much as it did several centuries ago.

The pressboard mounts with their primary records, except for a display panel in the anthropology department at the University of New Mexico, were—due to inadequate storage space there—transferred to the Museum of

106. Hull, 1916:330.

New Mexico in Santa Fe. The scaled drawings and canvas reproductions were also deposited with the Santa Fe institution. Notable simi-

larities have persisted in the costumes, style of hair dress, masks, ritualistic paraphernalia, altar decorations, and the like, to this day.

PL. VIII. Interior view, Kiva III, after reconstruction, with altar rebuilt, ladder in place over fire pit, and Layer N-41 frescoed onto the east and south wall. *New Mexico State Tourist Division photo.*

III. STEPS TOWARD UNDERSTANDING

STUDY OF THE PAINTINGS

It was the hope of Dr. Hewett that informants from each of the different Pueblo linguistic groups might be engaged to aid with
the study of the Kuaua kiva paintings. It was
realized that such informants should be found
among the older men who were versed in the
ceremonial dogma of their respective pueblos.
Dr. Hewett knew that such men as were thoroughly indoctrinated in their cultural mores,
and with whom we had sufficient friendly
relationships as to make possible the securing
of desired information, were of such an age
as to render this aspect of our project urgent.
Accordingly, in the fall of 1938, arrangements
were made for the author to initiate the study.

In September, certain of the quarter-size
copies of the kiva paintings were placed in the
hands of a Keres man known to be a ceremonial leader in his pueblo. The following
month, a trip was made to Zuñi, where other
copies were discussed with an old friend and
cooperative informant. In order to better record the information being derived, particularly to comprehend the Zuñi words, the assistance of Hulda R. Hobbs,[107] a member of
the museum staff at that time, was made available, and she accompanied the author on the
trips to Zuñi. This procedure was followed for
something over a year.

The Keres man wanted time to study the
paintings. Accordingly, certain copies were

left in his possession, for later reporting.[108]
Our Zuñi friend was willing to help, and he
identified certain figures without hesitation;
others required study. We soon realized that
we did not have the time to continue the
study, "cold," as it were. With him, too, a few
of the canvas rolls were left. As he found the
time, he gave them his consideration. Then,
after weeks had passed, he sent word that he
was ready to discuss the paintings.

At no time has there been an opportunity
to take up this study with Tewa- or Tiwa-
speaking informants, nor with the Hopi,
which we know would be most rewarding.
Certain individuals from both of these Tanoan groups, and other Keresans, have indicated some knowledge of the paintings; others
have seemed unacquainted with their significance.

As soon as we obtained information concerning a particular painted layer, we studied
the existing ethnological and historical liter-
ature, and endeavored to tie in the Kuaua
representations with known and recorded observations. In some instances, this was profit-
able and encouraging; in others, we could find
no corresponding records.

During this same period of time, the author
was made curator of ethnology at the Museum
of New Mexico, and was charged with plan-

---

107. Now Mrs. Finis L. Heidel, Lovington, New Mexico.

108. Ultimately, he divulged a certain amount of information, but his conservatism regarding sacred matters
caused him to withhold most of what he knew. Later, he
died, taking his knowledge to the grave, rather than reveal
it to the uninitiated.

ning the remodeling of the old Santa Fe Armory, which had become the property of the museum, and with preparing installations in the resultant Hall of Ethnology. This major undertaking demanded more and more attention through the succeeding years. About the time the new hall was opened to the public, World War II commanded the scene, and field work had to be curtailed. The mural study was carried forward only insofar as library research would permit, and as time allowed.

In the spring of 1945, the author did some further work at Zuñi with the informant hereinafter referred to as Zna'ote. That autumn, she was granted sabbatical leave from the museum in order to pursue studies at Columbia University. It was the feeling of Dr. Hewett that the Kuaua paintings might serve as suitable subject for a doctoral dissertation. Consequently, a full set of the quarter-size reproductions was taken to New York. The departmental staff at Columbia upon viewing them decided, however, that such an undertaking would be of too great a scope; and a subject capable of limitation was favored. For this reason, the mural research was put aside and full attention was given, first, to academic studies; then to preparation of a dissertation, the subject of which had little apparent bearing on the Kuaua paintings; and, then, resumption of museum duties in the fall of 1946.

Fortunately, about this time, a local artist, Miss Agnes C. Sims, became seriously interested in the study of petroglyphs—the rock carvings which so copiously adorn smooth lithic surfaces over great areas in the Southwest. Many people have become engrossed in similar studies, but in rare instances, if any, have their interests led them into exhaustive research with view to interpreting the petroglyphs and tying them in with archaeological and ethnological data and items of material culture. In this case, extensive field work, with library and specimen correlations, re-

sulted in valuable identifications and interrelationships.[109] The consequences were so striking that it was arranged to have an exhibition in the Hall of Ethnology, where petroglyph reproductions were shown in conjunction with archaeological and ethnological specimens, together with explanatory data. With the knowledge gained from these undertakings, it was a natural consecution that the study be extended to the Kuaua murals, as well as those from the Awatovi excavations,[110] which were initiated in Hopiland, northeastern Arizona, in 1935, at almost the same time that the discovery of the Kuaua paintings was made. Since both researchers were working along parallel lines and dealing largely with the same data, it was agreed that they should pool their knowledge. Miss Sims was appointed a Fellow of the School of American Research and, as such, worked closely with the author for several months, on the interpretation of the Kuaua mural paintings.

Something of what we have learned and suspect to be true is set forth herein. By her own choice, Miss Sims is confining her remarks to the appendix which appears at the end of this work: *Rock Carvings, a Record of Folk History.*

Watson Smith has included many references to Kuaua in his splendid presentation of the Awatovi murals.[111] During the last several seasons, the University of New Mexico, working at an archaeologic site known as Pottery Mound on the bank of the Rio Puerco, west of Los Lunas, New Mexico, unearthed sixteen kivas, all of which contained mural paint-

109. *See* Sims, 1949. Her work was supported in part by a Neosho fellowship made available through the agency of the late Frederick H. Douglas of Denver, Colorado.

110. Photographs of the Awatovi mural paintings were made available to us at the Museum of New Mexico, and photo copies of the Kuaua murals were sent to Watson Smith, at Peabody Museum, Harvard University. Information was exchanged freely.

111. Smith, 1952.

ings.[112] Studies of those have been initiated. Thus, there is coming to be a significant amount of material of this nature, and all should be made available for further studies along many lines of research.

It is this latter fact which has prompted the publication of the present work, as it is. Rather than hold up the work indefinitely, it seems only fair to make the Kuaua mural paintings available to all such investigators as may have the desire and time to utilize them in any manner.

The author realizes fully that the information is lamentably incomplete, and uneven in character. The study makes no pretense of being concluded. Other duties preclude the devotion of more time to the continuance of this undertaking. It could go on for years . . . and should.

CHRONOLOGY OF THE PAINTINGS

In the laboratory at the University of New Mexico, the stripping of plaster layers from the kiva walls showed that there were many layers of plaster. Seven sterile layers were removed before the first painted layer was revealed. According to the scheme of numbering, this was denoted as Layer A-8, indicating that it was the *eighth* layer of plaster, but the *first* of the painted ones encountered. Inasmuch as the first painted layer disclosed by the excavations and subsequent stripping was the *latest* to have been applied to the kiva walls, the layers more deeply placed were increasingly older. The practice of replastering domestic units and kivas is widespread,[113] but the interval of plastering is unknown.

Today, the custom prevails among the Pueblo peoples to replaster their structures—at least on the exterior—prior to fiestas.[114] We also know that, occasionally, excessive rains necessitate repairs and replastering at other times; and the same is true when structural features become weakened, allowing for pillars or posts, walls, or roof, to slump or otherwise indicate too much stress.

It was sometimes difficult, or impossible, to ascertain whether particular figures relate to one plaster layer or to another. It may be that full depictions never existed. At Awatovi, Smith found evidence that painting renewals did not always include the entire room. He states: ". . . sometimes two layers of plaster that were in immediate sequence on one wall correspond respectively to layers on a contiguous wall that were separated from each other by one or more different and unrelated layers."[115] As has been noted, the east wall of Kiva III apparently gave trouble when the chamber was in use, and a reenforcing wall was built over the original construction, covering the painted plaster. It may be expected that lesser repairs may have been made prior to taking this severe form of strengthening that portion of the chamber. These, too, probably would have disturbed the continuity of plaster layers and of the ceremonial representations thereon. At Awatovi, there were instances where patches of mortar over certain uneven areas only occurred.[116] At Kuaua, those figures which were indeterminate and between layers which contained definite murals were indicated by letters with numbers in prime position, for example: Layer O^1-44, fig. 105. Some of the paintings were very simple, with figures in limited areas only.

The next plaster layer under A-8 was also painted, and was accordingly indicated as Layer B-9. There was then an undecorated layer, which was followed by one on which

---

112. *See* Hibben, 1955:179-180; 1960:267-275. It may be noted that one of our northern Tiwa friends, upon seeing the depictions in Kiva II, remarked on the similarity of certain figures with those still being used in kivas in her pueblo.

113. Smith 1952 Table 2.

114. *Cf.* Parsons 1939:493, note.

115. Smith, 1952:12.

116. Smith, 1952:17.

there was a prominent yellow band that extended to the limits of the painting. Sections of the complete layers of plaster were found *in situ* at the extremes of the walls. This yellow band, on Layer C-11 (Pl. XXIII), enabled the technicians to determine the layers, either backward or forward therefrom. The final laboratory count of plaster layers was 85.

INDIAN CONCEPTS AND SYMBOLS

In order for non-Indians to comprehend even a little of the lore to which the Kuaua paintings pertain, it is necessary, first, to have some knowledge of the concepts fundamental to the Indian philosophy, religion, and social organization.

Primitive peoples live in a world of mysticism and symbolism. Each day, man had to derive his existence from the plant and animal world about him, and so these things were of the utmost significance. Their response to the environment and elemental factors were closely observed. And so it was that the Indian geared his life to the scene around him. The result was a culture which integrated the natural phenomena with mankind and all biota of his world. Between all there was universal interplay. This formative type of religion prevailed over wide expanses of the western hemisphere during the early centuries A.D., and in some regions long before.

The Pueblo Indians are agriculturists. Once agriculture is introduced into a way of life, whether it is the result of indigenous development or whether it is a borrowed trait, change is inevitable. Agriculture prescribes a sedentary mode of life; it requires a specific type of implements and procedures for handling them—and these provide the foundation for rites and ceremonies which grow out of continuing cycles of behavior.[117] Someone is

a leader, the one with the know-how, and he directs the formalities which agriculture demands; he introduces calendrical observances which, by the very nature of things, give eminence to the *sun*. The *earth*, though equally important, is here, always at hand; the Indian lives in it or on it, and from it. But the sun comes and goes, and alters its course; it is something with which man must reckon. The *moon* divides the year into time periods and is thus a factor to be considered, almost as the earth which gives sustenance. These simple origins give rise to cults and attendant procedures, to the priesthoods, formalization, and all that follows.

Pueblo religious societies, controlled by hierarchal priesthoods, "own," or have preemptive rights to the use of a kiva; they likewise own the particular ceremonies associated therewith and the paraphernalia pertaining to them. Some kivas are used exclusively by one society; others may be employed for the activities of more than one society, but are usually restricted to the use of one society at a time, or to the combined observances of associated groups. Some ceremonials extending over several consecutive days and nights are held at regular intervals; some are held annually; and some are of irregular occurrence. The ceremonials include alternating in-the-kiva rites and plaza functions: song, dance, and drama; magical acts, prayers, paintings; initiations, supplications for rain and well-being, cleansing and seasonal solemnizations, e.g., the solstice observances. The ceremonials represent and/or depict folk history with great symbolism.

As will be seen, there is not the slightest feature of the Kuaua murals which is without significance to the portrayals and all that lies back of them. Cushing gives proper attention to the way everything is ordered and interrelated at Zuñi.[118] Everything is animate. Directions are of utmost importance, with far reach-

---

117. *See* White, 1930:618, for hypothesis of ceremonial development.

118. Cushing, 1896.

ing relationships pertaining to each.[119] There are close ties between directions and colors.

At Zuñi, the association is thus: north, yellow; west, blue; south, red; east, white; above, mixed ("pinto"); and below, black. The Hopi and Keres follow the same scheme, though the latter have local differences regarding the above and below. Jemez (Towa) recognizes the same associations for the cardinal points, but evidences uncertainty as to the zenith and nadir designations. Of the Tiwa, Isleta shows a somewhat varying association: north, black; west, yellow (or blue); south, blue (or red); east, white; and considers the above and below together, as vari-colored. The Tewa use yellow for the west, and blue for the north, agreeing with the Hopi, Keres, Towa, and Zuñi for the south and east; nadir is vari-colored, and zenith is black. The customary manner of naming the directions is as here given, or anti-clockwise.[120]

Scanty evidence of Pueblo mural paintings has come from archaeological sites from time to time,[121] the earliest being discovered in chambers dating to the Pueblo II period, and thus probably prior to A.D. 1100. Smith calls attention to the fact that such art, at that time, occurred only in the northern and eastern parts of the San Juan drainage, and he suggests: "Just possibly this area may have been the cradle of an art form that flowered luxuriantly in later centuries both to the east in the Rio Grande Valley and to the west along the Little Colorado and its tributaries."[122]

In the succeeding culture period, Pueblo III (in general, A.D. 1100-1300),[123] occur-

rences of mural paintings are recorded over a much wider area.[124] Therefore, peoples moving into the Rio Grande valley around 1300 would, doubtless, have had a more or less developed concept of ceremonial art and its related ritualism.[125] About this time, an increase in religious representation and formal portrayals becomes evident. As we have seen, it was at this period that Kuaua manifested new cultural stimulus. The older black-on-white, carbon paint wares, dating from approximately 1250-1350, occur in limited quantities, but glaze-painted, red pottery is in great preponderance.

The fact that kiva paintings were noted to such a wide extent by the early Spanish chroniclers, and that excavations have disclosed them at Kuaua, Awatovi, Pottery Mound, and other locations, reveals religious fervor and expression of the Pueblo IV period (roughly A.D. 1350-1500), and makes it apparent that the florescence of ceremonial art was general throughout the Pueblo area of the Southwest.[126] Doubtless the influence

---

119. *Cf.* Parsons, 1939:365.

120. *See* Smith, 1952:170-171, for further discussion.

121. Smith, 1952, gives a record of known occurrences.

122. Smith, 1952:57.

123. Since the tentative assignment of dates to the periods set up by the Pecos classification, it has been determined that Pueblo III in the Chaco Canyon area is better covered by the dates A.D. 950-1150, while the Classic culture did not prevail in the Mesa Verde region until A.D. 1150-1300. To complete the record in terms of the Pecos classification, the earlier Anasazi periods mentioned

in this work are roughly covered by these dates: Basket Maker II, from around the birth of Christ to A.D. 400 or 450; Basket Maker III, about 400 to 800; Pueblo I, chiefly 800 to 900; with Pueblo II, about 700 to 900 or 950.

124. Smith, 1952:57-68.

125. At the ruin of Chetro Ketl in Chaco Canyon, a spectacular discovery was made a few years ago, when a lower, sealed room was opened during the process of stabilization. Placed there during the Pueblo III period was the almost complete assemblage of carved and painted wood items from a ceremonial outfit: elaborate bird forms cut from thin slats, painted realistically, and intricately assembled—obviously to permit of certain movability; lightning sticks, wands, flutes, stone points, and other items. Significantly, these specimens were tentatively identified by four elderly Hopi priests as comprising paraphernalia used today in their Blue Flute ceremony. This reveals a blending of art and religion among the Pueblo Indians for more than 800 years, and perhaps for as much as 1000 years. The Zuñi had comparable ceremonies. *See also* Haury, 1958:4, and Kidder and Guernsey, 1919:145-147.

126. From a cave in the vicinity of Monticello, New Mexico, a long, narrow, tabular specimen in wood shows a figure simply carved, with features, costume, and articles of adornment painted with native pigments in white, black, and red. This example, dating to the mid-1300's,

spread to neighboring peoples at that time.

When one recalls the vicissitudes and considers the impact of foreign cultures to which the Southwestern Indians have been subjected since 1540—through Spanish, Mexican, and "American" administrations—one begins to gain some appreciation of the universal strength and tenacity of the indigenous socioreligious structure. He finds that through all these centuries there has been little deviation in the recountings, by recitation and song, which had originated long before, with graphic portrayals such as those painted on the walls of ceremonial rooms at Kuaua. Five or six hundred years after the murals were placed in the Kuaua chambers, men versed in the esoteric dogma of modern Pueblo organizations are able to recognize the symbolism and can translate the events and ceremonies depicted as well as we can read a book.[127]

---

proves that for some 600 years Indians of the Southwest have conceived of dimensional portrayals of ceremonial figures, and that they achieved artistic results verging on sculpture in the round. Judging from the multi-strand necklace, pendant, and ear loops (presumably representing white shell), which are much the same as articles of adornment shown on several of the Kuaua mural figures, as will be seen later (e.g., Layer G-26, fig. 113), this being portrays one of the ancient Pueblo ceremonial personages. The shells, cloud-terrace headdress with small shaft sunk in the top to support an upright feather, and tasseled girdle bespeak a "rain maker" function.

Haury, 1945, describes material of ceremonial nature found in Double Butte cave, a site in the Gila valley, about two miles southwest of Tempe, Arizona, which includes wooden items that appear comparable in significance and age to the Monticello specimen. There are painted prayersticks and an early katsina form; carved shell figures show similarity to Kuaua depictions. See pp. 196-200; see also Hough, 1914.

127. One of the exhibits installed in the Hall of Ethnology included a set of authentic sandpaintings, which were made by an old Singer and his assistant, who were brought from the Navaho reservation to Santa Fe. As they were being taken back to their home, a stop was made at the Coronado State Monument, where Kiva III at Kuaua had been restored. Upon seeing the murals which had been replaced on the kiva walls (Layer G-26), the Singer immediately began identifying the personages depicted, in terms of Navaho mythology and ceremonialism. They were equally as well known to him as they proved to be to the

MYTHOLOGY

In general, the Indians acknowledge the omnipotent as a universal being, as the firmament above, observable in the Milky Way, but who pervades all space, and who is, or was, thought to have created the clouds and the great waters of the world.[128] Inasmuch as the basic pattern varies but little among numerous groups of Indian peoples, something of the Zuñi concept will be related, using Zuñi terms for later comparative purposes, particularly in view of the fact that information regarding Zuñi is relatively extensive. This is not to be construed, however, that the Zuñi language necessarily prevailed at Kuaua. Many Keresan words appear in this work, and in some cases the Keres data are more abundant than those for Zuñi.[129] The information at hand is not sufficient to prove that any one language, or languages, was spoken at Kuaua.

The Zuñi recognize a supreme, life-giving power, a spiritual force, or *Áwonawilona*,[130] which was made manifest in person and form of the sun, thus the Sun Father, the great god,

---

Pueblo sages. On another occasion, it was found that the Navaho wife of a Zuñi man had great familiarity with the Kuaua paintings. See also Smith, 1952:104.

128. In many instances it is impossible to know whether beliefs and practices are viewed in traditional manner, or whether they have been altered or replaced by modern teachings or experiences. Accordingly, present tense verb forms are used in this work in situations where concepts or traits may have changed in recent times, or may differ from one indigenous group to another.

129. Mr. Edmund J. Ladd of the pueblo of Zuñi, graduate of the University of New Mexico (where he majored in anthropology), views this as indicating that many aspects of present day Zuñi religion have been introduced from the Rio Grande curing societies, via Acoma and Laguna. He says: "As a matter of fact, many esoteric songs and some prayers belonging to the various societies are not Zuñi but Keresan. Some members do not even know what the meaning of these words are. Since the songs are of esoteric nature, only a select few know these—which have been handed down from one generation to another without explanation of meaning."

130. Kroeber, 1916:273, gives the fullest form as *Ho'p-aw-onna-w-ill-onna*, meaning "he who owns our paths," or "he who holds the ways for us."

giver of light and warmth, and "through the supreme power the giver of life."[131]

At the outset, then, it may be said that the basic religious doctrine of the Indians is monotheistic.

To continue with mythology, however, we find that associated with the sun was the moon, Moon Mother, considered to be his wife [or sister], the giver of light at night and divider of the year into months. Certain symbolization or insignia came to represent this Sun being, but he could assume any desired form, and this has led to much confusion in the identification of personages through which the work of the Sun Father is accomplished. An increasing array of manifestations became necessary as the religious leaders developed priesthoods and associated organizations.[132]

This is observed in that other associates were designated to carry on sacred duties: Below, dwelt the Rain priest *(Shíwanni)* and his wife *(Shíwanókia)*, the priestess of fecundity. These latter two were superhuman beings, "who labored not with hands but with hearts and minds." The Rain priest is said to have created the fixed stars and constellations from spittle bubbles of many colors. These celestial powers are represented in paintings and carvings. To portray her potency, the priestess similarly created the Corn or Earth Mother *(Áwitelin 'Síya),* a terrestrial being, the giver of vegetation.

Following Mrs. Stevenson, "certain subterranean members" of the deific assemblage are represented by persons wearing masks, and these are: Salt Mother, Corn Father, White Shell Woman, Red Shell Woman, Turquois Man, the Plumed Serpent *(Kolowisi),* and others. Those which the Zuñi do not personify, but which they represent by figurines carved in wood are: the gods of War, children of the Sun Father, who have their successors but not impersonators on the earth; *Póshai yanki,* the culture hero;[133] and the Corn Mother.

According to Mrs. Stevenson, the Rain priest and his wife were parents of the *Áshiwi,* the original people of Zuñi.[134] More familiar to the present day Zuñi is the belief that their ancestors were living in the four worlds below, "when the Sun Father wanted 'his children' to 'come up,' and thus caused them to come

---

131. Stevenson, 1904:22; *see* Cushing, 1896:379. Bandelier (1890:I.200) makes it clear that it is not the sun which the Indian reveres, but the spiritual being residing on or in it.

Bunzel (1932:480) says that with the Pueblo Indians the essence of religious participation is collectivism. She states: "The supernatural conceived always as a collectivity, a multiple manifestation of the divine essence, is approached by the collective force of the people in a series of great public and esoteric rituals whose richness, variety, and beauty have attracted the attention of poets and artists of all countries."

132. Bunzel (1932:547-548) has said that: "There is no single origin myth but a long series of separate myths. Each ceremonial group has a myth which contains, in addition to a general synopsis of early history, the mythological sanction for its own organization and rituals . . . . These separate myths are preserved in fixed ritualistic form and are sometimes recited during ceremonies, and are transferred like any other esoteric knowledge. . . . The main outlines of the origin myths are known to all, and great delight is found in recounting them. The history myth is not fixed in form or expression and varies in comprehensiveness according to the special knowledge of the narrator."

133. He and his associates were the possessors of "the secrets of Mystery medicine, and whom the Divine Ones changed into beasts to serve as guards for the six regions: cougar, north; bear, west; badger, south; wolf, east; eagle, zenith; and shrew, nadir; others were converted to rattlesnakes to 'preside with wisdom over the earth.' " These becoming the animal gods, distributed their medicines, tablet altars, and dry (or sand) paintings to the esoteric societies (Stevenson, 1904:409). *See* footnote 309 herein.

134. Stevenson, 1904:28. "The Áshiwi were queer beings when they came to this world. They had short depilous tails, long ears (at night they lay on one ear and covered themselves with the other), and webbed feet and hands, and their bodies and heads were covered with áwisho (moss), a lengthy tuft being on the fore part of the head, projecting like a horn . . . . After the Áshiwi moved to a spring not far distant from their place of nativity, which they named Áwisho, the Divine Ones amputated the tails and ears and cut the webbed feet and hands with their stone knives . . . ." See Pl. A-1, page 214.

forth."[135] Sun Father created two sons, the Divine Ones.[136] In order that they could pass from the undermost world to his presence, each was provided with a rainbow [or cloud bow], lightning arrows, and a cloud shield. The Divine Ones aided the people in their progress from the undermost world through the succeeding worlds, into this world.[137] The place of emergence is one surrounded by lore and occult meaning. This outer world was reached just as the Evening star rose above the horizon. He, then, is considered as second warrior to the Sun Father. The Morning star (Venus or Jupiter)[138] or *Móyachun thlánna,* is his first warrior. At Awisho, near their place of nativity, the Divine Ones organized four esoteric fraternities: *Shí wanna kwe,* the priesthood of the Priest people;[139] the *Néwe kwe* or galaxy fraternity;[140] *Saniya ki kwe,* priesthood of the Hunt (also called Coyote, *Sus ki kwe*);[141]

and the *Áchi ya kwe* (Great Knife people; "makers and defenders of pathways for the people")[142] or *Ha lo kwe* (Ant people). The first two fraternities are closely allied, the Shiwannakwe being regarded as the elder brother of the Newekwe.

It is said that the people traveled about for many years. Finally, the Rain priest decided to send forth two of his children, a youth *(Síwulu tsíwa)* and a maiden *(Síwulu tsíya tsa),* to look for a good place to build their village. The two ascended a mountain, where the maiden stayed to rest, while her brother looked over the country. When the youth returned and found his sister asleep, she appeared so beautiful that he desired her. His act enraged her; and this unnatural union resulted in the birth of ten (or twelve)[143] children, that same night. Thenceforth, they talked a changed language, but there was no change in appearance. The first born was normal in all respects, but the other children lacked the seeds of generation.

Realizing that it was not well for them to be alone, the youth hastened to make things ready for the coming of their people. He created two rivers and a lake with a village in its depths. The lake village is called *Kóthluwaláwa,* and it has the great ceremonial house of the gods in its center. This house has four windows through which those not privileged to enter may view the dancing. Mrs. Stevenson states that, "Only deceased members of the *Kóti-*

---

135. Ladd, manuscript notation. He knows of no specific mention in the folk history of the priestly couple being the parents of the Zuñi people.

136. Stevenson records these as *"Ków wituma,* the elder, and *Wátsusi,* the younger." Cushing (1896:381) speaks of them as ". . . the Beloved Twain who descended; first, Úanam Éhkona, the Beloved Preceder, then Úanam Yaluna, the Beloved Follower, Twin brothers of Light, yet Elder and Younger, the Right and the Left, like to question and answer in deciding and doing. To them the Sunfather imparted, still retaining, control-thought and his own knowledge-wisdom, even as to the offspring of wise parents their knowingness is imparted and as to his right hand and his left hand a skillful man gives craft freely surrendering not his knowledge . . . ."

137. Cushing, 1896:383, records these as *Ánosin tehuli,* "womb of sooty depth," *K'ólin tehuli,* "umbilical-womb, or place of gestation," *Áwisho tehuli,* "vaginal ['moss' or 'algae'—E. J. L.] womb (sex generation)," *Tépahaian tehuli,* "womb of parturition," and the present world, *Tek'ohaian ulahnane,* "world of light and knowledge." NOTE: When the author first went to Zuñi, it was found that the older people were still mourning because Cushing was not able to return from Washington. On various occasions, Zna'ote said: "What Cushy says, that is right."

138. Stevenson, 1904:26, and Bunzel, 1932:487.

139. Ladd says the members abstain from eating bee plant and jackrabbit.

140. At Zuñi today, "This society," says Ladd, "has two sections, one a medicine group, the other 'clowns'."

141. Ladd cautions that this society is not to be confused with the Suskikwe, or Coyote, clan.

142. Cushing, 1896:388. Ladd concurs in this, saying that the Achiyakwe and Halokwe are two sections of the same group; he says that "tHlé we kwe," as recorded by Stevenson (1904:410) is incorrect. The latter source tells of the initiation of members into the *tHlewekwe* (Wood or Staff people—sword swallowers) fraternity by its original director, who had "received the knowledge of sword swallowing from Áchiyalátopa (a being with wings and tail of knives) at Shípapolima." Her error, then, may have been primarily in statement.

143. *See* Cushing's accounts, 1896:400 and 1941:149.

kili (mythologic fraternity)[144] go within the walls."[145] She adds that the greatest of the Zuñi ancestral gods, *'Kianilona*, reigns there in Kothluwalawa, where the Council of the Gods appeals to him for water with which the rain makers may water the earth, "the male gods sprinkling with plume sticks dipped in gourd jugs of water and the female gods from vases."[146]

When the people came to the river,[147] the leaders[148] crossed the fearsome stream, but strange chills pervaded them; it was "as though they were themselves changing in being to creatures moving and having being in the waters."[149] The poor women who followed closely, with the little children on their backs, became crazed and terrified, as these, wriggling and scratching from fright, dropped into the water and became instantly changed into tortoises, water snakes, frogs, tadpoles, and other aquatic creatures. These transformed ones went from the river to the lake village, where they were restored to normal condition. As recorded by Stevenson, "They attained to the age of maturity at once, becoming the Council of the Gods, the prototypes of the Kómosona [whom she calls the director general of the Kotikili, or kiva society], first body of Ashiwanni [Rain priests],[150] and Gods of War."

The father and the nine last-born children became old dance men or *Kóyemshi* (all Mud Heads or masked clowns), the former (actually Siwulutsiwa) came to be known as *Awan tachu*, father of the newly created gods;[151] and the mother became old dance woman (*Kómo katsi),* the mother of the gods, who bear the name of Ko ko.[152] The first born became the

these transformed beings "becoming the Council of the Gods." He adds: "The Zuñi concept of life in the hereafter is pretty well defined. The *Koko* [Rain people] are those who have died, and as such reflect the earthly manifestations of the deceased." Further, Mr. Ladd says: "I do not know why the early authors failed to understand this, but as far as I have been able to find out there is no information on this aspect." He points out that the "first body of Ashiwanni" are separate, and are not related except in an overall religious cycle.

Throughout Mrs. Stevenson's work of 1904, Mr. Ladd finds many statements with which he disagrees, and of which he says: "They are not big errors, but one leads to another, and puts the whole picture out of focus." He does not profess to know all about Zuñi, in fact, he says: "There are a large number of individual items which I know very little about, but I know they are not exactly current." Where he is certain, Mr. Ladd has given this work the benefit of his knowledge. In some instances, he has indicated errors in recording, in other cases he has questioned statements; in certain situations he has not been free to reveal the correct information. Also, he feels that there are probably points which he missed in going over the manuscript.

151. *See* Kroeber, 1916:273.

152. Cushing, 1920:632, records the "Mud Heads" as *Ko-yi-ma-shi*, "the oracles (or *Kâ'-kâ*), of all olden sayings of deep meanings,"—the sages of the ancients (1896-:402), priest-clowns.

At Zuñi, as noted above, the Koko are considered as the ones who have died; these are represented by a society of the gods—the Koko organization.

When the Spaniards entered the Southwest, they became acquainted with the masked personages who took the part of the gods in Indian ceremonials. As shown on page 17, the early chroniclers recorded them as *catzina,* apparently approximating the sound of some Rio Grande Pueblo designation. This is thought to be a Keresan term, which is pronounced *kâ'tsi na*. The original Hopi recording was very similar. Subsequent pronunciations and spellings have varied considerably, both among the Indians and non-Indians who have made use of the word—which has come to have rather wide application.

Bunzel, for instance, uses the character "c" to represent the sound "sh," and she says: "The word *koko* is used

144. Kroeber, 1916:271, says a better rendering into English is "god-fraternity." Ladd translates it as "kiva society."

145. Stevenson, 1904:32. *See* Cushing, 1896:404-405.

146. Stevenson, 1904:21. Mr. Ladd knows of no ranking of the gods, and he says that every Zuñi who dies—women and children, as well as the men who are members of the Kotikili, or kiva society—goes to Kothluwalawa.

147. Identified as the Little Colorado, "where now flow the red waters" (Cushing, 1941:149).

148. Recorded by Cushing, 1896:403, as "the Bear and Crane father-people," and by Stevenson, 1904:33, as the *'Hlewekwe* or Wood fraternity.

149. Cushing, 1896:404.

150. This includes the Rain priests of the six regions, elder and younger brother Bow priests, and the priestess of fecundity (Stevenson, 1904:33, 319).

Mr. Ladd says that Stevenson is in error when she has

dancer for good, *Kó' k'oshi* [or *Kór kokshi*].[153] Father Koyemshi and the nine old dance men dwelt in the mountain which he had created to be his perpetual home, while the old dance woman and the first born dwelt in the lake village.

After the creation of the gods, which was the beginning of the veneration of the ancients, Father Koyemshi decided that these gods should not appear outside the dance house unmasked. Stevenson records that, "He therefore created masks by placing his finger to his mouth and rubbing the spittle in a small spot on the floor of the dance house, a mask appearing almost immediately each time the finger touched the floor. Masks were made in this way for each god."[154] The Divine Ones visited the Koyemshi at Lake Village, examined the masks, and returned to tell of them to the Rain priests.

Many conflicts occurred with strange peoples whom the Zuñi encountered in their journey of seeking the Middle Place of the world for their village. The Divine Ones grew weary of fighting, and requested Sun Father to send two others to take their place as warriors. The Sun "caused a heavy rain to fall until the cascade of the mountain side no longer glided placidly over the rocks to the basin below, but danced along; and in her joy she [the cascade] was caught in the sun's embrace, and bore twin children, who issued from the foam."[155]

The Divine Ones discovered the two little fellows, and questioned them. Finding that they were born of Sun and Laughing Water, were of good heart, and knew all about fighting, the Divine brothers told the diminutive ones of their wish to have them work in their stead. The newborn gods agreed to fight the opposing forces who were keeping their people from the Middle Place. Each was given a turquois rabbit stick and certain games. The elder War god bore the name, *Úyuyewi*, and the younger War god, *Ma'a sai wi;*[156] and the two were called *Áhaiyuta*. After the Divine War gods reached Zuñi and presented a Scalp dance, they disappeared from the earth forever. The priesthood of the Bow was organized, with Uyuyewi and Ma'asaiwi as its first directors.

As understood by Stevenson, in the Council of the Gods, the director general of the gods was *Paútiwa;* there was his deputy or *pekwinna* ('Kiaklo) —the Sun's speaker; and the deputy to the Sun Father, *Shúlawitsi*. In the Zuñi priesthood, corresponding positions are held by the *Kómosonna,* or the god director of the katsina or kiva society; his deputy, the god speaker *(Kópekwinna);* and the deputy to the Sun Father, who is also regarded as the Rain priest of the Zenith.[157] Also there are those whom the Zuñi call *Sáyatasha* (Long Horn), First *Yámuhakto, Hú tutu,* Second *Yámahakto,* and the *Sál imopiya*—warriors and seed gatherers of the lake village.[158]

There came a time, after the people were settled in their present location, when Pautiwa desired them to become personally acquainted with their gods, and to learn the details of their coming to this world and of their migrations. His deputy passed from Lake Village to the Middle Place *(Ítiwanna)* on the backs of the Koyemshi. He related the history, and announced that in eight days all of the ancestral gods would come. For this reason,

alike of the being impersonated and the mask wherein resides the power of transformation. The mask is the corporeal substance of the katcina, and in wearing it a man assumes the personality of the god whose representation he bears" (1932:847). *See* Kroeber, 1916:272, on recording of koko or *kokko*.

153. Practically every Indian word used in this work has been recorded in more than one form. In large part, we have employed the spelling used by a major researcher, and then have followed that rendering consistently, except where directly quoted otherwise. In numerous instances, the forms used by Mr. Ladd have been followed. Lastly, our own recordings have, of course, been used.

154. Stevenson, 1904:34.

155. Stevenson, 1904:35.

156. *See* Cushing, 1896:422, and Stevenson, 1904:35, each of whom records this name as *Matsailema*. We are following Ladd's recording.

six chambers were to be built, one for each of the six regions, and these were to be dedicated to the gods. Before the deputy left, a man of the Pitchikwe or Dogwood clan[159] examined his mask, and later made one like it. After the deputy had gone, the six *kíwitsiwe* — each designated today by the generalized word, *kiva* —were built and put in readiness for the Holy ones.

The gods came into the village wearing their masks. The Rain priests and others were gathered in the North kiva to receive them. When the gods entered the chamber, they removed their masks, and then Father Koyemshi told the assemblage to look well at the masks. The Rain priest of the North, a man of the Dogwood (or Macaw) clan, received Pautiwa's mask, made its counterpart, and wore it henceforth. The director of the Newekwe fraternity examined the mask of Father Koyemshi, and copied it;[160] others of this fraternity copied the remaining nine masks of the Koyemshi. Then, Father Koyemshi organized a fraternity to impersonate the deities, with a man of the Deer clan as director general of the katsina society; a man of the Badger clan as his deputy; and two warriors to the Zenith, known as the *Kópi tlasshwanni,* the first from the Deer clan, and the second from Badger. Others of the Zuñi were divided by the director general, regardless of clan, among the six kivas; the division

158. In the priesthood, these are shown to correlate with the Rain priest of the North (Kya kwemosi), Rain priest of the West, of the South, and of the East, respectively; and the elder and younger brother Bow priests— the earthly representatives of the War gods (Stevenson, 1904:33). *See* Cushing, 1883:22.

159. Mrs. Stevenson believed Cushing wrong in giving this as "Macaw people," instead of Dogwood. Actually, according to Ladd, the Pitchikwe sometimes use the two divisions, *Mu la·kwe* (Macaw) and *K'wa la shi kwe* (Raven); he substitutes *A·ya ho kwe* or Tansy Mustard (now a very small group) for Dogwood.

160. This information by Stevenson (1904:47) is felt by Ladd to be wrong. Kroeber (1916:273) notes with interest that according to all of Mrs. Stevenson's accounts, the Koyemshi "are partially but rather closely duplicated by the unmasked members of the Newekwe fraternity in actions and even in appearance." Kroeber says: "There is no trace of confusion in the Zuñi mind; but the same idea has clearly been worked over by them twice in the two connections."

157. Ladd finds the outline of Stevenson (1904:33) somewhat confused. He offers the following schematic representation of the major correlations:

Earthly Officials	After World	After Spanish	
1. Pekwinna	Pautiwa	Pekwinna	
K'ya kwe mosi	There are a large number of deities that do not reside at Kothluwalawa who are included here	K'ya kwe mosi	Governor and staff
A shiwanni	Ko'a shiwanni	A shiwanni	
2. Ko mosonna			
Ko pekwinna	Ko ko — Rain people		
Ko pitla·shiwanni u pa wan (kiva) — all have leaders, 6 groups	Ko'a·pitla shiwanni — all warrior gods		Kivas

1. Dogwood clan (Pit chi kwe). 2. Shówitaka, Elk clan. Certain of the above officers are clan owned, hereditary within the clan.

Ti·kya·we (Medicine or Beast societies) have no counterpart in the Koko system; each has its own origin. NOTE: *Pekwinna* and the shortened form generally used by writers, *pekwin,* are both used in this work.

remained permanent. The gods whose masks had not been examined were ordered to go to the other five kivas, where their masks were copied. There were six giant couriers to the rain makers (Ûwannami), the Zuñi Shalako [Shalakia·pithashiwanni—E. J. L.], one for each kiva. Thenceforth the gods were represented by human personators.

Not everything was to the good alone, for among the peoples coming out into this world, the last to emerge was a pair of witches. The Divine Ones tried to dissuade them, but the witches threatened to destroy the land if they were not allowed to come, and they held precious seeds which would be beneficial for the people. After magically producing rains, the two witches planted all their seeds in the wet earth. Next morning, the corn was a foot high, and other plants were of good size; by evening, all had matured. The people had new foods, and were instructed in fire making and cooking.[161]

SOCIO-RELIGIOUS ORGANIZATION

Through the centuries, rites initiated by the Indian leaders, ceremonies, and formalized concepts have been worked into a complex organization. Dr. Benedict has summarized it thus:

This ceremonial life that preoccupies Zuñi attention is organized like a series of interlocking wheels. The priesthoods have their sacred objects, their retreats, their dances, their prayers, and their year-long programme is annually initiated by the great winter solstice ceremony that makes use of all different groups and sacred things and focuses all their functions. The tribal Masked-God society has similar possessions and calendric observances, and these culminate in the great winter tribal masked-god

ceremony, the Shalako. In like fashion the medicine societies, with their special relation to curing, function throughout the year, and have their annual culminating ceremony for tribal health. These three major cults of Zuñi ceremonial life are not mutually exclusive. A man may be, and often is, for the greater part of his life, a member of all three. They each give him sacred possessions "to live by" and demand of him exacting ceremonial knowledge.[162]

The priesthoods are on the highest level of sanctity; the priests are holy men. They have their sacred medicine bundles in which their power resides. The priests do not hold public ceremonies, although members of the priesthood must be present to initiate or participate in many of the ceremonies of other groups. In June, when rain is needed for the corn, the priests hold a series of retreats "before their sacred bundle." The leaders of the Sun cult and of the War cult participate in these retreats. Dr. Benedict states that the "heads of the major priesthoods, with the chief priest of the sun cult and the two chief priests of the war cult, constitute the ruling body, the council, of Zuñi," a completely theocratic group.

The masked gods are more widely recognized. They are comprised of the masked gods, proper, or the Koko (Katsinas) ; and the katsina priests, the chiefs of the supernatural world, who, in turn, are impersonated with masks by the Zuñi dancers. When a man puts on the mask of a god, he becomes the supernatural one, for the time being. There are six katsina societies at Zuñi, each with its ceremonial chamber or kiva. Initiation into a kiva society usually occurs when a boy is six to nine years of age; it does not teach him of the esoteric mysteries, but establishes a bond between him and the supernatural forces. When a youth is old enough to assume societal respon-

161. Stevenson, 1904:30-31.   162. Benedict, 1934:59-60.

STEPS TOWARD UNDERSTANDING

sibilities, he is again initiated, this time receiving a katsina mask and being told some of the secrets of the organization. Like all supernaturals, the Katsinas are bringers of rain, but the power of fecundity is their special endowment.

The supernatural patrons of the medicine or curing societies are the Beast gods, of whom the Bear is most powerful. He is impersonated by the society members, just as the dancers impersonate the Katsinas. No mask is worn, but the skin of a bear, with forelegs dangling and claws in place, is drawn over the arms of a member, who goes about growling like a bear. The bear has the supreme power of healing, "by use of his bodily substance."[163] Members of the medicine societies possess great esoteric,

as well as practical, knowledge. Dr. Benedict says: "The doctors are the highest orders of all, those 'whose roads are finished.' Those who aspire to this degree must sit for years at the feet of those who already know."[163] The medicine societies have altars and sacred paraphernalia; and each doctor has a personal fetish, a perfect ear of corn completely covered by beautiful feathers, with especially cherished adornments. The public ceremony of pueblo healing comes at the conclusion of their winter retreat. The cults of hunting, war, and of clowning, are associated with the medicine societies.

With these steps toward understanding the Indian mythology, folk history, symbols, and deeply integrated society, we should now be ready to examine the Kuaua paintings with due appreciation.

---

163. Benedict, 1934:65.

BOOK TWO

PORTRAYALS FROM THE PAST

THE PAINTINGS OF KIVA III

Layer Q-59

It was found that the earliest evidence of painting in Kiva III, or the so-called Painted Kiva, appeared on the 27th layer of plaster which was placed on the chamber walls. This was recorded as a "copper" layer, "deteriorated and very fragile,"[164] and was designated Layer Q-59. Inasmuch as the Zuñi people consider the cardinal directions in a counter clockwise manner, starting with the north, that procedure has been followed in describing the Kuaua paintings. Where depictions remain, they frequently overlap the kiva corners, indicating that the portrayals represent a continuous recitation of events involving the personages. Especially at the northwest corner do significant features occur.

On the north wall, a zig-zag band was painted in black (fig. 104, *not* illustrated), with fragmentary green spots at the westernmost end, which came to within 3.5 inches of the northwest corner of the kiva. At its uppermost height, the representation was 33.5 inches above the floor; its greatest width was slightly over five inches, and its length 77.25 inches. This shows similarity to the depiction on Layer I-33 (figs. 72-73,75-76,77), which, as will be seen later (Pl. XIII), is identifiable as a serpent associated with an altar and rain symbolization. It is probable that Layer Q-59 was painted during a comparable ceremony, when Kiva III was put into use by a katsina group[165] on some occasion when the kiva was "open" to the pueblo.

Kolowisi, the great horned serpent, functions with the Rain makers or Uwanami, being the guardian of sacred springs and featuring in events of magical impregnation. Our Figure 104 would represent Kolowisi.

Mrs. Stevenson learned that the sacred fetish at Zuñi, said to have come from the Rain priest of Héshotayalla (that of the last of the Black Corn clan), was in the possession of one of the old priest's descendants. Since the latter was a friend of hers, she was allowed to photograph the chamber in which the fetish was kept.[166] Her old priest friend, being the keeper of this sacred object, had the privilege of painting an elaborate serpent on the wall of the chamber.[167] She notes that other fetish, or *éttowe,* rooms do not have this decoration.[168]

Thus, the Kuaua fragment may indicate that the kiva was used by the Rain priests; and there is a suggestion that it may have been in use by the Rain priest of the Black Corn clan.

---

164. Laboratory note.

165. If this were a Zuñi ceremony it would pertain, of course, to the Koko society with enactment by a kiva group. At Zuñi there is a Kolowisi for each of the directions except the Below—E. J. L.

166. Ladd says: "I don't know where this is, but I think the fetish is that belonging to the *A·yahokwe,* a non-functioning society. I recall that the rooms in which sacred objects are kept were decorated *'te·shi kwiya.'* This latter term is applied to the house decorations in the Shalako houses, and also to the ceremonial altar, as well as to men and women members, especially of the medicine societies and Koko, when they have planted prayer plumes and are observing certain religious abstinences."

167. *See* Stevenson, 1904, pl. XXXVI.

168. Stevenson, 1904:24. The *éttone* (singular), the most sacred fetish of the Rain priests, is a symbol of life, including rain and vegetation.

Layers 58-47

No paintings were found on Layers 58 and 57, indicating that the serpent painting of Layer 59 had been obscured by coatings of plain adobe plaster. The only thing significant about Layer 56 is that the south wall showed as another "copper layer," like that of Layer 59, but no paintings were found. Layer 55 was likewise devoid of paintings. Nothing was noted on Layer 54, but this was heavily smoked on the north side of the chamber. Layer 53 showed traces of mica in black paint, but no figures were detected. Layer 52 had no decoration. Evidence of red paint was seen on Layer 51, on the south wall. The succeeding layers, 50 and 49, gave no indication of decoration. Layer 48 was another "copper layer," with yellow and black paint on the north and south walls; and there were bits of red paint on the south wall of Layer 47.

Layer P-46

On the north wall, Layer P-46 shows two extremely incomplete figures (102 and 103, *not* illustrated). The latter occurs close to the northwest corner, 30 inches above the floor.

It is simply a black-painted area, eight inches in upright extent and 20 inches across. Far to the left of this and 39 inches above the floor are the remains of Figure 102, five inches wide and eight inches high.[169] The greater portion is green, with three short red lines thereon; along the right side a black area extends vertically. "The green appears to have been mixed with or painted over the black."[170] Nothing of importance is distinguishable.

Layers 45 and 44

Layer 45 showed traces of black paint on the south wall, and Layer 44 gave slight evidence of red paint on the same wall. A layer O^1-44 had one red splotch of color on the north wall, which the laboratory technicians indicated as Figure 105 (*not* illustrated).

Layer O-43

Here for the first time the paintings show recognizable features (Pl. IX). On the north,

---

169. Because of the significance connected with body parts, all of the directions herein are to be considered as if one were in the position of the personage represented, thus as if he were facing the reader.

170. Laboratory note.

PL. IX. *Layer O-43.* Rabbit Hunt with the Gods.

Fig. 61a, b, c

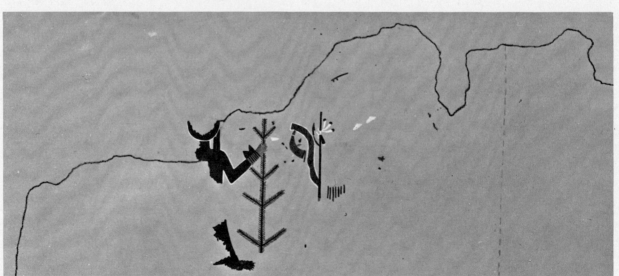

nearly 36 inches above the floor, there is a device (fig. 100) about 6.5 inches in diameter, representing the SUN, OR SUNSHINE. YA·TO KYA, YELLOW, according to Zna'ote.[171] The outermost of its concentric circles is black; it is about two inches wide. Within this is a band, about one-fourth inch wide, painted yellow-orange, followed by an unpainted one of equal width. The central portion is about 3.5 inches in diameter and is painted "green, mixed with black, as though the black were painted lightly over the green."[172] A faint trace of red occurs eight inches to the right of the sun, on the level of its center.

Figure 101 represents a personage although only skirt and sash remain. Zna'ote recognized this as an OLD WOMAN, OKYA.[173] The black skirt was incised into the plaster, forming a design of small squares. The sash of indeterminable color is tied off with four red knots, each with a yellow tassel which is tipped with three black

fringes. A narrow band "between the sash and body is irregular in outline. The body, from the sash up, is definitely grey."[174] It was noted[174] that the black paint on this layer is much more powdery than that henceforth used.

No paintings were found on the west wall. On the south, however, there are fragmentary remains of a very fine personage (fig. 61a). The body is dark grey in color. Only the lowermost part of the head remains, showing a round face mask painted black. Down the left side black hair hangs, cut off squarely at the base. A white line, probably indicating a cord, shows lengthwise in the hair, and is tipped with a red ornament.[175] The left arm, painted like the body, projects akimbo and upward, thus in a position of dancing, with the hand of adobe color extending in front of a coniferous tree, 31 inches high. The wrist is encircled by six narrow, black bands, above which a black,

171. Ladd says "yellow is symbolic of the sun, but only as applied to prayersticks."

172. Laboratory note.

173. According to Ladd, *okya* means "female," with no age indicated. Parsons, 1930:21, gives *oketsi* as "old woman."

174. Laboratory notes.

175. Ladd says that a red feather, *la·sho wannshi lowa*, is symbolic of the medicine societies and is worn only by members thereof. After initiation into a medicine society, the sponsor or ceremonial father presents such a feather to his new son or daughter.

Fig. 101. Old Woman, Komokatsi.   Fig. 100. Sun, Sunshine, or Sun Father.

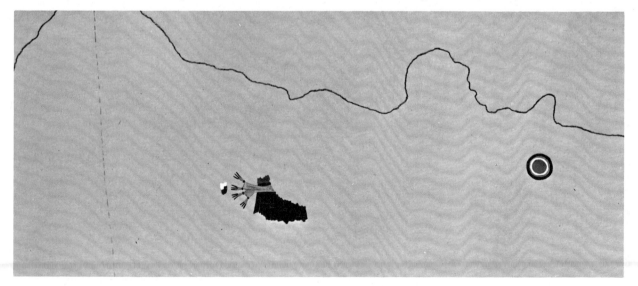

swallow-tailed element extends, as a wristlet.[176] There is a black skirt, with a sizable blotch of red color, irregular in shape, at the bottom-left corner. On the chest of the personage is a small red area, presumably representing the heart.

At first glance, the tree (fig. 61b) appears to be held by the hand of the personage, but inasmuch as the fingers are straight, with the red color of the tree trunk showing between them, the figure must be considered as standing in front of it. The trunk and four branches at each side are shown in red, with green needles alongside each.

To the left of the tree and close to the fingers is a small, white animal track. About three inches further is a complex of representations (fig. 61c). First there is a horn-shaped object painted in yellow and decorated with red. This appears to be a fire torch.[177] Above and to the left of this, is a loose S-shaped element,[178] painted green, with criss-cross in yellow, bordered in white, from end to end—identifiable as a rabbit stick. The base of this implement rests against an upright black shaft 20 inches long, near the top of which a cluster of four eagle feathers is tied on the left side, with a prominent knot on the right. Below the knot, a curving black object, with three or four white x's painted about midway of the staff, heads upward between the prayerstick and the rabbit stick, to terminate in a yellow point. Near the cluster of feathers are two more small animal tracks. Interspersed among these and the other elements are a number of small red marks or tracks. Near the base of the prayerstick are seven short, vertical red lines—perhaps a count of rabbits slain, or symbolic of the Seven Sisters. Just to the left of them, a patch of yellow color may be seen. Above this

and toward the southwest corner are traces of green and black; there is also a narrow green streak with two diagonal projections to be seen above the Figure 61b-c complex.

These depictions indicated a hunting ceremony. At Zuñi, rabbit hunts are held in which personators of the gods take part. The Rain priests meet in the ceremonial chamber of the Bow priests and spend the night. At sunrise, the warrior of the hunters fraternity,[179] who is either the elder or younger Bow priest, announces that a hunt by the Koko, or gods, will occur in four days. Preparations are made for this event, and inquiries are made concerning little boys to be initiated into the Kotikili (the mythical fraternity, or kiva society, of which every male child must become a member), or katsina society, as related with Layer Q-59.

In the folk history, it is found that a personage called *'Chá'kwena'okya* was considered as the original owner and keeper of the game.[180] The impersonator of the 'Cha'kwena'okya must be a man of the Badger clan. He dresses

---

176. Wristlets are a symbol of strength and bravery to the Pueblo Indians. Benedict (1930:68) says all warriors wore them, and a child might wear one "to make him strong."

177. *Cf.* Layers H-31:64, 67 and G-26:49.

178. *Cf.* Judd, 1926:147.

179. Saniyakikwe; it is also called Suskikwe (Coyote). The fraternity has two orders, Hunters and Fire (Stevenson, 1904:438). Cushing, 1896:387, says this priesthood served as "Keepers of the Seed-substance of Game." In most cases, a fraternity has but one warrior, owing to limited membership of the Bow priesthood (*Ápitlashiwanni*). At the installation of Rain priests, the warriors act separately, as fraternity members (Stevenson, 1904:168).

180. Stevenson, 1904:37, 39, 89, 90, records the 'Chá'kwena, as *Kúyapali'tsa*, the deceased female warrior of enemy peoples called, *Kiánakwe*. She walked at the head of her army, shaking her rattle. In one encounter she captured four of the Zuñi gods and held a dance in celebration of the captured ones, among whom was Ko'k'oshi, the first born, who became so angry and unmanageable that Kuyapali'tsa dressed him in female attire, saying, "You will now perhaps be less angry." The Zuñi say this was the first time that god or man appeared in woman's dress. It hung from both shoulders and was fastened up the front. Kuyapali'tsa was killed when Sun Father revealed that she carried her heart in her rattle (*see also* Bunzel, 1932:600 and Cushing, 1896:424), and a man of the Coyote clan pierced the rattle with an arrow. Her village in the south was conquered, and all of the game was freed to roam the earth. The scalp of the female warrior was divided, and a pre-battle ceremony held, with songs of thanksgiving for the scalps which bring good fellow-

in the attire of a woman. 'Cha'kwena'okya appears during rabbit hunts; and she comes during the Winter solstice ceremony, soon after dark of the fourteenth day, to be received by the Saya'hlia, the Whippers, in each of the kivas. As she proceeds to the kiva, "all pregnant women hasten to look upon her, that they may pass through the trials of parturition safely and without pain."[181] Pregnant women visit her in the kiva and wash the pinkish paint from her limbs; personators of her people, from the Corn kiva, also visit her. On the first day, the 'Cha'kwena'okya emerges from the kiva of the Nadir, wearing a face mask. She passes through the pueblo, telling the people that she will give them the game of the world and bountiful crops. The Salimopiya, warriors and seed gatherers of the six regions, announce that they will bring all seeds to the people. Various rites are performed.

On the night prior to the rabbit hunt, the hunters gather in their ceremonial room. Personators of the gods, including 'Cha'kwena'okya, wearing their masks and other paraphernalia, go into the hunters' chamber and dance "to the accompaniment of the rattle, drum,

and song of the fraternity."[182] At the same time, the Rain priests meet in their kiva. At sunrise the following morning, the hunters and Rain priests unite.'Cha'kwena'okya comes from the Nadir kiva and circles about the village following directional patterns and symbolic procedures which "may cause the rains to fall upon Zuñi."[183] She then enters the Rain priests' chamber. During the ceremonies which follow, the Sun priest attaches a downy eagle plume, colored red, to the scalp lock of 'Cha'kwena'okya. Then, accompanied by two Koyemshi, with lighted torches of juniper bark, and the younger brother Bow priest, she follows the hunters from the kiva "for the western road."[184] Other gods likewise pass over the road and take their positions. People of the village are notified that the hour of the hunt has arrived. All move past the gods and finally reach the hunters, awaiting them in timbered country.

Then a "low tree is fired near the base with a burning torch [by the Koyemshi] and the fraternity gods, and others, with prayers, cast bread into the flames as food for the gods." The hunters' prayers are for aid in the hunt; those of 'Cha'kwena'okya for many children (rabbits) for the Zuñi; and the prayers of the others for game and for rain. All but the gods pass their rabbit sticks through the flames for success in the hunt. The people and gods, excepting 'Cha'kwena'okya and the hunters, spread out in each direction, forming a great circle. Those remaining drive out the rabbits from among the trees, with their blazing torches, so that the others may kill them with their rabbit sticks.

The first rabbit killed is given to 'Cha'-kwena'okya by a maiden. 'Cha'kwena'okya rubs the blood from wounds on the rabbit caused by strikes with the rabbit stick down her legs on the inner sides, thus seeking to hasten the arrival of puberty for Zuñi girls, "that

ship between the deceased enemy and the Zuñi, "and therefore much rain." The other gods were *Itsepasha*, one of the Koyemshi; and a Blue Horn warrior god (*Sáya'hlia*).

It should be noted that the conflict, or encounter mentioned above, arose when the Katsina people and the Kianakwe went hunting and their hunting circles overlapped, causing them to fight. The Kianakwe claimed the deer; they said the mountain lions, mountain sheep, jackrabbits, and cottontails belonged to the Katsinas. The Katsinas also claimed ownership of the deer. Then the Kianakwe rounded up all the deer and hid them. A battle waged for days, while great rains fell. Finally, the Kianakwe won by using yucca strings for their bows instead of deer sinew which always slackened when wet; and the deer thus became theirs. The Katsinas took the seeds of corn and other things. Since then both groups have worked together (*from* Benedict, 1935-I:7-8,262).

Ladd identifies the village of 'Cha'kwena'okya as *Shunt·k'ya,* and says that when he was a boy he was told that you could still see the corrals where the Kianakwe put all the deer and game animals.

181. Stevenson, 1904:140.
182. Stevenson, 1904:90.

183. Stevenson, 1904:90.
184. Stevenson, 1904:91.

Fig. 61. a) ʻChaʼkwenaʼokya, Ancient Woman. b) Flaming tree. c) Complex, including fire torch, rabbit stick, lightning and prayersticks, tracks, feathers, etc. *Layer O-43.*

they may be prolific in childbearing."[185] After the hunt, further ceremonies are enacted, followed by dancing in the six kivas throughout the night. ʻChaʼkwenaʼokya, performing fertility rites, and the gods appear for three successive evenings; and there is more dancing. Any woman who has lost a child may remain in the kiva with ʻChaʼkwenaʼokya. In the end, ʻChaʼkwenaʼokya and her associates pass over the western road, deposit offerings[186] in a hole in the river bank, and recite long prayers. ʻChaʼkwenaʼokya removes her mask, and the ceremony is concluded.

Returning to the fragmentary depictions of this painting, one may infer that it related to ceremonies similar to those described at Zuñi. On the north wall, Figure 100, the colored disc, represents the sun, the Sun Father, who is represented in the ceremonies by Pautiwa. Figure 101 was identified as "old woman," thus Komokatsi, or old dance woman, mother

of the gods (*see* Pl. A-3b, Appendix herein, for depiction), and who before being defiled by her brother was Siwulutsiyatsa, who bore the ten Koyemshi.

No paintings of this layer were found on the west wall, but on the south were the partial remains of a significant unit, designated as Figure 61. From the Zuñi mythology, this may be identified as ʻChaʼkwenaʼokya,[187] with black face mask and red-colored downy eagle plume tied in her hair—the symbol of Mystery medicine. The conifer shown at her left side well illustrates the burning tree into which bread was prayerfully cast.[188] Nearby is a rabbit stick such as was passed through the flames of the burning tree, and with which the rabbits were then killed. The small tracks may be identified as those of the scampering rabbits. The presence of the War gods is symbolized by the fire torch. Here they assume an attribute of the Fire god, Shulawitsi. Doubtless, the red splotch extending from the bottom of ʻChaʼkwenaʼokyaʼs skirt represents blood of the rabbit, with which her legs were smeared.

Thus we have related Layer O-43 of the Kuaua mural paintings to a ceremonial enacted by the hunters fraternity, the Rain priests, and the Katsinas, in which the ʻChaʼkwenaʼokya plays an important part. It may,

185. Stevenson, 1904:92; *see* Bunzel, 1932:935.

186. For the increase and perpetuation of vegetable and animal life, including man.

187. *Kʼyákweina Ókʼyatsiki,* Ancient Woman of the *Kʼyakweina,* or ʻChá'kwena[ʼokya] (Cushing, 1896:424). When the warrior gods were created to serve the Divine Ones, the latter revealed that they had been unable to conquer the enemy, saying, "Many arrows have pierced the heart of the ʻChaʼkwena who leads the opposing forces, yet she continues to pass to and fro before her army, shaking her rattle; and until these people can be conquered or destroyed we can not proceed in our quest of the Middle place of the world" (Stevenson, 1904:35).

188. In describing a rabbit hunt which she says was held upon call of the governor at Zuñi, Stevenson (1904: 442) notes that a fire made by the Koyemshi "was burning in a low and symmetrical cedar tree, the flames spreading evenly and beautifully." She records that the Koyemshi represent the War gods, who intercede for rain to fructify the earth. Ladd notes that the hunts are usually called by the Bow priesthood, and he says that Shulawitsi makes the fire.

therefore, be considered as a portrayal of a Rabbit Hunt with the Gods. The painting might have been made at the time of initiation,[189] which usually occurs on the fourth night of the ceremony.

It has been reported that there was a Spanish priest at Puaray of whom the Indians thought kindly, and at the time of the Rebellion of 1680, they gave him food and under cover of darkness guided him off to the west. Near Pescado, an outlying community east of Zuñi, he was discovered by a party of the Indians hunting antelope, which took him back to the pueblo. He remained with the Zuñi, adopting their costume.[190] He is heard from again, when Vargas besieged the Zuñi who had fled to the top of Corn (or Thunder) mountain, when he participated in the peace agreement, and after which he traveled with the Spaniards when they returned to the Rio Grande.[191] Several authorities mention a priest who survived the 1680 episode and who was later seen among the Zuñi and Hopi peoples. It is also told that several Zuñi Indians followed the priest with Vargas as far as Laguna, where they took up residence. These latter are said to have introduced a new society to Laguna, an order called "Chaquin," which, according to Gunn, the Zuñi claimed had been taught them by the priest. He says, "not being allowed to practice it in Zuñi, on account of the opposition of the medicine orders, they had come to Laguna, which being a new pueblo, any new order would be welcomed. It is quite a popular order yet, and known as the 'Chaquin,' or the order of the Black Mask."[192]

If this were to have been the case, the priest credited with this introduction would have had to have phenomenal knowledge of the rites and accoutrement pertaining to similar ceremonies which had long been enacted in Mexico, for this has close kinship to religious portrayals which were held in Indian regions to the south. On the other hand, Mrs. Stevenson, observing the Shalako at Zuñi in 1891, says of one of the ʽChaʼkwena ceremonies that the songs are in the Laguna tongue, and that a Laguna Indian was instructing a group of young Zuñi men, who were not familiar with them.[193] Dr. Bunzel records that the Zuñi claim to have borrowed one of their ʽChaʼkwena dances from Laguna, while the Laguna say the ʽChaʼkwena dance is of Zuñi provenience. She gives further account of the credited exchange.[194]

Regardless of subsequent interchanges, from the occurrence of this hunting ceremonial featuring ʽChaʼkwenaʼokya at Kuaua, it would appear that this was well established in the tradition of the Pueblo Indians long before the time of Vargas or any Spanish priest who may have been in this region in 1680.

Layer 42

No paintings were found on this layer, indicating that it had served as a covering wash for the portrayal of the preceding hunting and initiation ceremony.

Layer N-41

This, the 46th layer of plaster applied, shows paintings on the fragmentary north wall and on the west. On the north, there is, first, indication of perhaps a personage representation (fig. 91a), extending westward 20 inches from the easternmost limit of the wall, 41 inches above the floor level. The "skirt"

189. When Mrs. Stevenson recorded this drama, it was given every four years, except in time of drought when it could occur oftener (1904:89). The Koʼkʼoshi dances begin with the close of the Summer solstice ceremonies, and are for rain to fructify the earth that the crops may grow (p. 162).

190. Gunn, 1904:309-310.

191. Gunn, 1904:324; see also Cushing, 1896:331.

192. Gunn, 1904:324-325. Ladd reports that there is a

story told at Zuñi to substantiate this information regarding the priest, but not of his introduction of the Black Mask dance. See Pl. A-3a for illustration of this mask.

193. Stevenson, 1904:262-266.

194. Bunzel, 1932:901, 1022-1023.

Fig. 93. Paiyatuma or Ne'paiyatama, with a rabbit stick (Fig. 90) under his rainbow wing. *Layer N-41.*

Fig. 92. Duck or 'Eya.

Fig. 91a. Unidentified personage.

Fig. 91b. Eagle feathers.

shows a line painted in indeterminable color along the right, and the left side is outlined in red. A black line shows across the bottom. To the right of this, 9.5 inches, the distal portions of two or three feathers are noted, each white with black tips of eagle character (fig. 91b), probably ornaments on an object held in the

right hand of the personage. Standing to the right of Figure 91 is a waterfowl, a duck, or 'EYA, as identified by Zna'ote, painted in the faded color, with body outlined in red (fig. 92). Two narrow, red bands encircle the base of the neck. The raised right wing is marked with black and white; the tail is black and

PL. X. *Layer N-41.* A major Winter ceremony.

Fig. 99   Fig. 98

Fig. 97. Ko'kothlanna, the great god, surrounded by falling rain.   Fig. 96

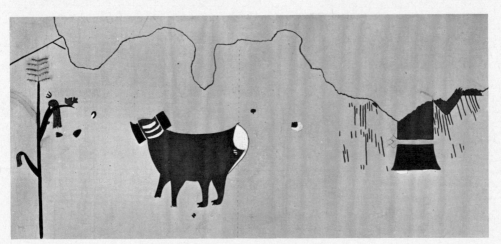

white. Bill and legs are shown in yellow-orange color. Black dots pour downward from the duck's mouth.

Rising to the eroded limit of the wall, a few inches beyond this fowl, is a prominent figure, and one of the few representations sufficiently preserved as to show the face mask and headdress (fig. 93). The lower part of the mask is painted black. The upper section is of the indeterminable color with two diagonal streaks thereof extending down into the black area, from the eye which is shown as two connected white circles outlined with black.[195] There is a white, down-curving protuberance at the front, below which are enlarged lips, black like the lower part of the face. Black hair hangs down on the right side of the figure, showing a white line vertically within and a red feather attached toward the bottom, depicting a cord with feather at its extremity.

Above the face is an elaborate headdress fashioned of red, white, and black feathers projecting upward stiffly; some are plainly eagle feathers. Around the forehead and extending to the back of the head, where it is secured with tasseled knots, is a narrow white band, very much in the manner of the usual waist sashes. The body of the personage is painted white, outlined in black at the front and with red toward the back. A leg—seemingly of human form—in the faded color outlined in red, is shown appended to the body, and a narrow red stripe projects backward horizontally from the neck of the figure.[196] Curving downward on the right side of the body is a large three-colored wing,[197] painted in orange-yellow, red, and the indeterminable shade, outlined in black. At the rear of the body is a large cluster of feathers, primarily white with black tips [eagle], but with the uppermost one yellow, tipped with black. A fragment similar to the latter remains, slightly back and above this figure. From it, a white crossed lightning symbol extends back and upward along the eroded wall.

This anthropomorphic being was identified

---

195. Stevenson, 1904:67. Lines radiating below eyes are symbolic of rain. *See* Cushing, 1896:406-407; *see also* Pl. A-9 herein.

196. *Cf.* modern costume, Stevenson, 1904-435.

197. Wings are symbolic of sunbeams. In the Wing world, the first world, the first glimpse of sunlight was seen, "the beams penetrating through the opening in the earth." Sunbeams are the sun's wings (Stevenson, 1904:75)

Fig. 95   Fig. 94   Fig. 93   Fig. 90   Fig. 92   Fig. 91b   Fig. 91a

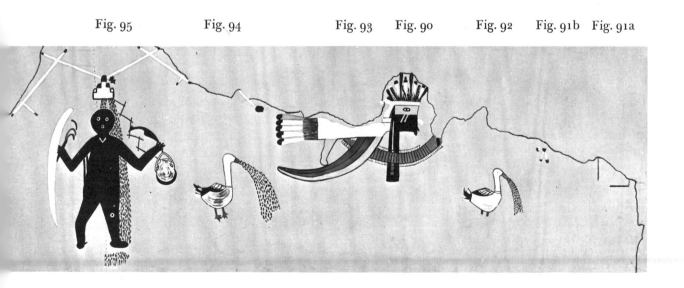

Fig. 94. Goose or Owa. *Layer N-41.*

by Zna'ote as: BETWEEN THE SKY, PAÍYATUMA. In the position of his wing is AMÍTOLANᵉ, THE RAINBOW.

At the right of the bird personage is a goose, OWA (fig. 94), as identified by Zna'ote (*cf.* Pl. A-5). Its body is shown in white with black and red outlines, and the side somewhat greyed. At the base of the neck there are red, white, and black encircling rings. The short-feathered tail is black and white, with a black band about the base. The raised wing is outlined in black, and has black markings on its midpart. As with the duck, black droplets spray downward from the mouth.

About eight inches westward from Goose, another complex of elements centers around Figure 95, a personage about 40 inches tall, placed directly at the juncture of the north and west walls, with his right foot within 23 inches of the floor. This figure is nude, with dark body outlined by a thin white line; eyes and mouth are shown by white circles, and a V-shaped necklace about the neck is indicated by a narrow white line. This being was identified by Zna'ote as KÁ'NASHKÚLE, THE BOSS. WHEN PEOPLE ARE HUNGRY AND WANT TO EAT, CALL ON HIM. ABOVE HIS HEAD, LIGHTNING AND

A RAIN CLOUD ALTAR. The altar is white, outlined by black. Above each lower step, rise white clouds outlined in black; above the second step and top are black clouds.[198] From the altar's summit, criss-crossed lightning extends upward, white with red end tips. From its base, black droplets of moisture fall down the left, back of the personage, extending nearly to the floor. This, Zna'ote said, is RAIN, THLI'-

198. Stevenson, 1904:21, gives something of cloud symbolism: cirrus clouds are considered as rain makers, passing about for pleasure; cumulus and nimbus indicate that the rain makers will water the earth; and wind clouds [black] send the cold winds from the northeast and northwest, and denote some offense to the Council of the Gods has been committed by the Rain priests.

Fig. 95. Ka'nashkule (priest-clown-medicine man) with a rain altar above his head; water jar in left hand, snare in right hand; white "worm." *Layer N-41.*

TO-PA'NINᵉ. At the right of the altar is a small black figure, called GETSICTLTO, A CRICKET, by Zna'ote.

Suspended from the personage's left hand, by a white thong attached to opposed handles, is a white water jar, or canteen, encircled with black.[199] Above this hand, a long, black curving and pointed object projects toward his head. From the water jar to the altar, crisscrossed lightning is shown in red-orange. In the right hand is TÁ'ATSIKONE, A SNARE, shown as a black stick with red crook at its upper end.[200] Just above this, similar curving elements are shown, one red and one black. Back of the right hand is a long, arced white object, asserted to be WÍ'KATHLO, A WORM, by Zna'ote, who says: KANASHKULE GETS ON THE WORM LIKE ON A HORSE. THEY ARE ALL DIFFERENT COLORS. LONG TIME AGO, KANASHKULE WAS LIVING WAY DOWN IN GROUND. HE WANTED SKIN WHITE; TOOK BLACK OFF LIKE A SHIRT. WANT TO DO SOMETHING MAKE HIM BLACK. GOT BLACK COMING OUT. WANTED TO SEE SUNSHINE. HAD NO EYES. HE TALKED FOUR TIMES. PEOPLE DIE AND CRICKET COMES UP. FIRST TIME DIE; SECOND TIME, SAME AS LIVING. FOURTH COME DOWN BLACK. THEN WANT TO COME UP WHEN SUMMER TIME; WARM. WHEN COLD OR SOMEONE KILL, DIE; NO MORE LIVE.

On the west wall, to the right of Figure 95, is a personage alongside a tall plant which measures 27 inches in height; its basal extent is 28 inches above the floor. Here, the body is painted dark grey, almost black, including both arms to wrist—where the hands are shown in red—and neck; the head is missing. Down

Fig. 96. Grey Newekwe with *Datura* or jimson weed. *Layer N-41.*

the right side of the neck, hanging over the shoulder is black hair, cut off squarely at the bottom. At the front of the neck an ornament is shown by short, vertical lines in red, bordered by white. Around the waist is a large, tasseled sash,[201] all in white except for a red knot where tassels are tied off on the right side. There is an all-black kilt. The disproportionately large left leg is painted white. Both arms are bent at the elbow; the left hand is held near the hip. On the right, the deep-grey stalk of the plant with three ear-like projections of the same color stands on a slight diagonal to-

---

199. Many of the Zuñi personages appear carrying gourd or pottery jugs, or baskets, covered with a netting of cotton cord, in the left hand, with a number of prayersticks (e.g. Stevenson, 1904:128); the vessels are for water from the sacred, directional springs.

200. The crook has considerable symbolism. It is a symbol of longevity; is a symbol of office; and it represents the rainbow, providing the means for the Cloud people to come down. The crooked prayerstick is "the walking cane of the Katsinas." *See* Parsons, 1939-I:480; Stevenson, 1904:111, and White, 1932:126.

---

201. Throughout the Zuñi accounts, sacred items are carried in these sashes, particularly kernels of corn or cornmeal; the same is true in the other pueblos where this type of sash is used. Corn is so important to Pueblo life that "it plays an all-essential part, not only in his daily but also in his industrial, religious, and mythologic life, and even in the tales with which he amuses the children about the fireside in winter-time" (Cushing, 1920:18).

ward the body. The alternating leaves at either side of the stalk are shown in the indeterminable color. Red and white flower-like features are shown on the nubbins which issue forth just above the leaves. To our eyes, this plant appeared more like that of corn than anything else, but one must be ever mindful of the mythical characteristics which may pertain to the mural depictions. Zna'ote readily identified Figure 96 as GREY NEWEKWE, ANOTHER HELPER. IN HIS RIGHT HAND HE CARRIES A PLANT, ÁNIKLAKYᵉ [a naklä kia or Datura]. WEED WITH WHITE FLOWERS, SEED POD SIMILAR TO COCKLEBUR. PEOPLE USE ROOT, DREAM, GO CRAZY [but not literally]. RUB WITH A LITTLE OF THE ROOT, DREAM AND KNOW IT.

Also on the west wall, to the right of Grey Newekwe, another personage is depicted (fig. 97). The upraised arms and upper body are painted in yellow, outlined with black. By the red left hand fragmentary colors remain in black and yellow. From this and from the area of the right hand, long dashed lines indicate falling rain, the source of which might be a large altar above and behind the personage. The black kilt, which has a red decoration at the bottom and extending up some distance on the left side, is secured with a sash shown in the faded color; it has four fringes at each corner.[202] Only the uppermost portions of the legs remain, these painted white. From the floor to the bottom of the kilt is 37.5 inches.

This personage was identified by Zna'ote as KÓKOTHLANᵉ [Kókothlanna]. HE IS MAN WHO CAN BRING CORN AND DEER.[203]

Next occurs an anthropomorphic being about midway between Figure 97 and the southwest corner of the kiva, toward which it

heads. It represents a four-legged animal with body, neck, and legs painted yellow. The belly line is 34 inches above the floor. Most of the head has been obliterated, but black features showing down either side of the neck are similar to depictions of hair on other of the mural beings. These are set off from the neck by a thin margin which is unpainted. Around the neck are three white bands, and above this an indication of orange-yellow color. At the rear, a white rump patch was painted, above which —where a tail could be expected—is a short, red fragment projecting upward. Curving downward behind the rump patch to the thigh is a narrow, white element, terminating in a point, the outer margin of which is outlined with red. Below the patch are three short, roughly horizontal white lines. The feet show two red toes to the fore. Below the left hind foot are two small red prints, like those made by a deer. Above the rump and toward Figure 97 is a fragmentary portion of a black element, now unidentifiable. Between this and the falling moisture, the distal portion of a white feather with black marking remains.

This figure was identified as MÁAWI, YELLOW DEER, by Zna'ote [má·awi has been recorded as meaning doe; but Ladd gives the translation as antelope—Figure 98].

Out 6.5 inches from the southwest corner, and on the right of Figure 98, there stands a tall plant, tasseled at the top, TEK'UWANNA. Its stalk extends for 40 inches and the inflorescence adds another eight inches. On each side of the black stalk, a black ear projects, of which Zna'ote said, CORN FIRST TIME COMING, TSAU·OLE [nubbin]. Each has a red silk protruding, HON OP CHI·A. The tassel is shown in the indeterminable color, as is a long leaf, SHI·YA CHINNA, issuing forth on the right side, and a short one on the left. Intersecting the tassel at its right, above, is a red lightning motif, with one short branch. Along with the ear on the left, a grey leaf extends across the

---

202. The four fringes on the sashes and skirts or kilts are symbolic of the four directions (cf. Stevenson, 1904:-174).

203. Ladd mentions two personages with the name, Kokothlanna, but he says neither has anything to do with deer or corn.

Fig. 99. Black corn.   Fig. 98. Yellow deer or Maawi. *Layer N-41.*

long silk. Above its exterior tip is an irregularly shaped splotch of yellow color. Below this and the pendant silk are two foot prints in red, showing five small toes each. Just at the side of the nearest ear, is a similar, but much smaller, red track. Above it is a tripartite track in black with white tips. Slightly to the north from the tip of the grey leaf is a fragmentary feature in black with white central portion—perhaps as a feather tip. Above the corn plant is a long, brownish yellow stick, branched at its upper extremity, which Zna'ote identified as a planting stick, 'TSEMᵉ.

Of this complex (fig. 99), Zna'ote said: KWÉ-INIKWAMITÁNE, ALL OF THE BLACK CORN. [*Kwé nikwakwe* means the Black Corn people; *see* Pl. A-13.]

Having identified the separate components of this portrayal, Zna'ote stated that this represents a PAINTING FOR HUNGRY PEOPLE. It seems an apt designation, for it concerns personages from whom the people sought assistance in obtaining food, particularly corn and meat, and those who could bring the corn and the deer.

Turning to the complex centered about Figure 93, Paiyatuma, the Duck and Goose, we find that these are the principal characters in the *Mólawiya* ceremony, enacted each year on the last day of the Shalako, at Zuñi; it is a dramatization of the search for the lost Corn maidens[204] [*see* Pl. XIV]. According to folk history, the Corn maidens belonged to the head Rain priest. Each had brought a number of stalks of white corn with her from the underworld: the Yellow Corn maiden and four sisters, who accompanied the elder son of the Sun, and the Blue Corn maiden and four sisters who accompanied the younger son of the Sun.[205] They were taken to the North kiva, where they sang and danced—without singers, drum, or rattles.[206]

At midnight they were led to a bower (*hámpone*) of waving corn, in the sacred dance plaza.[207] There the Corn maidens danced on a meal painting of cloud symbols which had been made upon the floor.[208] While the Rain priests and the Divine Ones slept, Paiyatuma discovered the Corn maidens, and seated himself in the bower. He thought all of the maidens beautiful, but considered the Yellow Corn maiden as the most beautiful of all, and he desired her.[209] The maidens understood his thoughts, and were frightened. They ceased their dancing, whispered together, and decided to run away when he fell asleep. Accordingly, they ran off by the first light of the Morning star.[210] On awakening all were dismayed to find the Corn maidens gone; they searched for them without success. From their distant sanctuary, the elder sister, Yellow Corn, sent the Black Corn maiden to tell the gods of their fears. Black Corn was accompanied back by Father Koyemshi and by Pautiwa, "both gods assuming the form of ducks"[211] (*see* Pl. B-7). The Corn maidens, hidden in a spring, were protected from view by the spread wings of these fowls.

After a time, witches destroyed the corn and other food of the people. The Divine Ones were called for aid and they instructed various birds to seek the Corn maidens, but they looked in vain. Then the twin gods, knowing that only Newekwe could find the lost maidens, summoned Bitsitsi.[212] He was the first Newekwe, and original director of that fraternity or cult. "Having special qualifications,"

204. Ladd notes that the entire ceremonies of the final day of the Shalako revolve around this corps of individuals, mo·la·wiya, or the men who take the part of the Corn maidens, mo·la·kwato k'ya (mo·la·—"round objects," in this case, squash; kwato k'ya—"bring in," or "cause to bring in"). "In the olden days, these men carried the mo·la·wau on their heads, as the women carried food, water, etc. Now, they carry this wrapped in a mi hya (Hopi red-and-white robe) over one shoulder." Again this is very complex, with the Pekwinna, Pautiwa, *Bitsitsi,* and Awan tachu (Koyemshi) playing major roles.

205. The Corn maidens have as their great or elder sister the Yellow Corn maiden, and as the younger sister, Blue Corn maiden. These two are the directors or leaders of the others. There are seven in all: Yellow, Blue, Red, White, Every-color, Black, and Sweet Corn [a late addition—E. J. L.]; also, there is an eighth maiden, Squash; a ninth maiden, Watermelon; and a tenth, Muskmelon maiden. Bunzel (1932:914) says the Corn maidens do not wear masks.

206. Stevenson, 1904:48.

207. *See* Cushing, 1920:41, in re preparation of the bower for the Corn dance.

208. Altars and dry (meal or sand) paintings which appear in the ceremonials are referred to as *téshkwi,* "not to be touched" (Stevenson, 1904:425). *Cf.* footnote 166.

209. Benedict, 1935:20, gives a version; *see also* Cushing, 1896:435.

210. The Black Corn went behind, as the Corn maidens left the people, "to make the road dark so that the people would not find them. Therefore, when anyone is very lonesome for someone who has died, they give him the juice of the black corn to drink to make him forget" (Bunzel, 1932:914-916).

211. Stevenson, 1904:49. Ladd says that when traveling *all* the gods assume this form.

212. An informant of Bunzel (1932:917) said: "We call Ne'we·kwe Bitsitsi when he brings the corn maids, and we call Pautiwa Móla·kwatokia and Á·towakwatokia." The latter means "Corn maiden."

he was appointed musician and jester. He remained with the Newekwe during the migrations of the Zuñi until they reached 'Kiáp kwena, which Stevenson identifies as Ojo Caliente.[213] The Newekwe visited Ashes Spring (*Lú kiana 'kia ia*), where, according to Stevenson, Kokothlanna appeared to them, and gave them strong medicine (excrement) to use with their medicine. Since then, she says, Kokothlanna[214] is personated at the initiatory ceremonials of the Newekwe.[215]

The same source records that before Bitsitsi disappeared in the waters of Ashes Spring, he told his fraternity that whenever they needed him, they should notify him with[216] prayer plumes and he would come to them. He went to live with Kokothlanna and to become musician and jester to the Sun Father.

Since that time, Bitsitsi has borne the name of *Ne'paiyatam'a,* or Newekwe Youth.[217]

According to one of several versions, Bitsitsi-Ne'paiyatam'a planted the seed of the cottonwood tree which grew to the sky, and up which he climbed to look around the world[218] (*see* Pl. A-7). He found the maidens hiding far off under the wings of the Duck, Pautiwa. He returned and reported to the Divine Ones and the Rain priests, saying that he would get the Corn maidens if the priests would do as he directed. They agreed. Prayer plumes of yellow, blue, red, white, spotted, and black were prepared; days of fasting were decreed. One plume was to be given to Newekwe each day, starting with the yellow one. Sandhill crane was called in to prepare him, Ne'paiyatama, for the journey, painting him and arranging his hair, and putting one grain each of the six kinds of corn in his hair knot and also in the belt over his stomach. A rabbit tongue was put in his mouth. Each day, before sunrise, one plume was planted. Each night was spent in the Rain priests' chamber.

213. Ladd does not know the location of 'Kiap kwena, but he does not believe that it is Ojo Caliente.

214. Stevenson, 1904:430. Here she notes that, "The Kokothlanna of the Newekwe is quite different from the patron god of the same name of the Great Fire fraternity." Ladd holds that Kokothlanna did not appear as stated.

215. The Newekwe or galaxy (Milky Way) fraternity (*see* Cushing, 1896:371, 388, 403, 439-442) is considered as one of the four original organizations of the Zuñi, having been established soon after they came into this world. It was comprised of two orders: the Life Givers, possessors of Mystery medicine (*Ónaye nakia*), and the Jugglers (*Itsepasho*), of whom the patron god was Kokothlanna. Stevenson (1904:429) reports that two other gods also appeared at times with the Newekwe, one of whom was *Mítotasha*. Ladd, however, says there are only two gods who appear with the Newekwe. They are both referred to as women, *Ho·máh* (old woman).

Stevenson observes that the Newekwe are great theurgists, but are seldom called upon except in extreme cases. She says that if one is cured by this group, he has to join the fraternity. Ladd says this is not correct; only under certain given conditions does one join this fraternity, and he can "buy back" the obligations. He adds that this is true for all societies. There are certain conditions where one *must* join, but not always by curing, although this is one aspect of recruiting members.

216. Stevenson, 1904:430. In other accounts, Pautiwa's attributes are assumed by personators designated by other names. Cushing, 1896:412, records Pautiwa as the "cloud-sender and sun-priest of the Souls." Ladd finds the latter quite right, being the Koko. Pautiwa, he says, appears twice a year; he belongs to the 'Tansy Mustard clan.

217. Here, Ladd tells us something of the evolution of ceremonial words. He says: "The word Paiyatamu, for example, has become associated with the magical plant, Tenatsali, which is personified by two young boys. From this, the meaning has been extended to 'boy gods,' and later to 'young man,' Paiyatam'a."

This may account for some of the diversity in the spelling of the name of this important personage. In his work of 1896, Cushing records it as *Paiyatuma;* Bunzel (1932) uses *Paiyatamu,* which she says "is the Keresan word payatamu, 'youth.'" One of the present writer's Acoma informants has given the rendering as *Paiyatuma.* Stevenson (1904) uses the spelling, *Páyatamu.* Benedict (1935-I:22) records *Ne'paiyatamu* for Newekwe Youth, thus agreeing in her understanding with Ladd, who indicates this manifestation of Bitsitsi as *Ne'paiyatam'a.*

It seems doubtful that the significance of this name, as given by Ladd, is always fully comprehended by recorders. It is certainly beyond the faculty of the author to distinguish the proper application at all times. The general usage of "Paiyatuma," herein, may include various aspects of this being, which will be indicated insofar as known.

218. Ladd mentions a version, wherein the Newekwe, or galaxy, being high above the world, could see far to the east, where there were always clouds and rain, and where it was known that the Corn maidens had gone.

The black plume was planted farthest to the west, "at the door of the house where the Corn maidens live, on the edge of the ocean."[219]

As Ne'paiyatama approached the hiding place of the Corn maidens, two geese (or white swans), Owa, a male [Old Man Goose] and a female [Old Woman Goose], saw him and told the maidens, advising them to prepare for their return journey. Unwilling to go back, because of their offender, each maid took "rubbings" from her body and made them into the shape of a corn ear, each ear colored like her maiden maker [origin of the sacred corn ear fetishes].When Ne'paiyatama arrived, the maidens agreed to go with him, but not to stay. Each placed a basket of corn on her head, and they all "came out," with Goose leading, followed by Ne'paiyatama or Bitsitsi,[220] Father Koyemshi, Duck or Pautiwa, and then the Corn maidens.[221] They returned thus to the house of the Rain priests.

The priests had waited in solemn silence all of this time.[222] When Ne'paiyatama came with the maidens he said to them: "The Corn maidens left us because one man desired them and wished to lay hands on them. We are their flesh and they give us themselves to eat. If they give it to us again and we plant in the spring for the rain to water we shall be fed again with their flesh. They will be our mothers and we shall be their children. If at any time we think evil thoughts or are unhappy, they will go away from us again and we shall have nothing. When we dance the Corn dance we shall carry their flesh in our hands. We shall not see them but they will be there in spirit. They will be among us and when we speak to them they will hear us."[223] The people said, "It shall be as you have said." Then Yellow Corn told the priests to send for her and her sisters, "at the end of the year," and she said: "My flesh is your flesh. When you put my flesh in the ground it sprouts and does not die. It is like your bodies. When they are buried in the ground they do not die. Our flesh is like your flesh."[223]

The people went to their homes. Late at night, when everyone was asleep, the Corn maidens came out of the kiva and went to each house. Yellow Corn first took one grain of yellow corn, bit it and dropped it in the first house, and proceeded on to the other houses. Blue Corn followed the same ritual with the blue corn; and thus did Red, White, Speckled, Black, and Sweet Corn, respectively. After each house had been visited, the maidens left the village. The next morning, each corn room in each household was "bursting with the flesh of the corn mothers." Everyone had plenty to eat.[224]

Thus, it would appear that the Kuaua Figures 92-95 relate to a mythological search for the lost Corn maidens, with Paiyatuma, Duck, Goose, and the Koyemshi-like character, Kanushkule.[225]

Another Zuñi tale pertains to a personage, "the all-hearing and wise of speech," who also seems identifiable as our Figure 93, (page 56) .

---

219. *See* Stevenson, 1904:49, 429; Benedict, 1935:34 ff.; Cushing, 1896:445.

220. While with the Corn maidens and soliciting their return to the starving people, Bitsitsi found a rabbit, and said: "This is an animal that is happy all the time. It is good to make the people glad." He killed it and made a whistle from one of its forelegs and bound it with sinew from the rabbit's back [Parsons, 1939-I:380, says the whistle carried in his mouth is referred to as "rabbit tongue."]. This is the whistle he played while leading the maidens back to the people (Benedict, 1935:23) [*see* Pl. A-8].

221. *See* Stevenson, 1904:52 ff.; Parsons, 1916:394.

222. Ladd tells us that during this observance at Zuñi, today, no one in the kiva (*mo·la winna kwe*) must utter a sound until all the Corn maidens have entered. He says that the whistle was put in the mouth of Bitsitsi so that he could not talk.

223. Benedict, 1935:24.

224. But, they say, never afterward were the ears of corn perfectly kernelled, never filled out to their tips, because a man had tried to "lay hands on Yellow Corn" (Benedict, 1935:24).

225. Mr. Ladd learned, on 23 September 1959, that his old grandfather at Zuñi knew this name, but not a figure thus identified; to him it was a word, no being who had ever been seen.

He was journeying alone "in the north land of cold and white desolateness," in search of the Middle Place, and became lost in the snow which covered the world. He was so cold that his face "became wan, and white from the frozen mists of his own breathing." He was dreary of heart and so blinded that he wept, "continually wept and cried aloud until the tears coursing down his cheeks stained them with falling lines . . . as may be seen on his face to this day when in due season he reappears." His lips were split from continual calling, and his voice grew shrill and dry-sounding, like the "voices of far-flying waterfowl." Water birds crowded around him, but none told him his way to his homeland and people.

Then the Duck (fig. 92), "the traveler and searcher," the most knowing of all creatures, and who was thus closely related to the man being, heard his cry which was so like her own. She bade him not be sad, and placing "talking shells" from his girdle on her neck and "singing shells" in her beak, set out to lead the blinded one, guiding him by the tinkling shells. They came to the borders of the Snow world, where wide waters lay in their way. Maimed as he was, the man being could not swim, nor could he fly as the Duck.

In that land of mists and waters, the Rainbow worm heard the sacred sound of the shells, and "he placed himself nigh them." As he requested, the suffering one gave him the lightest and choicest of his plume wands, and the Duck gave her two strong pinion feathers, that he might make of them far reaching and far-seeing pendants. Rainbow arched himself and stooped close to them, while the man being, breathing on the plumes, approached him and fastened them to his heart side, saying "the sacred words." The Rainbow shadow "gleamed full brightly on his forehead like a little rainbow . . . and became painted thereon." Then Rainbow addressed the man being as his grandson, and told him to mount

on his shoulders. He unbent himself lower so that he could be mounted, and then arched himself high among the clouds. Duck spread her wings in flight toward the south. Like an arrow, the Rainbow worm straightened out and followed, bearing the man being[226] to the Lake of the Ancients. On the plain to the north of the lake, he descended, weary and lame, and sat down to rest. Rainbow sped back quickly.[226a]

This myth seems to give our Figures 92 and 93 added significance. The latter, the body of which is shown in white, would bespeak the snow and frozen mists; the stains of his tears course down the cheek, and his lips appear splayed. The Kuaua personage shows a girdle-like band around the head, which could represent the girdle in which the shells of the man being, or Ne'paiyatama, were carried. The duck of Figure 92 apparently relates to that of this myth.[227] It was noted that the wings are spread in an attitude of flight.

When the Kuaua murals were being studied and the plaster layers removed from the walls in the laboratory, a large, curved element painted on the north wall was considered to belong to Layer M-40, and was registered there as Figure 90. Disconnected as it was from all recognizable complexes, it was identified by Zna'ote as A RABBIT STICK — TO KILL RABBIT AND JACKRABBIT. To our eyes, it appeared more like a giant millipede than anything else. We followed many unfruitful

226. Cushing, 1896:398, relates this being to the eldest son of the priest of the people, 'Kiaklo. Ladd notes that only the living can travel in this manner. Here, then, we seem to have a recounting of an old myth, in which the priest's son represents Ne'paiyatama (the Youthful god), with the latter "being either returned from the supernatural world, or being carried off by the beautiful spirit of the duck, rainbow, or eagle." Ladd says, "Zuñi myth is full of these, each to explain why, how, or what some feature is that cannot be explained any other way."

226a. See Cushing, 1896:408-409.

227. Ladd says the mask above described is that of Hehea', but that he was not lost in the north.

leads. In shape, it did suggest a rabbit stick or TLE·AYANNA. Remembering that the Hopi say that this implement was modeled after the wing of Sparrow Hawk, a great hunter, and the first possessor of the stick, "which he carried under his wing,"[228] this clue was followed. The succeeding plaster layer, the N-41 under discussion, has the anthropomorphized bird form, Figure 93. Measuring carefully, it was found that the two features could be fitted together harmoniously. Next, studying the photographic copy of the original painting, taken at the time that the stripping occurred, it seemed evident that the cracked and eroded plaster had given rise to erroneous correlation of the painted layers in this instance, for the down-sweeping wing of the bird certainly extends over the so-called rabbit stick, in proper proportion (*see* Pl. IV, page 28). Therefore, Figure 90 is shown, herein, as a part of the complex centering around the personage, Paiyatuma.

The element, Figure 90, has a yellow-orange central portion, four inches wide, bordered on each edge by a white decoration, one inch wide, segmented by closely spaced white dividing lines, and terminating in small black, dash-like units which parallel the sides of the main feature. Some segmentation on the main part of the element is also indicated by very narrow black lines which cross the yellow portion from side to side. A larger, black feature is at the figure's fragmentary fore end.

What appears as a great sweeping wing in the Figure 93 complex was identified as the rainbow. Our worm-like feature may, indeed, be a "rabbit stick," which was fashioned after a bird wing—here made of the pinions from the Duck and the fluffy plumes from the man being. Its attribute of "far reaching and far seeing" would be doubly meaningful. Paiyatuma is shown, then, as mounted on the back of the Rainbow, following Duck in flight back to his people.

With the Kuaua Figure 95 we have a personage with certain attributes of a Koyemshi. Inasmuch as Paiyatuma is a Newekwe [Ne'-paitama] it appeared likely that this "Kanash-kule" represented a being of that society, or one of similar nature. No other character of all the depictions gave such difficulty as this. Many false leads were followed, until it was finally decided that our recording must relate to the Newekwe being whom Cushing has called Ténatsali, and to whom later reference is made. Mrs. Stevenson, describing the retirement of the Koyemshi, in 1891, prior to the Molawiya ceremony, stated that four men and three boys of the Newekwe fraternity performed, adding to the amusement in the plaza. She records that all of those other than "the boss," wore old tattered clothing,[229] particularly cast-off uniforms from the army. The one was nude, with his entire body and head painted ash-grey in color; bodies and faces of the others were similarly painted. The soil used to decorate the Newekwe during ceremonials was obtained from Ashes Spring.[230] All wore ash colored skullcaps, with bunches of ribboned corn husks on each side. During the absences of dancers from the plaza, the Newekwe and the Koyemshi played the wool bag game. Finally there was a free-for-all between the two groups, and much excitement. In the end,

228. Parsons, 1939:187. At Zuñi, Chicken Hawk is considered one of the four messenger birds sent out by the two war chiefs to get permission from the Rain chiefs to "come out" from the under world. The fourth world was called "wing inner world because they saw their Sun father's wing" (p. 219).

Ladd tells us that when the Zuñi were ready to come up from the four worlds below, several creatures, including *Ha·tsu showe* or Cooper's Hawk (*Accipiter cooperi*)—called Chicken Hawk, here—were called by the leaders to find the opening through which they could come up. The hawk did not find it.

229. Part of their creed of disorderliness. *See* Cushing, 1896:414.

230. Stevenson, 1904:430. According to Ladd, ashes from corncobs are now used.

bunches of willows were brought forth, and whipping ensued among the members of the two organizations. Then the elder brother Bow priest gathered all the willows in his right hand, waved them to the six regions, and carried them from the plaza. When the dancers returned for the last time to the plaza, they were laden with cooked sweet corn, rabbits, and sliced watermelon.[231]

Mr. Ladd observes that there is a whole series of dances which are performed at this time, and which may have included the *Ha'wa hawe* dance. This is performed by the kiva, but has some connection with the Newekwe. Kokothlanna and Mitotasha occasionally perform in this dance, as well as Ne'paiyatama. Several Newekwe appear, acting as drummers and directors of the dance.

At this stage of the Kuaua study, it was concluded that our Figure 95 represents the nude one of the Newekwe fraternity, as mentioned by Mrs. Stevenson.[232] And thus it rested.

A myth which was published by Parsons,[233] tells of the son of a Rain priest, who lived alone with his grandmother off a little distance from one of the ancient Zuñi villages. Everyone hated them; they were mistreated, poor, and without food. The boy learned from his grandmother that they had relatives in the east, at Turkey Tracks, and he started there to find them. En route, some little turkeys took him into their home, where one of the turkeys gave him red beads and burned turquois, and each of them gave him a body feather. With these feathers he was to make prayersticks, which would summon the turkeys. They taught him prayers to repeat, and what to do with his beads when he got close to Zuñi. The boy returned to his village and did as he had

been directed. His grandmother gave him willow sticks; he made the prayersticks and planted them in the old fields which had belonged to his ancestors.

That night while the boy and his grandmother slept, the Turkey people came to their home. Through magical means, they produced buckskin, blankets, and corn, which they left. Then the turkeys scattered themselves everywhere. When the boy and the old woman awoke, they saw all these things, and different kinds of beads. Where there had been nothing, their rooms were filled with corn and everything to eat.

Later, because they were still poor, the boy went to the west to visit another relative of whom his grandmother told him. There, he learned his uncle's sacred song and dance, and was provided with turquois moccasins, high leggings with buckskin fringe, parrot feathers, kilt, and girdle—thus attire exactly like that of his uncle, a Koko (Katsina). These he took back to his home, where he told his grandmother "to clean the room,"[234] as his uncle had bade him. Grandmother cleaned the room, and then the boy "stood up and sang his song." When he had finished, all the beads shook and made a noise.

The boy went out to hunt, each time bringing home a deer; "he killed deer all the time." When spring came, he prepared prayersticks and planted seeds of yellow corn, blue corn, and all the other colors of corn; he planted watermelon [later addition—E. J. L.], pumpkin, and squash; then beans of all different colors. In a few days, everything had begun to grow; then everything blossomed. The

231. Stevenson, 1904:276.

232. Parsons, 1916:399, reported that the Zuñi Newekwe was then a fast diminishing fraternity. Today, Ladd says, it is probably the second largest.

233. Parsons, 1930:11-19; *see also* the Tenatsali tales, pp. 19-24.

234. Stevenson, 1904:423, "Prior to the occupation of a room by a fraternity the household moves out and gives the room a general cleaning. They do not remove, however, until just previous to the convening of the fraternity. Their presence in the chamber does not interfere with the meeting of the members to rehearse their songs and talk over matters." Ladd notes that the head of the household is usually a member; all non-members move out before the ceremonies.

field did so well that some witches became very jealous, and so they plotted together. They decided to make caterpillars *(amewiwe),* saying, "When these caterpillars begin to eat, everything will be dried up." One of the Rain priests who heard the conspiracy was the boy's uncle, and he went to the boy's house and told him about it. The burned turquois which the boy had was the proper antidote. Following his uncle's directions, he caught a caterpillar eating his corn *(see* Pl. A-10). The caterpillar begged for his life, and, holding him, the boy said: "All right. I will let you live. Now you go down to the bottom of the world. You will be always as you are now, but you will come out only in midsummer when weeds of all kinds have grown. That is the time you are to come out. You will live on weeds." He threw the caterpillar in, and walked away to his house.

A few days later, the plotters made a grey worm, which they thought would eat up everything in the boy's field. Again the uncle warned him, and told him to do as before. So the boy found a grey worm, and dispatched him to the bottom of the world, to come out only during the summer, and to eat weeds. Then a blue worm was created with the same intent, and with the same result. Next, a red worm was sent to eat the crops, but he met with similar dispatch. Finally, the witches met again, and their father decided that he would go to the boy; he said: "I will do it myself now. I will go as a butterfly when he goes to his field. I will go there as a butterfly and he will turn into a butterfly and fly away. I will go because I do not want him to have all the growing things."

Being warned by his uncle, the boy used cotton threads, his red beads, burned turquois, and a stick to fashion a special snare for catching butterflies. The next day he took it to the field, praying for a strong wind. The wind began to blow hard, and then he saw a butterfly, which blew onto his stick and was caught. The butterfly begged for his life. The boy saved him, but assigned him to the south forever, to live there in the winter, and to come forth only in midsummer to live among the flowers. This was the end of the trickery.

The next day, the boy went off hunting and brought home a deer. The following day, he went to the spring at Kyapkwena to get a drink, and a girl came for water.[235] She invited him to her house, and he went there and stayed. When he went back to his home in the afternoon, he had no deer. He went to the girl's house the next day, and she said that she wanted to go with him to his house. He said, "All right." So the girl put meal in a basket, carried it on her head and went with him, where they stayed together. He gave his wife clothes and moccasins. He told his grandmother "to clean the room," which she did. Then he told her and his wife to sit down. He donned the clothes his uncle had given him, and came out and stood in the middle of the room and danced and sang. When he finished singing, and gave his koko cry, everything hanging on the walls made a noise. The girl asked, "Do you live like this?" The boy answered, "Yes, this is the way we are to amuse ourselves because the people of the town are not kind to us." And they lived there.

Going to his field, the next day, the boy found his corn and everything had begun to ripen. That night, two Bow priests came and asked him to become their leader, their Rain priest to *take care of the people.* He refused, though they asked him four times. They left, but met again to talk about it. The priests decided to make him their society chief, even if he didn't want to be. He continued to refuse, and his wife did not want him to become the Rain priest. The priests sent two Bow priests to take the couple to the Rain priests' chamber, and there they asked him to be their father, to be Rain priest. They insisted that he should take his father's place, for "his

---

235. *See* version in Stevenson, 1904:135-137.

father used to be the head chief in the set of rain priests." The boy kept refusing, but at last, seeing that he was wanted so badly, he said that he would not be Rain priest while they lived in that outlying village, he wanted his people to go to the Middle place, or Zuñi, and there he would be Rain priest. The priests agreed that they would all join together. The boy said, "All the things I have planted have grown ripe. In a few days all the people will work for us (meaning his family), all the people will have corn and beans and squash for us. And everybody will take some for their own."

A few days later the Bow priest called out to the people, as the boy had directed, to work in the fields. The next day everybody went down to the field, men, women, and boys, and harvested the crop. The Bow priest said, "Everybody go for his own. The stronger one thinks himself, the more he may carry home."[236] Some went twice. When they had finished the work they lived on for a while.

Then the boy had his grandmother summon the Bow priest to his house, where he was told to call out to the people to be ready to move in four days, to the Middle Place village. They were called and the move was made to Zuñi.

Looking again to Figure 95 (page 58), we see that many of the features with which the Parsons' tale is concerned aid in explaining those of the Kuaua complex. Certainly, the "worm" shown at the right of our Newekwe representation may be related to the episode treating of the caterpillar and the worms of various colors, over which our personage attained power and thus provided abundant food for his people. The prayerstick held in his left hand probably represents one made of turkey feathers; and the snare in his right hand is well described as one like the boy fashioned to capture the butterfly. Being the son of a

Rain priest, and ultimately one himself, he was able to bring the clouds and the rain necessary for good crops, and these elements are depicted in the Kuaua painting. Likewise, he was a great hunter, who brought in plenty of deer. It would seem, therefore, that we may identify the boy-priest of Parsons' recording with that of the Kuaua depiction. When the people were hungry, they called upon the priest for aid, and he in turn invoked the bounty of the deities who by various manifestations enacted the Sun Father's dictates.

Above, or behind, Figure 95, the elements shown may be interpreted as the "sacred reclining terrace and roadway of prayer," along with other sacred things.[237]

We come next to a consideration of Figure 96, identified as Grey Newekwe, who is carrying a plant in his right hand—anaklakia, which produces dreams. Mrs. Stevenson gives this as the so-called jimson weed, or Datura, which is capable of causing one to dream and have visions.[238] She mentions a legend in which a mythic boy, Aneglakya [Anaklakia], and his sister knew too much. They could make one sleep and see ghosts, and see who committed thefts. Their constant talking displeased the Divine Ones, who caused them to disappear into the earth forever. Then, "Flowers sprang up at the spot where the two descended—flowers exactly like those which they wore on each side of their heads when visiting the earth. The Divine Ones called the plant *aneglakya,* after the boy's name. The original plant has many children scattered over the earth; some of the blossoms are tinged with yellow, some with blue, some with red, some are all white—the colors belonging to the four

236. Ladd says they carried for the priest four times; the fifth was their own.

237. *Cf.* Cushing, 1896:432.

238. Stevenson, 1915:46. Stevenson, 1904, 386 ff., gives uses for jimson weed. Bunzel, 1932:489, records anaklakia as *Datura.* She says it is used by the medicine men to detect witchcraft. Ladd says, "not witchcraft, but to locate lost objects." He adds that powdered Datura is placed on wounds. In classifying it, the Zuñi consider it "bad" medicine. *See* Yarnell, 1959.

cardinal points."[239] Mrs. Stevenson says that Datura is very sacred to the Zuñi and other Pueblo Indian peoples.

Dr. Benedict has recorded an account in which the search for the Corn maidens introduces the Tenatsali[240] youths and their brother, Jimson Weed, all of whom tried to locate the lost maidens. They were unsuccessful, and told the priests to summon the War gods. The tale goes on from there.[240a]

Parsons gives a myth which pertains to Tenatsali youth and Tenatsali maiden and their grandmother, all of whom go to visit the Ahaiyuta and their grandmother. By rubbing corn all over the grandmothers, Tenatsali youth transforms them into young girls. As such, they go and dance in the village plaza, accompanied by Younger Brother.[241] The myth treats of fructification; production of an abundance of food—particularly deer and corn with the grinding of cornmeal, during which the girls seem to become synonymous with the Corn maidens; and of the clearance of dirt and ashes from the houses of two boys—one who was destined to remain unmarried and be hated, and one who was to become a Rain priest. Ahaiyuta brings the Tenatsali fetish for the latter, his son, who is given the prayers and songs. Tenatsali youth and Tenatsali maiden assume the positions of Wood Carrier and Poker, respectively. In the end, they take

their grandmother to live with them at Tenatsali, "beyond Koluwalawa."[242]

At Kuaua, a Tenatsali-like being is portrayed by the priest-clown-medicine man, Figure 95. There is extensive symbolism which relates to corn, hunting, and to curing.[243]

In bringing the study of the Kuaua paintings to a close, it was found that personages of peculiar character occupy relatively the same position in the kiva, as does Figure 95, on Layers D-14, B-9, and A-8, respectively. As will be seen later, each of these representations had certain features in common. Consequently, Layer N-41 was re-studied. Going back to the accounts of the search for the lost Corn maidens, Cushing's recording became more significant. He says:

> Of a sudden, for the sun was rising, they heard Paíyatuma in his daylight mood and 'hlimnan [transmutable]. Thoughtless and loud, uncouth of mouth, was he, as he took his way along the outskirts of the village. Joking was he, as today joke fearlessly of the fearful, his children the Néwekwe, for all his words and deeds were reversals (iyati-'hlna pénawe) of themselves and of his sacred being.[244]

Continuing with Cushing as a source, we are told that the warrior priests came forth

239. Stevenson, 1915:46.

240. Bunzel, 1932:915, records tenatsali as an unidentified plant. Ladd has learned from his grandfather that this is held the most sacred of all plants. It does not grow at Zuñi, but in Arizona, near the junction of the Little Colorado river (with the Zuñi river). It has a purple, Morning Glory-like flower which grows on a bush, two to three feet in height. Tenatsali is used in healing. It is represented in myths by two small boys.

240a. Benedict, 1935:34-38. See Cushing, 1896:395.

241. Parsons, 1930:19-24, says this, the *Muaiya*, is a dance for snow, danced by two girls and one boy at sunset on the day of the *tLewekwe* dance, at Zuñi. Stevenson describes the ceremony, an initiation of youths and girls, in February (1904:450, 458 ff.).

242. Parsons, 1930:24.

243. Cushing, 1896:395, tells of the creation of corn and says that as the people gazed at the wonderment of it, out of the east came "Paíyatuma and Tenatsali of the All-colored flowers (God of the Seasons)" [and thus the Moon, as Paíyatuma represents the Sun]. Stevenson (1904:413) gives "ténastsali" as the name of a mythical plant which bears six-colored blossoms. The plant was used for a floral crown for Paíyatuma. And it was considered "good medicine for game." She says (p. 192) that tenatsali pollen is used to paint the faces of the flute players (for *tHláhewe*), and those so decorated sing the songs of Paiyatuma.

244. Cushing, 1896:439. Ladd says the Newekwe do not have this reversal feature. Since the *Siyapakwe* of the *Shuma·kwe* do, however, he believes Cushing may have confused the two.

and greeted him. Much "backwards" talk ensued. The chief priest, Pekwinna, begged Ne'paiyatama to search for the lost ones, continuing the lying speeches, until "in leaving," he advanced toward Ne'paiyatama and performed the proper rites to release the grand personage that he was from his vile aspect, whereupon the wise and good god agreed to search for the Corn maidens. Cushing records:

No longer a clown speaking and doing reversals of meaning—as do his children (followers) the Néwekwe, today,—was Paiyatuma, as he walked into the court of the dancers ere the dusk of the evening, and stood with folded arms at the foot of the bow-fringed ladder of priestly council, he and his attendant follower (ánsetone)[245] Shútsukya, brother of Kwélele! Nay, he was tall and beautiful, and banded with his own mists, and as wings carried upright in his hands, under his folded arms, banded also, the wingplumes right and left, of the turkey,[246] wherewithal he had winged his way from afar leading the Maidens and followed as by his own shadow, by the black being of corn-soot, who cries with the voice of the frost-wind when the corn has grown aged and the harvest is taken away—Shútsuk'ya.[247]

This seems to indicate that Ne'paiyatama was followed by *Shutsukya*, who is said to be the white god (*Koko hohana*)[248]—the god of fire. Shutsukya is closely associated with one designated as his brother, *Kwelele*, the black god (*Koko kwin·e*), who is known as the god of heat. In Cushing's poetic account, there is intangible evidence that both Shutsukya and Kwelele are part of the scene. This is suggested by the white and the black colors of these respective beings, by the presence of Shutsukya

as follower of Ne'paiyatama, and yet by the indication that the "black being of corn-soot" cries, "Shutsukya."

Since the white god characteristically carries items (yucca and a bull roarer) in his *right* hand, and the black god, a torch and fire drill in his *left* hand, it is the belief of the present writer that we have in Figure 95, or Kanashkule, a representation of the twain, the Divine Ones, sons of the Sun—the Beloved Preceder and the Beloved Follower, or their twin War god successors—otherwise manifest as Newekwe-like beings (*cf.* Pl. A-11). Ne'paiyatama, then, would bespeak the great god, Kokothlanna, or Pautiwa—actually the sun. This gives meaning to Zna'ote's phrase, BETWEEN THE SKY.

Shutsukya (who, according to myth,[249] married the daughter of Pautiwa) and Kwelele appear at Zuñi only once a year, when Shutsukya "brings the new year from the east," thus at the time of the Winter solstice.

In the Kuaua portrayal, the duality of character is indicated by the double outline surrounding the figure, white bounding the black body of Figure 95.[250] The Cushing account adds substance to the fact that Ne'paiyatama [Paiyatuma] as shown in Figure 93, traveled by the aid of banded wings, and it places Figure 90 in harmonious association.

Finally, it becomes evident that the myths connected with Figure 95 all relate to facts and ceremonies which were evolved from observance of the solstices—the movement of the sun from north to south and vice versa, as always, the Sun Father's way.

Here we have an outstanding example of the manner by which the priesthood increased its complexity and added to the manifestations of the holy one. When a new idea was to be effected and explained, a new visual concept was created and woven into the ceremonial

245. Ladd renders this as *a·tsanna*, meaning "children."
246. Ladd says this should be "primary flight feather of eagle," not turkey.
247. Cushing, 1896:443.
248. *See* Bunzel, 1932:923.

249. Bunzel, 1932:930.
250. Ladd says he could be *Ishana'*, Grease Boy.

fabric. By giving each character a position akin to familial relationships of father, mother, uncle, sister, son, daughter, and the like, and by relating each to a common pursuit such as hunting, warfare, or agriculture, the priests made their religious organization intimate and understandable to all people.[251]

We have noted above that Kokothlanna, the great god (fig. 97), appeared to the Newekwe fraternity members at Ashes Spring, where he gave them strong medicine. Following Stevenson, we learn that Kokothlanna talked long there with Bitsitsi-Ne'paiyatama, who told him of their insignia—an ear of corn covered with downy plumes and feathers of vari-colors[252]—their prayer plumes, and of their baton[253] of authority. Then it was that the great god of the Newekwe said, "That is well; that is well. Come and live with me and you shall be musician and jester to the Sun Father." Since that time, Kokothlanna is personated at the initiatory ceremonials of the Newekwe, and administers the medicine to initiates and fraternity members.

Nearby Kokothlanna, in the Kuaua painting, is the figure of a deer or antelope (fig. 98). Inasmuch as it is shown in yellow, the same color of the great god's body, the association of the two is indicated. Close to the animal, on his right, is the black stalk of corn, shown in its full maturity, and representing "all of the black corn" (fig. 99 and Pl. X)—bespeaking the Black Corn people. This leads to further mythical accounts.

During their migrations, the Zuñi arrived at one village,[254] "to find all the inhabitants but four either fled or dead from the effluvium of the Áshiwi. . . ."[255] In their reed and earth house, an old man and woman and their two grandchildren, a boy and a girl, were discovered "sitting by a meal symbol of clouds upon the floor. Their ears and nostrils were closed with raw cotton, and they were bending over a . . . urinal in which the old man had deposited sunflower and other medicine, the fumes of which they were inhaling to save them from the killing odors of the Áshiwi." The Zuñi thought they were dead, but the aged man said: "We are not dead; we were the Yellow Corn people; you have destroyed or driven off all but ourselves;[256] we are saved by

251. Bunzel, 1932:845, notes also that the Katsinas, like the people, have a village organization, in which Pautiwa is "the boss," and his messenger, ᵗKiaklo. Ladd notes that ᵗKiaklo does not live at Kothluwalawa, but has a special place of origin.

252. Symbolic of the life-giving or "soul power which comes from Awonawilona, the supreme bisexual power" (Stevenson, 1904:416).

253. Benedict (1935-I:103) says this baton is called *yamune*. Ladd explains that this yamune is a short prayerstick which is used specially for medicine. *See* Cushing, 1896:384-385.

254. This is recorded (Stevenson, 1904:44) as Heshotayalla, where there were extensive villages, with houses of reeds and earth [*jacales*] built in the heights. There were great fields, well irrigated, and the people had many possessions. This indicates that the location was in an area considerably to the south of present Zuñiland. There, the warriors' thoughts "were always of the eagle or mountain lion or other fierce creatures of prey" (Cushing, 1896:424). This denotes relationship with, or influence from, the great warrior societies of the Eagle and Jaguar of the Aztecs and their predecessors, the Toltecs, of central Mexico. Likewise, it may be noted, that it was here that the battle with the ᵗCha'kwena'okya, mentioned in connection with the painting of Layer O-43, is said to have taken place.

255. Ladd, here, raises an interesting question. He wonders if the gases expelled at the time of the eruptions at Sunset Crater and in the surrounding area might have been harmful to the people then dwelling in that region, and if the situation which pertained may be reflected in Zuñi mythology. He says there are myths which recur so often, and they speak of people who were "driven to the east by *K'o liwya*—not A·shiwi (*k'oliwya* [*k'o li*] meaning something with an unpleasant odor; and, later, 'a rusty piece of metal'—also associated with a taste.)" He questions whether the Zuñi could have been near that area during the period—the latter part of the 11th century.

256. According to Cushing's recounting (1896:417-424), the Divine Ones, the twin brothers, became angered by the warring tendency of the people, who having attained complete human character and self-esteem, were becoming too vain and insolent. Therefore, they caused earthquakes; great storms with thunder and lightning, rain and hail, winds and floods; and raging fires to descend upon the earth. From this cataclysm, there came forth the two gods, the beloved twain, strong "with the full

inhaling my medicine, but it has made our corn, which we hold in our belts, black, and we are now the Black Corn people." Since that time "they and their descendants have been called the Black Corn people" *(see* Pl. A-13).

Some wanted to kill these people, but because the old man had a sacred fetish, "which was immediately before him and over which he leaned to inhale the medicine from the bowl," they refrained, being pleased to find that he possessed a fetish (ettone). In the following four days, contests were held between the Zuñi and the old man of the Black Corn, whose songs brought much rain. They became friends, and the old priest and his family were adopted by the Zuñi. Since his death, it is said, his fetish has been in the possession of his descendants, the Black Corn people.[257]

We may conclude, then, that the complex of Figures 97-99, at Kuaua, depicts the great god, Kokothlanna, or the Sun, and assisting personages. The entire painting, doubtless, represents a major ceremony in which numerous activities took place over a period of several days, and which was open to the public.[258] The deities and their symbolic paraphernalia were placed on the walls of the ceremonial chambers;[259] myths were recounted, telling of

the origin of the Kuaua people, their migrations, the accomplishments of their ancestral ones, and of their coming to settle at this location; and, without doubt, the priests arranged colorful dance dramas which were enacted by masked Indians impersonating the katsinas—with antics performed by members of the jester orders, balancing the serious aspects with great merriment.

Layer M-40

Of this layer, which immediately followed Layer N-41 in the kiva, we have a limited expanse of the north wall and the full extent of the west, up to the height above which it is eroded away, giving fragmentary remains of three prominent figures and a considerable number of important small elements. Upon viewing the paintings, Zna'ote readily remarked: TSÁNYA AK KEH, HUNTING CEREMONY; COULD BE HELD ANY TIME, SUMMER OR WINTER [Saniyakikwe—hunters fraternity].[260]

At the juncture of the north and west walls, a large animal figure is painted, with its head portion on the west wall, and the back half of the body on the north, standing 32 inches above the floor (fig. 89). Its overall length is 34 inches. The animal has short, incurving horns which rise above the head; the back shows a long hump; a straight, rather bushy tail, 13 inches long and four inches at its widest part, extends upward over the rump; the four feet show more toe development than is usual on bovines, otherwise the animal appears to be a bison, and is so identified by Zna'ote: CÍBOLA, BUFFALO [bison]; RED SHOWS TONGUE AND HEART[261] *(cf.* Pl. B-1).

---

strength of evil, and armed as warriors of old." Few people had endured the furor, and the priests led them back to rebuild their houses. The twin ones assembled their warriors, the chosen few, who were taught the sacred knowledge of the warrior gods, and thus became the first Bow priests. Together, the Divine Ones and the new warriors sought the priest fathers of the people to aid in summoning the sleeping people that they might journey to safety. These were led by Ahaiyuta to a place of security. Those who failed to join them were choked by the black fumes, or were buried in the walls of their houses which fell "when presently the earth heaved with dire fumes, fire, and thunder."

257. Stevenson, 1904:45. *See* page 49 herein.

258. Ladd cites the Shalako at Zuñi as a likely parallel of modern times.

259. At Zuñi, Ladd says, under similar circumstances, paintings would be painted in each of the kivas, but they all would be different, involving other gods and personages.

260. Ladd says that the house of *su mosona,* the head of the society, was fully decorated at one time, and was used several times, but not for any one ceremonial at Zuñi.

261. Hodge, 1907:301, notes that the name "Cibola," which was applied to the Zuñi pueblo of Hawikuh, is believed to be a Spanish form of *Shiwina,* the Zuñi name for their tribal range, and that "*Cibolo* later became the term by which the Spaniards of Mexico designated the bison."

Fig. 89. Bison (big lying star) with foot prints before it, and turtle, woman's track, and medicine behind it. *Layer M-40.*

The animal is painted black, except for a red line which extends from the mouth to the heart, thus showing the "tongue and heart." A prominent penis is shown. From the mouth and penis, dashed lines flow downward. On either side of the mouth droppings, a crescent-shaped track, TÉ'ANÁNᵉ [*teanna*], according to Zna'ote, with two small dots close thereto is

shown in black. These appear to be in opposed direction to the footprints which the bison would make (fig. 89). Zna'ote explained them as representing a TRAP.

From both the mouth and anus of the bison, criss-crossed lightning elements painted in yellow extend to the limits of the eroded walls. Directly back of the animal and below the

PL. XI. *Layer M-40.* Hunting ceremony; Scalp or War dance with initiation; Shumaikoli society.

Fig. 86   Fig. 87. Racing stick and ring.   Fig. 88

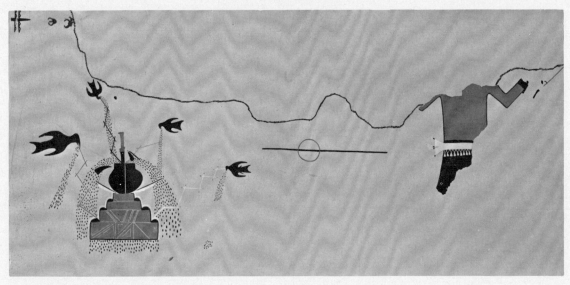

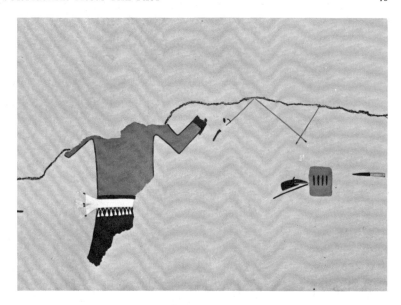

Fig. 88. Paiyatuma, patron of the hunt, with pollen bag and medicine rock at his left. *Layer M-40.*

lightning are three small elements. The first is a yellow TURTLE, ÉTO·WE'; SLOW. Next is a black and yellow footprint, a WOMAN'S TRACK; SLOW. Of the two, Zna'ote said: MEDICINE; CAN'T GO FAST; MAKES BUFFALO GO SLOW SO HUNTER CAN CATCH AND KILL HIM. And the third is a claw-shaped feature, identified as WEEDS; OPEN UP AND SLOW; MEDICINE.

Back of the weeds, down-falling dashed lines again occur, issuing as moisture from a source no longer evident, but indicating another symbolization of rain making.

Centrally located on the west wall is a personage (fig. 88), the bottommost part of which (the kilt) extends to within 19.5 inches of the floor. The body is painted yellow, outlined in red. Only an indication of the right arm remains, but this, like the left arm, shows the elbows crooked; the left hand is painted red, and appears to grasp, or come close to, a criss-

Fig. 89

crossed element painted yellow, extending toward the buffalo. There appears to be a wristlet, or bow guard, on the left wrist, indicated by two narrow black stripes bordering a white area. The personage wears a black kilt which has a red border at the bottom. About the waist is a white sash, tied on the right side; it is tasseled, and has red knots from which fringes project stiffly; pendant from the sash proper, a fringed or tasseled decoration is seen. Fragmentary as it is, this figure was readily identified by Zna'ote as PAIYATUMA, THE "BOSS"—HUNTER. AS IN DEER, ANTELOPE, OR RABBIT HUNT. MAKE CORRAL AND PUT CORN MOTHER IN IT. DON'T TALK; CALL LIKE A BLACK CROW. GET MAYBE FOUR HUNDRED ANTELOPE.

To the left of Paiyatuma is a yellow object, decorated with four short, black lines in its center.[262] It is four inches wide and five inches high. From the right side, two feathers extend. Zna'ote identified this as a POLLEN BAG; ALWAYS SAME COLOR AS MAN WHO USES IT. Close to the pollen bag, on the left, is a slender, pointed object, which Zna'ote said is a HEAVY ROCK; SLOW; A KIND OF MEDICINE. It is four inches long; about half of this length is painted black, coming to a point toward the pollen bag, with the remainder in faded yellow.

To the right of Paiyatuma, at hip height, is a unit identified by Zna'ote as TSÍ·KOHN ['tsí kon-ya]; STICK RACE. ZUÑIS HAVE TWO KINDS. BUNCH OF YUCCA TIED WITH STRING AND PAINTED YELLOW. BUNCH ABOUT THREE INCHES ACROSS (Pl. XI, fig. 87). There is a yellow, circular element about five inches in diameter, and a black stick 30 inches long.

Heading into the southwest corner of the kiva, high above the floor, is a figure which Zna'ote identified as SHU MAK LO·A' [shúmaikolowa]; SUMMERTIME AIRPLANE OVER WATER (fig. 86), which is recognizable as the dragon fly (cf. Pl. B-2).

Northward from the dragon fly, and diagonally downward, is a finely portrayed altar, the base of which comes to about 20 inches of the floor. The altar is painted yellow and outlined in white, with a linear decoration on the front, of which Zna'ote said: TSÍ NA' PA'; DESIGN LIKE ON POTTERY, "MARKED UP" [decorated]. The altar rises in four tiers, with three black clouds, also outlined in white, resting on the steps on either side. On the top rests a globular, black water jar, which has a white line running from rim to base. Curving upward from either side of the jar's base is a black and white feather, which Zna'ote explained, WANTS RAIN, TO MAKE LIGHTNING. This represents a pad or PILLOW to steady the vessel, and represents the feathers used throughout the ceremonies for sprinklers of sacred water, and for making yucca suds symbolic of rain clouds.

Extending from the mouth of the water jar is a narrow object painted black where it seemingly enters the vessel, and yellow on its upper portion. Of these, Zna'ote said: A BLACK JAR AND TASA KWINNA—A PLANTING STICK. At each side of this latter implement are a stick and triangle-shaped elements in black—now disconnected from other features, though seemingly projecting from within the jar.

Flying about the jar are four graceful birds painted black. Zna'ote said: KWAU WU' LOKWE'; A LITTLE BLACK BIRD, HERE IN THE SUMMERTIME; LIVES IN THE BIG PINE TREES. From the mouth of each bird, zig-zag lightning symbols, each in a different color (yellow, black, indeterminable, and black with yellow tips), extend down to the altar clouds, and two to the mouth of the water jar; also falling from each bird's mouth are black droplets.[263]

About 12 inches above the bird on the right, and thus back of the dragon fly, are two animal

262. Note importance of *four*, as in Bunzel, 1932:675.

263. The birds that sing before the rain are supposed to be messengers of the supernaturals, sent to announce the rain (Bunzel, 1932:639).

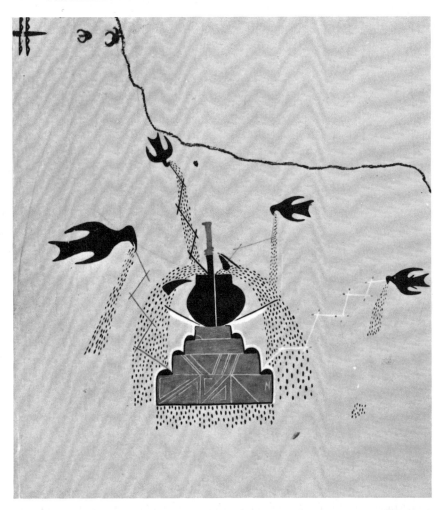

Fig. 86. Above, dragon fly and mountain lion tracks; below, altar with scalp jar on top—surrounded by feathers, moisture, clouds, lightning—and holding a planting stick; little black birds. *Layer M-40.*

tracks, painted in yellow. One shows claws projecting from a pad, the other, with more claws, shows similarity to a mountain lion track.

The most significant figure of the M-40 depiction is that of Paiyatuma, who is summoned to participate in hunt ceremonies. But the entire painting is a fine example of the use of sympathetic magic, for every feature shown has been portrayed because of its particular power to aid the hunter. That the depictions represent a complete recitation of myths, along with the painting of the symbolic, is evident. On this layer, the buffalo or bison is shown extending onto the north and west walls (fig. 89), indicating a ceremonial bison hunt.

Hunts were traditionally communal undertakings among the Pueblo peoples, and hunt orders were associated with the oldest of the fraternities. Inasmuch as the Kuaua painting portrays the bison, largest of all game animals known to the Pueblo Indians, and for which they had to organize hunting parties to go east of the Pecos river, into the wide plains, there were doubtless significant kiva observances in connection with the hunters society.

The Zuñi claim to have but little knowledge of the bison, as they say it belongs to the east.[264]

Among the Keresan pueblos, a supernatural Father of the Game, *Shaiya·ik,* was recognized, "the owner or keeper of the game." According

264. Stevenson, 1904:311.

to Acoma lore, the oldest man born in the Eagle clan (for the eagle is a bird of prey) was chosen to be the father of the game. His work was in the power of his songs, and when he sang and prayed to the animals, they and the hunters were to become partners.[265] This supernatural one set up his altar, prepared prayer plumes to be given to those going on a hunt, and taught the hunters his songs, which they sang all night. Thus the hunters society, *Shaiyai ka,* was formed at Acoma.[266]

Each man was given prayersticks and sent out into the wilds to pray. They prayed that they would have the power of the prey animals. Early on the morning of the fourth day, the priest started out to a place he had selected. Whenever he saw animal tracks, he took some dirt out of the track, and dung, and placed it in a cedar bark container. When he reached his chosen place, he tied both ends of the cedar bark with yucca blades. "He was going to scorch the feet of the game animals. Then he made a fire and scorched the dirt and dung so as to scorch the feet of the animals so they could not run fast."[267]

The hunters were told to bring sacred cornmeal[268] and pollen, and also to pick up dirt and dung from animal tracks. The priest signaled his location by building a fire and throwing on green branches to cause dense smoke. When the hunters came, they threw their offer-ings into the fire and uttered a prayer, naming any animal from whom they sought aid on the hunt. They named "birds for small game like rabbits; lion, wolf, wildcat, for deer and large game."[269] This appears to explain the small tracks (fig. 89) which are seen in front of the bison.

All hunters carry fetishes on the hunt, having been taught how to make them by the society leader. They should be made of hard stone. They represent the prey animals, and give the hunter protection, having been sung over and prayed to by the leader. The priest has stone fetishes which he uses about the altar. The Kuaua "medicine rock" (Figure 88) probably represents one of these fetishes. It is a pointed object, identified as a HEAVY ROCK, more "slow medicine," according to Zna'ote. The following statement given by Kirk's Zuñi informant seems to describe and explain its use:

Sometimes they don't kill anything. Then that fetish been put by their fire, they must use it. Making prayers over fetish and finding buffalo tracks and put fetish in the tracks and sticking it down there, hard; and praying over. Stick into footprints with this sharp thing and beside it putting medicine. I don't know if it is true or not, but beliefs is that buffalo won't disappear from hunting ground if this sharp things sticking in his foot tracks, and they put different sharp things besides. The points of iron and stone, and other different sharp things, also the fetish. Then they will have good lucks.[270]

265. Stevenson, 1904:368, says, "Game is a necessary offering to the Beast Gods to induce them to act as mediators between" the Zuñi people and the gods.

266. There, members were initiated during ceremonies which included the making of paintings and the performance of rites about altars, with songs to invoke the gods to give power over the game when on the hunt. Medicines were prepared to insure success in capturing game.

At Zuñi, Ladd says, the hunters "make medicine," but "most of this is done with songs and prayers before the hunt; prayersticks are usually prepared and a visit made to the Suskikwe society. There are no other objects involved except the animal fetishes."

267. Stirling, 1942:21.

268. Sprinkled cornmeal signifies a prayer to the gods for strength of heart and limb (Stevenson, 1904:129). *See* Benavides, 1945:43.

269. Stirling, 1942:21. At Laguna, on the eve of a hunt, meal or dough images were offered to animals and, if they disappeared, it meant that deer would be killed. At Acoma, cornhusk images of deer, rabbit, or quail were made and, early on the morning of the hunt, they were scattered outside the pueblo—to make plenty of game for the hunters, just as game and other creatures were created by the Corn Mother (*Iyatiku*), from images in her basket (*see* Parsons, 1939:316). The Zuñi make a small mound and cover it with meal and sprinkle meal round about. If deer tracks appear in the meal, a successful hunt is assured.

270. Kirk, 1950:140.

The information given by Zna'ote in reference to making a corral and placing the Corn Mother in it, the night before a hunt, is a variant of rites practiced generally by Pueblo Indians, to insure the ultimate success of the hunters. At Cochiti, a corral was made of juniper, a big fire built, cornmeal sprinkled on it, and in the morning each man prayed to Old Fire Woman, asking her help and making an offering of meal.[271]

Certainly, the pollen bag (fig. 88) represents such a one as that used by the hunt priest, here portrayed as Paiyatuma. Sacred meal was always used in connection with any hunt. Kirk's informant describes the use of ritual "blue medicine" on the second day before the start of the buffalo hunt:

> During four days ceremonies before starting out on hunting trip, use fetishes . . . . And on second day use blue medicine . . . I don't know what it is made of. Probably blue corn and maybe turquoise in it. The pouch it is in is about five inches long and about two inches wide. They have medicine shell spoon, just little one, about big as pencil and use just little bit of that medicine in ceremonial."[272]

Sacred meal and fetishes are also placed by the body of the buffalo at the end of the hunt.

From a tale recorded by Parsons, concerning a "ground cow," we get a hint as to the original symbolism shown with the Kuaua beast.[273] The Ahaiyuta were cautioned by their grandmother about this animal, who killed people, and they were warned to stay away from him. But younger brother was never afraid, and so the boys, aided by Gopher, sought out the ground cow. Gopher found him lying on the ground, and made a hole to him. He listened

and heard his heart beating. He cut the hair off to his heart and went back to the boys. Since Gopher had opened a hole to the beast, and had "cut the hair off straight to his heart," the boys argued as to who was to go in. The elder brother wanted to go in, but the younger one said, "No, you would not shoot him straight to the heart. I want to go." He went in and "pulled his bow straight where his grandfather had cut off the hair. He let loose the arrow. When he did that he ran back. The cow jumped up and looked around . . . . He looked down where he was lying. He saw the hole. There he put two horns into the hole and followed Younger Brother. The horn almost caught Younger Brother. When he got to where the other two were, the horn just touched him and the cow fell down dead." Gopher was pleased that the boys had killed this cow, which had been killing the people who came for wood.

The younger brother went to the beast and "knocked its eyes to see if it was dead. When he touched its eyes he saw it was already dead." He took off the hide and cut off the head. Ahaiyuta said: "Throw its head to the east side Now you go to the east (sic), you will be the big star that tells lies, mok' (star) kwanosina (lying) łanna (big)."—"Good for you, grandson, I have all the meat I need."

Modern Zuñi pottery frequently depicts deer with a red line extending from the animal's mouth to the heart, and this has been explained as "the heart line." In the Kuaua painting, as well as in the pottery portrayals, the significance of this heart line appears to be found in the above myth, and represents the cutting off of the hair "straight to the heart," so that the animal could be successfully killed by a shot arrow. It may be noted that the painting of the bison (perhaps a "ground cow"), shows no eyes. Here we may have a representation of the dead beast, whose head was assigned to the east, to appear as the big lying star (see Pl. XI, fig. 89). This mythical creature, then,

271. Goldfrank, 1927:87.
272. Kirk, 1950:138.
273. Parsons, 1930:32-33. Benedict, 1935-I:51, gives a similar Cloud Swallower tale.

with its bushy tail of little stars, is hunters' magic. Recitation of the historical myth during ceremonial preparation for a hunt, doubtless, would bring the power of the War gods to initiates or to hunters.

The easternmost element shown in our painting (fig. 89) is identified as WEEDS, which "open up and slow; medicine." From its shape, it seemed that this might represent martynia, commonly known as devil's claw, the pods of which hook about the fetlocks of burros and catch into the fleece of sheep, and would have clung in the same manner to the coat of the bison, thus serving, perhaps as a "slow medicine."[274] We know that the plant called *tenatsali* is considered "good medicine for game," and that the hunters society possesses its blossoms and roots,[275] and so it is probable that this is represented in the Kuaua medicines. This medicine is the property of the Rain priests and directors of the Little Fire[276] and Bed Bug fraternities, and is administered with great care by these directors only. The root is given as a narcotic, and the roots and flowers ground together into meal are applied to wounds. These properties would make the medicine especially desirable for hunters and warriors; likewise, the visionary attributes might be equally helpful to these particular ones. The property of causing drowsiness could make of it a "slow" medicine. Also, it is possible that these "slow" medicines may be of cathartic nature.[277].

The proverbial slowness of the turtle or tortoise is recognized, the world over; and it is a universal observation that women move more slowly than men, as represented by the woman's track. Here, the latter[278] probably represents the priestess of fecundity, Shiwanokia, who has been summoned, and who is an important participant in the Summer solstice ceremonies. And there is more to the tortoise representation than has been indicated.

During the Summer solstice ceremonies the katsina director and his assistant, each with his warrior, make a trip to Kothluwalawa, where they deposit prayersticks and pray that the tortoises may come out from their homes in the water, four deep holes which are supposed to exist in the walls of the lake. Members of the party accompanying the officers are sent out by the director who says, "Go, look for our otherselves." "Only members of the fraternity of Hunters may strike the tortoise with the rabbit stick; others pat them with their hands until the head is projected, when a string is tied around the neck."[279] A favorite place of the tortoises is said to be "the house of the deer," a spring not far from Kothluwalawa, where the deer come to drink.

To the Zuñi, tortoises [as well as water snakes, frogs, tadpoles, newts, etc.] are "our lost others," meaning the children dropped by their mothers in the first crossing of the river to reach Zuñi. The children floated downstream, and "their souls or 'in-being' sank to the city of the dead," where they were transformed to their former selves.[280]

It is thus understandable that tortoise meat is seldom eaten by the Zuñi; it is used as medicine for cutaneous diseases.[281]

We come now to the personage identified as Paiyatuma (fig. 88), who is here portrayed as patron of the hunt. The costume shown agrees

274. Mrs. Stevenson (1915:46) notes that flowers of the plant called "aneglakya" *(Datura)* are represented in Zuñi and in other pueblos by interlacing colored yarns around the desiccated fruit of *Martynia louisiana* Mill., which is attached to a leather band passing around the head.

275. Stevenson, 1904:440, 444.

276. Stevenson, 1904:550, 554, 555, gives information concerning Mystery medicine of the Little Fire fraternity. A tiny covered vessel contains blossoms and root of tenatsali, combined with hearts of butterflies and dragon flies.

277. *See* White, 1942:287.

278. Footprints show that the gods have come. Ladd gives *tla'ma k'a,* "to make like a woman."

279. Stevenson, 1904:156-157. Currently, according to Ladd, others than hunt society members strike the tortoises.

280. Bartlett, 1914:86.

281. *See* Stevenson, 1904:161. Cushing, 1901:243-254, relates a tale concerning Turtle and Coyote, which gives reason for the pimply skin of the latter.

in detail with the traditional hunting dress of the Hopi Indians, where Paiyatuma is strongly associated with the hunt, as well as with music.[282] As such, he is associated with the Sun, father of the twin War gods.

At Zuñi, Benedict says, the cult of the War gods is administered by the Bow priests,[283] with several other groups participating, such as the priests who keep the war fetish (*pa'-eton·e*), priests of the great shell, the scalp chief who cares for the scalps in the scalp house, and men who carve and paint the war god figurines.[284] People who have killed an enemy under any condition must join the Bow priesthood,[285] in order to receive magical protection from the vengeful spirit. Members are initiated during a Scalp dance ceremony which celebrates the victory and propitiates the ghost.[286] The Scalp dance is given to please the War gods, so that they will intercede with Sun Father and the Council of the Gods for rain.[287]

Rain is important to a good hunt, as well as to the growing crops. Mrs. Kirk's informant from Zuñi says:

> Several fetishes using before going out for buffalo hunting. One fetish [288] got rainmakers headdress on and his plumage just like rain prayer sticks. That is because don't want to go out dry times. They would rather have fresh rain to start out with, want to get out on fresh tracks for their better luck. That rainmaker fetish like sea serpent, coming out of water; belongs in big jar with rain making fetishes . . . .[289]

Since the Figure 89 complex of our painting clearly refers to hunting rites and magic,[290] its relationship to the warriors society is indicated, and thus to the Scalp or War dance, which is an invocation for rain. The Scalp dance is a twelve-day ceremonial which was formerly given every four years. Mrs. Stevenson has described in detail the one which she observed at Zuñi in October, 1891.

From her account,[291] we learn that the scalps were kept in a large, black pottery jar which remained permanently in the scalp house. The vessel shown in Figure 86 of the Kuaua paintings would seem to be identifiable as such a vessel. The white line extending through its

---

282. Mrs. Stevenson cautions that Paiyatuma of the Newekwe fraternity at Zuñi "must not be confounded with Páyatamu, the god of music, flowers, and butterflies, who lives in the spring *Shún te⁺kiaya . . .*" (1904:409). Benedict (1930:67) records that, according to Keresan belief, "The Paiyatamos lived in the east at the sunrise, and were referred to . . . as Sun Blossoms." See also Bunzel, 1932:1016.

283. She (1935:I-88) states that the elder brother Bow priest is the hunting society's executive or Bow priest. Ladd says, "He is associated with the society but is *not* its leader." This society is responsible for the ceremonial rabbit hunt.

284. Bunzel, 1932:525. Ladd corrects this statement by inserting "Arrow" instead of "great shell."

285. This is organized similarly to the medicine societies, as Mrs. Stevenson included it. Bunzel describes the organization, at which time Zuñi had but three members of the Bow priesthood [There are currently four. — E. J. L.]. Mrs. Stevenson explains that while this priesthood is embraced in the esoteric fraternities it is also distinct from them, and is "always referred to as a priesthood" (1904:577). The members communicate directly with the lightning makers, rather than invoking the aid of the gods.

286. *See* Bunzel, 1932:526, 674; Stevenson, 1904:578; Parsons, 1924. Ladd tells us that "any time a scalp is taken, there is an individual initiation; not like Koko initiations."

287. Stevenson, 1904:578.

288. Ladd changes "fetish" to "prayerstick."

289. Kirk, 1950:137.

290. At Zuñi, today, the hunt and its preceding ceremonies are still directed by the hunters fraternity. Stevenson describes the ceremonial chamber of this society as one of the few which extended north and south. On these walls were permanent pictures, the writer never having seen the walls without them except when it was undergoing repairs (Stevenson, 1904:438). Their intent was evidently the same as these of the Kuaua mural, the insuring of success in the hunt. Cougar, wolf, lynx, and coyote were shown in the chase after elk, mountain sheep, deer, jack rabbits, and cottontail who were fleeing those which prey upon deer (Stevenson, 1904:438-439). A large group of petroglyphs pecked on the rocks, with similar intent, may be seen on the basaltic cliffs at La Ciénaga, about fifteen miles southwest of Santa Fe.

291. Stevenson, 1904:578 ff. Ladd says that, today, there is no time pattern.

center is probably symbolic of the heart and center of the region.[292] In rites performed during the Scalp ceremonial, the roadrunner is symbolized, this bird being held valuable "because he can convey messages, and the enemy can not tell from his footprints whence he comes, for the feet point both ways." Again, the roadrunner feathers[293] are employed, the quill ends of two feathers, "one an upper tail feather and the other an under tail feather," for the feathers "give courage, for knowledge and courage come from this bird, who is the keeper of courage." These may be represented by the feathers shown resting under our black jar atop the altar. Two juniper twigs are prepared, each with a piece of scalp and a fluffy eagle plume attached, and these are carried by the victor and the elder brother Bow priest until they are ceremonially deposited. Perhaps the two, triangular black elements seen extending from the mouth of the scalp jar are representative of these twig-scalp-feather objects. Among the participants in the ceremony are scalp-kickers,[294] who "start the scalps with the left foot and so keep them before them, never using the right foot for this purpose," and never looking to the right or the left. On the fifth morning the scalp-kicker and her aid bathe the entire body of the victor, "when his blood-stained hands are washed for the first time since the scalping." This blood symbolism may explain the red hand shown on Paiyatuma (fig. 88).

At various times during the ceremony the scalps are washed by women specially designated as scalp-washers; they bathe them in yucca suds, after which they rub them with kaolin, "for rain," and "a bit of the scalp is taken into the mouth,[295] that the Zuñis may have brave hearts and that the Gods of War will empower them to destroy the enemy. 'Should the victor possess a good heart, the killing of the enemy brings much rain.' "[296] There is much rain symbolism shown about Figure 86: the altar stacked with clouds—of which yucca suds are representative—lightning,[296a] birds of the four directions, and falling rain.

In a later painting (Layer D-17[1], fig. 58), Zna'ote mentions black, white, and yellow lightning as being ALL RIGHT; RED LIGHTNING IS BAD; LIGHTNING HITS SOMETHING AND BURNS, ANA TSI ATI ["struck by lightning"]. Here, then, we may conclude that only good lightning is depicted.[297] The birds are probably "water bringing birds," the ones who sing before the rain.

On the final night of the Scalp dance, nightlong ceremonies take place in the society chamber, when a painting is made and the epic songs of the War gods are sung, and the novices are taken into the warriors society "to

---

292. Stevenson, 1904:507.

293. Ladd gives the information that it was the number of tail feathers in the roadrunner's tail that determined the original length of the ceremonial; twelve feathers were taken to indicate a duration of twelve days for important observances.

294. Stevenson, 1904:579, says the scalp kickers "must be paternal aunts of the victor and elder brother; if there are no aunts, then the nearest paternal female relatives, grandmother excepted." Ladd tells us that the scalp is kicked through the village by the clan aunt of the initiated, who alone may touch it.

295. Ladd tells us that: "During this whole ceremony, the Bow priests cannot use salt. If the scalp-taker wishes, at the time of the scalping, he picks up the scalp in his mouth, and throws it in front of him four times, each time making a sound like a coyote. Then he must wrap the scalp around his mid-section, next to his skin. This is the only time the scalp is put into the mouth; and this is optional."

296. It is of interest to note here that black corn grains are carried under the tongue of the Scalp chief and his associates to prevent pursuit by the ghost of a scalped one. *See* Bunzel, 1932:683. Ladd says it is an arrowhead, not corn, which is carried under the tongue.

296a. It has been said that the only ones privileged to use the lightning symbol are members that belong to the Bow priesthood and order of the Arrow in the Great Fire fraternity (Stevenson, 1904:270). However, Ladd says the symbol may be, and is, used by other societies and certain of the Koko.

297. Ladd says there is no real differentiation of "good" or "bad" lightning. Lightning represents power, and it is feared.

share their supernatural prerogatives."[298] A great dance occurs, the next day, in the plaza, and late at night the scalps are returned to the scalp house.

Bunzel has noted that at the full moon in March, the Bow priests of Zuñi make prayer-sticks for Ahaiyuta. They meet at night in their ceremonial room, where their altar is set up. During the night, songs of the "spiral," or Circle, dance are sung. Four days later, a kick-stick race is held under the special patronage of the War gods. "After this it is safe for the people to plant corn." Bunzel says this ceremony has never been described; she only heard of it.[299]

Two features have been mentioned—the ring and stick element shown between Paiya-tuma and the altar, and the planting stick projecting from the scalp jar. The former are identical with the reed-like stick and ring composed of yucca ribbons that are part of the implements for a game which was still played rarely at Zuñi in Stevenson's time. She reports that it was played only by order of Father Ko-yemshi, and used exclusively to bring rain.[300] She says a chosen number of women were supplied, each, with a slender rod, "longer than an arrow shaft, zigzagged in black, symbolic of lightning," and a ring about 2.5 inches in diameter. The women stood in line, to the left of a number of men who were provided with racing sticks, about three inches long, which they kicked. The women tossed the yucca rings from the ground with their sticks.[301]

Although it is not recorded, the objective probably was to capture the rings again, with the sticks. It was a contest between the men and women, for Stevenson says, though the distance covered is short, the women seldom won.[302]

Such billet and ring sets are common among the Hopi and Keresan groups, where miniature representations are included in offerings to the Sun, who must be placated, if there is to be ample rain; and there is further association with the clouds. Parsons cites other pertinent data.[303]

Acoma has four sizes of kick-sticks, the largest of which is called "over all" (*da·wa·k*^a). There, it is said: "If you watch the water coming down off a mesa during a rain, you will see that it does not flow evenly; it comes in spurts. That is because the katsina are running along, kicking their kick-stick." Again, they say that the water runs down the "road" [which is a flat stick] and washes the kick-stick into the annulet which then carries the stick into the fields, keeping them moist all summer.[304] Among the Tiwa, relay races on a set course are characteristic, rather than kick-stick.

With the Kuaua depiction, then, we may conclude that the ring and stick shown in Figure 87, symbolize a rain making contest enacted by the deities, and thus a supplication for rain to benefit mankind. Inasmuch as we also have the feature identified as a planting stick, which rests in the scalp jar, we may likewise infer that the Kuaua painting commemorates a springtime ceremonial which observed that the time had arrived for planting corn.

Remaining for consideration is the figure at the upper right end of the painting (fig. 86, above), the dragon fly, or *shúmaikolowa*, which is thought to have supernatural pow-

---

298. Bunzel, 1932:675. Ladd says there is usually only one novice.

299. Bunzel, 1932:527. Ladd reports that, now, no songs are sung. The kick-stick race is not held; however, at night, symbolic games are played by persons who make sympathetic magic for the coming year.

300. Stevenson, 1904:346, fig. 21 (*tSi kon-yá mune ti twane*). Currently, at Zuñi, it is played only during the retreat of the War gods.—E. J. L. There is a kick-stick game played by children.

301. Ladd points out that, here, Stevenson is describing certain games which are played during the afternoon performances by the Newekwe and Koyemshi, which are symbolic but have no highly esoteric implications.

302. Ladd says, "This is, or was, much like the shinny game of the Rio Grande Pueblos."

303. Parsons, 1939:306-307.

304. White, 1932:127.

ers.[305] It bears symbolic character both in rain bringing and hunting ceremonials. Kirk mentions a pottery jar used in initiation of youths at Zuñi, on one side of which was tied a fetish of Kolowisi, the great serpent, which plays a major role in that ceremony, and on the other side, was tied a dragon fly fetish. This, so her informant said, was because when Kolowisi spat up the seeds which the initiates kept and planted, the seeds must, of course, be assured water; and so the dragon fly was tied to the jar to guarantee rain[306] (*see* Layer Q-59).

Dragon fly is also a symbol of the *Shúmakwe* society at Zuñi, and as such is associated with game animals. The society is said to take its name from a spiral shell, because the fraternity treats for convulsions—terrible twisting of the body; it also treats for sore feet—perhaps providing medicine for the foot indicated in Figure 89, "slow" because it was sorely tired. The society consists of two orders, Shumaikoli and *Saiapakwe*.[307] The Shumaikoli of the six regions are patrons of the fraternity, together with their warriors, *Saiapa*.

The original home of the Shumaikoli was in Sandia mountain, at a place called *Chípia*, where the Zuñi claim that they formerly lived. It is believed that in that village, the culture hero, Poshai'yanki,[308] the Father of the Medicine societies, became known. Cushing gives us the following information regarding him:

He is supposed to have appeared in human form [thus as a priest?], poorly clad, and therefore reviled by men; to have taught the ancestors of the Zuñi, Taos, Oraibi, and Coconino Indians their agriculture and other arts; their systems of worship by means of plumed and painted prayer-sticks; to have organized their medicine societies; and then to have disappeared toward his home in *Shi pa-pu-lima* (from *shi-pi-a*—mist, vapor; *u-lin*—surrounding; and *i-mo-na*—setting place of—"the mist-enveloped city"), and to have vanished beneath the world, whence he is said to have departed for the home of the Sun. He is still the conscious auditor of the prayers of his children, the invisible ruler of the spiritual Shi-pa-pu-li-ma and of the lesser gods of the medicine orders, the principal "Finisher of the Paths of our Lives." He is, so far as any identity can be established, the "Montezuma" of popular and usually erroneous Mexican tradition.

In ancient times, while yet all beings belonged to one family, Póshaiank'ia, the father of our sacred bands, lived with his children (disciples) in the City of the Mists, the middle place (center) of the Medicine societies of the world. There he was guarded on all sides by his six warriors, *A-pi-thlan shi-wa-ni* (*pi-thlan*—bow, *shi-wa-ni*—priests), the prey gods; toward the North by the mountain lion (long tail), West by bear (Clumsy Foot), South by the badger (Black Mask Face), East by wolf (Hang Tail), Above by eagle (White Cap), and Below by mole. When he was about to go forth into the world, he divided the universe into six regions . . . .[309]

According to Stevenson,[310] Poshai'yanki distributed the Beast god medicines, the tablet altars, and sand or dry paintings to the esoteric fraternities. The first organization named (the priesthood of the Priests) was Shiwannakwe, or Meat Eaters—"people who do not fast from animal food."[311] The songs for rain given to them then were said to "have special influence upon the Council of the Gods, who direct the rain-makers."[312]

305. Stevenson, 1904:79, says *Pa'tsi* is archaic for *shúmaikolowa*, dragon fly—one of the rain symbols of Zuñi.

306. Kirk, 1943:45.

307. Stevenson, 1904:530, gives Fire and Shumaikoli, but Ladd says that she errs, that Shumaikoli and Saiapakwe are correct.

308. Ladd says that, like Paiyatuma and Achiyalatopa (Knife Wing bird), this being is not very well defined in Zuñi thought.

309. Cushing, 1883: 16 ff. *Cf.* footnote 133 herein.

310. Stevenson, 1904:410.

311. Stevenson, 1904:408.

312. Mrs. Stevenson says these songs are sung in the Zuñi and Santo Domingo [thus Keresan] languages (1904: 424; *see also* pp. 408, 429).

At Zuñi, it is told that one night, while a man of the Roadrunner clan *(Póiyikwe)* sat in his house, a Shumaikoli god and his warrior[313] appeared, unmasked. They told him that their present home was Chipia, near the Place of Mist. They remained but a short time, then returned to their home. The following morning, the Zuñi Sun priest was informed of the visit; he was so anxious to see the gods that he visited Chipia. There, he invited the six Shumaikoli with their warriors to visit his pueblo. The invitation was accepted, and the party came, this time each wearing his mask. During their stay, they initiated the man of the Roadrunner clan into the secrets of their medicine. They taught him the songs which the Sun Father had given them, and left their masks with the Roadrunner man, so that he could initiate other members into this new fraternity, the Shumakwe. After this, the Chipia gods came to Zuñi and organized other fraternities and initiated members.[314]

As shown realistically on our painting, the dragon fly doubtless symbolizes the carrying of a message for aid to the supernatural ones and the Shumaikoli priests. The animal tracks shown close to this figure are likewise indicative of assistance sought from the prey animals for aid in successful hunting.

Mrs. Stevenson says that the Shumaikoli order was common to the Keresan pueblos, and that in 1891, Zia, with no longer anyone privileged to wear Shumaikoli masks, decided to give their masks to the same order at Zuñi. In exchange, a Zia man was initated into the kiva society at Zuñi, and thus became privileged to personate the Koyemshi, and to teach the ritual to his fellow villagers.[315] The director of

the Shumaikoli had to be of the Roadrunner clan and his assistant, a child of that clan; other officers of the Sandhill Crane, Dogwood, and Frog clans, or children of these clans. The director of the Shumakwe was also a Rain priest or Shiwanni.[316] He had his fetish (ettone). In 1902, it is said, the six Shumaikoli masks from Laguna were also consigned to the Zuñi fraternity.[317]

While attending the ceremonial preparation of medicines for the Shumaikoli drama, Mrs. Stevenson discovered that the Shumakwe songs were being sung in the Pima tongue.[318]

It would seem that Layer M-40 indicates that the Shumakwe (one of the curing groups) was a functioning society at Kuaua. Paiyatuma, patron of the hunt, is representative of the great god, who is portrayed by priests performing ceremonials which will bring forth rain for ample meat and food supplies. Painted for an observance probably twelve days in length, mythical recountings involved hunts for game and sacred contests enacted by the supernaturals, in which the War gods played a prominent part. As an accompaniment, there were races and dances, visits to sacred places, and initiation of new society members. This ceremonial may have been given quadrennially.

Layer 39

No paintings were found on Layer 39, and so it may be assumed that this was a covering coat of plaster over the preceding painted layer.

Layer L-38

On this layer there were the remains of a painting on the west wall only, and this was recorded as Figure 85 (*not* illustrated). Forty-

---

313. Stevenson, 1904:535, records that the Saiapa personators at Zuñi wore around the waist a fringe of buckskin six inches deep and tipped with bits of conical tin. The latter doubtless replaced the conch shell tinklers of earlier days. Otherwise, this describes the sash worn by Paiyatuma (fig. 88) very well.

314. *See* Stevenson, 1904:410 ff.

315. Stevenson, 1904:531.

316. Ladd says that this is not necessarily the case.

317. Stevenson, 1904:547.

318. Stevenson, 1904:545 note. Ladd suggests that these may be very old Zuñi songs that sound like Pima.

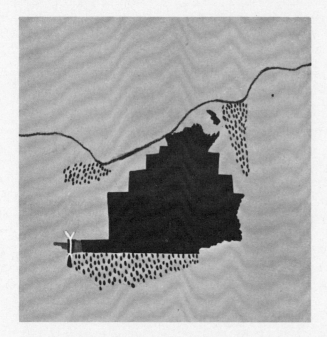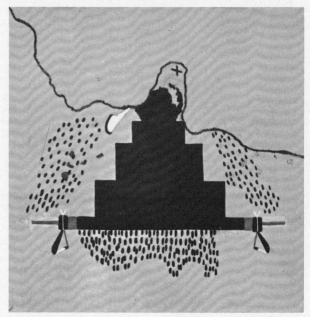

Figs. 83 and 84. Altars of Arrow order, Great Fire society. *Layer K-36.*

six inches above the kiva floor, on the left, and 49 inches above the floor, on the right, the wall was painted a grey-black color. The lower part of the wall has no paintings; thus there is merely this dark band extending the entire limit of the wall. In the plaster, brush strokes can be seen.

Layer 37

Here again no paintings occur, indicating that a sterile coating of plaster was applied over Layer L-38.

Layer K-36

Of this layer, a section showing decoration on the north wall and a like fragment on the west wall remain. An altar is shown on each, almost equidistant from the northwest corner of the kiva, and each a little over three feet above the floor. Both are similar, with the usual terraces.[319] It appears that a black jar

rested on the top of each altar, which is painted entirely in black.

Something of the painting technique by which the figures were produced is shown on this layer. A rather wide brush stroke outlined the altar, with the vertical lines projecting over and above the horizontal bounds, forming little tips, after which the interior portion was filled in with irregular strokes, and paint of varying intensity. Over this, "a sprinkling of green" was noted in the laboratory.

Each altar has, as the bottommost element —as if resting upon, or being directly back of —a long stick. These are painted black in midshaft and yellow at the ends, which project several inches beyond the base of the altar. That of Figure 83 extends toward the south a distance of eight inches, and shows a smaller

319. Cushing, 1901:386, says: "The words 'terrace,' 'sacred terrace,' 'terraced plain' *(awithluiane, awithluian-pewine),* and the like, wherever they occur, refer to the figurative expression for the earth in the Zuñi rituals ad-dressed to the gods, where they are used as more nearly conforming to the usage of the gods. The symbol of the earth on the sacred altars is a terraced or zigzag figure or decoration, and the same figure appears in their carvings and other ornamental work . . . As the conventional sacred emblem for the earth is a terrace, outspread or up-reaching, as the case may be, so the conventional sacred emblem for the sky is an inverted terrace."

yellow-orange segment projecting from the center of the main shaft. At the outer end of the larger stick, black feathers with white tips are tied with a white cord; the feathers hang pendant from the stick and the white tie rises above it. Features of the projections at the right side of Figure 84 are the same, excepting that a yellow feather is shown along with the black pendant plume. The opposite end of this stick shows similar projections, but erosion marred the details. In the copy which was made of this painting in the laboratory, the artist found evidence to portray each end in like manner.

From the jars, moisture drops curve downward on either side of the altars; and drops of moisture extend downward from each altar. On the right side of the jar in Figure 84, a white feather with black tip hangs down alongside the altar. From the left side of the jar in Figure 83, there is a small bit of black in approximately the same position, which may indicate another feather. Traces of black, zigzag lightning are shown above the north altar. The unusual feature of these altars is that no clouds are represented on their terraces.

Looking at these fragmentary representations, Zna'ote said: DE' TLI YA'KA; NIGHTTIME CLOUDS COMING UP [actually, "nighttime" or "belonging to the night"—E. J. L.].

With the limited features which remain, there was little on which to base identification with known ceremonies. However, attention was turned to the Great Fire society. Here we find the patron gods, Kokothlanna, Shutsukya, and Kwelele. The Great Fire society has several divisions among which are those of the Sword (*Pianni'hle*) and of the Arrow (*Shó-tikinna*), and a Navaho branch (*Pa·ti kyan-na*).[320] Mrs. Stevenson says that a ceremonial of the Arrow division occurred at Zuñi every four years, in February, in connection with the Spruce Tree ceremony. In February, 1891, she witnessed a ceremony of the latter type;

she also observed the activities of the Sword division. She reports the indoor activities of the Arrow order as substantially the same as those of the Sword, except on the fifth morning.[321] Then, with preliminary preparations and due rites, each member received the arrow he was to swallow. Of these, she says that:

> Some are covered with a glossy brownish substance, while others have it half over them, and others only one-third of the way. The arrows vary in size and form, many being slightly oval at the end, some are pointed, and all are rounded or oval where they are attached to the shaft, which is slightly curved at this end.[322]

Following further rites and dancing in the kiva, the group goes to the society house, each dancer carrying the arrow and a rattle in his right hand, and bow and arrows in his left. Both the swords and the arrows to be swallowed are *held horizontally*, and are "placed to the mouth while the head is erect, then the head is moved gradually backward as the instrument is pushed down the throat."

The Arrow dance is repeated three times in the plaza. After each appearance, the order retires to the ceremonial chamber, where, following the third dance, the director receives the arrows "and the dancers are provided with their swords for the closing dances." These are the zig-zag, or serpent form, swords symbolic of lightning. When the swords are carried for the first time, they, too, are swallowed in a ceremonious manner. After they dance, the Arrow order is joined by the women of the Sword order and another dance is performed, and there is further sword swallowing (*see* Pl. B-3). The director then collects the swords. Each dancer lays his sword on the arm of the director, who, "holding the swords with both hands, stands before the boxes and prays that Áchiyalátopa (being with wings and tail of

---

320. Ladd, ms. note.

321. Stevenson, 1904:511.
322. Stevenson, 1904:513.

knives) and the Beast gods will intercede with the rain-makers for cold rains and snows."[323]

From the foregoing, we feel that the items lying horizontally at the base of each altar shown in this painting (figs. 83 and 84) may represent the arrows swallowed by members of the Arrow order. Lightning symbolism ties the depiction to that order and to the Bow priesthood, and the representation of rain indicates the ever-present supplication for moisture. We noted the absence of the billowy white clouds by which summertime rains are invoked. Here, it seems, we have, in the "nighttime clouds coming up," solicitation for the cold rains and snow of the winter season. It is, therefore, believed that Layer K-36 of the Kuaua paintings relates to activities of the order of the Arrow.

Layer J¹-35

The plaster layer so indicated shows only a splotch of green paint.

Layer J-34

Due to the initial uncertainty in the laboratory, in relating three portions of this painting, the figures of Layer J-34 were submitted

to Zna'ote at different times. He received the section showing Figures 80-82, first, and interpreted it as being a SUMMER CEREMONY. CACIQUE[324] CALLING FOR RAIN. Later, receiving the segment showing Figures 56 and 57, he readily recognized that as a SUMMER OR WINTER DANCE. DANCE AT ANY TIME. DAYTIME DANCE. Of the final section which he received (fig. 78), he said: WINTER CEREMONY. CACIQUE DANCE. A CURING CEREMONY. WHITE CLOUDS WANTS TO HAVE SNOW; BLACK [indicates clouds] AT NIGHT. The yellow arch shows the POLLEN ROAD THE GODS WOULD FOLLOW. GO OUT AT EAST. Pollen road is ó·NAYE TLAN[a]. NOBODY SICK, NOBODY DIE, EVERYBODY HAPPY. NEXT SPRING MOISTURE CAN COME AND RAISE ANYTHING. As we shall see, the sections are harmonious, being a continuous painting on the north, west, and south walls of the kiva.

On the north wall there is a great terraced altar painted in black with tall, white clouds on each step (fig. 78). The altar has the usual four terraces, with black fragmentary remains above.[325] Curving upward in front of the altar,

---

323. Stevenson, 1904:509, 514.

324. A Haitian word used extensively by early chroniclers to designate the priest-chiefs; it was incorporated into the Spanish language with this significance, and was added to the Indian vocabulary in this region.

PL. XII. *Layer J-34*. Scalp ceremony.

Fig. 56   Fig. 57   Fig. 82

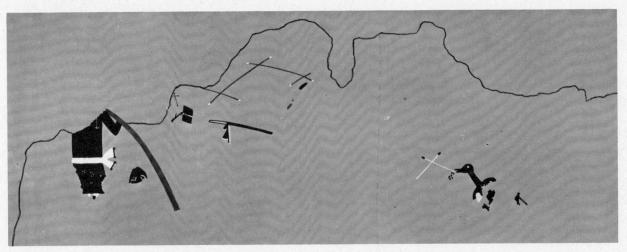

so that its arc obscures the lowest part of the altar at its center, is an arched rainbow which extends downward to the floor. It is yellow in color, outlined with red, and measures 45 inches from limit to limit. All across the upper part of the wall, and at the right extreme are green spots. There are a few black dots showing below the altar, at the right. Zna'ote said, BLACK IN ALTAR MEANS CLOUDS.

Extending horizontally, 20 inches above the floor at the north end of the west wall, a large fish is shown in black with yellow markings: two longitudinal elements on each side of the back, close to the fin representations, and yellow eyes. Black moisture drops spray downward from the fish's mouth, and yellow lightning zig-zags forward (fig. 80). A few inches beyond the limit of the lightning, there is a similar yellow fragment extending from the remains of some element painted in black, but now quite unidentifiable. Of the fish complex, Zna'ote said: KASHITA. FISH. LIGHTNING GOES UP AND WATER COMES DOWN.

---

325. Judging from depictions on other plaster layers, it seems questionable that the artist's license in showing an apical step with cloud above, when the replicas were made, is justified. The graph drawing and laboratory notes do not indicate the latter.

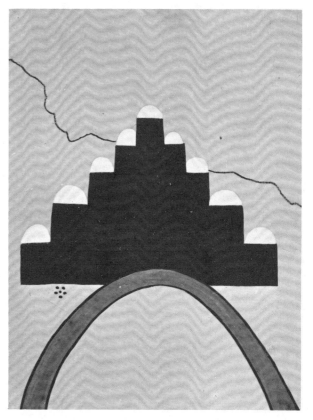

Fig. 78. Terraced black altar, indicating nighttime clouds; billowy white clouds, symbolizing winter snow; rainbow, signifying the pollen path. *Layer J-34.*

Fig. 81   Fig. 80   Fig. 78

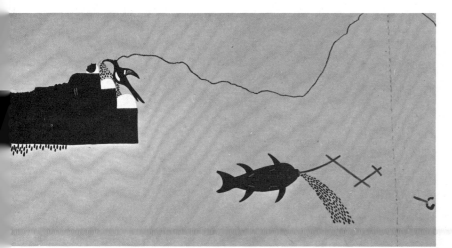

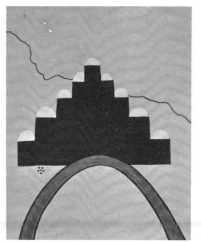

Fig. 80. Fish with yellow lightning and moisture. *Layer J-34.*

Midway in the west wall, with its base 36 inches above the floor, is a large altar (Pl. XII, fig. 81), painted black except for one small marking toward the left front—two short, parallel yellow-orange lines. On the altar steps, of which the remains of three are discernible, are billowy white clouds. The upper cloud on the left side is partially obscured by a large black element. On either side, a long-tailed bird is shown, perched atop the second cloud, and with tail extending over and beyond the lowermost cloud. The bird on the left is shown with long, black bill, black body with white breast and wing markings—the wing shown as in flight—and long forked black tail. This, Zna'ote identified as POY YE' [*póy yi*], ROAD-RUNNER. Of the bird on the right, only a long black tail, showing a small, rectangular marking near the body, remains. Of this, Zna'ote said: K'ATA TASHA.[326] LONG-TAILED BLACK BIRD. LITTLE ONE. LOTS IN SUMMER. SEE SANTO DOMINGO. From the mouths of both birds, the dashed-line rain symbols are shown, falling downward behind the clouds and altar. Below the altar, close to its base, there is evidence of falling rain.

On the right of the altar, in symmetrical position with that of the fish, is a long-necked

bird. Its lowermost portion comes to 11.5 inches above the floor level. Painted mostly in black, the bird has a white eye, and two white lines extend down the center of the neck; there is also a large, white marking on the wing. Traces of yellow paint may be seen toward the left of the bird, apparently indicating a leg. From the opened bill, crossed white lightning sticks tipped with black project toward the southwest corner, and black moisture drops downward from the bird's mouth. Zna'ote identified this (Pl. XII, fig. 82) as 'EYA, DUCK. LIGHTNING COMES UP AND WATER COMES DOWN.

Then on the south wall, there is a fragmentary figure of a prominent personage (fig. 56). The body is painted a grey-black or bluish color [327] and is outlined in black. There is a kilt of the same bluish color, with zig-zag decoration in black, extending vertically on the left and right sides and in the center; [328] in the right half of the kilt, there are small elements of white—perhaps representing stars. There is a white sash around the waist, tied on the left side; it shows red end and tie decoration. Limited remains indicate a right leg, painted

326. Ladd translates this as "magpie."

327. Stevenson, 1904:599, indicates that the water sprinklers and victor and his elder brother wear native blue shirts over a white shirt.

328. Stevenson, 1904:599, rattlesnake charms?

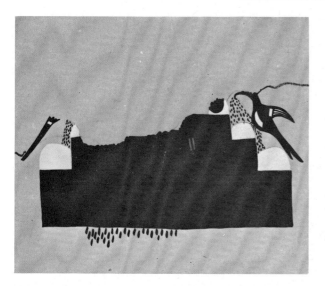

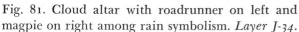

Fig. 81. Cloud altar with roadrunner on left and magpie on right among rain symbolism. *Layer J-34.*

Fig. 82. Duck or 'Eya with white lightning and moisture. *Layer J-34.*

in white, with a red "blotch" on the inner side of the left leg. Part of the left arm, held akimbo, was distinguishable, painted in black. There is also indication of black hair extending down the left breast, with a red feather ornament. This personage was identified as: A MAN. LIGHTNING MAN, PIʼKLASHIWAN [Apiʼlashiwanni] by Zna'ote. From the left shoulder of Lightning Man a narrow, yellow arc extends downward, terminating about two inches below the bottom level of the kilt, at a point some 20 inches from it. The arc reaches to about two feet above the kiva floor.

Between the personage and the yellow arc, a small black, winged creature is shown; only the wings and tail feathers remain. A short red line extends out from the tail, on the right side.

On about the shoulder level of Lightning Man, and on his left, is a black painted object, identified as a pollen pouch. CORN POLLEN BAG, said Zna'ote, IS BLACK BECAUSE BODY [of Lightning Man] IS BLACK [blue-black]. On its right side, a black feather with white side markings projects. Around the middle of the pouch is a narrow white tie dotted with red. Close to the tie are two short pendants painted in orange-red and yellow,

and on the pouch are two triangular elements, one at the upper left and one at the lower right of the top half of the pouch. Above and to the right is the end of yellow lightning tipped in black. To the left of the pouch, projecting downward on a slight diagonal, is a black stick with the first few inches of it, closest to the pouch, of adobe color. Tied on with a white cord at the junction of the colors are pendant feathers, shown in white and adobe color, with fine black lines crossing diagonally. This feature (fig. 57) was identified by Zna'ote as, KNIFE. TO KILL PEOPLE WITH. LANSA—lance, A CHI NAN—knife.

Above the lance is a criss-cross lightning symbol painted in yellow with white tips at the ends. At its upper extent the lightning reaches to 72 inches above the floor of the chamber. At its left extremity two small elements are directed toward the lance, the upper one black and the lower one yellow. We have no information on these, but suggest that they could represent the bull-roarers which are used in the Scalp ceremony to summon the rains.

In giving his information, Zna'ote said of this painting: ZUÑI SQUAW DANCE. STILL DANCE SQUAW DANCE. EIGHT-DAY DANCE; NAVAHO

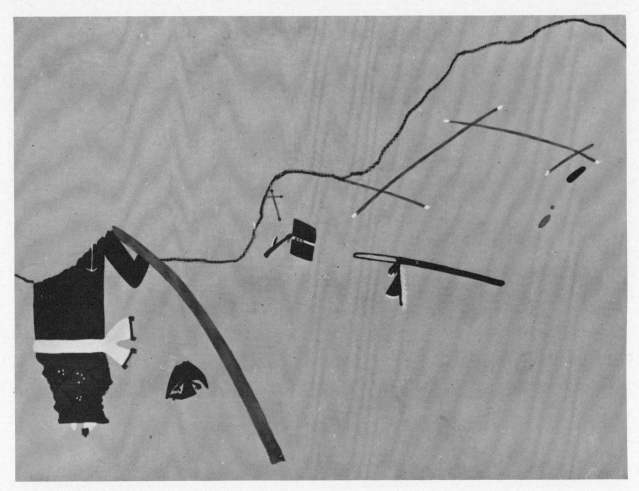

Fig. 56. Lightning Man, Kupishtaya, with pollen pouch on his left.

Fig. 57. Complex, lightning and feathered lance. *Layer J-34.*

SCALP ON POLE IN MIDDLE OF PLAZA. TAKE SCALP DOWN ON NINTH MORNING, AND TAKE TO TSÍHA U-PA [scalp house], CORNER WEST OF CATHOLIC SCHOOL.

With all of these manifestations of rain bringing: lightning, clouds, breath, rain, rainbow, birds, fish, and waterfowl, attention was turned again to the cult of the War gods, of which some mention was made in Layer M-40. The Bow priesthood of Zuñi is considered to have been created by the War gods, who were its first directors, and who passed on their duties to earthly representatives, the elder and younger Bow priests. Membership is exclusive with the males. Affiliations of the Bow priesthood are with the Rain chiefs, or priestly hier-

archy, the kiva organizations, and with the curing societies—two being assigned to each. Members of the Bow priesthood are privileged to be present at the meetings of all the societies.[329] Only two festivals are celebrated by this priesthood, the Scalp ceremonial or initiation of a victor of a killing into the priesthood, and the Harvest dance (*Ówina haiye*), an annual thanksgiving for crops, enacted in October. The Scalp festival was, or is, held every two, three, or four years.

Mrs. Stevenson has given extensive accounts of the Bow priesthood and of the ceremonials relating to the Zuñi Scalp dance,[330] citing some

---

329. Stevenson, 1904:498.
330. Stevenson, 1904:578-606.

of the mythology, but for the most part describing activities which she witnessed. On the other hand, Stirling, for Acoma, relates more of the legendary aspects.[331] The two reveal significant relationships.

It seems likely that the author would have failed to connect Layer J-34 with the Scalp ceremonies had she not had the assistance of Zna'ote. With his guidance, however, it was possible to ascertain that this painting does pertain to that observance. In the first place, scalps are symbolic of the Bow priests who bring the rain from the gods above. It is the special duty of the Rain priests to fast and pray for rain. Accordingly, the extensive rain symbolization in this painting bespeaks the invocations of this body. Terraced or serrated designs are symbolic of cumulus clouds, which bring the summer rains. The rain makers cover themselves with clouds as a warrior with a shield.[332] Thus, the billowy white clouds shown on the two altars (figs. 78 and 81) may be considered as masking the presence of the rain makers. It is believed that the Council of the Gods control and direct the rain makers, who "collect water in vases and gourd jugs from the six great waters of the world (springs of the six regions). They [these "shadow people"] are carried by the steam which rises from these springs to the upper plane, provided they are supplied with breath plumes." It is also believed that the rain makers pass to and fro, protected from the view of the people by cloud masks. The clouds are produced by the breath of the gods and smoke. The greater the smoke offering the greater inducement for the rain makers to work; thus, smoking is a conspicuous feature of Pueblo ritual. The greater the smoke offering the heavier the cloud masks will be. When it rains, the rain makers are pouring water through the cloud masks.[333]

A few lines from a War cult prayer, recorded by Dr. Bunzel, indicate something of the great symbolism involved. The Sun Father speaking, says:

> Near by, in the corn priests' court,
> Our two fathers [the twin War gods],
> The ones who hold the high places,
> With all their sacred things
> Made their roads enter.
> Yonder from all sides,
> Those who are our fathers,
> All the water bringing birds,
> Pekwins [human counterpart of all the summer birds], priests,
> Made their roads come forth.
> They made their roads come hither.
> With his hand,
> With his heart
> His fathers' cloud house he fashioned [the meal painting on the altar],
> Their mist blanket he spread out [the dotted moisture symbols],
> Their life-giving road he sent forth [the pollen road],
> Their perfect spring he prepared . . . .[334]

The rainbow is representative of the Cloud people, affording a means for them to "come down" (fig. 78b).[335]

---

331. Stirling, 1942:83-90.
332. Bunzel, 1932:662.
333. Stevenson, 1904:21.

334. Bunzel, 1932:684-685.
335. Bunzel, 1932:689, notes that after the priest completes his prayers of the War cult, he takes out his black corn and passes it around four times in front of him . . . . At the end, he again passes it around counter clockwise before him, as a rite of exorcism, and sets it aside for planting in the spring . . . . The following day he deposits prayersticks at a shrine called "where the rainbow bends over," a shrine to the War gods. The rainbow in the Kuaua painting probably relates to a similar ritualistic procedure.

The fetish of the Bow priesthood consists of "an ear of corn surrounded by reeds, six are colored, each for a region and are filled with grains of corn of the six colors and other seeds. The remainder of the reeds contain native tobacco. The reeds are obscured by a pyramid of eagle plumes (which must have been dropped by the eagle in his flight, not plucked) and the base is covered with cotton cloth wrapped with cotton cord to which shells and precious beads are strung . . . . One of these fetishes

At Zuñi, Rainbow is held to be a son of the Sun Father, and has power to call the rain makers from above and send them where he wishes.[336]

The small cluster of black dots shown below the altar and to the right of the rainbow—the pollen road by which the rain bringers come to the people—in Figure 78, do not appear to be representations of rain. It is possible that these portray the Morning star, which in myth is first warrior to the Sun Father. Mrs. Stevenson states that each of the first four nights of the Scalp ceremonial, the warriors assemble in the ceremonial chamber, where they sing and brandish the war club. Some say the original clubs were thrown from the heavens by this great star, warrior of the heavens.[337]

The white clouds in our painting symbolize winter snow, and the black altar, the clouds of nighttime.

Deceased members of the Bow priesthood are thought to become lightning makers of the six regions, where they collaborate with *Kúpishtaya,* chief of the lightning makers.[338] This, then, brings the lightning makers into our painting. Inasmuch as Figure 56 was identified as Lightning Man, we have here a representation of Kupishtaya. During a ceremony which Mrs. Stevenson witnessed in October, 1891, she recorded a prayer uttered by two warriors. It concerns the Sun Father, the Beast gods, ants of the six regions, and the mighty warrior-rain maker Bow priests: *'Sikiahaya,* "quick moving hair," who travels in the rain by day; *'Kia'lawanni,* who "looks like an icicle," and sometimes has long hair reaching to the knees, who travels at night [his long hair represents a meteor or comet]; and Kupishtaya, who travels in the midst of fog. These

beings are associated with thunderstorms and sudden tempests.[339]

The lightning-like symbols emitted by the fish and duck, in our painting, would seem to indicate the roads by which the deities were to enter, and the various colors call forth the gods from the respective regions: yellow for the north, white for the east, and so on. Also, shooting arrows, like this shooting lightning, are symbolic of the destruction of the enemy.[340] Zna'ote indicated certain symbolism by remarking that "the lightning goes up" (as from the fish and duck) and "water comes down."

On the kilt of Lightning Man, there is a zig-zag decoration, which may signify the rattlesnake, symbol of protection from the enemy, for members of the Bow priesthood are the only Zuñi who kill the rattlesnake. The fluffy red feather tied to the hair of Lightning Man is the insignia of Mystery medicine. Mrs. Stevenson notes that hematite is used to color red the objects sacred to the Bow priesthood.[341]

Since Kuaua was located on the bank of the Rio Grande, it is certain that the people dwelling there had full knowledge of fish which inhabited that water, and incorporated them into their rain making symbolism. We have the information of Villagra and Benavides, also, and the statement that the Indians were great fishermen (*see* page 14). Petroglyphs of fish are not common, but some occur on the rocks near Placitas, across the Rio Grande, to the east of Kuaua.

Shown on the front of the altar in Figure 81, the small element composed of two short, parallel lines in yellow-orange may be identified as representing the heart. Throughout Pueblo mythology, deific ones talk with the heart instead of speaking vocally. The heart, then, is a most significant symbol, and is similarly depicted on many of the Kuaua figures. Mrs. Stevenson describes the face painting

---

is carried to battle; the other remains at home" (Stevenson, 1904:598, footnote *a*). Ladd says that the idea of one of these being carried to battle is quite wrong.

336. Stevenson, 1904:169.
337. Stevenson, 1904:587.
338. Stevenson, 1904:21, 110, 149, 171.

339. *See* Stevenson, 1904:580, and Bunzel, 1932:513, 664.
340. Stevenson, 1904:586.
341. Stevenson, 1904:517 and 599.

and decoration of the victor and elder brother in the ceremonies of the Bow priesthood, in which the final act is to cover the chin, upper lip, end of nose, and forehead with eagle down, and a similar crown about the head, the whole symbolizing that "the heart must be pure that the prayers breathed into the plume offerings may be wafted to the deceased Ashiwanni [rain priests] that they may send much rain."[342]

Important among the persons who dance on the twelfth day of the Scalp ceremonial are girls, the *Hashiya* or Shakers, who dance successively in couples. The purpose of the dance (*Awek shuwaha*) is to cleanse the ground, thus a rite of exorcism. At Zuñi they dance on the so-called foot drum, consisting of two planks laid across an excavation, thus placed "so people will come, it draws them in their hearts." It is believed that these planks form the door for the people inside the earth, "the dead Apache, Navaho, Sioux, Hopi, Acomans and Mexicans (not for people of Laguna or Americans).[343] It makes their hearts shake and tremble."[344] It is probable that the heart symbol on the Kuaua altar likewise indicates the doorway into the earth.

We have seen that a roadrunner is perched above the clouds on this altar, on the left. This is a messenger capable of traveling with the prayers of mankind unto the gods above; it is also the keeper of courage.[345] The bird on the right, magpie, being a summertime bird, connotes another rain bringing feature.

The tie around the pollen pouch (fig. 57) is still another invocation for rain, inasmuch as Mrs. Stevenson notes that when one or more plumes are attached with cotton cord, the latter is dotted four times in black, symbolic of rain clouds.[346] On the eleventh day of the Scalp

ceremony which she witnessed,[347] a meal painting was made in the plaza, with images of the War gods on the east and west sides of it. The elder brother Bow priest and the elder brother of the victor stood to the east of the cloud symbol in the painting, and the victor and the younger brother Bow priest stood west of it, while warriors lined up on either side of the painting. All the sacred objects were guarded by two warriors standing with long spears at the south of the painting. During the dancing on this day, men in elaborate costumes participate, and the leader carries a spear, which Mrs. Stevenson describes as being about six feet long, "with an aigret of raven plumes and a single eagle tail feather attached where the spear joins the handle."[348] Obviously, the spear or lance identified in our Figure 57 relates to similar representations. It is suspected that one appeared on the right side of our Lightning Man, originally, thus these two in the position of guards.

We see that the Scalp dance is significant, primarily, as a rain making ritual, embracing priests who utilize all possible symbolism to invoke the favor of the gods and assure abundant moisture for the crops. Thus, the statement of Zna'ote that we have in this painting a priest calling for rain is fully confirmed, as well as his identification of the entire ceremonial. Corn, or maize, was the most important food of the Southwestern Indians, and elements of the Corn ceremonials are drawn into the Scalp complex. This does not relate well with known facts regarding the early Navaho, inasmuch as they were more nomadic than sedentary corn raisers.

Of the corn ear fetishes used in the Zuñi Scalp ceremonial which Stevenson described, two belonged to the Bow priesthood and one to the priest of the *'Sú 'hlánna* [large shell].[349]

---

342. Stevenson, 1904:600.

343. Ladd says this applies to any person, other than a Zuñi.

344. Parsons, 1924:21.

345. Stevenson, 1904:582, 584, 589.

346. Stevenson, 1904:172. Ladd says this is on all prayer sticks.

347. Stevenson, 1904:595. Parsons, 1924:7, says a 12-day observance with 8 nights of dancing.

348. Stevenson, 1904:595.

349. Ladd says that each member of the societies has a corn ear fetish.

The epic songs of the latter sung during the all-night rites in the ceremonial chamber were very old—so old that only four men of the Badger clan knew them in Stevenson's day.[350] These could derive from influences which reached Zuñi at a time prior to the days of warfare with the Navaho. There are numerous traits which occur throughout the Scalp ceremonies which suggest relationships with cultures in Mexico. It is beyond the scope of this study to introduce such evidence, but it is recognized that there has been a union, through time, of old agricultural concepts with those of warfare and blood fertilization,[351] and a shifting of recognition of earlier enemy peoples to the later Navaho.

At Acoma, we find that the Scalp dance ceremonies include women, who are referred to as *Kóchininako,* or the Corn maidens. There, the dance relates to the Warriors society and with the *Koshari* organization [a clown society]. According to legend, the Divine Ones were traveling in different countries, killing many people and bringing back their scalps. The rulers in the four directions were angered and decided that the twins should be punished, and so they called in Evil Spirit [*Pishuni hachtsa*—old man] to help them. Evil Spirit, disguising himself as an attractive young girl, gained the interest of the War twins and went home with them. As such, "she" crept between them as they slept, and turned to a corpse of an emaciated old hag. The boys awakened, were terrified, and ran away, pursued by Evil Spirit. They sought aid from all directions, and finally the Gambler in the south agreed to help them. He took his ball [a baby head] and his stick, and hit the ball toward Evil Spirit, who was struck in the chest. The ball splashed blood, frightening the spirit [Ko'ko], who turned and fled. Then Gambler ridiculed the twins, and told them why they had been punished. Henceforth they were not to kill for sport, nor because they felt brave. Gambler sent them back to their people, where they had to carry the scalps and wash them, and where they had to dance in public. He taught them how to dance and how to treat the scalps. The scalps were not to be thrown away; after the dance they were to belong to the people. The twins returned home to fulfill their instructions.[352]

As they came near their village they cried out with a war whoop; they entered into the midst of their assembled people, saying that the enemy was coming after them, and urging all the able-bodied men to get their weapons and food. The women encouraged the men, all of whom followed the twin warriors. They led "the attack," to the place where they had buried their scalps in an ant hill, representative of a hogan [Navaho house]. They shot arrows and threw clubs at the scalps, teaching the people how to do it:

> They would rush up to the hogan, acting as though they were fighting and cutting the scalp from an enemy. They would take one scalp after another and throw it over their shoulder. After they had gathered them all up, they told the people to get shoots of young cedar [juniper] and cut down a twelve-foot pole. The cedar shoots were tied to the top of the pole and from each twig a scalp was tied. After this was done they told the people, "We are going to take the scalps

350. Stevenson, 1904:598.

351. Blood fertilizes the earth. Bunzel, 1932:687, notes the idea that "wherever an enemy falls is formed an ant hill—a symbol, probably, of fecundity." Therefore, the Ant society figures prominently in Scalp dance ceremonies.

Parsons, 1924:33, says that a song recital regarding the War gods is performed at Zuñi not only in the Scalp ceremony, but every March, "at the corn-planting season, before the first foot-race by kivas." A four-night ceremony is held in the house of the Bow priests, wherein they, the Rain priests, the scalp custodian, the scalp chief, and people of the Coyote clan participate. The war fetish is set out on the altar; and the entire ceremony is for rainfall and good crops.

352. *Cf.* this with the tale recorded by Parsons, 1924: 29-33.

back to the village and we are going to sing the first song." As they came toward the village they sang. The younger brother carried the pole.[353]

As they neared the village, all the women came forth and gathered around the warriors. The pole was planted in the center of the plaza. Younger brother announced that they, the twins, would dance there in four days; he asked all of the people to practice this dance and to help them with it. He told the people that their mother (Kochininako) would have a part in the dance. She dances in and out among the warriors and then dances alone in the center of the plaza. Thus the Scalp dance or Squaw dance was brought to Acoma, where it is also called by its Mexican name, Montezuma dance.[354] By holding this ceremony, the people would pay tribute to the warriors if they conquered their enemies. At the end of the dance, the scalp is taken from the pole, as was done by the twins originally, when they told the people that anyone wishing to be brave might come and ask the scalps for power. The people were to go through this ceremony at any time that an enemy was killed. The dance would also pay respect to the slain enemy, so that his spirit would not haunt the killer.[355]

We have, thus, identified Layer J-34 of the Kuaua paintings as pertaining to ceremonies of the War cult, those commonly referred to as a War dance, Squaw dance, or Scalp dance, and which were enacted by personators of the twin War gods and their retinue, and by Rain priests who supplicated the deities to bring rain and success in conflicts with enemy peoples. The rites would include initiation into the Bow priesthood. We have also shown that Zna'ote's relation of two fragments of the painting to ceremonies of the priests' calling

for rain is fully confirmed, while his recognition of the other fragment as pertaining to the Scalp dance brings all together in complete harmony.

Pueblo Indian tradition is told and taught when a person is being initiated into one of the esoteric organizations. In preparing for a ceremony, that part of the tradition which may relate to it is recounted. The songs also contain much information. During the period that the priests are setting up the altar in their ceremonial chamber, they tell the legendary history. Thus the impersonators of the gods become thoroughly familiar with the parts which they will enact and the proper ritualistic procedures.[356]

It may, accordingly, be assumed that the painting here described depicts the traditional history as related during a ceremony which included the initiation of novices into the Bow priesthood at Kuaua.[357]

Layer I-33

This layer of plaster was applied directly over that of the preceding, painted layer; its remains are most fragmentary. The only figure on the north wall shows one angular segment, 6.5 inches wide and 24 inches in extent (Pl. XIII, fig. 77). It is painted green except for a one-inch border of white at each side. The laboratory notes say that a coat of black appears to have been added over the green paint; small dashes of red are scattered over the colored area. At the northwest corner of the kiva, heading onto the west wall, a similar zig-zag figure (76) extends for 65 inches; it lacks the red dashes. Below it are short black dash-dots falling from the angle farthest toward the right. In the midst of these dots are smears of

---

353. Stirling, 1942:83-85, 88.
354. White, 1932:101.
355. Stirling, 1942:89.

356. *See* Stirling, 1942:91.
357. Parsons, 1924:7, states that the last Scalp dance at Zuñi was performed in October, 1910, but that "like the ceremonial of 1891, it was not exactly authentic since there was no real initiation." Ladd says, "If there is a Scalp dance at all, there has to be an initiation."

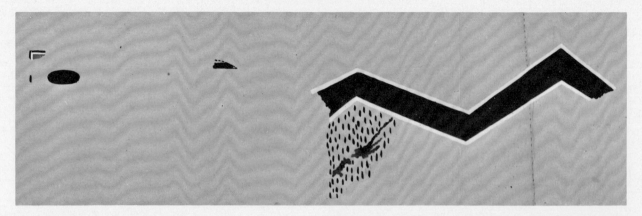

Fig. 74. Kiva niche with altar decoration.

Figs. 75-76. Horned serpent on left side of kiva niche-altar, with water symbols. *Layer I-33.*

red paint. The figure comes to within about two feet of the kiva floor.

Some 15 inches south of Figure 76, a small arc of grey color (fig. 75) appears on the west wall. Slightly less than three feet further, on approximately the same level, Figure 74 shows the small portion of a cornered element, yellow in color and bordered with white and grey bands. A short grey line is also shown below the upper one. This element, then, centers in the west wall, some 28 inches above the floor. Figure 73 is just a trace of red color painted

over with yellow. It is in the form of a forward reaching arc which ends in a point. Another zig-zag depiction, 56 inches in extent, occurs as Figure 72. This is outlined in black, around a body of indeterminable color. Black dash-dots fall from the foremost angle, ahead of a square element from which three heavy lines curve downward. Amidst the dots are one large irregular splotch of black, one of white, and a small one of red.

A small painted feature, listed as Figure 55, which occurred on the south wall of the kiva

PL. XIII. *Layer I-33.* Initiation into the katsina society.

Fig. 55   Fig. 72   Fig. 73   Fig. 74

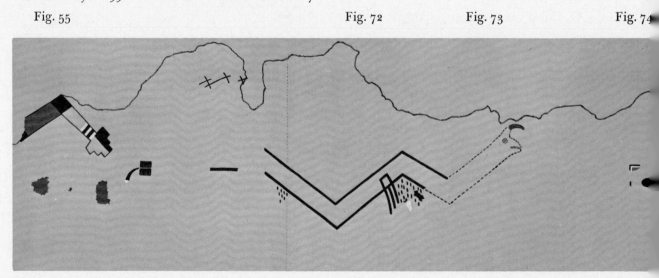

was difficult to place, but the technicians in the laboratory determined it to be a part of Layer I-33. Unfortunately, none of the recorded measurements tie this in with those on the west wall. It is noted that Figure 55c was 6.25 inches from the left edge of the wall, and the figure is shown in this position on the reproduction—which seems to indicate that it should appear further toward the right, or east. As it is, there is not space for prolonging Figure 72, as seems warranted.

If we recall that the kiva wall was eroded at this point, and assume that Figure 55 was 6.25 inches from its left remaining limit, we find that the complex relates to the figures above described. The most conspicuous feature is a unit in right angle position, as though part of a large, zig-zag element. The easternmost part is painted in black; there is then a portion painted yellow; the angle is black; and the remainder is adobe color for about two-thirds of its extent, terminating in white and black bands parallel with the base of this segment, which ends in a terraced altar design (*cf.* Pl. A-2b). The lowest point of the latter is 38 inches above the kiva floor. The altar measures

nine inches across its base. The upper or left half of the altar is painted black, and the remaining half is of adobe color. The entire figure is outlined in red.

Below the altar just mentioned, traces of green paint remain. About five inches below and to the left of the altar is an oblong figure shown in black, with "lines running up and down it,"[358] and a black feather tipped with white projecting on the right side. To the left of this about 19 inches, a segment of a black shaft is seen, nearly 30 inches above the floor and parallel with it.

Figure 74 may be identified as pertaining to an altar design, painted in the center of the west wall of the kiva. Projecting the lines of Figure 72, it is found that they and Figure 73 may be joined harmoniously, thus depicting a horned serpent, the head of which would have approached the altar on its south side. Similarly, the black arc of Figure 75 may be part of the horn of another serpent (fig. 76), to the north of the altar. From the heart region of each serpent, moisture drops and related symbolic elements extend toward the floor.

358. Laboratory note.

Fig. 75   Fig. 76   Fig. 77

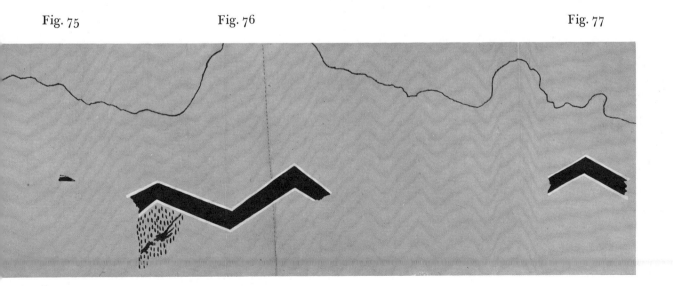

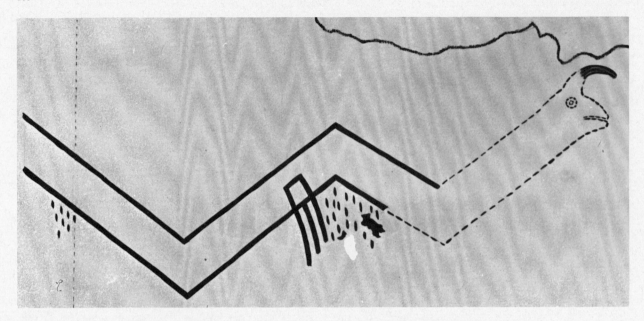

Figs. 72-73. Horned serpent on right side of kiva niche-altar, with fertility symbols. *Layer I-33.*

We are, thus, directed to the mythical serpent of Pueblo lore: the Water Snake of Acoma (*Tsits shuwi*) and Kolowisi of Zuñi, which we have noted in previous layers.

Stirling records a brief episode concerning the snake at Acoma.[359] The Divine twins were up to mischief, as usual. They found the Katsinas sleeping and stole, from the Katsina of the north, the staff with which he made snow; from him on the west, they stole the staff with which he made hail; from him on the south, they stole the staff with which he made lightning and the balls with which thunder is made; from the east, they stole the frost making staff. On earth, the people were in need of water. The twins thought they could handle the Katsinas' staffs as well as the owners. They buried the staffs on their homeward way. When the Katsinas awakened, they thought of bringing to life the Water Snake, "so named because it travels like a stream of water." They told it to chase the twins and to devour them.

Not far from where they had buried the staffs, the twins were approached by a cloud that was followed by a cloudburst. Lightning

struck at them, but the twins shielded themselves from the flints (a form of lightning) by buckskin shirts which their Sun Father had given them. It rained all the way back to their village, where the boys found that a lake had overflowed and driven the people away. Many had been killed by lightning. Those who were left, the twins shielded with their shirts. But it continued to rain, and the people were forced to leave their homes, taking only the altars and the things which they needed most. They moved onto a mountain in the south. The priests tried in vain to stop the rain.

As the story goes: The world began to fill with water and the dashing waves almost swept them from the mountain. So the twins, seeing the large waves, said, "That must be Water Snake. He is coming to kill us." They had never used the four arrows their father had given them and they said, "perhaps this is where we are to use these arrows." So they watched carefully until they saw the biggest wave coming up. They said, "This is where his heart is." Each shot an arrow into it. After they had done this the waves came slower and became a huge snake which wrapped itself

---

359. Stirling 1942:77.

around the mountain, where the twins killed it, using up the rest of the arrows, each shooting four times.[360]

From Stevenson, we have information regarding the coming of Kolowisi to Zuñi,[361] a dramatic ceremony relating to the initiation of boys into the katsina society. She tells of the ceremonies which she witnessed, and describes the making of the representation of Kolowisi which is used during the initiation rites.[362] The snake is carried by two men, in a procession followed by *Suti⁺ki,* a bird fetish, accompanied by Pautiwa, the Salimopiya (warriors and seed gatherers) from the six regions, and many other gods and men from the "corn house," or *Chú pawa.* Kolowisi[363] is carried to each kiva and is then deposited in the kiva of the Nadir.[364] This has its walls decorated with two paintings of Kolowisi, "which extend along the north and south walls, the heads almost meeting at the altar."[365] Probably the major difference in the depiction of the great snake is that at Kuaua it is shown with a horn surmounting the head, in the Rio Grande manner, while at Zuñi it is shown with plumes which obscure the smaller, forehead element, or *mi'tanna,* which is painted blue.

We then find a Zuñi tale which Cushing relates, in which the beautiful daughter of the chief Rain priest had a passion for neatness and cleanliness of person and clothing. She spent most of her time washing her clothing and bathing herself in a particular spring. This spring was sacred to the "Serpent of the Sea," Kolowisi, and he became angry at the sacrilege which the maiden committed. He devised a plan to punish her.[366]

When she came again to the spring, she found a lovely child seated in the water [the serpent in disguise]. Thinking someone had abandoned the baby, the girl took it to her home, to her room, where she remained to play with the child. When her younger sister came to summon the maiden to eat her meal, she saw what was going on, and hurried forth to tell their father. The thoughtful old priest sensed something of what was wrong.

As the child tired, the maiden lay down with him. She fell asleep, but he only feigned slumber. He became elongated by degrees, coming to be an enormous serpent that "coiled itself round and round the room until it was full of scaly, gleaming circles. Then, placing its head near the head of the maiden, the great Serpent surrounded her with its coils, taking finally its own tail in its mouth."

In the morning, the maiden's younger sister found it impossible to open the door to her room. She finally went up on the roof and looked down through the hatchway, where she saw that the serpent's coils filled the chamber and pressed against the door. Others joined the little girl, but her father walked out of the house, "deliberately and thoughtful, angry in his mind against his eldest daughter." He went to her room and pushed against the door, saying: "Oh, Kólowissi! It is I, who speak to thee, O Serpent of the Sea; I, thy priest. Let, I pray thee, let my child come to me again, and I will make atonement for her errors. Release her, though she has been so foolish, for she is thine, absolutely thine. But let her return once more to us that we may make atonement to thee more amply."

360. *From* Stirling, 1942:78. Ladd says the Zuñi counterpart is almost the same.

361. "Kóloowisi came from the waters of the west, appearing to the Ashiwi for the first time when they went to Tówa yallane [Corn mountain] to escape the great flood which swept over the earth. The impression of his head is still to be seen on the mountain side where he stopped to rest. Kóloowisi did not return to the western waters, but went to Kóthluwalawe, becoming the seed-bearer of the gods to the Ashiwi" (Stevenson, 1904:61, 84). Ladd disagrees that Kolowisi went to Kothluwalawe.

362. Stevenson, 1904:94-102; *see also* Cushing, 1920:614.

363. The effigy of Kolowisi which is used in this ceremony is kept by the Kolowisi priesthood, a group belonging to the Corn clan (Bunzel, 1932:516).

364. Ladd notes that Zuñi kivas have lost their directional significance.

365. Stevenson, 1904:95.

366. Cushing, 1901:93 ff.

Answering the priest's prayer, Kolowisi loosened his coils, causing the whole building to tremble violently. The maiden awakened, and cried to her father for help. As the coils loosened, she found herself able to rise. "No sooner had she done this than the great Serpent bent the folds of his large coils nearest the doorway upward so that they formed an arch. Under this, filled with terror, the girl passed." The priest remained, praying to the serpent, promising that the girl should be his, as he had said.

The old priest called the two warrior priest-chiefs, and these called together all the other priests in sacred council. "Then they performed the solemn ceremonies of the sacred rites—preparing plumes, prayer-wands, and offerings of treasure." After four days of laboring, these things were "arranged and consecrated to the Serpent of the Sea." The maiden was called by her father, who bade her "make ready to take these sacrifices and yield them up, even with herself,—most precious of them all,—to the great Serpent of the Sea; that she must yield up also all thoughts of her people and home forever, and go hence to the house of the great Serpent of the Sea, even in the Waters of the World."

Amidst the lamentations of her people, the maiden was dressed in her ceremonial robes and adorned with beautiful jewelry. "They painted her cheeks with red spots as if for a dance;[367] they made a road of sacred meal toward the Door of the Serpent of the Sea—four steps toward this spring did they mark in sacred terraces on the ground at the western way of the plaza." When this was done, the old priest instructed his daughter to go "forth on the terraced road, and, standing there, call the Serpent to come to her." The serpent came forth in great undulations, placed his head on the girl's shoulder, and the two started toward the west. Over the Mountain of the Red Paint, the serpent drew himself together again, and assumed the form of a handsome youth. He placed his scales, "now small," under his flowing mantle. He was a "splendid and brave hero, so magnificently dressed." Thus, happily, the maiden descended with him into the "Doorway of the Serpent of the Sea and dwelt with him ever after."

The tale concludes: "It was thus in the days of the ancients. Therefore the ancients, no less than ourselves, avoided using springs, except for the drinking of their water; for to this day we hold the flowing springs the most precious things on earth, and therefore use them not for any profane purposes whatsoever."

These narratives and observations give some notion as to the significance of Layer I-33. There are depicted two horned serpents (figs. 72-73 and 75-76), whose heads approach an altar (fig. 74), painted on the center of the west wall of the kiva, symbolizing the doorway through which Kolowisi and the daughter of the Rain priest descended into the waters of his sacred spring. This is a good example, too, of the moral stories whereby Indian children were taught right and wrong. The various colors shown on the body of Figure 55 would seem to represent his gleaming scales, and the angular elements, his undulations, and thus to be a portrayal of Kolowisi himself. The very zig-zags of his being are symbolic of lightning, which comes with rain. The stepped altar may depict the "four steps" on the terraced road toward the sacred spring.[368] In the kiva, as we have seen, it is directed toward the west, the way which the road followed. That the entire unit is outlined in red may represent the "Mountain of the Red Paint," where the ser-

---

367. Ladd notes this as a "later elaboration," since a woman's face was not painted with red spots before some new pleasure dances from the Plains Indians were introduced, and then it was not for ritual purposes.

368. Smith, 1952:248-249 and fig. 77a, found a few lightning representations at Awatovi not unlike the Kuaua portrayals. From his findings, we would seem to have a symbolization of "good" lightning, indicated by the blunted extremity.

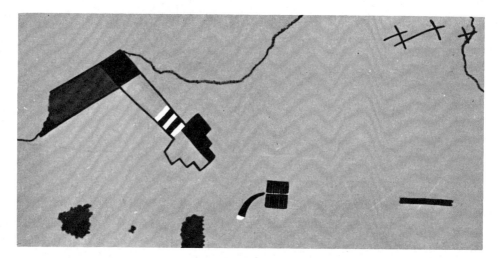

Fig. 55. Kolowisi, a manifestation of the Sun Father, with his dual fetish and staff. *Layer I-33.*

pent assumed human form. At least, it is the color of the War gods who participate in this ceremony.

The smear of red shown in the rain symbols beneath Figure 76 doubtless represents blood from the snake's heart—symbol of fructification. The three heavy lines pendant from Figure 72 would symbolize rain, according to Mrs. Stevenson.[369]

The rectangular, black figure (55, left) shown in association with Kolowisi, and described as having "lines running up and down it," causes one to look to the fetishes of the Rain priests Each Rain priest of Zuñi, other than the Shiwanni of the Zenith,[370] possesses a fetish of dual parts, which is supposed to have been brought in a basket from the undermost world by the original holder of this holy office. One part consists of four hollow reeds of finger length, one larger than the others, all of which contain paint. Ends of the reeds are sealed with black paint and native cotton.[371] This is referred to as "Father." The other part is composed of eight hollow reeds filled with all the edible seeds known to the Zuñi; the ends of these are closed with native cotton. This is spoken of as the "Mother."[372] Mrs. Stevenson

says: "Each group of reeds is wrapped with cord of native cotton . . . . A number of precious beads are attached to the cord wrapping of the ettone, and a fine arrow point rests on the top."[373] She notes that two of the fetishes are supposed to have come from the conquered Kianakwe.[374] Again, she observes that when a fetish of this dual nature is removed from its vase—which, since the invention of pottery has replaced the original sacred basket—the wrappings about each part form "a sort of square package,"[375] thus resembling the Kuaua Figure 55, which may be considered as representing the fetish used by the chief Rain priest in ceremonies to evoke help of the mythical serpent, Kolowisi, who is associated with rain making.

Nearby this object is a black shaft. It seems probable that this represents the staffs as stolen by the War gods, with which the priests brought the snow, hail, frost, and cold rains—all forms of wintertime moisture; or perhaps it represents the arrows with which they shot the serpent. Since the War gods are associated with the Morning[376] and Evening stars, it is

369. Stevenson, 1904:67.

370. The Rain priest of the Above—deputy to the Sun Father—has direct access to the Sun, and thus needs no fetish.

371. *Cf.* Stevenson, 1904:163.

372. Cushing, 1896:392. The "Father" is considered to be medicine seed of water and rain; the "Mother," medicine seed of grains.

373. Stevenson, 1904:163.

374. Stevenson, 1904:164, 446.

375. Stevenson, 1904:174.

376. Stevenson, 1904:95, says that at the rising of the

Fig. 69a, b. Bats with rain symbols; a rain making ceremony with the game, Sholiwe. *Layer H¹-32*.

concluded that the crosses shown above the black staff are symbolic of them. We know that the traditional manner of planting corn at Zuñi included the making of a cross on the ground in the center space of the hills in which corn grains of the six regions were planted, this cross to "symbolize not only the four cardinal points, but also the stars which shall watch over" the planter's field by nighttime.[377] The fragments of green paint may indicate some element symbolic of the earth's fertility and vegetation.

At one stage of the initiation ceremony, whipping of the people occurs; and the personators of the gods break large quantities of pottery.[378] Baskets are broken by other gods and burned by a lighted brand carried by Shulawitsi. The Koyemshi come into the ceremony as assistants in the actual whipping, in the

first stage.[379] Throughout, the painting, I-33, is an invocation for rain, and for fructification of the seeds planted in the fields.

It is thus evident that the Kuaua depiction relates to an initiation of young boys into the katsina society. Assuming that the personages pertaining to the Kuaua ceremony were those enacting the Zuñi rites, as recorded by Stevenson,[380] we would have the Snake priest, Pautiwa (director general of the deities or katsinas) and his deputy, the Salimopiya (warriors and seed gatherers) with corn of the six directions, the Little Fire God, Kolowisi, the Koyemshi, et al. During the ceremonial procedures, a sandpainting would be made by an artist of the Great Fire fraternity in the kiva. In this, Stevenson says, there would be as many gods represented as there were children to be initiated. There would be the combined activities of the War cult and of the Rain priests. All of the accoutrement used is symbolic of rain making and fructification.

Layer H¹-32

Nothing remains on the north wall of the painted fragments designated as Layer H¹-32. At the northwest corner of the kiva, though, a complex begins on the west wall. In Figure 69, painted entirely in black, there are two winged creatures. From the head of the one on the right (fig. 69a) there is a stick-like projection extending upward toward the corner. A longer stick extends both to the fore and aft of the other figure (69b). One long shaft crosses that ahead of "a" and extends downward to the left to cross over the posterior one of "b." At the head of "b" a similar stick crosses the one extending forward from the mouth and parallels the stick just mentioned.

morning star the gods who accompanied Kolowisi gather in the Nadir kiva and make offerings of grains of corn and other seeds, which are received by the director and deputy of the Great Fire fraternity.

377. *See* Cushing, 1920:177.
378. *See also* Cushing, 1920:615; 1896:415.

379. Ladd, 24 September 1959. He adds that the later "finishing whipping" may be done at the parents' consent at any time, usually within one or two years.

380. Stevenson, 1904:96. Ladd says Pautiwa is not in this ceremony but a god who looks like him, *E im'pi yonna*, one of the seed gatherers. He also says that the equal numbers of gods and initiates is not a fact.

There are a few dash-drops indicated as falling from the mouth area of each representation. Neither the graph drawing nor the laboratory notes indicate any further features, but the artist who reproduced the canvas replicas put legs with clawed feet on each creature. A small spot of yellow color occurs about four inches below the lower end of the right shaft. Of this complex, Zna'ote said: BAT, ESH OLTSI. CACIQUE CALLS ON BATS TO HELP; BRING MOISTURE.

With regards to bats, we find that the Zuñi Newekwe represent them in carvings along with their altar accoutrement, very like those painted on our kiva wall [*see also* Pl. XII, fig. 56 and Pl. B-4],[381] and they are believed to be of aid in rain making. "If a man sees a bat when he is on his way at night to plant prayer plumes, he is happy, for he knows that in four days there will be much rain."[382] The similarity of the criss-crossing lines or shafts associated with the bats to other depictions of lightning in our paintings would seem to make that identification here feasible. In another instance (Layer D¹17), Zna-ote indicated black lightning as being "all right, not bad." Thus this complex signifies part of the ritualistic formula employed by a Rain priest in soliciting rain for his people. In Zuñi chambers, lightning is symbolized by zig-zag carvings, in association with representations of Paiyatuma.[383]

To the right of the bats, the fragment of a black shaft, Figure 70 (*not* illustrated), occurs, extending diagonally downward for 14 inches toward the mid-point of the wall, and reaching to within 32 inches of the floor. Projecting toward the southwest corner, Figure 71 (*not* illustrated) shows two yellow sticks which cross near their upper extremities. The longer one measures 38 inches; these are black tipped. Upon viewing these representations, Zna'ote said: SUMMER RAIN CEREMONY.

Since Figure 71 does not show other than one crossing of shafts, even in its unusually long extent, it seemed questionable whether this was meant to represent lightning. Finding that a potent rain bringing feature at Zuñi is the game, *shóliwe*, attention was turned to this.

When Mrs. Stevenson went to Zuñi in 1891 she learned that a special play of the sacred rain ceremony, 'Hláhewe, or dance of the Corn maidens, had been given the preceding year, because of the fact that the former Sun priest had been impeached for having caused a drought, and it was necessary to acquaint the new incumbent of this drama. The special festival brought so much rain that the people had to dance in the mud. In 1891, the Rain and Bow priests again included this drama in their rain ceremony. Since that time, she says, it has never been repeated.[384]

It is of interest that Cushing notes that this, "the *Thlu-he-kwe*, or Beautiful Corn Wands ceremony, was observed and admired by Coronado on his journey of conquest." This made evident the fact that the ceremonial in its beautifully developed form had, by Cushing's day, been practiced for about 350 years. It is, he states, one of the few sacred dances of the Zuñi in which women assume the leading part.[385]

Mrs. Stevenson explains that this ceremony consists of two groups of dancers and choirs, one called 'Hlahewe (which means "rabbit skin blanket" and signifies fecundity), and the other, *Shóko we* ("Flutes") —having reference

381. *See* Stevenson, 1904: Pl. CIV.

382. Stevenson, 1904:432. Cushing, 1896:402, indicates *Éshotsi* as the mis-meaning name of one of the Koyemshi.

383. Parsons, 1920:91, suggested that the personage Paiyatuma was borrowed by the Zuñi from the Keresans. At Laguna, she found Paiyatuma impersonated among the katsinas, where he came with 'Chakwena in the mixed Katsina dances.

384. Stevenson, 1904:57. Ladd says that he saw this special ceremony in 1932 or 1933. He remembers little about it, and says that it has not been performed since then.

385. Cushing, 1920:38 and 631.

to Paiyatuma.[386] Arrangements of the drama—which commemorates the departure of the Corn maidens and celebrates their return—are made by the first body of the Rain priests.[387] Some of the parts are performed by permanent actors.[388] The elder brother Bow priest is prominent in this enactment. After procedures which, on the day of the drama, extend from sunrise to sunset, there are night-time activities. Around midnight, the groups visit the sacred springs and bring in water and rooted corn stalks, which the Sun priest receives. Rites continue; then, after a long prayer by the Sun priest, the elder brother Bow priest leads a procession to the bower which has been erected in the sacred dance plaza. He carries his corn ear fetish (*mili*) and a triangular kilt which has a broad band of blue-green (symbolic of the vegetation of the world) painted across it, "with a conventional design of the game of shóliwe at each end of the band." [389] Mrs. Stevenson tells how this is made:

> . . . . The design is formed by the use of a number of yucca splints crossed at right angles to form squares. These are laid on the cloth, and yellow and black paint is applied in the squares, which denote the sholiwe reeds grouped ready to throw. The yellow indicates the north country, whence the

Áshiwi came, over which the Kíakwemosi, Shíwanni of the North, has care, whose breath must be pure so that this region may always be fruitful and beautiful to look upon. The black is symbolic of the earth over which the Shíwanni of the Nadir has care, whose prayers must be pure that the earth may be made good for man to walk upon. The diagonal line through each square is symbolic of the straight road of the Sun Father.[390]

A fluffy eagle plume is fastened to each point of the kilt. The arrow reeds of the game, sholiwe, with plumes attached are tied to one corner, and the gambling stick, *tikwane*, is tied similarly to another corner.

According to Zuñi mythology, the ceremonies of initiation into the kiva groups are supposed to be performed by direct command of Pautiwa, chief of the masked gods. Pautiwa decided that one of the gods must go to Itiwanna (present Zuñi) and relate to the people their history after leaving the undermost world, and prepare them for the coming of the gods "to bless the male children with the sacred breath of life that they might enter into the everlasting happiness of the sacred dance house," in the depths of the sacred lake, Kothluwalawa. Pautiwa chose his deputy, ᵗKiaklo, to perform this service.[391]

Mrs. Stevenson states that the drama reenacting this myth was performed every four years, beginning in April. Members of the Council of the Gods take turns in personating ᵗKiaklo, who as in tradition is brought forth on the backs of the ten Koyemshi. The drama includes many other gods.[392] In her description we find that the body of ᵗKiaklo was painted with clay, over which his attire was added. And this included a kilt similar to that mentioned above, for the elder brother Bow

386. The dances for which Paiyatuma played during the Corn maidens' dance are called "shokowe," being the name of his flute (Stevenson, 1904:569). *See* Layer H-31.

387. Ashiwanni—priests of the six regional directions—who fast and pray for rain, elder brother Bow priest, younger brother Bow priest, and Shiwanokia—priestess of fecundity.

388. The drama was enacted every four years, in August (Stevenson, 1904:180).

389. In another account, Mrs. Stevenson tell of a Sun dance of the Bedbug fraternity, which she observed in March, 1904. In this, a personage whom she speaks of as the Sprinkler wears the same kind of kilt, decorated with the sholiwe game. This quadrennial ceremony was celebrated alternately by the Bedbug (*Cimex*) and Little Fire fraternities. It is believed that the original fire was the gift of Sun Father. The ceremony formerly included acts of jugglery (Stevenson, 1904:564, 566). Ladd notes that a priest usually wears a plain sash.

390. Stevenson, 1904:189.

391. *See* footnote 251, page 72. ᵗKiaklo is the keeper of the rituals of creation (Cushing, 1896:373).

392. *See* Stevenson, 1904:181.

priest during the rain ceremony, 'Hlahewe, The narration of 'Kiaklo takes place in each of the kivas, where it is recited in full, after which the personator runs away, over the western road, to his special dwelling place.

Turning to accounts of sholiwe, we find that it is one of the games of the War gods (and which became the great indoor gambling game of the Zuñi).[393] According to Stevenson's recording of a legend, the game was played for rain by the War gods and the Rain priests. The latter considered it so efficacious in bringing rain that they organized a society for the express purpose of playing the game for rain, and they called it *Shówekwe*, or Arrow Reed people. There were ten original members, and their prayers were certain to bring rain. After the Koyemshi gave their songs and prayers to the fraternities, the Newekwe and Showekwe alternated annually in personating the Koyemshi.[394]

In the game, each player takes the side of one of the War gods. There are four pieces of split reeds, two representing the side of the elder War god, and two the side of the younger War god. Each piece has a distinctive decoration. One reed of the elder god has the concave side colored black, symbolizing the *whole day;* markings on the convex side denote the three periods of the day—*morning, noon,* and *sunset.* His second reed indicates *white medicine;* it has a daub of black paint at each end of the concave side, which, like the markings on the other side, show *morning* and *evening*

or *sunrise* and *sunset.* One reed of the younger War god has a daub of black in the middle of the concave side, denoting *midday,* and the markings on the convex side have the same significance. His second reed has a black mark on one end of the concave side; this and markings on the reverse side denote *sunrise,* "which to the Zuñis is the first light of day, or the white light which comes first." [395]

Mrs. Stevenson gives the procedure by which the jointed reeds are slipped one into another, and the method of placing them in playing the game. She gives an illustration (her fig. 13), which shows two reeds in the same relative position as the two shafts crossing in the Kuaua painting, Figure 71. Inasmuch as these are shown in yellow, the natural color of a reed, and have black tips, this unit may represent the reeds of the younger War god; while our Figure 70, painted in black, may represent the reeds of the elder War god. It is presumed that the playing sticks used by the gods would have been of larger size than those used by their earthly successors.[396] Thus, it is believed that the Kuaua figures portray the playing of the ceremonial game, sholiwe, as a means of bringing rain to the people. Figure 69 may represent the Rain priests' part in the drama, and the sticks of Figures 70 and 71, the War gods' part. This was probably painted on the kiva wall during an initiation of new members into the Arrow order of the Bow priesthood, as part of a ceremonial lasting over many (perhaps twelve) days, an outstanding feature of which was the great Corn dance and drama.

Layer H-31

With the painting of this, the 56th layer of plaster in the kiva, a new feature is introduced, an encircling band which reaches the full extent of the wall, from the floor upward

---

393. The once infamous gambling house at Zuñi had ceased to exist by 1902 (Stevenson, 1904:332).

394. Stevenson, 1904:328. She says the Great Fire and the Cactus fraternities are more recent accessions to the personators of the Koyemshi. At Zuñi, the four fraternities came to personate these gods, in turn. She also reports that the Showekwe degenerated into a body of professional gamblers, bearing no relation to the original organization of the Rain priests. However, the game continued to be played by the priests and others in all sacredness for rain. No games are played while the Rain priests are in retreat (Stevenson, 1904:330). Ladd detects error in this recording, but is unable to correct it.

395. Stevenson, 1904:331.

396. Stevenson, 1904:328, in fact, states that, "The rain priests thought the reeds used for the game were too long, so their length was measured from the tip of the thumb to the tip of the middle finger, both extended."

for a width of 19.5 inches. A white stripe, one-fourth inch wide, is painted between the black band and the adobe color of the remainder of the wall. This is said to occur in the most sacred rituals only, and represents the "firmness on which we rest or stand, the firmness of the earth," according to Lapajo, a Laguna informant.

Farthest toward the east on the north wall is a complex (Pl. XIV, fig. 68) showing a personage standing before a large black, terraced altar, each step of which is capped with a big white cloud. The altar is symbolic of the Earth Mother, around whose horizon the terraces represent the mesa and valley formations which enclose the Pueblo world, and above which the billowy rain clouds rest. Zna'ote said of this altar: A·WE TLU YANNA [cloud] ALTAR; WHERE CORN MOTHER PRAYERSTICKS ARE PLACED. CLOUDS ON TOP. MIDDLE OF THE EARTH. The base of the altar, which measures 46 inches across, is 10 inches above the dado. Each end is outlined with white.

The personage is centrally located with reference to the altar, but the head is missing, and no feet are shown. The torso and arms are painted yellow and are outlined in white; the hands are red. The left arm is raised akimbo, with extended finger tips reaching to a stalk of corn which occurs as the easternmost feature of the painting. The curved implement held in the right hand was recognized by Zna'ote as a RABBIT STICK, TLE·AYANNA, but may be better identified as a torch. On the wrist is a notched ornament. The bottom of the cornstalk rests on the dado, from which the plant extends upward as far as the wall remains. This and a companion stalk on the opposite side of the altar—both showing arced leaves and ears in silk—are painted in the faded yellow color, and are identified as YELLOW CORN, TLUP TSI·KWE, by Zna'ote. The silks are shown realistically, in reddish-brown.

Returning to the personage, there is a black kilt, bordered with white at the bottom, with fringes on the left side; the kilt is decorated on the front with small white circles arranged in certain patterns (fig. 68). The first of these, according to Zna'ote, represents SEVEN, A PLANET [Ursa Major or *kwillilek'akwe*].[397]

397. *See* Cushing, 1896:432-433, for symbolism.

PL. XIV. *Layer H-31.* Great Corn drama or ᵗHlahewe.

Fig. 54   Fig. 64   Fig

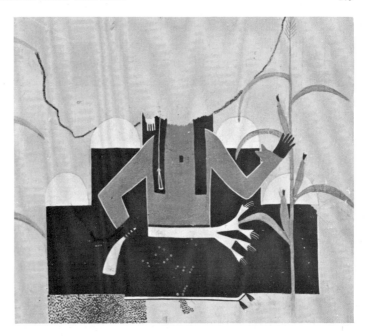

Fig. 68. Paiyatuma, manifest as god of music. *Layer H-31.*

The second is the SOUTH PLANET. GOING DOWN THIS MONTH (April) [Venus]. Next, is represented THREE BIG STARS IN SOUTH [Orion's Belt]. Another is KO PA'KWE [chupa·kwe], BIG BUNCH ABOVE AND TO THE NORTHEAST—the "seed stars" or Pleiades; and the last represents THE TWINS, MOK'WAN-OSIN·NA [Castor and Pollux]. About the waist is a large white sash with prominent white fringes, tied on the left side of the body. Down each side of the figure, over the shoulders, long, black hair hangs in a wide swatch, that on the right measuring three inches across. Extending longitudinally through its center is a white line, or cord, at the lower extreme of which is a white feather, which Zna'ote identified as LÁ SHO

Fig. 66   Fig. 67   Fig. 68

WAN[e], STRING WITH FEATHER ON END.[398] A small white feature resembles an ear ornament on the right side of the neck of the personage. Of this, Zna'ote said: COULD BE PART OF RAINBOW SIGN.[399] On the breast is a small rectangular element painted in red, said by Zna'ote to be, IK'A·NNA SHI LO WAH, PAINT ON TOP OF THE HEART.[400]

To the right of the personage a mass of black dots fills in the area between the altar base and the dado, and a similar small area shows in the space which might appear to have been occupied by the legs of this individual. This representation may have extended entirely across the altar-dado area, but the lower left segment of the painted features was eroded away, and the wall had been patched. Zna'ote said it symbolizes MOISTURE UNDER GROUND, COMING UP TO HELP SEEDS GROW.

This personage, Zna'ote considered as, PROBABLY THE SINGER.

From the outset, it was evident that the paintings of this layer had to do with corn ceremonials. Turning to Mrs. Stevenson's volume, we have her recording of the 'Hlahewe ceremonial referred to in the preceding painted layer to give aid with the Kuaua portrayals. Because of the symbolism associated with Figure 68, it is possible to identify it as Paiyatuma, who in this instance is manifest as the god of music, as well as representative of the Sun, or Sun priest. On his kilt, various stars and planets are portrayed. As an example, the seven sisters or Pleiades are explained by a journey which the two chief priests of the Bow made to the cavern of the Rainbow, seeking new blessings for their people. As they neared the cave they heard the sound of a drum and strains of song. When Paiyatuma received them within, they explained their mission, saying "our fathers have sent us to seek and greet ye, it having been declared by our children that the song-sounds and the customs thereof so far surpass our own, even those of our beloved [Corn] Maidens, makers of the seed of seeds." Paiyatuma bade the visitors to sit, watch, and listen. They saw that, "to the left, grouped around a great world-bowl, clad in broidered cotton vestment, were a splendid band of players, long flutes in their hands and the adornments of god-priests on their faces and persons. In their midst, too, was a drummer and also a bearer of the song-staff; aged, they, and dignified with years." The recounting continues:

Paiyatuma scattered a line of pollen on the floor, and folding his arms strode to the rear of the cavern, then turned him about and with straightened mien, advanced again. Following him, lo, and behold! came seven maidens beauteous like to the Maidens of Corn, but taller and fainter of form. Like to them also in costume, yet differing somewhat in the hue of the mantles they wore. And in their hands they carried, not tablets of the sun, moon, and each her star with cross symbol of the Corn priests above them, but, verily, wands of cottonwood from the branchlets and buds of which tiny clouds flowed forth.

"These be the sisters of our Maidens of Corn, of the House of the Stars, seen these too, as they, so these more faintly, as, when above are seen the stars of the House of Seven, others seven are seen below in the waters. Like in form of gesture is their dance custom, but fertile not of the seed, but of the water of life wherewith the seed is quickened," said Paiyatuma.

He lifted his flute, then took his place in the line of the dancers, as the *yá poto* does in the line of the Corn dance. The drum sounded until the cavern shook as with

---

398. Stevenson, 1904:182, says that for the *láshowawe* (singular, *láshowane*) one or more plumes are attached to a cotton cord. Each consists of a tail and a wing feather of the mountain bluebird (*'thlai aluko*). The two feathers are joined at the quill ends, forming a V, and are wrapped with cotton cord (Stevenson, 1904:182).

399. *See page 65.*

400. Ladd renders this as "having a red heart" (*Ik'annon shi lo wah,* "red heart").

Fig. 67. Nighttime Woman or Moon, with prayerstick in left hand, and gourd rattle in right. *Layer H-31.*

thunder. The flutes sang and sighed as the wind in a wooded canyon whilst still the storm is distant. White mists floated up from the wands of the maidens and mingled with the breath of the flutes over the terraced world-bowl, above which sported the butterflies of Summerland, about the dress of the Rainbow in the strange blue light of the night.

The visiting priests were awed and entranced. When they rose to go, Paiyatuma, smiling, "gave them his breath with his hands," and said, "Go ye the way before, telling the fathers of our custom, and straightway we will follow."[401]

To the right of the Singer, or Paiyatuma, is another personage (fig. 67), lacking head and legs, but who obviously stood above the dado. A tiny fragment of white indicates the right leg's position. The patched wall included this area. This figure is shown wearing a dress with sleeves which end at the elbows—both of which are bent upward. The dress is black, outlined with red. It has black fringes at the lower right edge of the skirt, with red stitching

shown above. The lower arms are painted white with red outline, and the hands are red. About the left wrist is a yellow band with notched end projecting upward, identified as a LEATHER WRISTLET by Zna'ote. On the breast, a white necklace with triangular pendant is indicated. About the waist a large white sash, with two fringes on each end, is tied on the right.

This personage was recognized by Zna'ote as NIGHTTIME WOMAN. In the left hand, she carries a long black shaft onto which four white feathers with narrow black tips are bound with a white cord. These hang downward; if there were corresponding feathers above the binding, these are completely obliterated. This is A PRAYERSTICK, TLESH NANᵉ; PRAYERSTICK WITH TURKEY FEATHERS AT TOP AND EAGLE FEATHERS BELOW, as stated by Zna'ote. A feathered object is held in the right hand. It is painted yellow and decorated with black, adobe, red, and yellow stripes, and the entire feature is outlined with white. The feathers are black with white tips. This was identified by Zna'ote as ᵗCHÍ MUNᵉ, [*chi'mon-na*], GOURD RATTLE WITH TURKEY TAIL FEATH-

401. *From Cushing, 1896:433-434.*

ERS.[402] The Nighttime Woman is identifiable as the Moon-Tenatsali personage who is the marker of time, and who also represents the Blue Corn maiden. This layer of the paintings involves great multiplicity of characters.

Alongside Nighttime Woman on her right is a black cornstalk, with leaves and ears in the faded yellow color; the ear silks, or blossoms, are red-brown. This plant, Zna'ote identified as BLACK CORN, MITAN KE KWI; ALSO PURPLE.[403] Within a few inches of the northwest corner, is another yellow stalk, extending from the dado to the wall's extremity—some 50 inches —and showing, in addition to the leaves and ears, the corn tassel also in faded yellow. Above the uppermost leaf on the right side of the yellow stalk, and thus at the western limit of the north wall—again in the northwest corner—two black footprints of an animal are shown (Pl. XIV, fig. 67), which Zna'ote identified as BEAR HANDS,[404] BEAR TRACKS; TE·ANNA WHA, TRACK. Just above these is a small pointed element (fig. 67, extreme upper right of personage) also painted in black, which he said represents an ARROW.

After viewing Layer H-31 briefly, Zna'ote said that it pertains to, A CURING CEREMONY.[405] Pointing to the bear tracks and the arrow point nearby, he said: ARROW GOING AWAY WITH THE DISEASE, WHICH WAS CAUSED BY A BEAR. SAYS "GO AWAY BEAR."[406, 407]

It is possible that, at Kuaua, as an accompaniment of the ceremonies pertaining to the corn's growth and earth's fructification, there may have been curing rites. If so, we may infer that patients troubled with Bear disease were duly treated during the performance of proper rituals and chants by the possessors of Mystery medicine.[408]

---

402. Bunzel, 1932:677, observes that turkey feathers are used on prayersticks for the dead. Ladd says, "eagle and turkey feathers are always first on the stick, and not always for the dead; the last feather on the stick denotes the dead, or for the Koko, and this is usually a duck feather."

403. Ladd notes that *k'wi ni kwe* means "Black corn"; *mi*—"corn ear"; *milah*—"corn"; *k'e*—"purple."

404. From time of the legendary past, the people of Zuñi are said to have been divided into dual groups. They were given the choice of selecting from two blue and two dun-red eggs—like the turquois sky or dull colored earth. Those who chose the blue eggs, which hatched ravens, became Earth people; those who chose the dull ones, which hatched into beautiful macaws, became the Sky people. Those creatures and things of summer and the southern space pertain to the South or Summer people—children of the Earth Mother; and those of winter and the northern space, to the North or Winter people—children of the Sky Father. To one or the other of these divisions, all of the people belong. For instance, the Sun, Toad, Turtle, and Frog; Seed, Tobacco, Fire or Badger peoples are affiliated with the South or Summer group, whereas the North or Winter group is comprised of Bear, Coyote, Deer, Crane, Turkey, and other peoples, or clans *(from Cushing, 1896: 386-387)*.

405. Ladd states: "As far as my information goes there are no paintings at Zuñi for curing, other than those depicted in the winter world cleansing ceremony when a floor altar is painted. The room is usually left undecorated. The ceremony is not held in a kiva." He adds that: "The Koko manifestations can be, and are, depicted by mural representation."

406. Stevenson, 1904:217, tells of a theurgist's activities during one of the dances; he walked back and forth between the lines of dancers, "passing down the body of each, to carry off disease, two eagle-wing feathers," while repeating an audible prayer.

Cushing, 1920:29-30, recorded that the Bear and Crane clans possessed hail medicine *(mû ettone)*, and he states, "When more than one clan possessed one of these magic medicines, they formed a secret society, like the first four, for its keeping and use. Thus the Bear and Crane peoples became the 'Holders of the Wand'—who bring the snow of winter and are potent to cure the diseases which come with them. In time they let into their secret council others, whom they had cured, that the precious secrets of their band might not be wasted . . . ."

407. *See* Bunzel, 1932:531-533, for Bear curing rites.

408. Stevenson, 1904:426. "For Mystery medicine the face, body, upper arms, and legs of the males are colored brownish red. The feet, the legs halfway to the knees, the hands, and the arms halfway to the elbows are colored with a white paint made of kaolin. A black woven breechcloth, embroidered at the ends, is worn. With females only the feet, the lower portion of the legs, the hands, and the arms are painted, kaolin also being used for this purpose. They wear the usual woven dress. An owl and a raven feather [Ladd says *no* owl feather, and Red Tail hawk instead of a raven feather], held in place by yucca ribbons, are crossed on the top of each wrist, the owl feather pointing outward, the other pointing inward. Similar feathers are also crossed on the outside of each leg below the knee, the owl feather pointing to the knee, that the child of Mystery medicine may be up early with the raven and go

Fig. 66. Fire Man or Shula-witsi, with feathered wand in left hand and torch in the right. *Layer H-31.*

Close to the corner, on the west wall, is another black corn stalk similar to the one previously described, which has a black tassel (*cf.* Pl. A-12). To the right of this stands a third personage (Pl. XIV, fig. 66), who was recognized by Zna'ote as ÓP TINKLE ON, FIRE MAN, SUNSHINE. His feet rest just above the white stripe of the dado. They appear to be dressed in white moccasins, above which are black anklets. The legs are white outlined with red. The feet are directed toward the right. The head of the figure is defaced, leaving only strands of black hair to fall forward over each shoulder. A red feather tipped with white hangs in the middle of the hair on the right side. The torso and arms are painted in the faded color, with hands yellow. Around the left wrist is an end-notched red wristlet. Over the heart, a small rectangular element is painted with a red stripe lengthwise through the center, bordered on each side with yellow. This, as with Figure 68, symbolizes the heart.

Around the right wrist is an elaborate and delicately painted feather ornament, showing white feathers with fine black markings at the wrist, with a pendant cord decorated with black feathers along each side, and a white feather with black tip at the lower end. Held in the left hand is a black stick, 25 inches long, like that held by Nighttime Woman. Here, however, feathers are shown above and below the black tie which is slightly above the midpoint of the shaft. Those above are black with narrow white tips, and those below are red—two plain and two with fine black markings, with black and red tips on each. This TLESH-NAN[e], said Zna'ote, has TURKEY FEATHERS AT TOP AND RED CHICKEN HAWK TAIL FEATHERS BELOW.[409] A fragment of an object carried in

about at night, without fear, like the owl. The chin and the upper lip are covered with a paste of kaolin, a circle of which is put round the top of the head, and hawk or eagle down is dotted over the kaolin, symbolic of the clouds of the world. . . ."

409. Parsons, 1939:187, states that at Zuñi, Chicken Hawk is one of the four messenger birds sent out by the two War chiefs to get permission from the Rain chiefs to "come out" from the underworld.

Fig. 65. Yellow Corn maiden or Meleyonako, carrying a rain jar. *Layer H-31.*

the right hand remains, showing red handle and the beginning of a decoration in black, with both delimited by a white line. Of this, Zna'ote said: HAS TORCH; CLOUDS, NICE DAY.

Secured at the waist by a white sash, which is tied on the left side, is a black kilt bordered with red at its bottom. The kilt has black fringes on the lower left corner; a splotch of green paint intermingles with the fringe. The sash has two knots at each end decorated with black, and from each of which four white fringes extend. This sash, said Zna'ote, is a RAIN SASH, A WHITE CEREMONIAL BELT, MO'LE MOP'EKWINNA.

This Fire Man personage is identifiable as Shulawitsi, deputy to the Sun, who goes about setting fire with his torch. One of his duties during the Corn drama is to keep the fire ever burning so that the Corn maidens may be watched and guarded against any desecration.[410]

----

410. *See* Stevenson, 1904:202.

Southward, on the right of Fire Man there are two more stalks of corn, both in the faded color, and quite like those already described. In every instance of showing, there are three ears in silk on each stalk, two on one side and one on the other, these being rhythmically alternated in the painting.

Then another personage (fig. 65) is shown directly in the midsection of the west wall. This time, a fragment of the left side of the head remains. Face, arms, and torso are painted in strong yellow color. At the upper side of the head, on the left, a bit of red paint is seen; in the area of the left eye, there is a fleck of white. A tiny rectangle painted in red shows in the position of the mouth. Around the neck is a black choker necklace with a rectangular ornament in white, at the front.

The hands, which are red, extend across the front of the figure and support a globular, black vessel[411] with low neck and outcurved rim; through its center a white line extends vertically. Long, wide, black tresses of hair extend down from each shoulder, reaching to the hands. In the right tress, a white cord hangs downward through the center, with a red feather pendant. The figure is wearing a black skirt supported by a white sash which allows a portion of the skirt to show above it. White fringes extend from each end of the sash, on the right, as do the black fringes at the lower corner of the skirt. The latter is bordered with red and shows red stitching along the side for a few inches above the fringes. The legs are white outlined with red. There are black anklets, and white moccasins. This personage was identified by Zna'ote as: A WOMAN, MÉLE YO NÁKO[412]—MAN-WOMAN BOTH. BOSS OF THE WOMEN. RAIN. CARRYING CANTEEN OF WATER BY THONG AROUND NECK, WITH HAIR ON TOP OF IT. Here we have a being bespeaking the uni-

----

411. *Cf.* Stevenson, 1904:202.

412. Ladd does not recognize Meleyonako as being pertinent to Zuñi. It is known to be familiar to the Keresan people.

versal deity, as the Yellow Corn maiden; who is represented by the priestess who directs the women participating in the Corn drama, and thus, Shiwanokia.

At the right of Figure 65 is another stalk of yellow corn. Then, rather than a second stalk, there is the fetish (Pl. XIV, fig. 65) or POLLEN BAG WITH EAGLE FEATHERS, as Zna'ote recognized it, which pertains to Meleyonako. It is painted in the same yellow color as this personage, is outlined in white, and has a white cord encircling it and attaching the black and white feathers which extend below.

Becoming expansive at this point, Zna'ote said: FIGURE 65 IS RAIN. CORN FIRST, THEN WANT RAIN, THEN SUNSHINE (fig. 66), thus indicating that the painting depicts a summer rain ceremony for the growth of corn and other seeds.

Beyond the pollen bag, on the right, is another yellow corn stalk and, then, a final personage (fig. 64), directed toward Meleyonako, very much like that of Figure 66, to the left. As before, the head is missing. Viewing these north and west wall paintings as a whole, it is evident that the heads of the five personages had been destroyed intentionally. Between them less significant features are intact.

The body and arms of this Figure 64 are of the same faded color, outlined in red. Heart symbol is likewise shown, and the tresses of hair, excepting that the feather pendant on the right is of plain red. There is a white ornament on the left wrist, on which short lines parallel the direction of the arm, probably indicating a shell bracelet. This is set off from the red hand by a black line. In this hand is a feather-bedecked prayerstick. Those above the white and black tie are white, with fine black markings and white tips; those below are of the faded color, with stepped tips in black. Here, Zna'ote said: PRAYERSTICK WITH TURKEY FEATHERS AT TOP AND EAGLE FEATHERS BELOW. 'KWIN Nᵃ, BLACK [*ha k'winna*].

Fig. 64. Lightning Man or Kupishtaya. *Layer H-31.*

The right hand is also red, and the wrist is banded by a yellow ornament with three notches at each end, and these outlined with black. This again is a LEATHER WRISTLET, by Zna'ote's identification. The long gourd rattle clasped in the right hand has a yellow handle. Where the gourd expands, there is a decoration consisting of a wide black band, then narrow white, red, white, black, and white bands. The head of the instrument has decoration similar to the one carried by Nighttime Woman, with black, white, yellow, and red colors. The entire rattle is outlined with white. From its upper end, two black feathers with white tips extend. To the right of the rattle handle, two tiny white tracks are identifiable as those of a rabbit (fig. 64).

The personage wears a black kilt, at the bottom of which, from each leg outward, there is a narrow border of red, white, and red again. On the right edge of the kilt red stitches extend upward a few inches. Across the front, the border is painted yellow. Around the waist is a very wide white sash with white fringes, tied on the left side. Hanging below the sash, in an arrangement of V-shaped white cords and triangular-shaped pendants, is an ornament which represents small conch shell tinklers. The legs are white with red outline; there are black anklets, and white moccasins.

Zna'ote identified this personage as KU PISH TA' [Kupishtaya], ONE OF THE KATSINA BEINGS. A MAN, TLASH SHI; SOUTH MAN; ASSISTANT TO THE BOSS.[413] He, then, represents the Sun priest's pekwin or assistant. Near his upraised right hand there is another stalk of black corn. With leaves of the two mingling, there is then a yellow stalk, its leaf tips reaching to the southwest corner of the kiva. The rabbit tracks mentioned above are painted over the middle leaf of corn on the black stalk, on the left, and are thus closely associated with Kupishtaya.

Considering this series of personages, Zna'-ote said: AFTER THE SINGER [Paiyatuma] COMES KU PISH TA'; THEN NIGHTTIME WOMAN AND MELEYONAKO, SIDE BY SIDE; BEHIND THEM COMES SUNSHINE [Fire Man or Shulawitsi]. Thus we have the order of the assemblage in processional form. It would seem that Figure 68 (Pl. XIV) bespeaks the Sun through Paiyatuma, attended by Figure 64, pekwinna to the Sun, here Kupishtaya—perhaps as certain of the stars or a comet. Figure 67, the Nighttime

Woman, doubtless is a manifestation of the Moon, with Figure 65, Meleyonako, representing the priestess of fecundity. Finally, Fire Man or Figure 66, with his torch, indicates Shulawitsi of the twain, probably the Morning star.

We come now to the south wall, where the most complete figure of all those portrayed in the kiva was revealed (*see* Frontispiece and Pl. XIV, fig. 54). This is odd in light of the willful destruction which obliterated the heads and adornments of all of the other personages relating to this layer.

Again the laboratory notes fail to tie in this figure with reference to the southwest corner of the chamber. However, since it is stated to be 13.5 inches from the easternmost limit of the remaining wall, we have fitted it into the space thus provided, which brings it close to the corner. The figure is lacking the lower part of the legs and feet, otherwise it is complete. It is headed toward the east, as indicated by the colorful mask which covers the face, thus directed toward the rising sun. The upraised arms, with elbows akimbo, measure 41 inches from finger tip to finger tip.

The mask consists of a yellow band across the forehead and eye area, in which a square, white eye hole is bordered with black, with the latter color swinging upward in a curve from the lower left corner. Below this band is one of black which includes the nasal area and steps down to cover most of the lower face, onto the neck.[414] The muzzle portion is shaped like the beak of a macaw, this covering the chin; it is painted in red and shows the nasal opening of such a bird as a small white circle. Above the mask, a white sash is bound, with elaborate knots and tassels hanging toward the back. A red outline extends down the front of this headband and continues to border the yellow and black bands across the face; such also separates the headband from the yellow

---

413. It is to be recalled that deceased members of the Bow priesthood join the Kupishtaya and become lightning makers, the mighty warriors who control the lightning arrows (Stevenson, 1904:20-21).

Although Mrs. Stevenson gleaned a considerable amount of information concerning Kupishtaya at Zuñi, and Zna'ote evidenced familiarity with such a personage, it appears that this being, or beings, is much better known among the Keresan peoples, and it is probable that the Kupishtaya were introduced to Zuñi by Keres associates of that organization. Today, Ladd reports a *Ha'k'u kwe*, or Acoma curing society, as affiliated with the Kupishtaya at Zuñi. He says that there is one family belonging to this society, which "some say is a bad witch society."

---

414. *Cf.* Stevenson, 1904:198.

Fig. 54. Universal Deity: Corn (Earth) Mother and Sky (Sun) Father. *Layer H-31.*

band, and outlines the back of the head, to the lower extent of the black band.

Returning to the headband, the upper part of each knot is painted red,[415] below which is a black element, and then a patterned area of criss-crosses and dots in black, ending in a large, red-bordered tassel of white, from which red and black fringes project.

Extending upward at the rear of the head is a panache of feathers and flowers, rising from a small red basal portion, which may represent a wrapping. There is a yellow feather (fig. 54) which Zna'ote identified as a MACAW FEATHER; next, SOME KIND OF A FLOWER, which is shown as a red calyx on a black stem and with black corolla; and, lastly, there is a long black feather with two prominent, oblate spots of white, which is an EAGLE FEATHER. All of these, Zna'-ote explained, COME UP BACK OF HEAD.[416] To the fore of this feature is a short, red and black element, incomplete. From the back of the head, as if pendant from the panache, a large, triangular black feather hangs downward, and

from its lower end a long white cord crosses the left shoulder of the personage and comes to an end in a big red feather or LÁSHO WAN[e], tied on with string bows. Two small footprints or tracks are shown below and to the left of the black and white feather, and are identifiable as those of a rabbit, as shown also near Figure 64.

Around the neck of Figure 54 there are several strands of white, interspersed with small red features, which cross as a triangular pendant on the breast. This obviously represents a shell necklace with red bead ornamentation. The pendant hangs just above the small rectangular feature which as previously seen identifies the heart symbol, here shown with a yellow band on either side of the red central unit—just as appears on Figures 64 and 66.

This personage is garbed with an elaborate dress of adobe color outlined with black. Where the sleeves—apparently of three-quarter length—terminate, each lower arm is painted yellow. About both wrists are wristlets; that on the right is white, with V-notches at each end and the upper end tipped with

415. Laboratory note says "pink."
416. *Cf.* Stevenson, 1904:194 note.

black, like eagle feathers. The wristlet on the left arm projects above only; it is red, v-notched, and has two large x's as decoration. The hands are painted red. The right one holds what appears to be four sticks, several inches in length, painted "black, yellow, and red," according to the laboratory notes; the reproduction shows the outer two sticks in yellow with a red and a black stick between them.

Attached to the left wrist of Figure 54 by a long red thong is a great, two-part quiver, or SHÓ·PONᵉ [sho·ponna], as identified by Zna'ote, painted in blue-grey color. This is the first appearance of this color of paint in the murals.[417] Where used it is outlined with white. The arrow-holding portion of the quiver, from which five feathered shafts and apparently one plain, black shaft project at the top, terminates at its bottom in a large pointed element painted yellow. The flap of the quiver[418] ends in a rounded element, likewise in yellow, and outlined with black. Where this unit adjoins the flap, there is a decorated area composed of five segments or crossing bands: first one of white, then one of blue-grey, white again, blue-grey with a black x over it, and a final white unit. About these five small blocks, a

black stripe extends inside the white outline, but not separating the uppermost white block from the main part of the flap. Both quiver and flap are criss-crossed with black lines which form a diamond pattern. Within each diamond, then, a yellow crescent is painted.

In the quiver, each arrow (fig. 54), identified by Zna'ote as SHAÚOLE', is shown with a red feather extending from a red shaft, where small fluffy, white plumes are tied on each side. Each feather has a large, elongated black spot on its left edge, outlined in a brighter tone of red. Along the opposite edge, there is a row of small black dots and some of the brighter red, like tiny buttons along a border. The rachis has three narrow, black bands paralleling the rounded extremity of the feather, which is tipped with white. These seem to represent hawk feathers.[419] The arrow to the right shows a red and a yellow feather at the shaft juncture, as well as the white plumes. A short, black projection at its right, distal end may belong to it or represent an unfeathered shaft, as suggested above.

Alongside the arrow farthest to the left, or east, is a five-pointed star painted in black, which Zna'ote indicated as MÓYA' CHUNᵉ. The two lower points of the star are tipped with red. Diagonally below the star, to the left and thus roughly paralleling the quiver flap, just where the wall is broken and the corner plaster warped, two feathers similar to those used for the arrows are shown. One points its quill downward, and the other upward and to the left—as though going out from the kiva at the southwest corner. An irregular red splotch occurs next, and finally an element not unlike the rain symbol shown coming from the heart of the serpent in Layer I-33, fig. 72, page 100.

We must look again to the dress of Figure 54. Scattered over it are small rectangular elements painted always in two colors, red or black alongside white. Twenty of these small

417. It was the source of considerable wonderment that no turquois color had been used in depicting the Kuaua ceremonies. Archaeological excavations in the Rio Grande drainage do not produce much in the way of turquois specimens until after A.D. 1300. It may be that the introduction of new cults into this region during the 14th century gave rise to the importance of turquois as a ceremonial requisite. Likewise, the blue-grey color here introduced in the paintings may indicate the initiation of a cult, or cults, hitherto unrepresented at Kuaua, in which turquois color was highly significant.

Stevenson has recorded that *blue* symbolizes Awonawilona, "the supreme life-giving power," and is the color of the Sun; again, that the blue-green [turquois] color symbolizes the vegetation of the world (Stevenson, 1904: 189, 537). Bunzel has commented that turquois, above all else, was the gift to the War gods at Zuñi (1932:669). Ladd says, "yellow is for the sun, blue for the moon"; he adds that turquois, mixed with cornmeal and shell, was the gift to all Zuñi gods.

418. *Cf.* Thompson, 1939:131, fig. 1a.

419. *Cf.* Stevenson, 1904:199.

figures occur, ten each of red and white and of black and white.[420] The bottom of the dress is deeply scalloped, with the sides flaring widely, thus giving the personage the appearance of a huge bird with spread wings, which indeed it is. It, the skirt, is representative of waves or water, and is thus a rain symbol; and by extension, of fertility. The moon is sometimes considered a water goddess, and she is associated with the flowers of the earth.[421] The legs are separated from the dress by black outlines, which continue down on either side of each leg.

When the identity of Figure 54 was disclosed, the painting became even more meaningful. Zna'ote knew this to be, A WOMAN, KíAʰ EK APA, THE CORN MOTHER, CORN FLAT. Furthermore, he said that, THE CORN MOTHER OF ZUÑI TODAY IS EXACTLY LIKE THIS. Of the mask, he pointed out the symbolism thus: YELLOW, POLLEN; BLACK—LIKE COAL BLACK, HA K'WINA [hakwin·e, black mineral pigment]; and RED—ÁHO·K'O [ahoko, red pigment—hematite].

Great as the Corn Mother is, this magnificent portrayal is even more. The macaw mask and form of the entire figure represent the Sky Father, whose all-seeing eye beholds everything that transpires. The scalloped skirt represents water and thus bespeaks rain necessary for the fructification of the earth, while the dun-colored garment itself symbolizes the Earth Mother. Phallic symbols which appear on the serpent-like quiver—which contains the arrows that shoot forth as lightning—indicate the union necessary for all reproduction; here, too, divisions of time as indicated by the Moon are symbolized. The crosses represent the Corn priests of Above; the star signifies the War gods. The heart symbolizes the "middle place," as well as the good and true. Corn is

symbolized and other seeds of vegetation. Feathers represent the birdlife, serving as messengers from this world to that of the Below and of the Above; while downy plumes symbolize the clouds of the world.

Blood bespeaks death, not as a permanent state but as a progressive step—fertilizing the earth and giving birth to new life. Animal tracks give heed to their importance in the scheme of things; they too are messengers; but above all the rabbit tracks symbolize happiness. The wrist ornaments denote strength, and the seashells wisdom. The black and white feather which crowns the head probably represents the Winter people, those who chose the raven eggs, rather than those of the macaw, which represents the Summer people. Tassels indicate the regions or directions of the world. And the single flower is likely the symbol of defloration.

Thus, in this one portrayal at Kuaua, we have the entire universe of the Indian before us, a graphic illustration of that which developed through the millennia from observations of natural phenomena, and the practice of agriculture.

One of the major themes of this entire painting is that of corn, the substance of life to the Indians. In Layer N-41, ten layers previous, abstractions have been given of tales which account for the Yellow Corn and Black Corn peoples, which have told of Paiyatuma's search for and return of the Corn maidens, and which have related Tenatsali and the Newekwe organization to the scene. Mr. Cushing wrote an entire book, many articles,[422] and recorded accounts on the subject of corn. He and Mrs. Stevenson[423] have told of its significance and

420. These are doubtless of calendrical significance, e.g., *see* Bunzel, 1932: 534-535 in re solstice ceremonies.

421. Ladd says this is not the case at Zuñi.

422. "Zuñi Breadstuff," *Indian notes and monographs,* vol. VIII, Museum of the American Indian, Heye Foundation, 1920; "Outlines of Zuñi Creation Myths," *13th Annual Report,* Bureau of American Ethnology, 1896; and others.

423. Stevenson. 1904:31-32, 48-49, *51-57,* 180-204, 277-283.

described the dances which celebrate its relationship to the Zuñi people—particularly the ʻHlahewe drama which was enacted every four years. Its main theme was that of rain and the growth of corn, with prayers made to Pautiwa, "that the sun may embrace the earth that she may be fruitful." This presentation was arranged by the first body of Rain priests, assembled in the house of Shiwanokia, the priestess of fecundity.[424] They decided who should perform the parts in the drama for which permanent actors were not provided.

Here, it should be stressed that there is nothing so precious to the American Indians as is corn, the seed of seeds. The extent to which they perceived its every aspect is an indication of their interpretation and symbolization of all life. The following quotation from Cushing is given as an illustration of the philosophy that lies back of the portrayals which we are considering:

> The Zuñi has observed that the corn plant is jointed; that its leaves spring from these joints not regularly, but spirally; that stripped of the leaves the stalk is found to be indented, not regularly at opposite sides, but also spirally; that the matured plant is characterized, as no other plant is, by two sets of seeds, the ears of corn springing out from it two-thirds down and the tassels of seeds, sometimes earlets, at the top; also that these tassels resemble the seed-spikes of the spring-grass or pigeon-grass; that the leaves themselves while like broad blades of grass are fluted like plumes, and that amongst the ears of corn ever and anon are found bunches of soot; and, finally, that the colors of the corn are as the colors of the world—seven in number.[425]

Cushing points out that, according to the Zuñi mind, nothing in this world or universe occurred by accident, rather, everything was initiated by a personal agency or supernatural. Thus, the Indian immediately begins to see, in these characteristics of corn, traces of his peoples of olden times, as recorded in his myths:

> Lo! men lived on grass seeds at first, but . . . there came a time when, by the potencies of the gods and the magic of his own priests or shamans, man modified the food of first men into the food of men's children. It needed only a youth and a maiden, continent and pure, to grasp at opposite sides and successively the blades of grass planted with plumes of supplication, and walking or dancing around them, holding them firmly to draw them upward until they had rapidly grown to the tallness of themselves, then to embrace them together. Behold! the grasses were jointed where grasped four times or six according to their tallness; yea, and marked with the thumb-marks of those who grasped them; twisted by their grasp while circling around them and leaved with plume-like blades and tasseled with grass-like spikes at the tops. More wonderful than all, where their persons had touched the plants at their middles, behold! new seed of human origin and productive of continued life has sprung forth in semblance of their parentage and draped with the very pile of their generation. For lo! that when the world was new all things in it were *k'yaiuna,* or formative, as now is the child in the mother's womb or the clay by the thoughts of the potter.[426]

Then it was held that in order that the corn seeds should not be lost, the deific ones should play their parts: Paiyatuma, the god of Dew and the Dawn, should freshen the newly made plants with his breath; Tenatsali (or Moon), the god of Time and the Seasons, should mature them instantly with his touch and breath; Kwelele, the god of Heat, should ripen them

---

424. Stevenson, 1904: 181, 188.
425. Cushing, 1896:376.

426. Cushing, 1896:377.

with the touch of his Fire brother's torch and "confirm to them the warmth of a life of their own."[426]

Also, it was recognized that, annually, the creation had to be repeated, "since man aided in the creation of the corn, so must he now ever aid in each new creation of the seed of seeds." The Indian sense of drama is as highly developed as is his philosophy. Thus it but follows that the yearly re-enactment of the drama of the origin of corn reproduced all details of the myth with scrupulous fidelity, giving the summer ceremonies while the corn seed was ripening.

Where such extensive symbolism and interrelationships exist among the characters with whom this painting is concerned, it seems astounding that our informants have retained so much ancient lore in their memory. Outwardly at least, the Corn drama has ceased among the Acoma and Laguna, yet much of its significance lived and died with our informant from the latter pueblo.[427]

In our Kuaua painting, the Singer (fig. 68) is relatable to the Sun through Paiyatuma. Nighttime Woman (fig. 67) has attributes of Tenatsali and the Moon, as regulator of the seasons and of time, and is recognizable as Blue Corn. Fire Man or Sunshine, relates to Shulawitsi bearing his torch (fig. 66). Meleyonako (fig. 65), as Yellow Corn, has attributes of the supreme life giver, and relates to the priestess of fecundity, Shiwanokia. Figure 64, as Kupishtaya, one of the lightning makers, appears here as the Sun priest's pekwinna.

Since these personages have reference to the very heart of the Indian philosophy of life, and embrace, in one way or another, everything which is known, it would be impossible to summarize this complicated ideology.

Because of the close relationship of subject matter here, and separation from similar cere-

monies, it appears most likely that Layers H[1]-32 and H-31 rightfully belong together.

Layers 30-27

After the great Corn drama with its ceremonies, dancing, and curing rites of Layer H-31, Kiva III appears to have been the scene of no other mural decorations for a time. Four plaster washes were applied over it, with no decorations on any of them.

If one layer of plaster was applied over the H-31 paintings upon completion of the ceremonies, as has been stated was the common procedure, it is possible that the succeeding sterile layers may indicate annual applications during the four-year interval which Mrs. Stevenson noted.

Layer G-26

When Layer G-26 was disclosed, it proved to have the most complete of all the paintings recovered—a complexity of figures from limit to limit. This, like H-31, had a black band, 14 inches wide, painted above the floor, thus indicating another very sacred portrayal. Above the black band was a separating white stripe, then one of yellow, a separator of adobe, one of red, and then a final white stripe; each of these stripes was $\frac{3}{8}$ of an inch wide. The black band, as was observed with Layer H-31, represents the earth. According to our Laguna informant, Lapajo, the yellow stripe represents ethereal or spiritual feeling; and the red symbolizes ethereal spirit higher than the yellow in order—the spiritual atmosphere next to the gods.

All but a few feet of the north wall remained, and at its easternmost limit an anthropomorphic figure appeared (fig. 63), unfortunately minus the head and whatever features existed from there to the corner. With this figure, the forepart of the body is painted yellow, with a red outline surrounding the belly and right leg which shows slightly. Inasmuch as the figure is headed toward the east, from what

427. *See* White, 1932:94-96, for Corn ceremony at Acoma.

would have been its mouth area (or similar source of some other depiction above), black dash-dots symbolic of moisture reach to the dado. Apparently held in the right hand of the being is a white stick, feathered toward the top with white plumes tipped with black (fig.63). This, Zna'ote identified as TE TLNANNA,[428] A STICK WITH SOME KIND OF FEATHERS. THE KIND OF A STICK THE OLD MEN USE FOR WALKING.

A tress of black hair hangs over the right shoulder, cut off squarely, just above a small rectangular heart symbol painted horizontally in white, red, and adobe color, from the upper part downward. From the back of the head, a white cord hangs pendant across the figure's side. It has two small white plumes on its right side and a white eagle feather with stepped black tip at its lower end. Recognizing this to be a headdress ornament, Zna'ote identified it as LÁSHUA, OR LASHOWAN[e].

Around the middle, or waist, of the figure is a large white sash, at the upper extreme of which fragments of white knots with red trim

428. This, says Ladd, refers to a special prayerstick; Pautiwa carries one.

may be seen. The sash allows a narrow margin to show toward the front—this and the rear of the animal are painted black as though representing a black kilt, following the natural lines of a quadruped, however. Two tiny teats are shown in the udder position. The being shows a white rump patch and short white tail tipped with black.

From these features, Zna'ote identified Figure 63 as a DEER [or antelope]. THE DEER HAS A HAT OR HEADDRESS. YELLOW MEANS DEER. And Lapajo recognized it as a supernatural, "the sacred deer, who helps to bring rain when properly invoked or propitiated." He said, also, "The one who invokes the deer usually gives it something sacred to him: corn meal, turquois, or coral, for example."

A fragmentary element, as though the butt end of a thrust arrow, shows a few inches above the rump of the deer, and directed toward it. This is feathered with black and white feathers, with one of red with black markings attached to a black shaft. Slanting diagonally toward the posterior of the animal is another portrayal of falling moisture, from some source

PL. XV. *Layer G-26.* A depiction of the Universe, with the major deific characters participating in weather control, planting rites, and hunting ceremonies. (*See also* color Pl. XVI following page 126.)

Fig. 106

Fig. 51   Fig. 52   Fig. 53   Fig. 107   Fig. 108   Fig. 109   Fig. 110   Fig. 111   Fig. 112

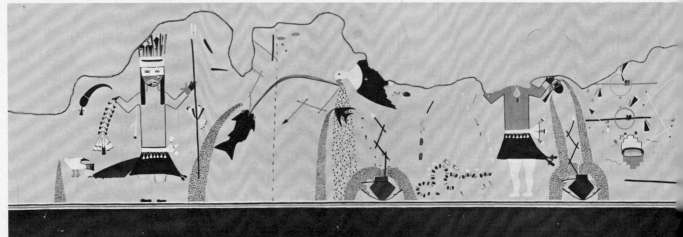

Figs. 50 and 62. Rain jar and bat, both accompanied by lightning arrows.

Fig. 63. Pautiwa manifest as a deer. *Layer G-26.*

. 113 Fig. 114 Fig. 115 Fig. 48 Fig. 49 Fig. 62 Fig. 50 Fig. 63

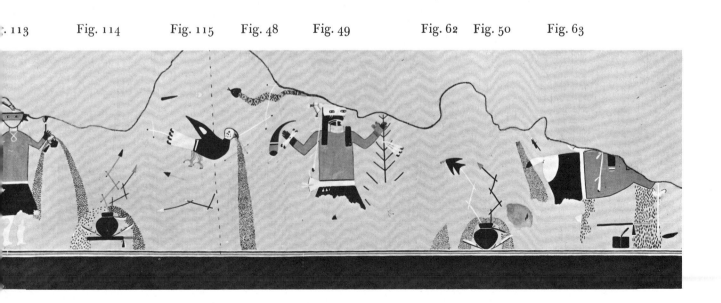

now unknown. Likewise, similar dash-dots appear below the belly of the deer. At the right limit of the latter, there is a remnant of some white object, with fine black decoration along its left edge—tiny black, horizontal dots.

Below the deer, between the object just described and the white staff, and parallel with the dado, is a rectangular item painted black, and tied around with white cord. White, red, and yellow form the tie above the item, where a black feather is attached. This, Zna'ote described as a STONE WITH A FEATHER, ÓLA KÍ ILA,[429] TOMAHAWK STONE.

Here, we have a sacred object or medicine bag which is associated with the Deer being.[430] Above the bag and horizontally placed is another shaft, painted black in its distal portion, and adobe color toward the fore, toward the white staff. Where the two colors join, a black feather with white tip is tied. This, said Zna'ote, is a PLANTING STICK, TSEMᵉ,[431] and he added: A LONG TIME AGO THIS STICK WAS USED FOR PLANTING. THE PICTURE WAS USED, MAYBE, BY SOME SHIWANNI, OR DANCE DOCTOR, TO MAKE PEOPLE WELL.

Ritual concerning the deer is most sacred with the Pueblo peoples. We find this especial-

ly developed among the Keresans as well as the Zuñi. Preceding each hunt, certain rites have to be performed. Stirling gives information from Acoma, in which it is recorded that when a deer is killed,

> . . . it is cut up where it falls; the legs are cut off and the ribs taken out. The head, the backbone, and the skin are all connected in one piece. When cut open, the entrails are placed to one side on the ground. The bladder is taken out and placed in the center of the entrails; the vulva or the penis and testicles are placed in the stomach;[432] and the hunter prays that the deer be reborn and that he will have good luck with game. He has corn meal and pollen and pieces of beads and shells which he sprinkles on.[433]

Stirling further records:

> When a hunter kills an antelope or a deer he brings it into the pueblo. The father or mother of the hunter's house comes out with some corn meal in her hand with which she makes a "road" into the house . . . . they help the hunter with his pack, and lay the deer on the floor with its head toward the fireplace . . . . Beads [and precious mantles] are laid on the neck. (Beads of lignite are preferred, as the hoofs of the deer are supposed to be made of this substance.) The deer would wear these back. They are taken away when they think the spirit has left, in about an hour. If relatives of the hunter come in, they go up to the deer and touch it and then rub their hands over their faces because they say the deer is pretty and not lazy. They say, "We are glad you have come to our home and have not been ashamed of our people." A dish of corn meal is placed near by and all visitors feed a little to the deer asking him to come next to their house, as they believe the deer will be reborn.

---

429. Mrs. Stevenson (1904:438) records that the Zuñi say there is an eagle (*Pósh kwa*) which has perfectly black plumage, and which, like the ordinary eagle (*kiakiali*) and the hawk (*pipi*), surprises the deer when grazing and kills him by striking him with his beak, first on one side of the jaw and then on the other. There is also the butcher bird (*súlulukia*) which is said to peck at the deer's head when he sleeps, and thus kills him. Another (*kiewia; Oreospiza chlorura*) kills the deer by pecking at his eyes.

Ladd gives *Póshi kwa*, golden eagle, and *Pa'k'o ha*, bald eagle; both are great hunters. He identifies "pipi" as the Red Tail hawk, which "is supposed to have killed nothing bigger than rabbits; the main diet is lizards." He says that *sulu'lu'kia* or Loggerhead shrike do not kill deer.

430. Ladd identifies this as a symbolic weapon of the Bow priests; later, a copy of the Plains Indian type of tomahawk. Stevenson, 1904:441, notes that the medicine bag of the hunters fraternity contained tenatsali. She says the bag was placed by the side of killed game.

431. Stevenson, 1904:177, gives *ᵗseme* as an ancient bean planter. Ladd says the word means any long stick.

---

432. White, 1942:294.

433. Stirling, 1942:22. With the Zuñi, says Ladd, "this offering is placed in a hole under the entrails, which are left for other animals to eat."

After this the deer is skinned. The head with horns attached is boiled in a pot, along with corn, pumpkin seeds, and piñon nuts.[434] Neither the hunter nor any man is supposed to eat the eyes of a deer, "lest he always have water in his eyes (tears) and not be able to see far."[435] Stirling adds:

> After the meat is all eaten from the head, it will be placed on top of the house to dry. When he has time, the hunter takes it back into the mountains where he prays that it will come alive again. First it must be painted as the deer was originally. A black line is painted down the middle of the face; under the jaw is white. Balls of cotton are stuffed in the eye sockets and the centers painted black. Then a string is tied across the antlers and to this feathers are attached. . . .

This is the way the first hunting society was made at Acoma.[436]

Upon viewing Figure 63, Zna'ote said: THE PICTURE WAS USED, MAYBE, BY SOME SHIWANNI, OR DANCE DOCTOR [Rain priest] TO MAKE PEOPLE WELL.[437]

From the facts at hand, we can partially reconstruct the features which were originally shown in the painting. Also, during the excavations at Kuaua, a fired clay figurine of a deer or antelope was unearthed. Its antlers are broken off, leaving the figure about six inches high. The head and back are painted yellow, and the belly white, similar to the kiva painting; the eyes are globular pellets of clay, like the stuffed eye sockets mentioned above. It may be suspected that the figurine had its place in the hunting rites. From the game animal dances which are currently performed in the pueblos during the winter season, one may derive further knowledge of the impersonators of the deer beings and of their costuming.

Inasmuch as Pautiwa assumes the form of a deer on occasion, just as did Sun Father, it may be assumed that the personage shown in Figure 63 is symbolic of that celestial body, and that the deer may be recognized as Pautiwa.

Behind Pautiwa and resting just above the dado is a black pottery vessel, globular, but somewhat pointed toward the base, where a pot rest is indicated, on either side of the jar. A yellow stripe extends down the center of the jar from neck to bottom (fig. 50). Zna'ote identified the vessel as TE'·ILI,[438] and the feature below it as a PILLOW, BÁ YAN.[439] PERHAPS A FEATHER. TÉ'·ILI [pot] KINA [wet] BÁ YAN. Thus we have a "feather pillow" or ceremonial pot rest. This is composed, apparently, of a black quill feather which projects upward at an angle of about 45 degrees on each side of the vessel, and which has white barbs along the upper side of the shaft, only. The one on the left has the barbs resting close to the vessel's base, that on the right has them directed away from it. On each, the two anterior barbs are painted red and yellow, respectively (or these colored elements may indicate ties). Around the high, slightly out-flaring neck a white cord is tied at the juncture with the body of the vessel. From the left side a black feather extends downward. This is secured to the pot with a small red and yellow tie, like those on the

---

434. These are called the deer's ear rings (Stirling, 1942:24).

435. Ladd says this is true for *all* animal eyes among the Zuñi.

436. Stirling, 1942:24, 29. *See also* White, 1942:292–295 (Santa Ana), and Stevenson, 1904:440–441 (Zuñi). Rodeck, 1954:117, in his study of the Durango, Colorado, animal and bird bones, notes the "tremendous predominance of deer bones in the collection," which he takes as indicating that venison was the principal meat diet. He also observes that paired bones were frequently found, but that certain skeletal parts were missing. From this he suggests the possibility that "animals usually were butchered in the field and the portions of the skeleton not wanted for the making of tools and ornaments left behind." This suggests that in the early days of our era, deer were not treated ceremoniously after the kill, in the north at least.

437. But *see* footnotes 405, 449, and 459, herein.

---

438. White, 1942:119, says that a Santa Ana informant called these Kuaua portrayals "Kaowata bowls."

439. *Cf.* Stevenson, 1894:82, 83, 103, 109.

feathers below it. At the right side of the vessel, the tie is of white. This feature Zna'ote described as a NECKTIE, DECORATION OR DESIGN, TÁ·KUNᵉ[ta·kunna]. On each side of the pot, black dots arise and curve downward from the mouth to the floor, passing behind the pillow.

From the jar's mouth, on the left, a crossed-stick motif in black arises to end in a yellow, triangular point, which Zna'ote recognized as an ARROWHEAD, TÍ MO·SHI. On the right, a similar white, lightning arrow, which he identified as WÍ LOLO NÁNᵉ, terminates in a large, black element in the shape of a projectile point with expanding-stem base, and from the point of which small black dots extrude (fig. 62). This is like the bats on Layer H¹-32:69—harbingers of rain. All of the black dotted features of the Pautiwa-jar complex were recognized by Zna'-ote as representing STEAM, SHÍ POLOLÓWE. EACH PLACE WHERE IT OCCURS IN THIS PICTURE, IT IS STEAM. IT MEANS, ALSO, THAT THE ARROW AND THE EAGLE [see below]—EVERYTHING—IS SENDING MESSAGES TO HELP BRING THE RAIN AND TO HELP THE SICK. LONG TIME AGO, EVERYTHING TALKED. THE ANIMALS DID NOT LIKE TO BE KILLED. THE GRASS DID NOT LIKE TO BE KILLED. THE ANIMALS' WHISKERS WERE ARROWS TO KEEP THEIR MOUTHS SHUT.[440]

"Shipololowe," or Shi pa·pulima, as we have seen previously, is the Place of Mist, where in the beginning "all was shipololo (fog), rising like steam," where Awonawilona, with the breath from his heart, created the clouds and the great waters of the world.[441] Mr. Cushing has given further explanation of the Zuñi concept of this phenomenon:

> The universe is supposed to have been generated from haze *(shi-wai-a)* produced by light (of the All-container, Sun-father) out of darkness. The observed analogy of this in nature is the appearance of haze (both

heat and steam) preceding growth in springtime; the appearance of the world, of growing and living things, through mist seemingly rising out of the darkness each morning. In harmony with this conception of the universe is the correlative one that every being (as to soul, at least) passes through many successive states of becoming, always beginning as a *shi-u-na ha-i* (haze being), and passing through the raw or soft *(k'ya-pi-na)*, the formative *(k'yai-yu-na)*, variable *(thlim-ni-na)*, fixed or done *(ak-na)*, and finished or dead *(a-shi-k'ya)* states; whilst the condition of the surpassing beings (gods) may be any of these at will *(i-thlim-na,* or *thlim-nah-na,* etc.). There are many analogies of this observed by the Zuñi, likening, as he does, the generation of being to that of fire with the fire-drill and stick. The most obvious of these is the appearance, in volumes, of "smoke-steam" or haze just previously to ignition, and its immediate disappearance with ignition. Further, the succession of beings in the becoming of a complete being may be regarded as an orderly personification of growth phenomena as observed in plants and seeds; for example, in corn, which is characterized by no fewer than thirteen mystic names, according to its stages of growth.[442]

Approaching the northwest corner we have a splendid personage (fig. 49; *see also* Pl. XVI, insert), erect and fore facing—this time with a face mask almost intact. The neck, trunk, and arms to the forearms are shown in yellow, outlined with red. About each forearm is a red band, and about each wrist a decorative element. That on the right shows two black-tipped, white eagle feathers arranged in V-notch form, KYÁ KALI KYÁ TEWE, ["eagle tail feathers"], according to Zna'ote, extending from each side of the wrist. At the center of the ornament there is a small, red oblong. On the left, the wristlet is painted yellow and shows two rounded elements projecting above, each

---

440. "Now," says Ladd, "the two War gods are responsible for animals at Zuñi not being able to talk."

441. Stevenson, 1904:23.

442. Cushing, 1901:400-401.

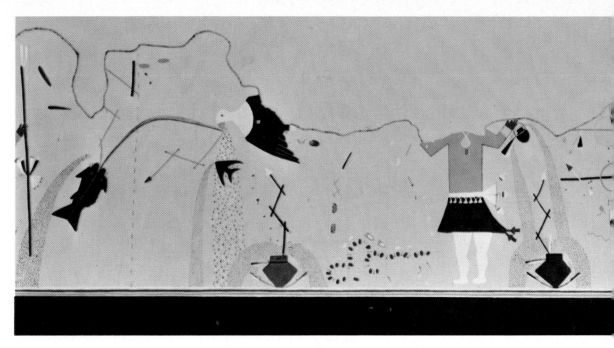

PL. XVI. *Layer G-26.* A depiction of the Universe.
Figures 48, 49, 53, 106-115. *See* Pl. XV.

PL. XXII. *Layers D¹-17 and D-14.* Autumn ceremony for fructification.
Figures 21, 23, 25-27, 28a, b, 58. *See* Pl. XXI.

Figs. 48 and 115. Rattlesnake and eagle, both messengers for bringing rain.

Fig. 49. Fire god, Shulawitsi. *Layer G-26.*

decorated with a red X. This, Zna'ote said, is SOME KIND OF SKIN BRACELET, KÉMPA-SIK WÍN [*kém pas si-kwi-we*—bowguard].

The face mask is painted white from its top to a line across the cheeks. Each of the eyes, consisting of two small, adjoining white squares, is outlined with black. Below each eye, thus extending down into the black, lower section of the mask, are two outward slanting diagonals, in white, like falling tears. The black portion is outlined with red, above and along each side, and is separated from the chin portion by an adobe stripe. Below this, the chin area is divided midway by a vertical white stripe which turns a near right angle and continues to the left extremity of the mask. Below the white, an adobe stripe extends parallel with it. The remainder of the mask, almost triangular in shape, is black. On the right side of the chin, a red stripe is shown in opposing position to the white one. Adobe follows this and parallels the vertical white line, leaving another triangular black area to complete the portrayal. Zna'ote said this black paint is

HAKWINA, mineral pigment. He identified the personage as PAIYATUMA.

Around the neck of this figure, eight white lines represent an ornamental necklace, which Zna'ote identified as BEADS, TAKUN[e]. From each side of the head, black tresses of hair, TÁYA AWE, as indicated by Zna'ote, hang over the shoulders, each cut off squarely on the lower end. About the forehead is a large white sash with red trim, tied on the right; there are prominent knots decorated with black cross elements, and large white tassels. This headdress, Zna'ote identified as OLTH PAN [headband—E.J.L.]. Extending from the back of the head and crossing over the right shoulder is a white cord with two white plumes attached on its right side, and a white, black-tipped turkey feather at the lower extreme. This is the same as the feather, LÁSHUA, which hangs pendant from the headdress of Pautiwa.

Tied around the waist by a large white sash, KÉMU KWIN—also secured on the right side—is a black kilt, PÍTHLAN [*pitlanna*], APRON, said Zna'ote, decorated with a red border at the bottom. The sash has red decoration at each end; the tassels are white. Suspended from the sash, across the front of the figure, are small white triangular elements, recognizable as conch shell tinklers.

On the left side of Figure 49, there stands a tree, TSÍ TON [*tsitónna*] said Zna'ote; it is obviously a conifer [spruce or piñon—E.J.L.], painted in red. A few inches down from the top, three white eagle feathers with the characteristic black tips are tied with a white knot. The similarity of this to the tree shown in Layer O-43, fig. 61 (p. 54), indicates that this personage assumed attributes of Shulawitsi, the Fire god. To the right of the extended fingers of his right hand there is a horn-shaped element identified by Zna'ote as a gourd or SHÓ PA'—LIKE A PUMPKIN, which he said, WAS USED TO HOLD WILD TOBACCO. The author believes this to represent the torch of Shulawitsi. It is painted red, with the larger end decorated: an adobe stripe uppermost, then one of white and one of black; the head of the object yellow, with a rounded black portion at the extremity. At the center of the head, two small white feathers with fine, black cross marking and tips are tied—UKYA HAYÁWE, LITTLE WHITE TAIL FEATHERS, according to Zna'ote [down feathers—E.J.L.].

With its yellow-tipped tail showing above and to the right of Shulawitsi's headdress, at the eroded limit of the wall, is a serpent 26 inches long (fig. 48). Its heart-shaped head, painted red and outlined with black, reaches to within two inches of the northwest corner of the chamber. There are two small, white eyes, with a black crescent between them and the mouth, from which a short black, forked tongue projects. The serpent's body, in zig-zag position, parallel with the floor, is painted with a thin greyish wash, across which black lines form diamonds and triangles from end to end; these are embellished with black crescents, each with a black dot at the center [thus appearing as an eye representation]. At the

posterior end there are five crossing stripes in grey and black which separate the body from the tail tip. This decoration of the serpent is the same as that of the quiver associated with Figure 54, Layer H-31, and has the same phallic significance.[443] Zna'ote identified the serpent as a RATTLESNAKE, 'CHÍ TOL[a].

Extending downward from the upper limit of the chamber wall and bisecting the serpent is a crossed-lightning element of white with black tips. As we have seen previously, the serpent is associated with rain bringing. Lapajo says, "Snake signs are lightning symbols, messengers of the gods—the Rain god." This figure appears to represent the serpent of the earth as a messenger for rain bringing from the Below. The crossed lightning continues downward to the right, joining another crossed lightning depiction in adobe with red tips (fig. 115), at the mouth of an eagle which is painted partially on the north and partially on the west wall.

Here, Zna'ote explained that the lightning with Figure 48 represents SMOKE LIGHTNING, and that with Figure 115 represents CLOUD LIGHTNING—both of which he called PÓNE E WI [cigarette—usually cane or cornhusks—E.J.L.]. He said: EAGLE WANTS TO HELP THE PEOPLE, TÉKOHANAN-SHÉME-A ["asking for life"—E. J. L.]. SORT OF TELEGRAM GOING OUT OF HIS MOUTH TO HELP THE MAN. IT IS CALLING EVERYBODY. YELLOW, BLUE, RED, WHITE, PINTO, AND BLACK ARE DIFFERENT KINDS OF LIGHTNING.

Black dots indicative of falling moisture extend from the eagle's mouth to the dado. The eagle, then, appears to represent a messenger for bringing rain from the Above. Zna'ote said, the eagle, KYÁ KALI [*kiakiali*], IS GOING TO HELP THE MAN, PAIYATUMA.

The eagle has a black body with white patch on the underside of the upraised wing, and a

---

443. Stevenson, 1894:69, says that at Zia (Sia), two of the Snake cults, the *káspanna* of the West and the *quissera* of the East, hold esoteric relations with the sun and moon; their bodies are painted with crescents.

white band around the rear, just before the tail, which shows four long white feathers with the usual stepped, end marking in black. Legs and beak are yellow, the latter outlined with black; the legs have tiny white and black markings, like fuzz, down each side; each claw is tipped with a black nail. White marks indicate down along the eagle's breast and at the crest of the white head which, like the beak, is outlined with black. The eye is yellow outlined with black and with black pupil. Six black dashes show further head markings.

Projecting backward from the eagle tail is white lightning with black tips, seeming to indicate that the lightning passed through this bird as it did through the serpent (Pl. XV, figs. 48, 115). It was identified as SÉ-WIK-SHI, by Zna'ote. Above the eagle tail is a single red hawk feather with white tip and Y-shaped point, directed toward the corner and toward a white track-like element in the form of a rounded triangle with three scallops at its back, close to which two small white dots occur (fig. 115). Zna'ote recognized the hawk feather as an ARROWHEAD, TIMO·SHI, and the other feature as SOME KIND OF TRACKS, TÉ-ANAN[e].

Below the eagle, on the west wall, is an adobe colored shaft with large red point directed upward and toward the right, which Zna'ote identified as a HUNTING ARROW. USED TO KILL SOMETHING—STRAIGHT ARROW, SHAÚOLE'. Below this is another crossed lightning element with red shafts and white tips and point, which Zna'ote recognized as LIGHTNING, WI-LOLO-NAN[e].

To the right, 31 inches from the northwest corner, is another assemblage of features (fig. 114), similar to Figure 50: a black globular jar with a yellow stripe extending, from a white cord which is tied about the neck of the vessel, to the base; a white feather with black quill extends to the left of the jar neck, with short, slanting features, one of black directed toward the jar about midway of the quill, and one of

Fig. 113. Yellow Corn maiden or Kochininako.
Fig. 114. Water jar from which snow and rain emanate and below which are a feathered pad and planting stick. *Layer G-26.*

yellow directed away from the jar at the neck. There is the same pot rest motif of Figure 50, though the feathers are in reversed positions—like the neck feather, with black quill above and white barbs below; and in addition to the small red and yellow motifs at the juncture of barb and quill, midway of the latter, a black and white element is directed toward the jar, on each side. Rather than resting on the dado, this vessel rests on a planting stick, like that shown in Figure 63, page 123. It has a black hilt and yellow blade. At the junction of these colors, a black and white feather is pendant from the implement, tied with white cord with knot above, and the red and yellow ornament below. The planting stick is parallel with the dado and three inches above it; it measures 16.25 inches in length.

From the mouth of the jar, toward the left, black moisture drops—again recognized as steam by Zna'ote—rise upward and curve gracefully to the dado; to the left, similarly, white dash-dots are thickly interspersed with black ones, and identified as SNOW SMOKE, ÓPI NÁWE, by Zna'ote. On the left, a red criss-cross lightning element, with yellow tips and a large yellow point, extends upward toward the eagle tail; on the right, one of yellow, with black tips and large black point, roughly parallels its direction. Both are identified as representing lightning.

There next appears, about one-third of the way southward on the west wall, another fine personage in almost complete detail, with feet slightly above the dado. This figure also wears a face mask (fig. 113). The mask is shown with a narrow black stripe across the flat top, below which is a yellow band that extends to the cheeks. The eyes appear about midway of this band, and each consists of a central black square, bounded on each side by a white square outlined with black. The yellow band is separated from the adobe colored chin section by a narrow black stripe; and black outlines the adobe portion. The yellow paint, Zna'ote knew as ÓNE-AYE. At each side of the head, the hair is done up in spool-shaped whorls, through which three narrow bands of small, red dots indicate decorations. Of this, Zna'ote said: HAIR, MÁ-TSI-KWÁ-WE. LIKE THE HOPI. ZUÑI WOMEN WORE HAIR LIKE THIS FOR RAIN DANCES [hair puffed out in whorls on each side].[444]

At the juncture of the hair and each side of the face, a rounded feature is shown in red, and from this two parallel, white pendants hang down on each side, representing ear ornaments: SHELL PENDANT, KÓHA-KWA SÁTO·WE, or white shell ear loops, as observed by Zna'ote.

Above the head a feathered headdress is shown, consisting of white feathers and tie, from which a small rectangular element in red and yellow stands centrally erect. To the right of this, white barbs of a feather reach downward from a long black quill, and above it other feathers are indistinct due to the wall's erosion.

The personage's body and upraised arms are painted in yellow, outlined with black. The hands with extended fingers are red. Zna'-ote said: RED FINGERS, ÁSI SHÍLOA [red hands]. About the neck is a five-strand bead necklace, with lowest strand hanging pendant in the form of a figure 8 on the chest.

From the left hand, a black shafted, feathered prayerstick is shown, as held erect. The feathers are of white, black, red, and adobe colors, and show the small red and yellow element at the tie. Zna'ote referred to this as the SAME AS THAT HELD BY FIGURE 63, TLESH NANᵉ. Hooked over the little finger by a narrow thong is a small, black pottery vessel. This has a sharp shoulder with pierced lugs on opposed sides, rather pointed bottom, and a relatively high, outflared neck. To the right lug, a black and white feather is tied. From the mouth of the vessel, which Zna'ote called a POT, MÉ HE TO [canteen], black moisture drops rise and curve downward. Those on the left coalesce with the snow and rain drops from Figure 114; those on the right pass back of Figure 113 and end in the distortion of the plaster at that point. As though held in the right hand, is a long yellow stick with the same feathered decoration as appears on the headdress. Two tiny white dots are shown near the tie.

The personage wears a black skirt secured by a narrow, white sash which has large, white knots decorated with red and black, and red tassels, tied on the right side. This, Zna'ote remarked, is a BIG BELT, PAÚ TAWE, LIKE RIO GRANDE CORN DANCE BELT. The skirt has a red border at the bottom and up a few inches on the right side, from the lower corner of which large red tassels and black and red fringes extend. The figure has white legs and feet, of which Zna'ote said: PAINTED WHITE LEG, SÁ KWI KÓHAN. He identified this personage as the FIRST SISTER, KOCHININAKO,[445] thus the Yellow Corn maiden.

444. Stevenson, 1904:197, says that Zuñi girls' hair is put up on whorls for ᵗHláhewe dance.

445. Ladd says this "simply means woman, or women; it is not a Zuñi word."

Near the sash tassels, two red hand prints occur, one with fingers extended toward each tassel (Pl. XVI, fig. 113). Zna'ote recognized these as RED TRACKS, ASI TE·ANAN[e]. Directed downward from the tassels are two white elements, like footprints. A few inches upward and southward from the handprints is a small white dot. Above it, pointing upward and to the right, is a white feather with black tip and Y-shaped point (like fig. 115), obviously carrying a message upward, as does its likeness, seen a few inches above it, and approaching a black X, which denotes the gods of War.

Layer G-26 brings a new feature to view (fig. 112). Here, in the center of the west wall, 28 inches above the floor, a greyish ellipsoid was introduced, two inches high and eight inches across. Above and below it, terraced altar designs were placed—a white one outlined with black as the upper, and a yellow one as the lower. Four layers of sterile plaster were put on after Layer H-31 was painted and before Layer G-26 was applied. The laboratory notes state that there was no indication of a niche in connection with Layer H-31, or the ones preceding it. However, the common practice of sealing over such sacred features might have permitted the plastering for Layer H-31 to obliterate the evidence of such a small compartment;[446] and the following sterile layers would have further hidden it. There was no indication that the ellipsoid feature, or cavity, had any overt connection with Layer H-31. However, since this cavity was found to extend back into the kiva wall for a depth of twelve inches, it probably was a feature of the original building, which was sealed over when not in use for particular ceremonies.

The niche[447] was identified by Zna'ote as a

HOLE IN THE WALL, HÉ MO KWAN[e]—LIKE A WINDOW; the decoration below it as a YELLOW CLOUD, A·WE TLÚYAN TLÚ SIN·NA; and that above as a WHITE CLOUD, A·WE TLÚYAN KÓHAN. Inasmuch as this Kuaua chamber did not have a small hole in the floor, symbolizing the "sipapu" or place of emergence, it appears that this wall niche represents a similar concept, thus signifying the entrance to the undermost world. Mrs. Stevenson remarks that the "Water moss world" is next above the undermost, and "if the door be opened, the rainmakers may come from there and be present" in the kiva.[448] This katsina niche, then, relates closely with the doorway mentioned in Layer I-33, in connection with the myth of the serpent, Kolowisi, and the daughter of the Rain priest.

From the left side of the white altar above the niche, a long white lightning element in four sections, with black tips on the crossing shafts, extends upward, passing the black X on the right of Kochininako (see Pls. XV and XVI). Near its emergence from the altar, a narrow, wavy red line extends for a few inches behind it. In the position opposed to that of the white lightning is a short yellow shaft with a small terrace outlined in red at its upper extreme. A short yellow line undulates as does the opposing red one. A similar yellow zig-zag is shown below and to the right of the yellow altar, now at least detached from any other feature. All of these, Zna'ote identified as LIGHTNING.

To the left and right, just above the white altar is a small, rounded, black animal track showing three curved claw prints with crossing bar through the center. Between the right track and the small terraced element are three short segments of crossed lightning in red.

Slightly to the right and just above the white

---

446. The laboratory notes do mention a plaster patch that destroyed part of the figure (H-31:65) which was painted over the position of the niche.

447. Roberts, 1932:78 ff., found similar "katsina niches" in kivas in the Nutria area, east of Zuñi pueblo. All were well smoothed and plastered; one had decorations around it.

448. Stevenson, 1904:146. Ladd refutes this. He gives the order thus: Top—Earth; (1) *Ti k'o ha*, (2) *Sula hayan Tiletonna*, (3) *A wisho-Tiletonna*, (4) *Anosia Tiletonna*; Bottom—South Room Darkness. *See* footnote 137, page 42.

Fig. 110. Blue Corn maiden, or Meleyonako, carrying a small vessel from which moisture streams toward Fig. 111, a black water jar. At the left, Fig. 112 includes two hoop and stick sets of the kick stick game, shown above the katsina niche with altar designs and lightning arrows. *Layer G-26.*

altar is a yellow circlet with a black stick, 22.5 inches in length, passing horizontally behind its center. A large black feather with white tip and plume and a narrow grey feather with fine black cross markings are tied with white cord toward the anterior portion of the stick, and, likewise, to the upper left side of the hoop. Crossing the distal end of the stick is a white arrow shaft with large red point of the hunting type. Between this and the hoop are two small red tracks of the same form as the black ones above described; three small black dots; and a triangular element in white. Within the circlet, three short black markings are featured with the shaft.

Above the yellow hoop and again slightly to the right a similar assemblage is portrayed, differing only in opposed placement of the shaft, which is painted yellow with three red marks behind it, within the circlet painted of the decayed color, and that a small black feather is tied with the others at the top of the hoop. Close to the anterior end of the stick, two yellow tracks with black nails are shown, like the red and black ones lower on the painting. However, Zna'ote identified these yellow "tracks" as representing YELLOW STAR, MO YA-'CHUNᵉ TLU·P OSIN·NA. This may indicate that red and black ones have similar celestial significance. Between the hoops and close to each is one elongated red dot.

Here we have the same features as occurred on Layer M-40 (page 76), relating to the kick stick game, shown in association with a katsina niche. Of the latter, Lapajo said that it represents "the earth complete," *ha·shi'*. Then, referring to the hoop-stick symbolization, he said: "The upper round figure denotes life, health, sound reasoning, and everything that is good in right living on the earth. Everything must be held with the greatest veneration and reverence to it; it occurs in the most sacred ceremonies of the Pueblos. The central idea is reverence and right living." In addition to the information given with Layer M-40, Zna'ote said of the hoops: ROUND, TSÍ KO OWE. TIED TO THE STICK; and he added: USED IN CURING CEREMONIES BY THE SHIWANNI.[449] ASHIWANNI HAVE WHITE LEGS.

Kick stick races are of religious character, as we have seen previously, and have two mani-

449. Ladd observes that there would be no curing by the Shiwanni unless he should hold an office in a curing society, and he says that they do not use hoops.

festations at Zuñi, one in which members of the kiva groups participate, and one in which the clans take part. Mrs. Stevenson says: "Both . . . are for rain to water the earth that the crops may grow. They take place some days previous to corn planting . . . . These religious games must precede the betting games of Tíkwawe . . . ."[450] From further information which she gives, we may gather that the upper hoop and stick shown in our painting pertain to the older War god, and the lower set to the younger War god. At Zuñi, the religious enactments are carried out by members of the kiva groups, whose director general is preferably a man of the Deer clan. Six days prior to a race, the Bow priesthood convenes and remains in session all night. The next morning they prepare prayer plumes to the War gods and to the deceased members of the Bow priesthood. Representatives from each kiva take part in the race, three siding with the elder and three with the younger War god.

From the right side of the niche, about midway between that and the dado, a similar, but unadorned, black stick slants downward to the left, toward Figure 113, Kochininako. Our informants made no mention of it.

Near the complex just described, on the right, another of the water jar units is portrayed (fig. 111). Here the all-black vessel is sharp shouldered and has a definitely pointed base. It rests on a feathered "pillow" which shows the barbs in almost equal proportions of black and white, long black quills, and a short black and white projection from the upper edge directed toward the jar on each side. Tied around the straight sided neck, on the right, is a similarly depicted feather. From the vessel mouth, wide bands of black moisture drops curve to the dado, and a long black, four-sectioned lightning arrow with white point rises at the right side, while a short, two-section segment of white lightning rises along its left side.

Standing close to the right of this unit is

another personage, lacking the head and lower right arm (fig. 110). The body and arms are painted yellow, outlined with black. Around the left wrist is an eight-strand ornament, doubtless representing white beads. The red hand with fingers extended holds the thong of a small, high shouldered globular jar. Around the shoulder is a white tie to which a black and white feather is secured on the right, with a white knot on the left. From this vessel, long streams of black dots pour forth on opposite sides and reach downward to unite with the moisture dots from the large, basal jar resting above the dado (fig. 111).

On the chest of the personage, a strand of white beads supports a shell-shaped pendant which is painted in the decayed color, outlined with white. Just below this, in the position of the heart, is a small, rectangular element painted from right to left in red, yellow, black, and white vertical stripes. The figure wears a black skirt with red border at bottom, large red tassels with red and black fringes projecting on the left side, and with red cross-stitching showing for several inches up on the side. The skirt is held in place by a white sash, likewise tied on the left. The sash ends are decorated with a red border, white knots crisscrossed with black, separated from the large white tassels by red bands, and white fringes pendant from the tassels. In each instance, three fringes show rather than the usual four. From the sash, seven triangular features hang pendant, representing conch shell tinklers. This, again, is the big Rio Grande type of dance sash used in rain ceremonies.

The legs and feet of this being, which rest a few inches above the dado, are painted entirely in white. Zna'ote identified the personage as the SECOND SISTER, MELEYONAKO.[451]

For a considerable distance to the right of Meleyonako, the wall is covered with a variety

450. Stevenson, 1904:318.

451. Ladd does not believe that Meleyonako is a Zuñi word, although he admits the possibility that it might be ancient Zuñi; he favors a Keresan origin.

of features (fig. 109 and Pl. XVI), pointed feathers and arrows, lightning motifs, tracks of several kinds and in differing colors, and a configuration of tiny, red, jar-shaped units interspersed with pointed arrows. Two of the tracks shown in yellow, with black nails on each of the five toes, and with a white footprint in the mid-part of each foot—like a continuation of a path of other white prints—were identified by Zna'ote as BEAR TRACKS, AÍNSHAN TE·ANAN[e]; and below them he recognized RED ARROW POINTS AND STONES.

Mrs. Stevenson tells of the race [*tikwane*] which is an important part of the kick stick game. The Rain priest instructs[452] each runner as to the course he is to follow. She says:

> One of two mesas must be ascended at this time; there are rock markings on each. The man never begins to run until he is a half mile or more from the village and on his return always stops running about the same distance from the town so that the people may not suspect him of starting or returning from a run. The mesa north of the village to which the runner resorts was the one visited by the writer. A rocky, picturesque trail leads to the mesa top. A few feet below the summit there is a stone heap 6 to 7 feet high and fully 15 feet at the base, and just before reaching this spot the runner takes a small stone in each hand; he expectorates on the one in the left hand and carries it two, three, or four times around his head from left to right or the reverse and throws it upon the stone heap that he may be rid of his tired breath so that he can start the run with new breath and not lose it.
>
> There is an exposure of rock surface 125 by 60 feet about half a mile north of the stone heap on the summit of the mesa. A running course is cut or worn upon the surface of the rock. The course has six loops, symbolizing cumulus clouds of the six regions. All but one of these loops are to the east; the first one winds to the west. The distance between the first two loops is 24 feet; between each succeeding two 12 feet. The line extends 6 feet beyond the last loop, making a total distance measured in a straight line of 78 feet. A second stone heap stands a short distance beyond the line. The stone carried in the right hand is deposited on the near end of the line and is pushed over the course beneath the right foot. As the man must move rapidly and the stone can not be restarted when once it gets from under his control, not infrequently the stone is left behind, in which case it is moved with the foot a short distance off the line to make room for other stones and runners, where it must remain until the runner makes another attempt at passing over his "luck line," as this marking is called, for one is never sure of success until one has carried one's stone to the end of the line with one's foot and cast it upon the second stone heap. When this has been accomplished a man may be sure of winning the race or may risk high wagers on the races, as he has gone over his luck line to the end; but when he has passed with his stone only partly over the line, he is very cautious in betting. The run continues across the mesa to a shrine where prayers are offered and meal mixed with crushed turquoise, kóhakwa, and abalone shell is sprinkled to the Gods of War for good luck in the race.[453] Then he runs, down the mesa over a regular course directed by the rain priest over the Ojo Caliente road and around to the south and back to Zuñi, the distance covered being about 25 miles.[454]

It would seem that the Kuaua representa-

---

453. It was probably a shrine of this nature which Espejo observed in 1583, as mentioned on page 10 herein.

454. Stevenson, 1904:323-324; *see* for further details. Ladd tells us that: "This shrine is on the trail to the peach orchards, above the CAA power station. As youngsters, we used it, but not for the purpose described above. The Rain priest has no power over this shrine, and no specific person has the exclusive right to use it; any one traveling the trail may use it. It has some connection with a god called *Ólolowishka*. When one uses this shrine, there is a specific little chant that goes with pushing the rock through the game."

Fig. 106. Eagle spewing forth all kinds of seeds, rainbow and lightning.
Fig. 107. Bat or winged arrow point.
Fig. 108. Blue water jar with moisture and lightning.
Fig. 109. Footprints, arrow points, and stones. *Layer G-26.*

tions of this complex involve similar running along a prescribed course, with stone piles, directions, and ceremonial symbols indicated.

To the right of the racing depiction there is a fourth water jar complex, showing another pointed bottom vessel (fig. 108), but this time painted in the blue-grey color which was introduced on Layer H-31 for the quiver of Figure 54. Likewise, the feathers of the underlying pot rest, which adjoins the dado, are shown with grey-blue quills, from which white barbs project downward. Both quills have tiny white and black units pointing toward the vessel, and the right quill shows a slim, red element erect before the white and black unit. Around the straight sided neck of the jar is a black cord securing a black and white feather on the right. This, too, has the tiny white and black projection directed toward the vessel, and a similar, yellow and red element directed from the vessel at the tie. A single, four-section black lightning arrow with white point stands erect in the jar, from the mouth of which black moisture dots flow downward to each side, to

the dado. Thin, short dashes of red are shown about the jar neck and about its mouth, rising along the black shaft of lightning. There is also a row of widely spaced black dots which extend upward from the jar alongside the arrow on its right, ending in two dots side by side.

The black lightning arrow is pointed toward a large black eagle (fig. 106), the white head of which reaches to within 18.25 inches of the southwest corner of the chamber; the lower wing tip is 28.25 inches above the dado. The eagle is in frontal, horizontal position, with all-black wing feathers extended toward Meleyonako (fig. 110). A fragment of white shows at the rear, with a spot of yellow which indicates a leg, and two long, slender claws with black nails are seen. Outstretched toward the latter is a red hand. In the heart position, a small rectangular element is painted from top to bottom in adobe, red, yellow, and white bands. The two-part beak and the eye are painted in yellow, the latter outlined with black and showing a black pupil.

This eagle is the center of a multi-featured

complex. Streaming downward from its bill is a great flow of dash-dots in white, red, yellow, and black, which reach to the black moisture dots on the right of the grey-blue vessel, and to the dado. In these, Zna'ote recognized ALL KINDS OF SEEDS, TÁU SHAU WE. EAGLE WANTS TO MAKE GOOD CORN; CALLS LIGHTNING; WANTS TO MAKE A RAINBOW; TELLS FISH[455] TO MAKE A RAINBOW. FISH HAS ALL COLORS LIKE A RAINBOW. This eagle, Zna'ote added, BELONGS TO MELEYONAKO. HE WANTS ALL TO HAVE SOMETHING.

The rainbow, or AMITOLAN͏ᵉ, as Zna'ote mentioned, arcs from the mouth of the eagle down across the southwest corner of the chamber onto the south wall and enters the mouth of a large black fish (Pls. XV and XVI, figs. 106 and 53). The rainbow is painted with a narrow red line, above which is a much wider band of less intense red—rather blurred. Also projecting from the mouth of the eagle is a three-sectioned, yellow lightning symbol, with large red point and red tips at the crossed ends of the shafts. A few inches below the eagle's beak, a winged black creature (fig. 107) overlies the multi-colored seeds, in flight position, rising toward the yellow lightning. It has a tiny, clawed limb at each side of the body. From the foremost point of the figure, black moisture drops extrude to the dado. This, like Figure 62, was identified as an ARROWHEAD, or TI MO·SHI, by Zna'ote. Its living aspects relate it to the similarly portrayed bats, which are recognized as rain bringers.

At the uppermost limit of the wall, directed toward the corner, are two yellow footprints and below these, two red dots. Just beyond these, on the south wall, a black vertical shaft crosses over a diagonal yellow one. Below these, crossed yellow lightning zig-zags into the mouth of the fish (fig. 53), which is entirely

on the south wall, 14 inches above the dado. From its union with the rainbow, a thin yellow line extends through the fish to the caudal fin. Crossing this at midsection is a thin red line which curves as a loose S from the left side of the fish and ends short of the tail (see Pl. XVI). Pectoral and ventral fins are shown, though the latter is missing on the left. The eyes are indicated by yellow circles. From each side of the mouth, barbels project forward around the curved lips. To the right, black moisture drops arc to the dado. Zna'ote spoke of this fish as KA·SHITA, ANY KIND OF FISH. Mrs. Stevenson gives *káshita 'siponipon*[456] as a "fish with bearded mouth," which well describes our fish.

We have, next, another fine personage who commands the south wall toward the southwest corner (fig. 52). Again it is nearly complete, lacking only most of the right hand, and the lower part of the legs. Body, upraised arms, and legs are shown in adobe color, outlined with red. About the left wrist is a yellow wristlet with a wide V element at the top and an element of the same color showing above and parallel with the wrist for a few inches. The red hand holds vertically a black staff, 50 inches long. Its upper end is decorated with two white feathers, which reach nearly to the limit of the wall; its lower extreme reaches into the moisture drops emanating from the fish. A few inches below the hand, a cluster of white feathers with black tips and black feathers with white tips is tied around the staff.

The personage wears a face mask and elaborate headdress, called LA PAK TON [war bonnet] by Zna'ote. The headdress shows a wide white band, or sash, around the crown of the head—set off from the mask by a thin black line; across the front of it is a red stripe. Above the flat top, a variety of feathers stands erect: black and white, white with black, yellow, yellow with black tip, red with white and black,

---

455. Ladd tells us that fish never were as important in ceremonies at Zuñi as were frogs and tadpoles. It is his opinion that this fish is purely of Rio Grande origin and interpretation . . . as are the subsequent fish depictions.

456. Ladd translates *'siponipon* as "whiskers," and identifies this as "catfish."

Fig. 51. Goose or Owa.
Fig. 52. Lightning Man or
Kupishtaya.
Fig. 53. Fish. *Layer G-26.*

red and adobe, white, red with black and white markings, black, and red with white. Among these, eagle and hawk feathers are recognized.

The mask is painted white from forehead to cheeks, with eyes indicated in black as two adjoining circles, or figure 8 on its side. Below each eye, overlying the thin red line, which separates the white section from the yellow cheek portion, and the yellow paint, are two tiny white feathers with black tips which represent tears (*see* Pls. XVI and B-6). The remainder of the mask is outlined in red; the chin is decorated in the same manner as that of Figure 49, but with a differing color arrangement. Here the separating stripe is of adobe color, below which on the left is a red and white stripe, with the lower part in yellow; on the right, there is a yellow line below the adobe outline, an adobe stripe, and the lower part in black; a vertical white line separates the black and yellow sections of the chin.

Black lines at each side of the head emerge as tresses of hair which fall over the shoulders and are cut off squarely at the bottom. Seen

as pendant from the back of the headdress, and showing below the right armpit, is a white feather with black tip, tied to a long white cord, again a LASHOWAN[e], according to Zna'ote.

From the right wrist a beautiful feathered ornament hangs pendant on a white cord. Near the wrist, two small, triangular, black feathers with red quills are tied on opposite sides. Below these are seven larger feathers of the same form and position. At the lower end of the cord is a cluster of white plumes showing fine black tips or bands; with these is one red feather with white tip. This ornament was recognized by Zna'ote as BÍTSI ME, COTTON STRING WITH LITTLE BLACK AND WHITE FEATHERS.

The personage wears a black kilt bordered with red at the bottom, with tassels of red knots, black cord, and three fringes, and red stitching on the left side. The kilt is held in place by a white sash which allows a narrow margin of black to show above it. The ends— which tie to the left—have white tassels and four-string fringes, attached to the belt with red knots. From the sash, seven conch shell tinklers are hung.

The legs of this figure show red outline or a red fringe—the latter being plain on the right of each calf. Smudges of black indicate the feet, just above the dado.

Back of the personage, which Zna'ote recognized as A MAN, KÚPISHTAYA[457] [thus a lightning maker]; ALSO A SHIWANNI, is a large triangular splotch of red, which he identified as a TAIL PIECE, PROBABLY PAINTED BUCKSKIN, KÉM SHE LOA.

To the right of this red element is a waterfowl (fig. 51). Its head, body, and raised wing are white; the top of the latter is black. Around the neck are fine black markings. Beak, eye—outlined with black, and with black pupil—legs and claws, and undertail are shown in yellow. Back of the yellow portion of the tail is a scalloped black band, followed by white, a larger area of black, and ending in three white scallops. From the wing tip a black outline surrounds the tail, excepting the white scallops. Toenails are painted black. From one claw and the anus region, three fine-line shafts project on a downward slant, one parallel to the other; one, two, or three small branching elements are indicated. From the mouth of the fowl—identified by Zna'ote as ÓWA, the goose—black moisture drops sweep downward to the dado.

Near the right hand of Kupishtaya, as with Figure 49, is a handsomely decorated object, seemingly a lightning stick or torch. The curved portion is painted red; the head, black. The juncture between these colors is banded from tip to head thus: black, red, yellow, and red with a border design of pendant triangles over the black. At the head of the implement, white, white with black tips, and a black feather with white tip are tied. This completes the paintings of Layer G-26.

Because this was the most complete of all the plaster layers recovered from Kiva III at Kuaua, it was thought that it might bring forth explanations readily. Apparently, however, we chose one of the most comprehensive and significant of all the ceremonial representations. This was undoubtedly unfortunate insofar as our Laguna sage, Lapajo, was concerned. When we questioned him as to a probable dating of the Kuaua paintings, we were quite unprepared for his answer: "The date of the murals is after the beginning of creation, after Shipap', because the people were told when they emerged that they were to practice these things." Under what circumstances would such paintings be made? "The occasion for painting the murals would be the performance of rituals in the kivas; masked dances. All dances are prayers for rain, for life."[458] Who would have made these paintings? "One or two who have been initiated do the painting. No other man can come and say 'I'll paint the sacred green'—only those designated."

Lapajo explained further: "This is one of the most sacred paintings, none other than the universe. The figures represent all that is good, well-being on earth that the Indians wish. These figures do not occur just anywhere, but only in the most sacred places, the kivas; they should not be used otherwise. The birds are those held sacred to Pueblo rituals. Feathers are used in all their ceremonies; they are a part of the whole [thus sympathetic magic]; that is why they are there. Furthermore, the eagle represents a mythological figure; he casts away all evil. The parrot [macaw] is a sacred bird, and the feathers are used in the sacred doings. Feathers are the signs or symbols of the Great Spirit, or Father, spirit of Indian things. The handprints are his signs. The figures mean that he wills the message."

Regarding the color symbolism, he said:

---

457. Ladd believes Kupishtaya to be primarily Keresan.

458. And this is what lay back of Coronado's observation, when he said, "water is what these Indians worship," as stated on page 7, herein.

"The yellow paint is almost like that with which they paint the dead. It has a meaning. Yellow means pollen. Green means life; it is the color of the fir, which represents long life, ever green, ever youthful. Piñon is ground up in the green paint. White means fruitful; white paint is sacred, and used in the ceremonies."

Of the fish (fig. 53), the same informant told us: "The fish figure represents water because they are connected with water." Again, he said: "When a deer is brought in from the hunt, it is laid to the north. Beads are put on it, and it is welcomed. They say, 'You will always come to our home,' and treat the deer as brothers. They think arrows came from the sky; the points represent lightning." All of the pottery vessels shown in the murals were recognized as "sacred water jars." The "rain drops and lightning symbols pertain to rain."

Fortunately, Zna'ote was willing to discuss this painted layer in greater detail, supplying most of the interpretative information given above. He stated that: ALL IS TO MAKE CORN, RAIN, AND TO HELP THE PEOPLE PRAY, FOR GOOD WISH AND GOOD LUCK. EVERY FEATHER HELPS FOR PRAYERS, ALL HELP. And he added. MAYBE SOMEBODY WAS SICK. THEY PAINTED PICTURE AND GAVE CEREMONY TO MAKE HIM WELL. SOME SHIWANNI USED PICTURE TO MAKE PEOPLE WELL.[459]

As I have studied the evidence, it has come to be my conviction that the complex array of deities pertaining to these religious portrayals is reducible to four major characters: father (sun), mother (moon-earth-corn), and two children (morning and evening stars), through whom all palpable attitudes of the great god,

the Sun, are enacted. From the simple familial core, there were evolved elaborate aggregates of personages who became identified with respective groups of Indians. The gods reflected the knowledge, wisdom, opinions, and motivation of the priests who devised them. Then personators were selected to appear as earthly representatives of the deities, under the manipulation of the priests and their expanding priesthoods.

It would seem, thus, that whenever deific ones are depicted in the folk paintings, or personated, there might be a multiplication of manifestations. That is to say, any or all of the basic, celestial family group might appear more than once, in varying or multi-guises. It was along such lines, apparently, that the religious organization of the Zuñi Indians, whom I am using as generally illustrative of the local indigenes, developed.

I well realize that there are numerous priesthoods with specific officials and definite characterizations, each with his own attributes and duties. However, I consider this situation as a magnification of the basic or nuclear idea of Indian religion. Consequently, when I appeal to cut through the great maze of accumulated ceremonialism, and suggest identifications which may seem contrary to general knowledge, I trust that I am not confusing the issue. When the Sun, through his speaker, the priest, causes a certain act to be performed, it is carried out by a personage called by a particular name; when some other task is done, the personage may have another name, and so on. I know these personages are "different," yet I feel that they may be regarded as representative of certain basic archetypes.

This situation is indicated in Layer G-26 at Kuaua. Among the main personages are the following: Pautiwa (fig. 63), the Cloud sender and Sun priest of souls,[460] as a deer being, representative of the Sun himself. Figure 49

---

459. Here, Ladd takes issue with Zna'ote. He says again that the Shiwanni has nothing to do with curing. He says also that no paintings are used for curing. "At Zuñi," he adds, "what might be called a 'house call' is very simple. Even the four-day curing rite is very simple, with only a small altar which is removed each night . . . and it is not used by a Shiwanni."

460. *See* Cushing, 1896:412.

is identified as Paiyatuma, primarily patron of music and hunting, and director of the Newe-kwe clown order, but who here appears to assume attributes of Shulawitsi, the Fire god (who is also called "Sunshine"), and likewise displays insignia of the War gods (*cf*. Pls. A-4 and B-5). The symbolism of the serpent (fig. 48) relates with lunar observances, and suggests representation of the Moon. Again, there is close affinity between the moon and earth and fructification, as portrayed by the Corn sisters, Kochininako (fig. 113) and Meleyona-ko (fig. 110). Lastly, Kupishtaya (fig. 52) indicates lightning, and probably represents the Sun's speaker.

The Earth and all above it are symbolized in the band forming the dado. The presence of the War gods is indicated by the wristlets worn by Shulawitsi and Kupishtaya, and by the hunting arrows. The eagle, serpent, goose, fish, and bats, all important in rain making, are prominently featured as messengers of the gods; and many other animals and birds are represented. From beginning to end, rain symbolization is the theme of the painting, and prayers for fertility and growth indicated.[461]

Considering Layer G-26, then, in its entirety, we recognize that everything in the universe is indeed portrayed, from the creation down through the ages. We can be sure that the paintings were placed in the sacred chamber during a ceremonial which lasted for many days, and that the history of the Indians was recited and given in song while hallowed rites were reviewing their ancient lore and practices.

To say more would involve lengthy quotations from already published sources. Instead, the reader is referred to certain of these, particularly, at this point, to Stirling.[462]

Layer G-26 Altar

It was determined in the laboratory that the first paintings identifiable on the altar, a structural feature of Kiva III, related to the wall paintings of Layer G-26. Some of the design which covered the adobe plaster remained on the south end of the altar, with lesser fragments extending onto the east and west faces —the latter toward the fire pit.

On the south, Figure 16 shows an animal resting on its small hind feet, five inches above the floor, and reaching upward so that the forefeet come to the eastern limit of the construction, where the left foot appears to grasp a long black shaft which expands toward the top, in line with the altar corner. The animal is all black, except for a hemispherical area of white which parallels the back and curves in line with the stomach, and short, stubby tail, small blunt nose, and circular eye — all painted in purplish-red. The ears are indicated as long, rounded, and at relatively right angle to the back. Each foot shows four thin claws. Parallel with the back is a greatly elongated, black, tear-drop feature, of the same shape as that held by the animal, the blunt end directed downward. Above this an extended hand is painted white, palm toward the west. Zna'ote identified this as a RIGHT HAND, ASI TE·ANAN[e]. The animal he recognized as SÚLA, A GREY AND BLACK CAT WITH LONG EARS AND SHORT TAIL, WHICH LIVES IN THE MOUNTAINS.[463]

---

461. This may appear at odds with present day facts. For instance, at Zuñi, Ladd tells us that: "All rain making activities of the Ashiwanni are held in their own homes, or in a room especially cleaned and prepared for this purpose —*not* in the kivas. In the room there may be a few wall decorations, usually rugs, blankets, animal skins, etc., but, again, not in the kivas." At the small settlement of Kuaua, where new forms of ceremonialism were being introduced and assimilated, we know not what ritualistic procedures may have been prescribed by the priests.

462. Stirling, 1942; *see also* Mrs. Stevenson, Frank Hamilton Cushing, Ruth Bunzel, Elsie Clews Parsons, and Ruth Benedict.

463. Ladd says that the animal that he knows as *súla* is the pocket gopher.

ceremony: A WINTER CEREMONY TO CURE THE CHILDREN; CALLED BY THE WINTER CACIQUE.[464]

Fig. 16. Altar decoration; Sula (animal appearing on south end of altar). *Layer G-26.*

The fragment on the west side of the altar shows a heavy black rectangular element with a white stripe extending its full length. A square of adobe is outlined by a black projection on the left. Adjoining this and the upper part of the main motif is a large area of purple-red color.

On the east side, a large element is shown in yellow, crossed with narrow stripes of purple-red at its upper limit, and similarly through its center. Above the latter there is a large, broadly pie-shaped area of black. Extending from the south end onto the east face is a large black scallop, which joins another similar scallop. From these remains we have not found the depictions decipherable.

Like the wall paintings, Zna'ote indicated the altar portrayals as relating to a curing

Layers 25 and 24

No paintings were found on either of these layers, indicating that they were sterile washes applied over the great ceremonial paintings of Layer G-26.

Layer F-23

Layer F-23 was the 64th to have been applied to the kiva walls. Due to the fact that the paintings on the north wall were most fragmentary, though shown on the graph drawings prepared in the laboratory, these were not copied, originally, with the figures on the west wall as a continuous layer. Rather, Figures 46 and 59 were reproduced on separate scraps of canvas, and these were not included with Layer F-23 when it was submitted for interpretation.

No dado was painted on this layer. At the extreme east, on the north wall, fragments of a complex show a personage with a black kilt, white sash tied on the right about the waist, with five white shell tinklers remaining in front (fig. 60). Red decoration is shown at the sash ends. Legs of the personage are painted white which, according to Zna'ote, indicates one of the Rain priests. Close by this figure on his right is a rectangular element painted black, with narrow yellow border at each end, and with a white feather tied above it with red and black cords. At its lower left corner, there is a fragmentary line directed downward. This rectangular unit, identifiable as a pollen pouch or sacred bundle, is relatable to Figure 60, signifying him as an important personage. It may be that the latter is represented by the Rain priest of the Nadir, whose directional color is black.

A short distance to the right of the pollen pouch and slightly lower is a white point with a short part of the white shaft remaining.

---

464. Here, Ladd disagrees with Zna'ote completely.

Midway between this complex and the northwest corner, there remains another fragmentary portrayal of a second personage (fig. 59). The most significant feature is an element painted in blue-grey color and of such form as to suggest a quiver similar to that associated with Figure 54, Layer H-31. It shows the same cross marking in black, and there is a yellow area at the left end. Along the edges of the quiver at the right are short yellow fringes. Below the quiver is a portion of a white apron. On the right, paralleling this, and perhaps pendant from the quiver (which is in the position usually held by a white sash), are two fringed tassels, one of red and one of blue-grey decorated with diagonal black lines. From the blue-grey color it might be inferred that the representation is that of Pautiwa. Mrs. Stevenson records that blue symbolizes Awonawilona, "the supreme life-giving power."[465]

In the upper northwest corner, a large bird is depicted. It is in a horizontal position (fig. 46), 46 inches above the floor, with head to-

ward the east. Wings, body, and legs are painted black; squared tail and head are white, the latter with fine black markings around the red eye, with black pupil and outline, and from the lower edge of which a small black feather suggests a tear. Across the white beak, a band of black appears at the fore, and after a separating white area, one of red occurs. Along each leg, red fringe is shown. The four slender claws on each foot have black nails. From the beak, dash-dots of black and white sweep to the floor. At the beginning of these, the remains of a red shaft cuts across, presumably part of a red lightning motif. Crossed red lightning with white tips shoots forth from the rear of the bird and extends onto the west wall. On the foremost shaft, two small white, V-notched feathers are tied.

Toward the upper limit of the wall, above the red lightning, two crossing shafts of black lightning with white tips are shown, and above these are two eagle feathers, white with stepped black tips. At the end of one, a red point is shown; the like portion of the other is missing. These represent prayers being carried to

---

465. Stevenson, 1904:537.

PL. XVII. *Layer F-23.* A summer rain ceremony, Summer solstice.

Fig. 40. Prayerstick.

Fig. 41. Pollen pouch of the director and yellow fish.   Fig. 42   Fig. 43   Fig. 44

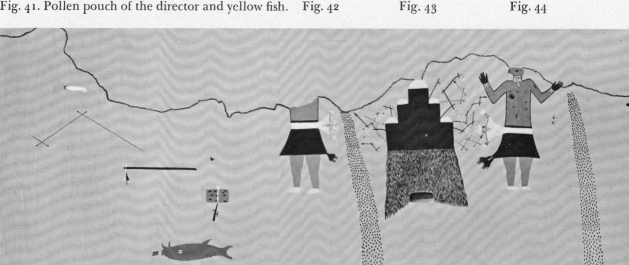

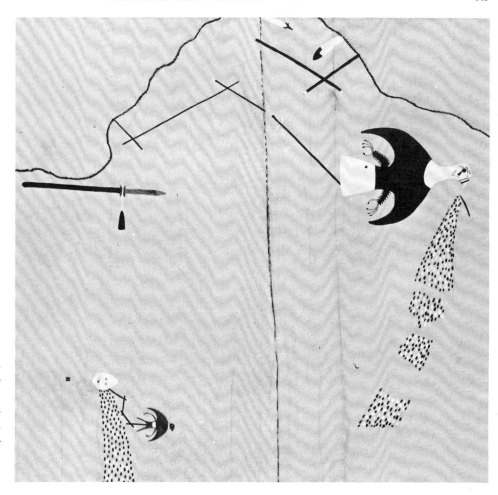

Fig. 45. Planting stick above moisture symbols.

Fig. 46. Eagle-messenger, with rain bringing symbols. *Layer F-23.*

Fig. 45   Fig. 46   Fig. 59   Fig. 60

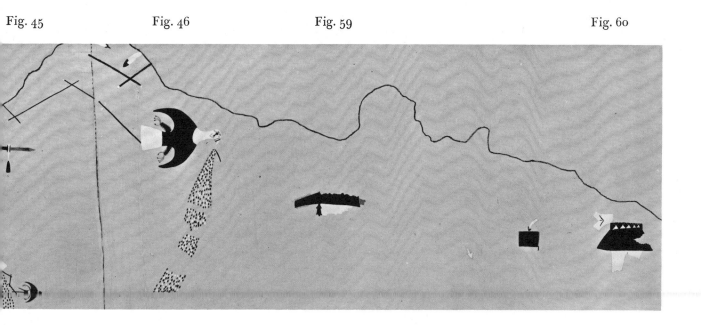

the Above. The bird would seem to be a species of eagle.

The next feature on the west wall is a planting stick (fig. 45), placed horizontally, 58 inches above the floor, and five inches below the red lightning shaft. The implement is 24.5 inches long, with black handle and yellow blade. A spool-shaped element of yellow is shown at the juncture of the two colors, and from this a black feather is suspended by a white cord.

Roughly in line, below the planting stick, is a small clustered complex. Uppermost is a strange little representation painted white, like an egg with a widely pointed base, lying on its side. It has two tiny dots like eyes, and a small round mouth from which barbels project laterally; all of these features are painted in yellow. At a distance about equal to the creature's greatest extent, toward the right, a tiny rectangle painted transversely, from top to bottom, in yellow, red, adobe, and red, may represent a heart, or a kernel of corn. From the lower side of the creature, a flow of black and white dash-dots reaches to the floor, similar to the flow from the eagle's mouth; these, Zna'ote identified as SNOW AND RAIN. From the same source, a fine black line with white tips portrays a four-section lightning symbol four inches in extent, which connects with the anus of a lovely little grey bird. This has sweeping wings, as if in flight, with thin, clawed legs following the curve of the wings, and tail forking from either side of a narrow body. Just behind the wings, a white area is indicated, and a narrow ring of white encircles the neck. The head and beak are grey, and the eye appears to have been left in adobe color. The wing spread is only 4.75 inches. Zna'ote identified this as a LIGHTNING BIRD,[466] WILOLONANᵉ — YELLOW LIGHTNING TOWARD END OF DAY. The shape of this bird is

very much like that of the little birds shown on Layer M-40, fig. 86.

In the center of the west wall, the katsina niche is again utilized (fig. 43). Painted above it is a black altar, 18 inches wide, with base 42 inches above the floor. The two steps on each side, and the top of the altar, are capped with white, cumulus clouds. From each side of the altar, a shower of fine-line lightning symbols shoot outward and up. These are painted: red with white tips and red point, red with black tips, white with black tips, white with yellow tips, yellow with red tips and red point, black with yellow tips and yellow point, black with white tips, and some of the points show as variegated. Zna'ote commented that RED MEANS BAD,[467] YELLOW MEANS GOOD. Together, these symbolize WINDS BRINGING THAT KIND OF WEATHER.

From the altar an exceedingly heavy shower of black dash-dots extends downward, passing each limit of the niche and terminating below it.

To the left of the altar stands a third personage, complete with exception of most of the head and the left hand (fig. 44). The face, body, arms, and legs are painted yellow—all but the latter being outlined with red. The hands with extended fingers are red. About the neck is an eight-strand necklace of white beads interspersed with red beads; the lowest strand supports a pendant in the form of a bi-valve shell on the chest—this also with red decoration. In the center of the body a tiny rectangle painted vertically in black, white, and red—from right to left—indicates the heart. On either side of this, nipples are indicated by little red dots, around each of which a larger circle is indicated by eight minute red dots. An extended red hand grasps at the right breast. There are four other minute symbols in red on the body; two show now as irregular dots, in staggered

---

466. Ladd notes that, "although this type of bird is depicted on the altar, it is not a 'lightning bird.' "

467. "This," says Ladd, "depends on how it is used in ceremonies; it has no standing quality of being bad."

Fig. 42. Director or mosona.   Fig. 43. Katsina niche with altar decorations.   Fig. 44. Bishininako. *Layer F-23.*

positions below the nipples, one on each side; another is a short horizontal band with four or five little lines erect above it, like the teeth of a hand rake; and the final element, slightly to the right of the navel position, appears to be a tiny point on a shaft, which is bisected by a short line at right angle (this might be a star or War god symbol) .

Around each wrist is a five-strand ornament of white and red beads. From the lobe of the right ear, a short pendant is shown in red. The mouth of this personage is made up of two lines, the upper one red and the lower black.

Obviously, this figure held a small water vessel in the left hand, for a long stream of black moisture dots springs from a source in that position, and reaches to the floor. The unit, 45 complex, pertains to Figure 44.

A set of two small tracks is seen below the left elbow, between the personage and streaming moisture. Each is made up of two little triangles with apices toward the back, and two minute dots to the fore.

Around the waist of the being is a magnificent white sash, tied on the right, showing great ends decorated with red borders and big knotted tassels of white decorated with fine black lines, or threads, which form diamonds, each of which has a black dot in the center; four white fringes extend from each tassel. Here we have a fine representation of the Rio Grande Pueblo type of sash worn in the Corn dances, the knots of which contain corn kernels wrapped in corn husks.

The sash supports a black skirt which shows slightly above the sash, and which has a red border and large decorative tassels at the bottom right. These are red, decorated with crossing black lines about the knots; from each, four long black fringes extend, amidst a cluster of short red ones. The feet are painted white.

Zna'ote recognized this personage as A WOMAN, A BOSS. HER NAME, BISH INI NAKO.

In comparable position to the right of the altar-niche complex is another personage (fig. 42), but only the lower body and pedal extremities remain. The body is yellow, outlined with red; legs are yellow, and the feet white. About the waist is a sash tied on the left; it is white except for a narrow border of red at the ends and setting off each knot, which is encircled by four fine black threads; each tassel has four fringes. The personage wears a black kilt which has a red border at the bottom, and at the left lower corner, two red tassels from which four black fringes and several shorter red ones extend. The kilt bottom is 39.5 inches above the floor of the chamber.

With no more features represented, Zna'ote pronounced this personage to be A MAN, THE BOSS, MAW SONª [mosona], or the director.

Associated with this personage, to his right, Zna'ote identified a rectangular POLLEN POUCH, painted in yellow, with three rows of elongated black dots placed horizontally. A white cord with tie above secures two black and white, barbed feathers at the bottom. Zna'ote explained that this pouch contained CORNMEAL, POLLEN, AND TURQUOIS, MIXED.

The feathers project toward a fish painted entirely in yellow except for two short, white horizontal lines which probably represent the heart. The caudal and dorsal fins are indicated; at the head, two horny projections curve up and backward. Four short, parallel lines appear before the mouth, and a small dot of black is seen in position of the anal fin. Zna'ote identified this simply as KASHITA, FISH. That it is painted yellow shows that it is to be associated with Figure 42, the director of the ceremonies.

Above the pollen pouch a small tip of what appears to be a red hawk feather is to be noted. To the right of this is a horizontal black shaft, 20 inches long, and 45.5 inches above the floor. At its southern extreme, a black feather with white tip appears to be tied with black and white cords. Zna'ote recognized it as a PRAYERSTICK WITH FEATHERS (fig. 40).

A crossed lightning symbol in yellow with black tips extends toward the corner, above the feathered end of the prayerstick. Above it is a white feather with black tip; at the fore is a white point, thus a prayer messenger. Zna'ote identified this as an EAGLE FEATHER, and said, the EAGLE FEATHER, THE ARROW, PRAYERSTICK, AND THE POLLEN POUCH ALL BELONG TO THE BOSS, or director.

With these features we have all that remains of Layer F-23. But Zna'ote recognized in it a CACIQUE CALLING THE RAIN, A SUMMER CEREMONY.

Layer F-23 Altar

Seeming to corroborate the identification of Figure 14, which occurred on the altar built in the kiva, as pertaining to Layer F-23, is the recognition by Zna'ote that the depictions thereon represent a CACIQUE'S CALL FOR RAIN DANCE—A SUMMER DANCE; PART OF THE SUMMER SOLSTICE CEREMONY. The two relate harmoniously and make the meaning of each more understandable.

The altar was painted over the adobe with a coat of blue-green paint, which Zna'ote called BLUE,TLÍ A KANʰᵃ [tli á kwa or tlianna—green or blue], and which is said to represent the supreme, universal being. Next, black dots were stippled over the blue surfaces; and, finally, much larger, elongated yellow and red dots were painted over the smaller black dots, for these show through the lighter paints in some instances. These surrounded a central motif of zig-zag lightning in yellow, with black tips, which extends the height of the altar. Shown in midsection of the lightning of each remaining panel of decoration is a large black point on

Fig. 14. Altar decoration—bats, lightning, moisture. *Layer F-23*.

which tiny legs are indicated, thus symbolizing the bat, flying upward to bring rain.

The yellow lightning represents FLASH LIGHTNING, TOWARD END OF DAY, WILOLONANᵉ. WILOLONANᵉ, said Zna'ote, is ANYTHING CROOKED, AS A ROAD. He added: THE OLD PEOPLE USED TO HAVE A LIGHTNING DANCE AND CARRY LIGHTNING STICKS (thin sections of wood jointed together) THAT WOULD SHOOT OUT.[468] THE OLD TREE DANCE AND OLD FIRE DANCE ARE NOW GONE, TOO.

Throughout this study, references have been made to ceremonial enactments, rites, symbolizations, and the like, but we have not presented any of these in relation to the pattern to which they pertain as a whole. Inas-

much as Mrs. Stevenson, fortunately, recorded information at Zuñi which further elucidates the significance of Layer F-23, this may be used as an example of a complex extending over a period of days and nights, and involving many interlocking events.

Mrs. Stevenson enumerates the first body of the Rain priesthood, as noted on page 43 herein. She says these are assembled when pekwinna notifies the elder brother Bow priest that the summer sun has reached its place of rest (where it strikes the same point five consecutive days). Pekwinna makes prayersticks and offers them to the Sun Father and Moon Mother, and to the deceased Sun priests (*Ápekwin*). Then he announces that the Summer solstice will occur after eight days. He instructs the people to make prayersticks for the Sun and Moon—blue ones for the Sun, yellow for the Moon—and for the rain makers; and

---

468. Fewkes, 1892:66, illustrates such a shooting lightning stick, as used by the Hopi Indians. Ladd says this was performed by the *Tli wa·kwe* society at Zuñi; it was part of a very long ceremony which was held in the winter.

the Bow priests to make them for Kupish-taya[469] and for the deceased Bow priests who become lightning makers and work with Ku-pishtaya, chief of the lightning makers.

Two days before the solstice, says Stevenson, the first body of the Rain priests gather in the ceremonial chamber of the Rain priest of the North and prepare prayersticks; the director of the koko or katsinas and his assistant pre-pare prayersticks in their respective houses. All the fraternities except the Wood people and the Bow priests convene on the day previ-ous to the solstice and remain in session throughout the day and night. Altars are erected in the ceremonial chamber and fetishes and feathered ears of corn—symbolic of the sacred medicine—arranged. Medicine water is consecrated and suds are made, symbolic of clouds. Prayersticks to the Council of the Gods are prepared. During the night prayers are offered to the Beast gods, invoking their influ-ence upon the rain makers. The Bow priest-hood offers special prayers to Kupishtaya,[470] to their rain makers, and to Paiyatuma.[470]

According to Mrs. Stevenson, pottery is made and decorated by the women and girls on the three following days, and is fired on the fourth. "A bit of wafer bread, the spiritual es-sence of which is believed to feed the spirit of this object, is deposited in each piece of pottery as it is balanced on stones to be baked."[471]

On the fifth day, the first body of the Rain priests gather in the ceremonial chamber of the priest of the North and make prayersticks, preparing those for the priestess of fecundity, Shiwanokia, and making them for the Sun and Moon, the regional rain makers, and the de-ceased priests. The North priest carries the prayersticks in a netted gourd jug to a sacred spring. Upon his return he goes into retreat with his fetish (ettone) for eight nights, ac-

companied by his associates and the priestess. During the retreat, the pekwinna visits those in retirement.

On the final night of the retreat, pilgrims return from Lake Village, and ritualistic pro-cedures are continued. And on the eighth day the priests are joined by the Rain priests of the West, South, East, Zenith, and Nadir, and by the elder and younger brother Bow priests, when other prayersticks are prepared. The di-rector of the katsinas and his assistant, with their two warriors to the Zenith, the person-ator of the Fire god, and many others, assemble in a ceremonial chamber and make offerings to the gods who will be represented. The Koy-emshi are carrying on their rites at the same time, in their ceremonial room.

Near sunset the katsina director makes a meal painting in the West kiva, deposits sacred objects, and offers a long prayer "for rains to fructify the earth." Members of the Great Fire fraternity visit the kiva and invoke the Beast gods to intercede with the rain makers for rain.

The next morning a pilgrimage is made to Lake Village,[472] with the director, his warrior on the right, leading the party. At their night camp on a mountain, the director requests the party to dance. Early the following morning they go on, dividing into two groups, one of which ascends a mountain while the other en-ters a sacred cave to deposit offerings. The two parties gather on a hill to the east of the lake. The director and his assistant deposit the prayersticks which they have brought with them from the pueblo, sinking them into the water with attached weights. The director also deposits old fire sticks in the water, and offers a prayer for much rain. Dancing follows these activities, after which the party returns to the hill and retires for the night.

Early the following morning the katsina di-rector sends most of the party to collect tor-toises from certain springs. He, his assistant, and their respective warriors, return to the

---

469. Ladd says "no" to this statement.

470. Ladd asserts that this is incorrect.

471. Ladd finds this entire paragraph to be contrary to fact.

472. See Roberts, 1931:7.

lake and gather cattails, and recover the fire sticks. When they return to the hill from the lake, the sacred fire is made by wood friction in ritualistic manner. When combustion occurs, "the one who produces the fire lifts the fiber, holding it in partly closed hands, moving them back and forth that the fiber may be fanned by the breeze. The breath must never be blown upon it, as this would so offend the Council of the Gods that there would be no rain. If rain is not the result of the fire making, the hearts of those who work with the drill are not good."

A juniper brand is lighted from the burning fiber, which is then thrown into the spring with a prayer for rain. The one who produces the fire and lights the brand is spoken of as "Shulawitsi." He places the brand on the ground, burning end to the east, which is the signal for the return to the pueblo. As they go along, they sing, and the two warriors whirl rhombi,[473] imploring the rain makers to water the earth. As they proceed, Shulawitsi "runs about setting fire to grass, trees, or whatever comes in his way, that smoke may rise in clouds like the breath clouds from the gods of Kothluwalawa."

The party returns to the mountain campsite where they spent the first night. Shulawitsi builds a fire and places his firebrand pointing toward the east. The katsina director and his assistant place their gourd jugs of spring water alongside the brand. The party dances until midnight, rests until early morning, and then continues on to the pueblo, visiting several springs en route.

About a mile and a half from the pueblo, the party is met by the Ko'k'oshi, or Long Hair dancers. A bonfire, just like that of the camping place, is lighted with the firebrand, burned end toward the east, and with the water gourds beside it. The Koyemshi have visited their place of origin, near the junction of the Little

Colorado river.[474] The Ko'k'oshi, wearing masks and ceremonial gear, and the Koyemshi, masked, but with scanty attire, then dance. After this Fire dance, the brand is lighted at the bonfire and is carried into the pueblo by the boy[475] who is to personate Shulawitsi in the Shalako ceremonial of the coming autumn.

Processions and dancing in the various plazas take place, and rites in the ceremonial rooms are performed. At night, the Ko'k'oshi dance alternately four times in the kopekwin's house and in the kiva. When the Ko'k'oshi are not present in the kopekwin's house, Shulawitsi, the Koyemshi, and others dance. The night is passed in dancing. At daylight, the bodies of the Ko'k'oshi are painted,[476] and the tortoises distributed. Later, the cattails are presented to the priestess, Shiwanokia, who descends from the ceremonial chamber of the North priest to receive them, and returns to place them near the meal painting on the floor.

The Ko'k'oshi enter, followed by the Koyemshi. Accompanying the Ko'k'oshi, says Mrs. Stevenson, are two who "are younger brothers of Pautiwa, director-general at Kothluwalawa. One of the brothers stands midway of the line and leads the dances. There are eight goddesses. One walks beside the foremost dancer in the file . . . . The others are companions to the gods."[477] They dance in two plazas and then enter a third. When they do this, the Rain priest of the North begins playing his flute in the ceremonial chamber. He descends from there after the first dance, and sprinkles with meal the cattails which the gods and goddesses carry; finally receiving them from the dancers.

---

473. "All members of kivas who will represent Shalako for the coming year, do this," says Ladd.

474. Information from Ladd.

475. Ladd says, "He is the one who originally starts the fire at the spring and carries it all the way."

476. *See* Stevenson, 1904:160.

477. As to this statement, Ladd says: "There may be a personage called *Ú pó yona* ("cotton over the head, or hat"), who usually stands midway, but who does not lead the dance." He substitutes the term *Ko pekwinna* for that of Pautiwa, and says there is no set number of "goddesses," who are men dressed as females.

Dancing in the four plazas of the pueblo is repeated four times before noon. Great feasts are then enjoyed.

Following further rites, there are four afternoon dances. Finally, then, with ceremonial smoking and head washing in yucca suds, the Summer solstice ceremonies are concluded. However, Mrs. Stevenson says, "yet it is but the beginning of the Korkokshi [Ko'k'oshi] dances for rains to fructify the earth that the crops may grow." The Ko'k'oshi and other summer dancers are personated, in turn, by the five other kiva groups.

We have seen that Layer F-23 of the Kuaua murals is vitally concerned with rain making, and Mrs. Stevenson has shown that every possible approach which might accomplish the bringing of rain is utilized during the Summer solstice ceremonies. Although somewhat obscured through earthly manifestations, the main deity concerned in each case is seen to be the Sun or Pautiwa, and his warrior, the elder War god or Rain priest of the Nadir. Pautiwa, in turn, is represented by the director of the katsinas. Though we have not established specific concordance between the personage iden-

tified as Bishininako, by our informant, Zna'-ote, and any recorded elsewhere, her association with the Rain priest and the Bow priesthood or warriors is indubitable; that she is one of the Corn personages seems certain, which may well identify her as the priestess of fecundity, and thus Shiwanokia (fig. 44).

Layer 22

This was a coat of plain plaster applied over Layer F-23. After this, however, the laboratory technicians encountered difficulties due to the fragile condition of the plaster layers and the extent of erosion which had occurred. Although no paintings could be related to Layer 22, there were well defined representations on Layer E-19, and between the two were a frustrating number of fragmentary records.

On the south wall, nearly five feet from its easternmost limit, was the partial representation of a black water jar with a white band just below its neck. This depiction was 7.5 inches wide at the vessel mouth and seven inches high. The laboratory personnel noted this as Figure 38, Layer E^3-22 (*not* illustrated).

A slightly more intelligible aggregate of

PL. XVIII. *Layer E²-21*. A curing ceremony.

Fig. 36   Fig. 13   Fig. 37   Position of niche

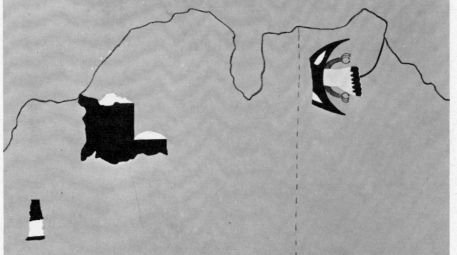
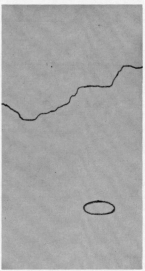

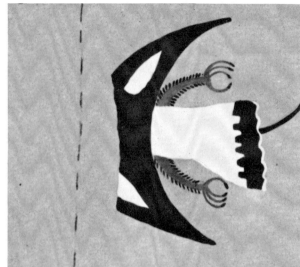

Fig. 35a. Unidentified personage (probably represents Pautiwa). *Layer E²-21.*

Fig. 37. Eagle-messenger in northwest corner. *Layer E²-21.*

fragments appeared on a plaster layer designated as E²-21 (Pl. XVIII). The first is a depiction which occurs in about the center of the remaining north wall, 33 inches above the floor (fig. 35a). This portrays a personage with yellow body outlined with red, wearing a black kilt. Across the front of the kilt, five small, round white features are shown in a diagonal

position, with a larger, white circular element below and toward the left. Around the waist and tied on the figure's right is an elaborately decorated white sash. At each end of the sash, there is an intricately designed portion made up of opposed elements in red and black—triangles, criss-crossed units, clouds, etc. At the ends there is one narrow red band; at each cor-

Fig. 35a

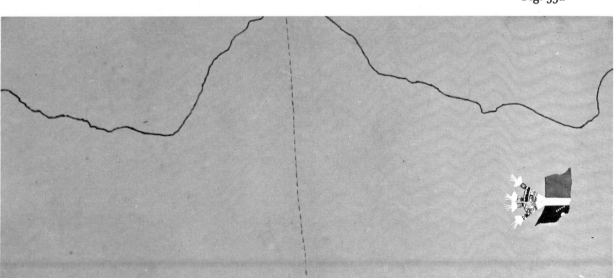

ner, a decorated knot from which large, bell-shaped tassels and fringes all in white, project. Figure 35a was identified by Zna'ote as PÍ KWI WE[h] [pekwinna], BOSS; IS BOSS OF MAWSON[a]—THE DOCTOR-BOSS. BOSS OF THE SUNSHINE. BOSS IS ALWAYS NORTH. This probably bespeaks Pautiwa.

Nothing is to be seen on the west wall except at the southwest corner, where all that remains is the after portion of a bird (fig. 37), 56 inches above the kiva floor. Seven inches of the upper wing is shown. The body is black; a black border outlines the central white portion of the wing and the scalloped white tail. The upper leg and scanty remains of the lower one are shown in yellow. It is observed that the legs are longer and more slender in proportion than those of other birds depicted in these murals.[478] Zna'ote identified it as an eagle, without particular comment. He said: EAGLE BRINGS CLOUDS AND RAIN, LIKE THE WIND. THE BOSS TELLS THEM TO SEND WIND. WIND BLOWS BECAUSE SOMEONE IS BAD. WITCH DOCTOR BRINGS WIND. WITCH, HA·TLI KWI. Projecting back and

upward from mid-tail of the bird is a slightly curved black line, probably denoting lightning.

On the south wall a small portion of a stepped altar was found, with white clouds on the terraces (fig. 13).

Just above Figure 38 (Layer E³-22) on the south wall and 20 inches below its upper extent, traces were noted of an unidentifiable figure, red at the upper part, with an underlying black expanse, then a white bit, and a final black fragment. In all this measured 8.5 inches high. It was recorded as Figure 36 (Pl. XVIII).

The entire portrayal was recognized by Zna'ote as a CURING CEREMONY. HELD ANY TIME.[479]

Next, depictions were found on the north wall, on a layer designated as E¹-20. At the easternmost limit of a complex recorded as Figure 29, there are such stepped red lines, white feathered motif tipped black and a surmounting red feather, and red and orange splotches, as may indicate a personage similar to that

---

478. Laboratory note.

479. Ladd says, "There are different medicine men, one for night and one for day, but no specific altar or other items are used in these curing rites at Zuñi."

PL. XIX. *Layer E¹-20.* Undetermined ceremony.

Fig. 35b. Eagle tail, in southwest corner.

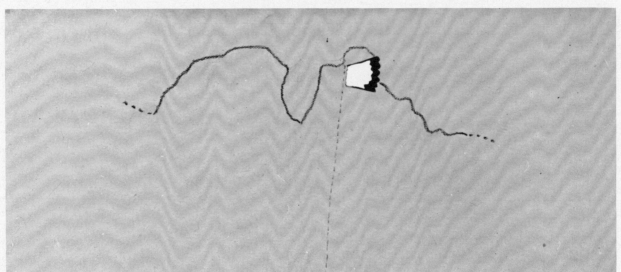

shown on Layer N-41:93. About a foot to the right of this unit, there occurs a white feathered stick, about 20 inches in vertical extent. Between the stick and the enigmatic unit is a circular feature, five inches in diameter. This is 44 inches above the kiva floor. It is outlined in red, with slightly less than the upper half filled in with red. In proper position to be holding the stick, which is undoubtedly a prayerstick, are the remains of a red hand. Extending from the hand downward to bent elbow and rising again toward shoulder position is a white arm outlined with red. Not quite connecting with this member at the right, the body of a personage is indicated. The trunk is white outlined with red, down to the fragmentary black kilt. The white color suggests that the personage is a priest, or Shiwanni.

Nothing is to be seen on the west wall until the southwest corner is reached, where the white tail of a bird is shown bordered in scalloped black (Pl. XIX, fig. 35b). Width of the tail is 8.5 inches. The figure is 62 inches above the floor. No features were discernible on the south wall.

Layer E-19

The first figure preserved on this layer (Pl. XX) is that of a bird on the north wall, close to the northwest corner, shown with white neck, head, bill, and tail (fig. 33); the head and neck are outlined with black, but the bill and tail are not so delineated. There is a yellow eye outlined with black, and a black pupil. Body and wings are black. The legs and long claws are painted yellow, the former showing black feathery fringe on each side, and the latter showing the nails in black. Zna'ote identified this as an eagle, but added: A DIFFERENT KIND, PA'·KO WA, [*pa'k'o ha*, bald eagle—E.J.L.]. TAKING MESSAGE. The wings, shown spread in flight, measure 18 inches from tip to tip. Extending backward horizontally from mid-tail of the eagle is a portion of black zig-zag lightning, 15.75 inches above the kiva floor. About one foot above this, two bolts of black lightning with white tips cross near their points.

Among the Pueblo peoples, birds are generally considered as messengers and scouts.

The next depiction of this layer occurs on the west wall and is that of a personage whose feet rest on a level 14 inches above the kiva

Fig. 29. Unidentified personage on north wall.

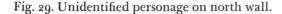

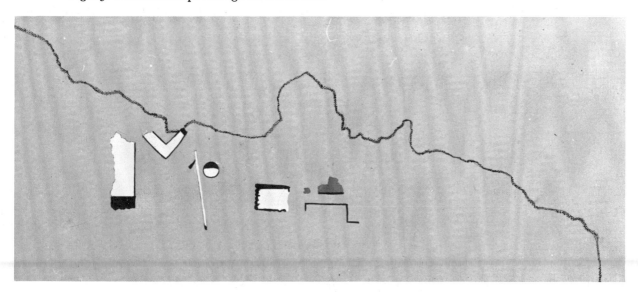

floor, and whose now existing height is 40 inches (fig. 32). The arms, hands, neck, and head are gone completely. The body is shown in adobe color outlined with red, apparently indicative of bare trunk. A black kilt, with red border at its bottom and red tassels with black fringed ends falling downward from the right side, is secured about the waist by a large white sash which is tied on the right side. The sash has white tasseled ends set off by narrow red bands, and a knot at each corner; these carry a framed criss-cross design in black. On the legs, white leggings extend from the kilt to black anklets. At the front of each, a narrow red stripe runs the full length, meeting a red band at the bottom, just above the anklets. Along the back of each legging is a row of five black, oblong elements suggestive of ornamental buttons; below the knee, each shows a square, red patch—the same color as that of the moccasins on the feet.

Paralleling the left side of the personage is a long white feature composed of two cords with an eagle feather tied to the lower end of each;[480] at the tie there are also downy white feathers.

Small flecks of red, black, white, and yellow colors are discernible at the upper extremity of this prayer plume. Then, alongside this, a few inches further toward the left, is another delicately feathered element shown entirely in white. On the right of Figure 32, in the shoulder position, a fragmentary patch of black probably indicates hair. In the center of the chest, two narrow, vertical red stripes bespeak a heart symbol, though a pendant from a necklace might be indicated. Slightly to the upper right of this figure, a cluster of white feathers, some showing the black tips characteristic of the eagle, are tied together with a yellow knot. The position is such that this feature was doubtless held in the right hand of the being. Again, this was identified as a prayer plume, TLESH NAN^e. Fragmentary colors in black, adobe, red, yellow, and white, close above this feathered article, indicate another symbolic element, which was identified as the

480. Stevenson, 1904:120, says of this feature, "Those prayersticks having this bear the prayers for rain, and those without are for clouds and other things." Ladd says there are only two kinds of sticks—"the dead or 'cloud people,' and the Koko. Women plant only for the dead."

PL. XX. *Layer E-19*. Salimopiya participating in a ceremonial rabbit hunt which precedes initiation into the katsina society.

Fig. 34   Fig. 30   Fig. 31 and Katsina niche

rainbow. Zna'ote said: RAINBOW. LIVING IN THE SUNSHINE. THAT IS WHY THIS ALL NICE COLOR. THESE PEOPLE CANNOT KILL ANYTHING. EVERYTHING TO HELP. The personage was identified, then, as K'ó HAN'ONA, one of the White Salimopiya who live in the east.

It is about 40 inches from Figure 32 to the niche, which is as usual the central motif of an altar decoration. The orifice is surrounded by a rectangle of black, which is bordered by narrow bands of white and red, then a wider expanse of adobe, a very thin black band, another of adobe, and a final framing of white. Above this composite, a two-tier altar is painted in yellow. From its lower step on the right, red crossed-lightning projects; on the left, a similar portrayal of yellow lightning, with a fragment of black lightning extending toward the north, is shown. From the altar base on the right, white crossed-lightning with black tips extends upward. On the south, or right of the central feature, yellow and red lightning zig-zags toward the personages at either side. The red lightning is tipped with yellow; the yellow lightning on the left has red tips and a white arrow point at its outer end,

Fig. 32. White Salimopiya, K'ohan'ona, from the East. *Layer E-19.*

that on the right has a red arrow point. From the lower left-hand corner of the adobe altar, black, red, white, and yellow lightning extends toward the kiva floor, the last named showing red tips and two red arrow points.

According to Zna'ote, the figure just described consists of these elements: HEMO KWAN^e, HOLE [the niche in the kiva wall]. YEL-

Fig. 32

Fig. 33. Bald eagle

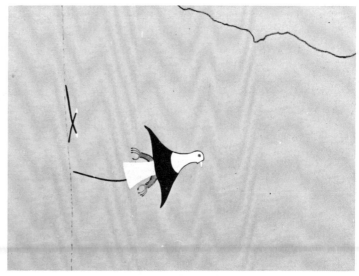

Fig. 31. Yellow Salimopiya, Tluptsinona, from the North. *Layer E-19*.

LOW TERRACE AT TOP IS FOR WEST AND OTHER IS SOUTH. MEDICINE IS PUT IN HOLE; HOLE IS SHUT. THEN OPEN SOME TIME AND MAKE PICTURE. PICTURE IS TAKEN OFF AFTER CEREMONY. NOT STAY ALL THE TIME.[481]

The cardinal directions are often used as a frame for the conduct of Pueblo ritual, or for securing repetition in prayer and song.

The sealed niche, when opened during the excavations, was found to contain an assortment of ritual objects; ground turquois, traces of meal, some projectile points, and small, rounded medicine stones.

At the south of the niche, 20 inches above the floor level, stands another personage with upraised arms akimbo (fig. 31). The hands and head are missing, but around the neck is a multi-strand necklace, apparently of beads in white interspersed with red; the lowest strand extends a little way down over the breast. Body and legs are painted yellow and are outlined

with red. In its present extent the figure is 24 inches high. Held about the waist by a large white sash is a black kilt at the bottom of which is a narrow red border. Long black fringes extend from the lower right corner of the kilt. The sash is tied on the right side, and thus *away* from the niche. It has a narrow red band across each end, which extends back a short distance on each side of the sash. From each corner, three-unit white fringes project stiffly. White moccasins and black anklets complete the costuming. This being was identified by Zna'ote as TLUPTSINONA, a Yellow Salimopiya, who comes from the north; he is regarded as "elder brother."

Another prominent personage is shown standing at the right of the Yellow Salimopiya. Here again the head is gone, but even so the figure measures nearly 40 inches high. Its feet are just 12 inches above the kiva floor. The trunk and part of the left arm remaining are painted in a faintly yellowish-adobe color, outlined with red (fig. 30). Two small, red dots show on the chest and indicate a neck ornament. There were black elements extending

481. Ladd suggests that this last statement might be due to Zna'ote's contact with the Navaho. He says, "In the past, the kiva was decorated and all decorations kept for several months, sometimes for years."

downward over the shoulders on each side of the body, which apparently portray hair, rather than some sleeveless garment as the reproductions might lead one to believe. Paralleling the hair, on the right side, and extending slightly beyond it, is a long, yellow feather with black, branching markings. This may represent a hair ornament. To the left of the personage is a long, feathered prayerstick, painted yellow below the clustered feathers, and adobe color above, with turkey feathers uppermost, and eagle below. Projecting upward from behind the upright turkey feathers are four straight reed-like elements in the adobe color. The upper end of this prayerstick terminates in the area of the missing left hand and was probably held therein, along with other tassel and/or feather elements shown in black, white, and red, and in red, yellow, white, and black, respectively. The personage is dressed in a black kilt with narrow red border and two black, fringed tassels at the lower left side. The large white sash which encircles the waist is likewise tied on the left. Both ends are bordered with red, and large white knots with bell-shaped tassels decorated with black terminate at each corner in white fringes which show four parallel cords. White leggings, fringed in front, extend from the kilt to black anklets which surmount red moccasins. This being is the Many Colored Salimopiya, Íto pa ná' nona, who, according to Zna'ote, LIVES ABOVE THE WORLD. IN HIS LEFT HAND, STICK OR CANE FOR WALKING. [It] HAS ON IT TURKEY AND EAGLE FEATHERS.

Between the Many Colored and the Yellow Salimopiya, and on approximately the same level on which the latter is shown, is a rectangular object painted primarily in yellow, with narrow white bands at each end, and dotted with red, white, and black dots. Two tiny, black tipped feathers form an inverted V-shaped element below this object, while large black and white feathers and a small, black tipped yellow one extend upward from it. This

Fig. 30. Many Colored Salimopiya of the Zenith, Itopana'nona, and his pouch of many-colored seeds. *Layer E-19.*

represents a pouch filled with many-colored seeds, which is associated with the Many Colored Salimopiya.

Salimopiya are called "seed bearers" by Mrs. Stevenson, who says that at the Zuñi Winter solstice ceremonies, for four visits, these deities dance and distribute seeds from baskets to all present. The seeds which they give away are said always to yield bountifully.[482]

There are twelve Salimopiya masks at Zuñi, two for each of the six color directions. These permanent masks are ancient, and are brought out only for the initiation into the katsina society.[483] But masked dancers made up as Sali-

482. Stevenson, 1904:140. Ladd says that the Salimopiya "carry the seeds (usually corn, squash, and beans) fastened onto the butt end of the yucca whip, which is carried in the left hand; or they may be carried in the sash; or they may be carried in both places." They are not, he adds, distributed to the people. "Men may take the seeds from the Salimopiya after the last dance or song."

The Salimopiya may equate with the Tewa personators, three dancers who carry seeds of crops at the winter ceremony at San Ildefonso, and who are named by a Tewa informant as *Tsa we, who comes from the north like Kossa.*

483. Ladd tells us that "there are others that are 'made' for winter dances."

Fig. 34. Mythical rabbit with rain symbolism. *Layer E-19.*

mopiya appear on different occasions. The taking of the permanent masks from their repositories is thought to cause windstorms, since the Salimopiya are warrior katsinas of the cardinal directions and wind is associated with warriors. For this reason, Salimopiya appear only in the winter, never in the summer when wind might ruin the crops.[484]

At the southwest corner of the kiva, a long-eared animal is shown, about half on the west wall and half on the south (fig. 34). From the lowermost hind foot to the floor is slightly over 38 inches. The measurement of the animal is 20.5 inches from the topmost ear to the lower, back foot. At first glance, this appears to be a rabbit, but Zna'ote was emphatic in his identification of this as something other than such a rodent. The creature's body and ears are painted white: the latter have black tip markings not unlike those of eagle feathers.[484a] There is a rump patch and tail—both black—

_____

484. *See* Bunzel, 1932:853. "When a mask is put away it is wrapped in buckskin or in cloths to keep out the dirt and is hung from the roof or placed in a jar. The dangerous ones are all kept in jars and all the old masks are kept in jars like ettowe. The mask is never placed on the floor."

484a. *Cf.* Chapman, 1927, fig. 6 (Sikyatki).

suggestive of a deer. The rump patch is surrounded by a semi-circular area, reaching midway up the back, of thin, elongated, light-grey dashes, indicative of the markings of a fawn. The animal has a large yellow eye outlined in black, and a black pupil. The seeming hooves are red, with the same color extending upward on the front of each leg for a short distance (*cf.* Pl. A-6b).

Two human hands, also in red, are shown in the position of grasping the left, hind leg of the animal. Back and somewhat below the hands and feet, two composite footprints are shown. The anterior portion appears to be a pair of tracks side by side, made by human feet, painted in red. The posterior portion is shown as two round, black dots. Together, the prints remind one of those made by the moccasin clad feet of a modern Deer dancer, who carries a stick in each hand and simulates the front feet of the deer as he manipulates them in walking as a four-footed beast, and symbolizes the road for deer to come forth. Two red elements similar in shape to the red prints just mentioned, and in such proportion as to indicate human size, are seen back of and paralleling the rump of the animal and extending upward toward the north, thus toward Figure 30, the Many Colored Salimopiya.

Extending through the little beast from belly to back is a red shaft, broken off a few inches below the body, and at the upper end of which a large white lance point is attached. At the hafting, the outer borders are shown in white, the center section in red. Emanating at the mouth of the animal, which is outlined in yellow, is a spray of black dots which falls downward to within a few inches of an outstretched human hand, painted red, 32 inches above the kiva floor. A segment of wrist is shown in yellow, outlined by red. In a position feasible for the occurrence of an upper arm and shoulder which might relate to this figure, there are further patches of red paint. Projecting upward diagonally toward the east from the hand, and intermingled with the moisture drops, is a black line, suggestive of a lightning stick. A large expanse of black moisture drops is shown to the right of the elements just described, originating in some no longer remaining source high up on the south wall. However, above the animal on the south wall, a few inches from its ears, fragments remain of an element undoubtedly related to this complex.

A wide black arc rises toward the east. Somewhat beyond its mid extent, a patch of white paint remains; at a common point of origin with the black arc, a thinner black element follows more of an angle, upward and toward the east. This appears to indicate the tip of an outspread wing of a huge bird—the source of the bountiful moisture drops.

The figures of this composite—mythical rabbit, animal tracks, footprints, moisture, spear, the personages, and the two hands grasping at the animal—combine to symbolize a rabbit hunt. Such ceremonial rabbit hunts are reported to always precede the initiation of little boys into the katsina society, at Acoma "and Zuñi." Ladd, however, says it is not true at Zuñi.

In all, then, this painting relates to a ceremonial rabbit hunt and preliminary initiation rites held during the winter for small boys who are to be inducted into the katsina cult; and it portrays those supernatural beings who play important parts therein, primarily represented by the Salimopiya.

Layer 18

This, again, was merely a covering wash which followed the ceremonial depictions of Layer E-19.

Layers D¹-17, 16, 15, D-14

At the eastern limit of the north wall on the layer listed as D¹-17, there occurs a rain bringing complex. This consists of a black water jar, TE'·ILI, POT, as identified by Zna'ote, resting on feather "pillow"[485] (fig. 58), such as occurs on

Fig. 58. Unidentified personage concerned with weather control. *Layer D¹-17.*

several of the painted layers previously described. The jar has a yellow stripe extending from almost the rim, down the middle of the straight sided neck, nearly to the pointed base. Around the neck a white cord with tie on the right secures a black feather which projects to the left. The feathers on opposing sides of the base are black, with black and white barbs pointing toward the vessel from near the outer extreme, and a white V at the juncture of quill and barbs pointing in the direction of the vessel. The jar rests on a black border, five inches wide, which surrounds the chamber, thus indicating this as one of the more sacred paintings. From the mouth of the jar, moisture drops are indicated with black dots which rise and flow to either side, reaching the border. Also emanating from the vessel are fine-line, crossed lightning features. That on the left is of black with white tips, and to the left of this is a white shaft with black point of the hunting variety; to the right of the black lightning is a red point, and then crossed red lightning with yellow tips and point. To the right of this is a three-section

485. Mrs. Stevenson, 1904;174, speaks of this as a *cincture pad,* upon which medicine bowls may be placed.

lightning symbol in yellow with black tips. Between the red and black lightning are five red dots arranged in the form of a little dipper.

Above these elements is a black object, nearly five inches square, with two black feathers tied on the left—probably representing the dual fetish. At the base of the tie a short red cord is seen, and toward the outer end of the lower feather a unit of cords projecting upward shows a white one between two black ones. Above the pouch is a white feather, 12 inches in length, outlined with black and with black tip; the quill end bears a white point, at the left side of which is a small red feature, and to the right is a short red line. On the right of the feather there is an irregular area of red, with a Y-shaped element pointing toward the pouch.

Flowing downward along the right side of these symbols is a heavy shower of black dots. A few inches above its union with the black border, a branching red symbol is painted.

Twenty inches above the floor, on the right of the moisture representation, the white feet of a personage appear. The left leg is indicated in yellow, outlined with red, and red fringe extends along the left side. Black anklets are also shown.

Zna'ote recognized this complex as pertaining to a CURING CEREMONY. BLACK, WHITE, AND YELLOW, ALL RIGHT; RED, BAD—LIGHTNING HITS SOMETHING, ANATSI ATI, AND BURNS [*ana tsi ati* —"struck by lightning"—E. J. L.]. RAIN COMES AND PERSON GETS WELL. It is thus to be assumed that the personage portrayed was a deity concerned with weather control. This relates well with Layer D-14, and is thus included with the figures thereof. The plaster layers listed as 16 and 15 show no paintings.

Toward the northwest corner of the chamber a large bird is painted on Layer D-14, the lower wing tip being 63 inches above the floor (fig. 28a). Spread wings and body are black, neck and squared tail are white outlined in black. The head is missing. Legs are yellow outlined with red, claws are yellow and show black nails. From the posterior of the bird, which Zna'ote identified as an EAGLE, PA'K'OHA [bald eagle], a curving black element reaches upward.

Below the eagle, with its tail on the north wall and its head on the west wall, is a small

PL. XXI. *Layer D¹-17 and D-14.* Autumn ceremony for fructification. (*See also* color Pl. XXII following page 126.)

Fig. 23   Fig. 24   Fig. 25   Fig. 26

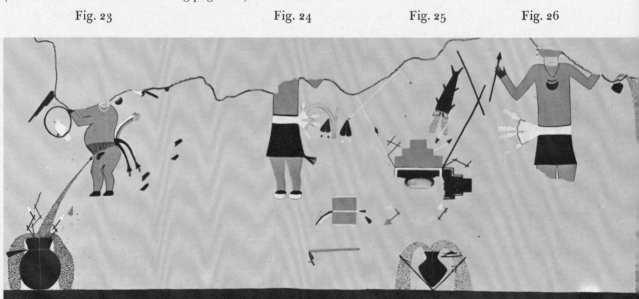

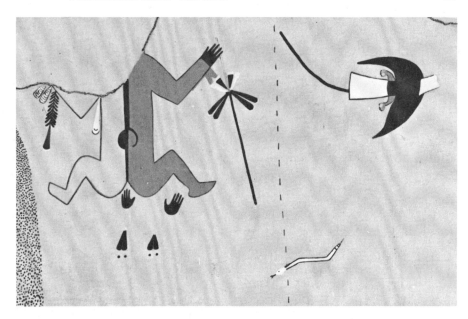

Fig. 27. Neipatch (dual personage).
Fig. 28a. Bald eagle.
Fig. 28b. White snake.
Layer D-14.

white snake, outlined with black except for the head (fig. 28b). An eye is shown by a black dot; the forked tongue is black, and three narrow black bands encircle the posterior end, before a yellow tail tip which is divided in two by another black band. The snake in zig-zag position, diagonally directed toward the Below, measures 12 inches long. Zna'ote identified it as 'CHÍ TOLᵃ KÓHAN, WHITE SNAKE.

Close to the corner, then, on the west wall, 36 inches above the kiva floor, there appears an intriguing personage, but, alas, without head (fig. 27).

Here, duality of character is represented, wherein the portrayal is recognizable as one individual seated on his buttocks, with knees spread and elevated, and heels drawn inward. The two-color painting of the body, the left

Fig. 27   Fig. 28b   Fig. 28a   Fig. 58

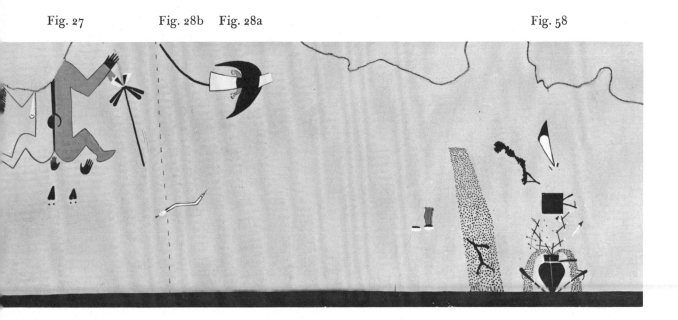

half yellow and the right half a dirty white, separated by a black line which expands from bottom to top, makes two persons visible, haunched back to back (Pl. XXI).

The left hand of the personage is painted red. A yellow W-notched wristlet hangs below the arm, and points toward a black shaft which is feathered at its upper end. There are two small black feathers with fluffy white tips, and two white plumes at either side of them, shown erect above the shaft head; and two red feathers with black markings and white tips hang downward on opposing sides.

In the middle of the body of the dual being is a circular symbol, solid black on the right side, and a black broken circle, opening toward the bottom, on the left. That this figure was bedecked with headdress and mask is indicated by a white feather with fine black tip marking which shows below the right armpit, as though pendant from the back of the head. Feathered ornaments, one fashioned of tiny black feathers and a pendant red hawk feather, and another of two white feathers with black, cross markings, hang from the right wrist; these Zna'ote called PASIKWIN.

Two extended red hands reach toward the bottom of the yellow half of the being (said by Ladd to be defecating), and below these are two animal tracks—one slightly larger than the other—composed of black, wedge-shaped elements with a small black dot before each of the greater ends. Zna'ote identified the handprints (fig. 27) as ÁSI (hand) TÉANAN[e] (tracks); of the larger animal track, he said: NADZI KEN TÉANAN[e], DEER TRACKS, and of the other, NADZI TÉANAN[e], LITTLE DEER TRACKS.[486] From this we may infer that a doe and fawn are represented.

Zna'ote recognized the dual personage as NE I PATCH, HELPER; ONE SIDE GREY, THE OTHER YELLOW.

This layer again features the niche midway

in the west wall, showing a terraced altar in yellow above, and one in black toward the left; the latter shows a panel of white bordering the two lower steps, with black, lateral outlines. The cavity itself was painted around with black and banded with yellow, white, and red, with the same symbolism as that of the dado of Layer G-26. Fine black, crossing shafts project from the upper and lower left corners of the altar, the former with white tips; and heavy black, white tipped shafts extend upward to the wall's limit.

From the center step on the left, a white shaft with red point is directed upward; just above it is a similar shaft with black point directed downward. This latter cuts across a moisture symbol of black dots which originates as a two-part element, at the anterior end of a black fish, the head of which seems to be cut off. The body is delimited by a crossing white band edged with black; then two elongated, bluntly pointed features, shown in adobe outlined with black, extend outward diagonally to either side, each being a source of the moisture drops. Between these projections, short black, opposing barbels are shown with a small white unit between them. Two fins occur on each side of the fish, and the caudal fin. Of this (fig. 25), Zna'ote said: KYA SHITA. SOMETHING LIKE A FISH.

Standing to the left of the altar is another personage (fig. 26). The body, arms, neck, face, and legs are painted yellow and outlined with red. The upper part of the head is missing, but the right ear lobe remains, with a white and red bead pendant; and a similar left ear pendant. Around the neck is an eight-strand necklace of white beads, below which a red strand supports a shell pendant which lies on the chest. This is painted yellow, with a narrow band of black across the pedicle portion, and about one-half of the shell in red.

By the red right hand is a black shaft, with black point of the hunting type. The left hand is missing, but it held the thong of a small

---

486. Ladd gives: *nadzi*, "fawn"; *ken*, "belonging to"; *teanane*, "tracks."

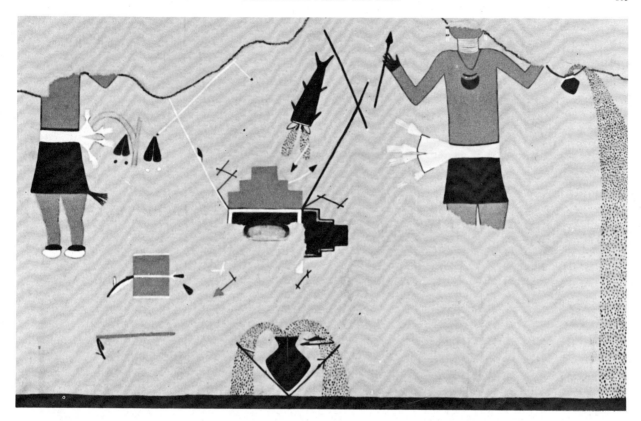

Fig. 24. Pekwinna to "boss" ('Kiaklo?, deputy to Pautiwa).   Fig. 26. "Boss" (Pautiwa?). *Layer D-14.*
Fig. 25. Fish-like representation above niche.

black water jar with pointed bottom. About
the base of the neck, which shows a vertical design in black and white, a white cord is tied
with a knot at the right. From the vessel a
great flow of black dots reaches to the border
below.

About the waist of the figure is a large sash,
all in white but for red borders at the ends, separating off the tassels tied on the right. The
close fitting black kilt, which Zna'ote said is
a DANCE SKIRT, PITHLAN, has a red border at its
bottom, likewise. Only the upper part of the
legs remain.

This individual is THE BOSS, KÓMI SHIWAN-
NI,[487] according to Zna'ote.

Standing to the right of the niche is a third
personage (fig. 24), the head and arms of which

are gone. The body, left elbow, and legs are
painted yellow, outlined in red except for the
latter. A white sash is tied on the left, showing
a thin red border at each end, with white knots
with black decoration at the edges, and white
fringes, of which Zna'ote said, TÁKUN IKWÍN.
There is a black kilt with red border and black
fringed knots projecting toward the left. Black
anklets are shown above the white feet which
are outlined with red, and rest 25.5 inches
above the floor.

Zna'ote identified this figure as KOK WAU^m
PEKWIN,[488] thus the pekwin to the "boss."

Between his feet and the niche is a yellow
object, six inches square, with white border at
each end and a white cord tied about its center,
with a small red feather tied on the left (with

487. Ladd comments that this is not the name of a god,
but says that "Pautiwa is sometimes called this."

488 Ladd suggests Ko pekwinna, since several are
called by this term.

a similar one close, but now disassociated from it), and a black and white feather at the right. At the tie of the latter, a small red thread is included. A small white barb, outlined in black, projects upward from the feather. This is the sacred bundle of the katsina leaders (Pl. XXI). A few inches to the left of it is a fragment of crossed white lightning, and one of red with yellow point. These were symbols which issued forth at the lower right corner of the altar design surrounding the niche. Below the sacred bundle is a yellow shaft in horizontal position. At its southern extreme a small red and a black feather with black and white barb on the right are tied, representing a prayerstick.

To the left of the sash tassels of Figure 24 is a fragment of a yellow cornstalk with one leaf. On the left side of the stalk is a large pair of deer tracks painted in black with white dots apart from the fore prints; and to the right of the stalk is a similar set painted red with black dots apart. These connote the opening of the hunting season. The fore of the black set points toward and almost touches the crossed shaft of a large white lightning motif with black tips, which reaches from the upper limit of the wall to the upper right corner of the altar painted above the niche. About midway of the lowest shaft a small black feather is tied on the upper side. Paralleling the white lightning a short distance from the altar is fine crossed lightning in red with black tip.

Toward the southwest corner of the chamber, with his right foot 30 inches from the corner and 26.25 inches above the floor, we find a fourth personage (fig. 23), shown in semi-profile. Most unfortunately, the head is missing; from the surrounding fragmentary indications, it must have been elaborately adorned. Bits of red and red-marked feathers, with one from an eagle tail, are shown back of the head, as though from a great headdress. What appears to be the long red tail of a bird projects to the right of the head area. About the being's neck is a multi-strand necklace of white beads,

the lowest strand of which hangs high on the chest. The body is painted yellow and is outlined with red.

In the red left hand is a black hoop, seven inches in diameter; and on the bottom of the circlet a white bird, which Zna'ote identified as WÁTHLANA, is perched. This has a small black eye, yellow beak outlined with black, red legs, and a red band separating off the tail, which projects in four fine, parallel "fringes." The hoop symbolizes the whole world, and the tail indicates the four regions.

The personage is pot-bellied, with a wide girdle[489] surrounding his belly and tied at the back, where two long black ends with six large white scallops outlined on each edge curve downward, ending in red-knotted, black tassels with red, white, and black fringes. Above the back tie, there projects a curved element painted in white, red, and yellow, with a transparent adobe wash over all, which ends in a small, terraced altar of yellow. Of this, Zna'ote said, TAKUN IKWIN, or decorated sash. Behind this figure are two sets of red tracks, as though indicating the path he had followed into the scene.[490] He has red feet with narrow black anklets about the ankles. A greyish patch on the groin indicates pubic hair. The yellow penis, not outlined but showing red foreskin, directs a thin stream of black dots into a very large, black, globular jar which rests on the black border below. From the flared neck of the vessel, streams of moisture dots flow upward on each side, and fall to the border. From the rounded rim to the base, a central line was painted in black [this was left adobe color in the reproduction in order to make it evident]. About the vessel neck was an adobe line indicating a cord which secured a black feather on the right.

---

489. The laboratory notes say that this "has a striped effect, the yellow body lines showing through at regular intervals."

490. He has a peculiar dance step, as he trots up and down the line of dancers, which is probably represented here.

Rising from the mouth of the jar, amidst the moisture symbols, are two black, crossed lightning representations, each with a white point, and red lightning between them. To the left are three sets of two yellow dots, each, and a black one. Above these, a yellow point is directed upward toward the personage, whom Zna'ote recognized as ÁLA LA WISHKA, or the Ololowishka [or Ololowishkya] of other recorders.

Viewing this painting as a whole, Zna'ote pronounced it: I·PU AWE, AN INITIATION. MUST SEE THE PICTURES BEFORE THEY DANCE. CHI·ANI USE PICTURES LIKE THIS AS MEDICINE. THIS KIVA MUST BE A KATSINA HOUSE. ALL MIGHT BE HELD IN THE SAME KIVA. THIS LOOKS LIKE SHIWANNA HOUSE—THE NICHE, AND ALL.[491]

Mrs. Stevenson, in 1896, witnessed the winter retreat of the priest of the Nadir, which explains some of the symbolism and significance of the paintings of Layer D-14.[491a] The black pottery jars doubtless represent those in which the fetishes, sacred bundles, and other ceremonial articles are kept when not in use. As the priest painted a meal painting on the floor of the fetish house, cloud symbols were outlined with six scallops. This indicates that the similarly scalloped element on the sash ends of Ololowishka (fig. 23) may have like meaning, probably indicating clouds from all the directions.

Arrow points of various sizes were distributed over the cloud forms, and an arrow point was placed at the end of each of two lines radiating from the extreme end of the meal and pollen circles—formed by placing the scallops together. This gives a result similar to our paintings around the niche, all rain bringing magic. The circles, like our hoop, symbolize the world. In the Zuñi meal painting, strings of

Fig. 23. Ololowishka. *Layer D-14.*

precious beads were placed within the circle; with our depiction they are worn by the personages.

Mrs. Stevenson noted that the Zuñi priest placed six concretion fetishes[492] "for fructification" into water in a medicine bowl and prayed to the respective rain makers. An associate formed a cross of powdered root and encircled the cross with it, afterward sprinkling the root over the water. It seems possible that the branching red, root-like element shown in the moisture emanating from the personage of our complex had a more realistic representation at Kuaua. Eagle plumes were dipped into the water and sprinkled to each direction. The eagle feather shown above the fetish in Figure 58 probably bespeaks the same function.[493]

491. It is Ladd's belief that the dance cited has nothing to do with *E·pu a* [I·pu awe] initiation, or with curing. The dance, he says, "is a public one, a very simple ceremony, held in the plaza usually during the summer dances."

491a. Stevenson, 1904:173-178.

492. Such concretions are especially sacred to the Corn Mother of the six regions (Stevenson, 1904:186, 277). Cushing (1896:366-367) gives significant information on concretion fetishes, the "stone ancients."

493. "Spitting, spurting, or spraying medicine is one of the most common ways of applying it" (Parsons, 1939-I:418).

Mrs. Stevenson recorded the appearance of Ololowishka,[494] who appeared among the god personators of the rain makers, at the retirement of the Koyemshi following the Shalako ceremonies.[495] She says:

> This god is supposed to sweeten bread by micturating upon the meal ("His urine is sweet like honey"). The penis is represented by a gourd with white fluffy eagle plumes attached pendent. During the dance of the Wátem⁺la [Mixed Katsina] the Kómosona approached the Ólolowishkia and most reverently prayed while he sprinkled the mask and artificial penis with sacred meal.[496]

During the day of the Koyemshi payoff, Mrs. Stevenson reports that large quantities of corn were collected from the dancers, and carried into the kivas. The pekwinna, younger brother Bow priest, and the Kopekwinna received several ears of corn from the dancers, and the Kopekwinna received corn also from Ololowishka. After these had prayed and sprinkled the gods with meal, they returned to their kiva.

Forced, no doubt, by non-Indians critical of their natural personations, the representative of Ololowishka covered his privy parts, but still continued the symbolization of old. By Bunzel's time, he was wearing a turquois mask decorated with deer, eagle, turkey wing and macaw feathers on its crown; had a ruff of raven feathers about his neck; and wore two girdles of raven feathers around his chest and waist. He wore a white skirt, embroidered kilt, white sash and red belt, from the back of which a fox pelt was suspended.[497] He had fringed leggings, blue moccasins, and hanks of yarn with tinklers at his knees. The phallus was supported by the belt. Bunzel says that "The brownish fluid ejected from the phallus in the course of the ceremony is a sirup made from peaches (formerly yucca fruit)." She notes:

> There is considerable esoteric ritual connected with the impersonation of Olowishka, the operation of the phallus and the preparation of the fluid. There are magical prayers, of course, for all these incidents. Only three men "know how." The performer in 1927 was severely criticized for clumsiness. Omens are read from the character of the flow.[498]

If the flow is smooth and unbroken, the token is favorable; if uneven, unfavorable, and there will be sickness in the community.

In a ceremonial Rain dance which Dr. Bunzel witnessed in September 1927, but which could be given in summer or winter (*hekshina shilowawa*—red paint), two *Hehe'a*[499] (*see* Pl. B-8) and Ololowishka had prominent parts, along with the two katsina maidens and four flute players.[500] Bunzel is quoted as follows:

> They come into the plaza. Each of the maidens carries an ear of corn in each hand and a basket of fine meal. The two Hehe'a carry the two grinding stones and the buckskins. They prepare a place for the girls in the center of the plaza. They spread out the

---

494. Petroglyphs of this figure occur at Cienaga, south of Santa Fe, and Mrs. Stevenson reported them near a spring south of Zuñi.

495. Stevenson, 1904:275; *see also* Parsons, 1922:195-199.

496. Plate LXXI of the Stevenson report gives a front and back view of the mask worn by *Nawisho* (which is said to be another name by which this personator is called) at that time, and Bunzel (1932:pl. 33d) gives a more detailed illustration of Ololowishka.

497. Bunzel, 1932:870, notes that the fox skin is worn by practically all of the dancing katsinas and many others, and that it is considered as a relic of the earliest days of man, for the katsinas "were transformed while mankind was still tailed and horned" (*see* Pl. A-1).

498. Bunzel, 1932:1007. Ladd says that yucca fruit, *t'spechi'*, is still used.

499. These have been equated with the Keresan *Heruta* and closely resemble the *Kurena;* a similar personage is recognized at Jemez; and the same character is known among the Hopi (*see* Parsons 1922:205).

500. These are always chosen from the Little Fire fraternity at Zuñi.

buckskins and place the two mealing stones down on them. The Koyemshi help them. The plaza is full of people. Then the four flute players take their places on both sides of the grinding stones. Then the girls take their places. They are on the south side of the plaza, and the dancers stand in line around the plaza, always men and women alternating. They then sing the grinding songs and the two katshina maidens grind. When they have finished one song they pile up the meal in the bowls. Then when all the meal is piled up in the bowls Ololowishka pretends that he wishes to pass water. Then the Koyemshi say, "Hurry up, children, our grandfather wishes to pass water!" Then they take the bowl from one of the maidens and set it down in front of Ololowishka. Ololowishka carries an old long-necked gourd sticking out of his belt. Then he stands over the bowl and pours some of the liquid into it. Then he goes to the second bowl and does the same. Then the Koyemshi put their hands into the bowls and mix the contents thoroughly and carry the two bowls around among the people who are standing in the plaza and on the housetops, and the people take some of the meal from the bowls.

While they are doing this the katshina maidens have gotten up and they begin to dance like the Corn maids, each maiden holding an ear of corn. . . . The katshina maidens dance that the women may have good luck in grinding, and Ololowishka comes to purify the men so that if any of them have venereal disease they may be cured and not give their diseases to the women.[501]

Mr. Ladd does not know of any personage such as that of Figure 27, who has been identified as "Neipatch." Inasmuch as Mrs. Parsons speaks of Newekwe participants in the Ololo-wishka ceremonial which she observed at Zuñi, on 15 September 1918,[502] it seems that the

Kuaua depiction relates to a similar representation—bespeaking the jesters of the powerful composite organization of mighty warrior-wise priest-medicine man membership. Again, there is the duality of character which was observed in Figure 95 (Layer N-41). Mrs. Parsons notes[503] that the Newekwe are *yatokya ancha'le*, Sun his child, "because like the sun they have no mask." Since the Sun Father has twin sons, it may be that this may be another

---

Kohashtoch, as danced at Laguna each autumn to open the hunting season (1939:537).

A striking portrayal occurs as interior decoration of a Mimbres polychrome bowl (Nesbitt, 1931, Pl. 23b—Mattocks ruin, near Mimbres, New Mexico), where a male figure, clearly identifiable as Ololowishka, holds in his left hand a hoop within which a yellow bird is perched; in his right hand is a crooked stick. The latter crosses a similar stick held in the left hand of a facing, female figure, in whose right hand is a short stick on which a yellow bird with black wings is standing. The male figure is painted black, and the female, yellow. The only thing worn by the male is a spindly head ornament with "eye" motif, and a wide, white girdle with two arcing projections toward the left front. These appear as parallel rabbit sticks, or batons, each painted yellow, and with a tiny face indicated at the terminal end. The phallus is prominently shown, as are the breasts of the female, who apparently represents the priestess of fecundity. Her only attire is a wide sash about the waist, from which long fringes hang downward, and sandals. On the cheek of each personage a warrior symbol is painted. Near the feet of the male is a bow and two arrows; and back of the female is a burden basket, on the top of which a yellow bird rests. Mr. Nesbitt identified these three birds as parrots, or macaws.

Mimbres vessels with polychrome decoration are not known to date later than A.D. 1200, according to Mrs. Lambert. Therefore, it may be assumed that the Mimbres branch of the Mogollon culture, at that period, embraced a highly developed priesthood and organized cults, with warrior-hunt society and recognized importance of women in ceremonial functions. In passing, it may be noted that fish are commonly used in decorations on Mimbres pottery.

502. She observes that Ololowishka never appears except in this ceremonial. This is in agreement with Ladd, who detected an error in Stevenson's recording of Ololowishka's appearance during the retirement of the Koyemshi; he feels that she has confused two different ceremonies. He tells us that the last performance of the Ololowishka ceremony occurred at Zuñi about 1945.

503. Parsons, 1922:204, note 98.

---

501. Bunzel, 1932:1008-1009; *see also* Parsons, 1922:195-199, who reports the same ceremonial under the name of

portrayal of the twain, thus of the Divine Ones or their successors, the twin War gods.

Obviously, the Kuaua painting pertains to the re-telling, during some lengthy ceremony involving the pueblo, of exploits which centered around such ancient deities as Paiyatuma, Ololowishka, Hehe'a, Koyemshi, Newekwe, et al. It appears that there is a subtle relationship between Ololowishka and Paiyatuma, especially since the latter shows a baton tucked into the rear of his girdle,[504] and since he is patron of the hunt.[505]

Layer 13

This was a plain layer of plaster, applied over the paintings of Layer D-14.

Layer C¹-12

On a section of plaster which was identified as Layer C¹-12, there occurred, on the south wall, partial evidence of a white skirt outlined in black, with red border at the bottom. Below

---

504. *See* Stevenson, 1904:27.

505. Mr. Ladd disagrees with me on this. Here, as elsewhere in the manuscript, he says, "Although I disagree with certain identifications, I have nothing better to offer."

this were indications of white legs outlined in red (fig. 17—*not* illustrated). The skirt fragment measured nine inches in width. Following the statement of Zna'ote that the Rain priests have white legs, it may be assumed that this was a personage of that character.

The north wall of this layer had three extremely eroded representations. At the eastern limit of the wall, a black vessel had been shown (fig. 22—*not* illustrated), the lowest fragment being 11.5 inches above the floor. And at a distance of 82.5 inches to the west of this, another jar had rested 7.5 inches above the floor (fig. 21—*not* illustrated). For the first time there is evidence of colored decoration on pottery. This globular jar was painted in red and black. A heavy black band extends from the left side of the rim down across the vessel diagonally; on each side of this band, fine red diagonal lines cover the neck and body. The fragment measured 8.5 inches in height. To the right of the red jar there is another element, a long irregular area of black with red dash-dots like buttons along the right edge.

It is evident that a ceremony concerned with rain making was depicted.

PL. XXIII. *Layer C-11.* A blessing ceremony. Fig. 20a. Water jar decorated with white triangles, below a yellow-orange band. Fig. 20b. Water jar with incised decoration, below a peach-colored band (path of the gods).

Fig. 20b   Katsina niche   Fig. 20a

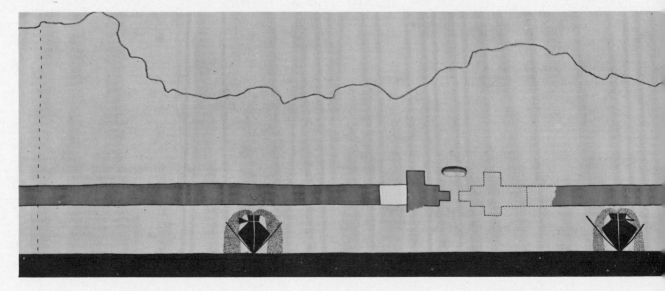

Layer 12

No paintings were found on this layer, thus indicating that it had been a covering wash for the preceding painted layer, C¹-12.

Layer C-11

In this painting there is a black band, about nine inches wide, encircling the chamber at floor level, representing the earth. On this, there are depictions of two black jars, both on the west wall. The one to the left of the niche (fig. 20a) appears to have a rounded base, that of the jar to the right of the niche (fig. 20b), a pointed base. Each rests on a "pillow" composed of two black feathers, one directed upward diagonally at each side of the vessel. Both jars show a white cord tie around the neck and a white line extending centrally to the bottom. A black feather with white tip is tied to the left side of the neck of Figure 20a, and a black feather, to the right side of Figure 20b. There is a design in white of triangles joined at their apices on the neck of the left jar, and larger designs of the same shape on the vessel body. The laboratory notes mention "scratches" in the paint of the other vessel. Moisture symbols

of black dots rise from the mouth of each jar and flow to the border below. The jars are 93 inches apart, and the one on the right is 10.75 inches high; the other is an inch less in height.

Thirteen inches above the black border, a peach colored band extends from the extreme of the south wall to the area of the niche; and from the limit of the north wall, a yellow-orange band is similarly placed. Each is outlined in black. The peach, or right, band shows a white segment as it approaches the niche, set off by a black line on each side, after which a terraced altar in lateral position is painted at the end of the band. This terminates just short of the niche. The orange band in opposed position is lacking most of its terminal features, but the laboratory technicians were able to determine that it also had an altar design at the left side of the niche. If a white segment had existed, that portion of the decoration was too eroded to show it.

Below the colored bands, smatterings of red and of yellow paint indicated features too indistinct to identify. At the southern extreme of the west wall, a fragment of a red and white line below the peach band was noted in the laboratory.

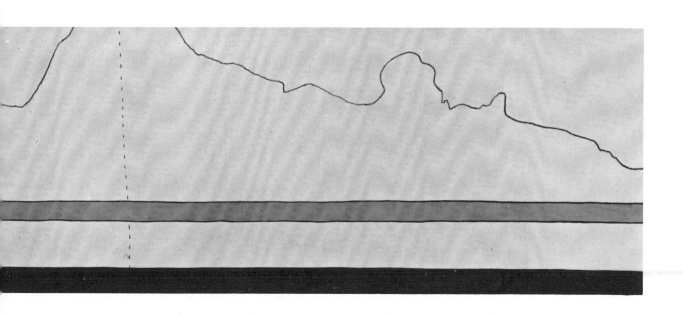

Zna'ote recognized this painting as the FIRST PAINTING WHEN KIVA WAS BUILT, A BLESSING CEREMONY. The colored bands represent THE ROAD, ONAYE TLAN[a]. THE GODS COME ON POL-LEN TRAIL.[506] The WHITE SEGMENT REPRESENTS THE CORNMEAL. THE GODS COME IN FROM THE SOUTH WALL, TAKE OFFERINGS FROM NICHE, AND GO ON OUT TO THE NORTH WALL. The pottery vessels with their moisture represent WATER—LOTS FOR GOOD, LITTLE FOR BAD.

Inasmuch as Kiva III was in use long before this layer of plaster was applied, the possibility of its being the "first painting" could relate only to a time of rebuilding and redecorating, after which a blessing ceremony might be in order. Otherwise, its appearance as a "first painting" might indicate the initial use of this kiva by a society which had not held ceremonies in it previously, and thus had to dedicate it.[507]

------

506. This trail or "road" represents a line of pollen which is symbolic of "the road of life and truth, the road which must be followed in order to win the favor of Awonawilona." It must be followed in order to receive the gifts of the gods (Stevenson, 1904:169 and 171).

507. Ladd says that the painting of the colored bands is

Layer B¹-10

On the plaster layer so identified, on the west wall, a representation was listed as Figure 20 (sic.). The laboratory notes state: "This figure is just one layer below B-9 and is directly below figure 6 of that layer"; indeterminate black is all that remains. This does not appear in the graph copies.

On the south wall, Figure 10 is noted. The laboratory record says "Layer B¹-10 is classified with B-9; it is a fragmentary layer between the two complete ones."

If Layer C-11 is indicative of kiva repairs or rebuilding, this confusion of the painted layers may be the result.

Layer B-9

In this instance, Zna'ote looked at the paintings and said: KÓ HANO. KO HANO MEANS WHITE MAN, LIKE THE WHITE OF THE MOON [light]. PICTURE FOR INITIATION. He then proceeded to identify the personages represented

------

done in most major ceremonies, in the kiva or in special houses, at Zuñi. This would appear to fit the facts at Kuaua.

PL. XXIV. *Layer B-9.* Initiation into the katsina society.

Fig. 10   Fig. 8   Fig. 7

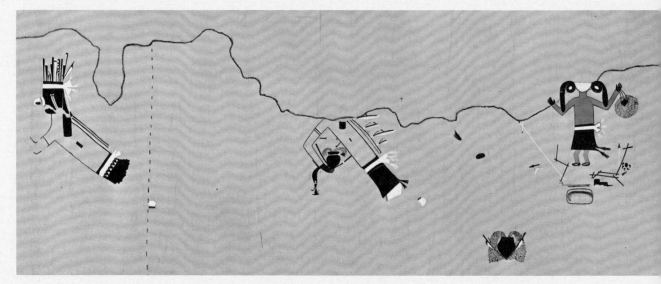

and the accoutrement accompanying them. Thus, we had sufficient information from the start to guide our research in seeking further data.

This was especially fortunate in regard to the fragmentary representations on the eastern portion of the north wall (Pl. XXIV). Figure 19, the first, appeared as a large, irregular area of black with a prominent encircling element painted in orange, reaching to 32.5 inches above the kiva floor. On approximately the same level, midway between Figure 19 and the northwest corner, was a small portion of the body of a personage, 7.5 inches wide, painted in adobe color outlined with black. Below this was a small indication of a black kilt (fig. 18).

Then, in the corner high on the north wall was a personage 38.5 inches tall, whose feet were 33.5 inches above the floor. This brought his head close to the upper limit of the chamber, and his right hand to within 9.5 inches of the corner. The figure (11) is painted white without outline. The long and slender body is disproportionate in all respects. The head is egg shaped. The circular, black disc eyes are

Fig. 11. Kohano (K'ohan'ona), White Salimopiya, Itsepasha, or Anahoho (warrior and seed gatherer—dual personage). *Layer B-9.*

Fig. 6   Fig. 11   Fig. 18   Fig. 19

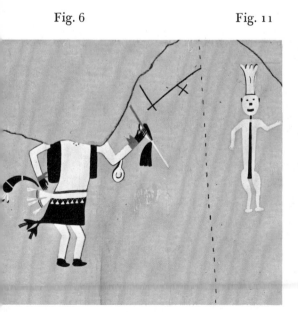

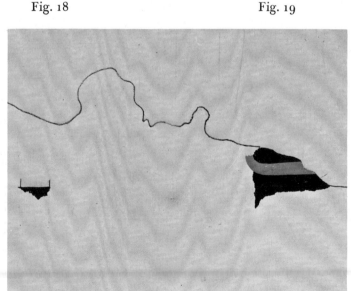

Fig. 6. Shulawitsi with fire torch. *Layer B-9.*

lopsided; and the mouth and nose are unsymmetrical, slightly rounded black rectangles. Relatively small, red oval ears protrude from the upper part of the head. A peculiar headdress is perched atop the head. This was identified as PÓAYANᵉ, HEADDRESS, by Zna'ote. It is outlined with black across the head and on the right side; four irregular scallops on the crest are outlined on their right edges only; and a fine black line cuts into the white on the left of the headdress and arcs to the lower left limit. A black square occurs on the front of the neck, separated by a white block of equal size from a black band which extends down the front of the personage, expanding slightly, to the crotch, where it is squared off like a narrow breechclout. This was the character that immediately identified the painting.

On the west wall, the niche is again the center of painted altar, lightning, and arrow symbolization (Pl. XXIV). To the left of this assemblage is a large animal track: five red claws with black nails, surrounding a red, circular pad, which Zna'ote thought was a mountain lion track. Occupying the space between the

niche and the corner, on the left, is a fine personage whose head had been destroyed (fig. 6). Nevertheless, Zna'ote recognized it as representing a SHIWANNI, or the head priest. The costuming is elaborate. The upper body and arms are painted white, outlined with red. About each wrist is a yellow leather wristlet with W-notch standing erect. Hands are red. The left one grasps a shaft which is yellow above, and white below a cluster of feathers; one each of black and white project upward, and three red ones outlined in black hang pendant. This was identified by Zna'ote as TÓM TLESH NANᵉ, and the white, globular object outlined with black, seen at the left elbow of the priest, as a rattle, or ᵗCHIMUNᵉ. Near the right hand, which is held near the right hip, is a horn-shaped object painted black with red and white encircling bands of decoration, and three small eagle feathers pendant from the head end. Of this, Zna'ote said, SHÓPA TÓMᵉ, thus another kind of rattle. It apparently represents a fire torch.

On the chest of the personage three red dots are shown, suggesting a neck ornament. Here, there is definite indication of a garment about the shoulders. Perhaps a black mantle is represented, but it appears to be vest-like, with arm holes, and reaching only along the sides of the individual. Around the waist is a white sash with three red bands of decoration at each end, tied on the right. Seven white pendants hang from the front of the sash, like conch shells. There is a black kilt with two red bands across the bottom part, each with a triangular border on the upper edge; there is a red band at the bottom also. Large red tassels with black fringes hang at the lower right corner of the kilt. The legs are white, outlined on the fore side with red and black, alternating, fringes. The moccasins are red, and black anklets surmount them. The bended knees indicate an attitude of dancing.

In corresponding location, between the niche and the southwest corner of the cham-

Fig. 8. Sun's speaker, ᵗKiaklo.

Fig. 7. Shiwanokia above katsina niche. *Layer B-9.*

ber, was another personage with elaborate costuming (fig. 8), this identified by Zna'ote as ANI ZA TON, the assistant, or pekwin [pekwin-na]. He is bent over in profile position *(cf.* Pl. B-9). He, too, wears an upper garment, shown in adobe color, outlined with red. The left arm is bent at the elbow, the red hand turned backward and supporting a small black jar, rather lopsidedly pointed at the bottom. This rests on a feathered pillow. These feathers are black, the one toward the personage showing a small white, rectangular unit about midway. Tied on the flaring jar neck with a white cord is a small black feather, also directed toward the personage. Two areas of black moisture dots arc upward from the mouth of the jar and fall downward for a short distance at either side.

Around the upper arm is an encircling band painted in black, red, and white. About the

wrist an ornament, or PA SI KWIN, is secured. It is painted black, sweeps downward in a curve and has an attractive end decoration. The pointed end is red, back of which is a fine white band, then a similar black one from which a white triangle with a black dot in its center is directed in opposition to the red point. A red feather with a small arc of black and white at its lower extreme hangs pendant from the wristlet's lower end. Along its posterior side a tiny black and white barb projects upward diagonally. At the tip of the wrist ornament a small black hook extends forward. One fine black line and a white one with black tip are seen parallel with the arm, back of the wristlet.

Within the area inclosed by the personage, his arm, and the water jar complex, three small red linear figures occur; the one just back of the arm has a forked end; one projects forward from the body toward the mouth of the vessel and ends in a tiny square; the third, very short one, extends at a diagonal from a few inches under the armpit. In the center of the body a small red rectangle occupies the heart position. A short tress of black hair shows, cut off squarely, on the left shoulder. The personage wears a close fitting dance kilt of black, supported around the waist by an all-white sash with tasseled ends. A short distance below the sash, a fine white stripe encircles the kilt; it has a red border and red separates off the black fringes which project backward. A small part of the left leg shows, painted white with red outline up the front along which are fine white fringes with black tips. Elevated behind the body, one white heel shows, surmounted by a black anklet. The pekwin is clearly in a dancing position, like that assumed by the animal figures in the winter dances still observable among the Pueblo Indians.

Along the back of the pekwin, a long white stripe outlines the red color from neck to waist. Back of this is an equally long white element outlined in red, with an orange stripe through the center, lengthwise (cf. Pl. B-9). From this feature, four white feathers, black along the quill, project to the back, large and small ones alternating. They are tied on with white, in the shape of small, shafted points. Back of the points, tiny red and white feathers with black tips form an angle with each of the larger feathers. From the latter, the frequently noted barbs, in black and white, extend diagonally toward the back of the pekwin (fig. 8). Here, Zna'ote said, UKYA' AN^e, FEATHER. BLACK FEATHERS FROM A LITTLE BLACK BIRD. LOTS OF THEM AT SALINA POINT. NAVAHO CALL HIM "NI ANI." The figure complete is a STREAMER, WYA·-ETO'.

In the area between the pekwin's feet and the niche, 14.5 inches above the kiva floor, is a black water jar, which, like that carried by pekwinna, was called K'APE by Zna'ote. It rests on the usual pillow, with black feathers projecting upward at each side of the vessel. From the lower side of the right quill a white feather with black end marking is tied. Short barbs— presumably tiny feathers—are seen on each quill about mid-section, and black barbs near the outer extremes. The rim, neck, and shoulder of the jar are outlined with red.

Above the niche in the west wall, another personage is portrayed, and this represents a female character (fig. 7), standing 37.5 inches above the kiva floor. Although the upper portion of the head is gone, whorls of black hair, which Zna'ote called MATSI KWAWE, dressed about a white "spool," shows at either side, with tresses falling over each shoulder. The lower part of the face was painted white and outlined with red. Body, upraised arms, and legs bent at the knees—all suggestive of a dancing position—are yellow, outlined with red except for the legs. Hands are red, though most of the right one was eroded. The left hand holds the thongs from a small tri-lobed, black vessel; two of these thongs are black, the central one red. A heavy shower of black moisture surrounds the jar, formed into a dotted sphere. Zna'ote said this is a SEED OR WATER PITCHER.

About the waist, tied on the left, is a white sash, with a red border around each end, separating off white-fringed tassels. There is a black skirt with red border at the bottom and red tassels with black fringes at the lower left corner. The moccasins are red.

In this personage, Zna'ote recognized SHI-WANOK' [Shiwanokia], priestess of fecundity.

At the southwest corner, there remained still another personage, this one with his head and upper body nearly intact (fig. 10) on the south wall. This is also in an attitude of dancing, like that of Figure 8. The elbow shown is 44 inches above the floor.

The body and left arm are painted adobe color, outlined with red. The arm appears to have been elevated and fore-reaching; a narrow band of red and white encircles the upper arm. The head is covered with a black, face mask in the form of a bird, which Zna'ote called WA·U TAN·NI. It has the curved beak of a macaw. The upper bill is painted white, the lower black; and the entire nib is separated from the posterior portion by an encircling stripe of red. The eyes are formed of two white dots separated from each other by a small intervening area of black—thus as a figure 8 on its side. From each eye, a long diagonal tear passes across the cheek, as two parallel white stripes separated by a red, longitudinal stripe.

An elaborate feathered headdress crests the head, held in place by a white, fringed sash, bordered at each edge with red; the spread out fringed tassels extend toward the rear. Zna'ote spoke of the headdress as PÁ PÓAYAN^e, saying, SHUMÁKO·NI IS A ZUÑI HEADDRESS SIMILAR TO THIS. The feathers show various combinations of white and black, red, red and white, and red and black, representing eagle, macaw, and perhaps others. At the back of the headdress, a white cord hangs down to the left shoulder with a red feather pendant [mystery medicine].

The back of the figure, like that of Figure 8, shows a white stripe outside the red of the body; and a similar paralleling element, this time red at each edge and adobe in the center, but without any indication of feathered trailer.

There is a black dance kilt, supported by a white sash, with shell pendants hanging from the front. Part of the white leg with red fore stripe and black fringe is seen at the juncture of the south and west walls.

Viewing the entire painting, Zna'ote remarked: NOBODY BUT THE SHIWANNI COULD GO INTO THE KIVA. AFTER THE CEREMONY, THE PAINTINGS ARE COVERED OVER. JUST DURING THE INITIATION ARE THERE PICTURES. EVERY FOUR OR EIGHT YEARS, A CEREMONY; AT NIGHT, FOR FOUR NIGHTS. IN THE MORNING, TAKE IT AWAY, LIKE A NAVAHO SANDPAINTING.

Taking Ko·hano as clue, it was found that the White gods of the Kianakwe were honored

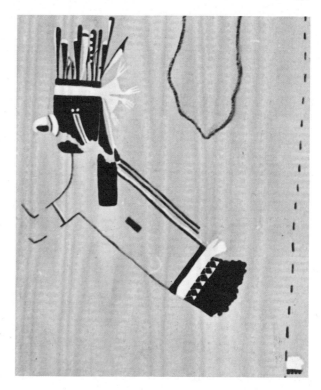

Fig. 10. Shumaikoli. *Layer B-9.*

by a dance given in four-year intervals at Zuñi, which Mrs. Stevenson observed in 1884 and on two later occasions. She notes that the personators of the Kianakwe are always members of the Corn clan and of the "corn house," or South kiva. Particularly significant to this study is the fact that the songs sung during the ceremonies were "archaic" [or ceremonial], and in the tongue of the Zia Indians, which the Zuñi said "was the language of the Kianakwe,"[508] thus Keresan.

In describing the ceremonies, Mrs. Stevenson says those who are to personate the Kianakwe "and their prisoners"[509] assemble south of the pueblo and paint their bodies with a very thin wash of pinkish clay, after which they dress themselves in their sacred embroidered blankets and masks, and return to the village. She says the priest leads, followed by his deputy. "They wear white cotton shirts, white embroidered blankets, each having four

508. Stevenson, 1904:918. *See* White, 1944:161 167.
509. *See* Layer O-43.

dark fluffy eagle plumes attached, front and
back, in the form of a square. They wear leggings of white cotton, knit in fanciful designs,
and dance moccasins. A tortoise-shell rattle is
carried in the right hand and a pottery meal
basket and *télikinawe* [prayersticks] are carried in the left. Each mask is finished at the
base with a collarette of spruce tipped with
popcorn" [and she illustrates these masks in
color, Pl. XLIII].[510]

She then says that the leaders wear dressed
deerskins instead of the embroidered blankets,
"and they wear bow wristlets and carry tortoise-shell rattles in the right hand and bows
and arrows in the left." In those features which
are comparable, the Zuñi impersonators dif-
fered little from those portrayed at Kuaua
some 500 years earlier; and where the Kuaua
features are lacking, Mrs. Stevenson supplies
helpful data.

The captives which she mentions are then
identified.[511] The first is *Kóthlama* [a man who
has permanently adopted female attire], whom
she describes thus:

He wears the woman's dress of black, embroidered in dark blue, and caught at the
waist with a red woven belt. A white embroidered sash passes from the left side of the
waist to the right shoulder, where it is tied,
the embroidered ends falling. A piece of
white commercial cotton hangs over the
back. The neck and arms, which are exposed,
are painted white; the hair is parted from the
forehead down the back of the head, and one
side is done up over a wooden form, while
the other side is tied with red and blue yarn
and left hanging. The mask covers only the
face. A rattle of deer scapulae is carried in
the right hand, and three ears of corn, tied
together with yucca ribbons and telikinawe,
are carried in the left [and she illustrates the
mask, Pl. XLIV].

This appears as a likely description of the personage represented by the fragmentary features of our Kuaua Figure 18 (Pl. XXIV). Another captive is identified as Saya^{t}hlia, or Blue
Horn (a warrior god), who:

wears a large deerskin, dyed reddish-brown
and elaborately ornamented with various
colored designs, an emblem of the sun being
on the back. A white cotton embroidered
sash is tied around his waist under the deerskin and falls at the side. The mask of the
Saya^{t}hlia is of a native cotton cloth, colored
with paint made from the pinkish clay. The
mouth of the mask is bearded with lynx
skin,[512] and the projecting teeth are made of
corn husks. Gray goat's wool falls over the
top of the head and forehead, and padded
eyeballs are conspicuous beneath the wool.
A red fox skin is worn around the neck at
the base of the mask [shown in her Pl. XVI].
The Saya^{t}hlia carries a tortoise-shell rattle
in the right hand and a bow and arrows and
telikinawe in the left.[513]

This seems to explain the features of Figure
19, which were perplexing, for the large deerskin would have obscured what might otherwise have given a lead to identity (*see* Pl.
B–11). Of course the Zuñi personage whom
Mrs. Stevenson describes had access to items of
embellishment which the Kuaua Indians did
not possess. The reference to a lynx skin may
support Zna'ote's supposition that the animal
track shown to the left of the niche complex
might be that of a mountain lion, indicating
that some large cat was important in this ceremony—perhaps referring to the cougar, Beast
god of the North.

510. Stevenson, 1904:218-219.

511. *See* her account of the destruction of the Kianakwe,
1904:36-39. *See* footnote 180, herein.

512. Ladd adds an important feature to the mask's description, that of the horns at each side, which are painted
blue, thus giving name to this figure. He notes that the
whole mask (which is made of buckskin) is painted black,
with crescents in blue and yellow below the eyes—the
same as shown on Kolowisi. Today, the mouth is bearded
with coyote skin, rather than lynx (*see* Pl. B–11).

513. Stevenson, 1904:219.

Mrs. Stevenson then mentions "the last captive," Ítsepasha (game maker),[513] one of the Koyemshi, who wears a "short, ragged skirt of native black cloth, and the three-cornered piece of the same at the base of the mask, the body and mask being colored with the pinkish clay." None of the Kuaua figures are painted with the pinkish color of Zuñi clay, rather, where comparable personages are represented, they are colored with the greyish-white clay of the Rio Grande. The Kuaua representation indicates an impersonator not unlike Itsepasha of Zuñi.

On viewing this being (fig. 11), Zna'ote said, KOHANO, which indicated *Ko'hanonna*, one of the White Salimopiya. The figure appears to be a clown, and it was observed that he occupies the same position in the northwest corner as do other personages of similar character (figs. 95, 27, and 4). Mentioned as a participant in the initiation ceremony of Zuñi is *Anahoho*, whom Ladd identifies as a member of the Salimopiya.[514] Bunzel says that his body is painted with white paint. He wears two sashes sewed together and worn as a breechclout instead of the regular kilt. As the only decoration, he wears crow feathers, "because the crow always comes when everything is quiet and no one is looking for a fight and they bring bad luck."[515] From this, it may be inferred that the black feather decoration on the headdress of the Kuaua personage represents crow feathers. He carries sticks which have turkey feathers and other feathers of little birds attached to them.[516] There seems little doubt but that this identifies the Kuaua figure.

Bunzel says that the Salimopiya do not like the Anahoho (for whom there are two masks); they chase them about and knock them down. The sticks which the Anahoho carry are not used for striking anyone; they are "just to take away the bad luck."[517] She explains that "ana" is an exclamation of distress, and *anahoho* means "take away bad luck."[518]

The same source says that the Anahoho were responsible for the welfare and protection of the people. In their role of guardian, it was natural that their appearance bespoke trouble at hand, such as the approach of enemies in days gone by, particularly the Navaho of later times. Thus it is told that the Anahoho "came like the crows to warn the people of bad luck. And in the evening the Navaho came and they began to fight. Many Navaho were killed, but none of the Zuñi. Then the elder brother Anahoho dipped his right hand in the blood of the Navaho and put it on his face and the younger one used his left hand. That is how you can tell them apart."[519]

The present writer believes that Anahoho may be considered as a manifestation of the Divine Ones, or the subsequent twin War gods. Here, it should be stressed that the religious concept held by the Indians of the Southwest, of Mesoamerica, and elsewhere, was one of monotheism. As stated previously in this work, the Indians of this region recognize a supreme being, a great spiritual omnipotence. Very much like the Holy family of the followers of Christianity, practical leaders related the ideas of Indian religion to the biologic family. In our use of Zuñi terminology, we have, then, Awonawilona, power that is manifest through the Sun Father, the

---

514. Parsons, 1922:200, notes that: "Theoretically there are two *salimpopia*, older brother and younger brother, for each of the six directions after which they take their color . . . but practically the impersonation, like several others, admits of reduplication." Cushing, 1896:399, records twain *Anahohoátchi* as the next younger brothers of Kyaklu [ᵗKiaklo]—who went to the north; they to the south.

515. *See* Bunzel, 1932:993-994.

516. Roadrunner, hawk *(tsilelika)*, blue jay *(maiha)*, swallow ? *(anilawa)*, and hummingbird *(tanya)*—Bunzel, 1932:993.

517. Bunzel, 1932:994, stated that the Anahoho had special secret prayers for "taking away the bad luck," but that only one person, an albino woman with no ceremonial connection, knew them at that time.

518. Ladd says, "This is a literal translation; it cannot, in fact, be translated."

519. Bunzel, 1932:994.

great god. His female counterpart is provided. These two are "married," and they produce offspring commonly identifiable as twain — but sometimes coalescing into one being, and sometimes appearing as boy and girl.

I have come to the conclusion that the terms, "elder brother" and "younger brother," as used by the Indians, relate to the twin War gods themselves (as successors of the Divine Ones) or to various earthly personages who display manifestations of them, for instance, the "elder brother Bow priest" and the "younger brother Bow priest," and, in the present case, to the Anahoho.

Here, the Anahoho depiction (fig. 11) occurs in the upper northwest corner of the kiva, in a position noted previously as significant, and which seems to indicate that from there, messages, prayers, and perhaps the causes for maladies passed upward from the sacred chamber. Furthermore, it suggests that each of the so-called clown figures that appear in similar location were members of medicine societies; it is possible that they symbolize curing rites which were part of a total ceremonial enactment for the welfare of those who dwelt at Kuaua. The Anahoho beings represent, also, the wise priests and mighty warriors; indeed, they are multiple personages.

Referring again to the initiation ceremony into the Shuma·kwe, in the dance of the fourth day, there appear six Shumaikoli personages, representing the regional directions, who come from Chipia, each accompanied by two warriors (Saiapa), and each god with a mask of appropriate color. Mrs. Stevenson describes the Shuma·koli of the North [and she illustrates the Shumaikoli of the Zenith—her Pl. CXXIII], which, but for color of the mask, kind of feathers, and slight temporal alterations, might well be the personage shown as our Figure 10.[520]

Finally, Shiwanokia enters the scene, stand-

ing just back of the priest and his pekwinna, thus much as shown in our portrayal, the priestess of fecundity above the decorated niche, with the priest to her left, and his assistant to the right. Her chief duty is to collect the gifts of corn, meat, birds, plumes, etc., which are brought in great quantities, and to give them proper attention. There are dances, of course, in which men and women participate.

Dr. Bunzel reports that when an initiation into the katsina organization is to take place at Zuñi, the priests prepare prayersticks for Pautiwa, thus summoning his presence. She says that the initiation ceremonies at Zuñi were so timed that the final public rites fell "on the day of the full moon of the third month following the [Winter] solstice."[521] She enumerates personages represented by the katsinas. All of the officials of the katsina society gather in the kivas, where Pautiwa comes and re-tells the "talk of the first beginning." When he leaves, each kiva appoints the impersonators of two Salimopiya and of the other gods who accompany them. Prayersticks are planted and an eight-day retreat observed.

On the day that the initiation is to take place, the katsina officers and dancers meet the children in the plaza, where they are divided into two groups. The katsinas line up and begin whipping the youngsters (a rite of exorcism), in turn. When they have been whipped by the last katsina, Shulawitsi, the boys enter the North kiva, where they look at "the pictures on the wall," and take "the feather from one of them." It is explained that the boys always want to be whipped first, so as to get the feather of an important katsina like Pautiwa, "or one of the nice-looking" katsinas. There is a katsina for each boy who is whipped. "The boys just go down into the kiva and get their feathers and come back to the plaza."[522]

Inasmuch as Zna'ote explained the Kuaua

---

520. *See* Stevenson, 1904:536-537.

521. Bunzel, 1932:975.
522. Bunzel, 1932:980.

Fig. 3. Duck or 'Eya. *Layer A-8.*

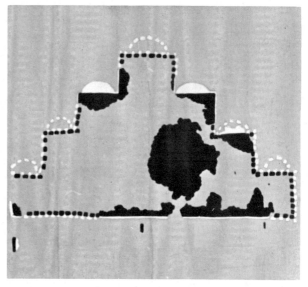

Fig. 5. Altar surmounted by white clouds. *Layer A-8.*

paintings of Layer B-9 as pertaining to an initiation, we may assume that he was referring to a ceremony very much like that mentioned above. It is plain that Zna'ote is thinking of the earthly representatives of the deific ones when he identifies the characters of this painting, and others, in terms of the priest, priestess, and their assistants. We know, as Ladd points out, that these are not depicted in paintings, as a rule; they have no counterparts in the Koko group. Rather, the mundane are visible manifestations of the Sun, Moon, and their associated celestial bodies.

Layer A-8

This was the final plaster layer in the kiva which bore decorations. At the extreme east of the north wall there remained the fragment of a large white waterfowl, shown with four-scallop tail and tip of the upraised wing outlined with black. The legs and webbed feet are yellow, the latter located 30 inches above the kiva floor. A red hand overlies the rear of the bird,[523] as though grasping it (fig. 3), but

---

523. Handprints are a fairly common expression of sympathetic magic, signifying the desire of the maker of the print to bring forth whatever is depicted; a deity, clouds, etc. The red handprint bespeaks the elder War god.

actually symbolizing the call for deific assistance. Above the bird about five inches is a red arced line, indicating a bow for him to descend upon. This complex would seem to signify that of the duck, 'EYA, which immediately brings to mind Pautiwa, who commonly appears in that guise.

Midway between the fowl and the northwest corner is the indication of a large altar of dull carbon black color, outlined with white, and surmounted by white clouds, representing the cumulus rain bringers. A large patch had been made over the altar, obliterating much of its features; these are indicated in our illustration by dashed white lines (Pl. XXV, fig. 5).

At the northwest corner, in the same position as that occupied by the clown-medicine man, Anahoho, of the preceding plaster layer (B-9:11), is another personage of peculiar mien (fig. 4)—and this was the one discovered initially, on that historic day of the excavations.

The nude body is painted a dirty white color, with black outline which, along the outer side on the right, is then bordered with white from neck to crotch. Along the inside of the right leg, a long, narrow, triangular area is painted black. The right fingers of the up-

Fig. 4. Luᵗkia, dual personage (brother and sister). *Layer A-8.*

On the left wrist another ornament is shown, a white wristlet with apparently three short, red parallel marks at the front center, and deep, red crescents projecting above and below the wrist. Below the left knee was a white band, to which a plume or tassel was secured, this black with red outline.

The head of this personage is covered with a mask and headdress of sorts. Only the right side of the head remained, and this is painted in orange-yellow and outlined with black. Traces of white on the left side are discernible [indicated in our illustration by dashed lines]. The grotesque muzzle is shown as a solid black circle, bordered with white, then a red circle, and white again separating it from the face. It would seem that this depicts the front view of an element which projected some distance from the face, like the snout of modern katsina impersonators. The eyes, shown in knobby projections above the face, are solid white circles with red outline. These doubtless represent knobs which also projected out from the mask. Here, a red line separates the eye from the erect, rounded ear or horn, which is painted white and outlined with black.

raised hand are black also. Alongside them on the right is a rounded, red element, from which two branched units extend, as though representing the antlers of a deer, which the personage is carrying. From this wrist an ornament extends toward the right. Since a white, pointed tie is shown to the left, this probably represents a wrist ornament secured with a white cord. It shows a small red crescent pointing away from the wrist, at the beginning of a short white section which becomes less in width, and terminates in a curved, black claw.

Probably because this figure was the first

PL. XXV. *Layer A-8.* Ceremonial of the Sun cult.

Fig. 15   Fig. 1   Fig. 2

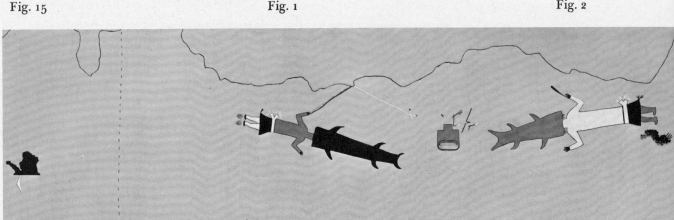

Fig. 2. Elder son of the Sun, Shutsukya or Shulawitsi, the Fire god. *Layer A-8*.

one to be disclosed and salvaged from the Kuaua excavations, it was reproduced as a single figure, originally. It was thus presented to our informants for identification without association with the other figures of this layer. Zna'ote, upon looking at it, merely remarked: JUST LIKE A MUDHEAD, LÚʿKIA.

The west wall features the niche again. This has a simple altar painted above the cavity, in yellow with red outline. From the upper left,

red, white and black crossed lightning and arrow symbols are directed upward; one red point remains in similar position on the right of the altar.

In a recumbent position, to the left of the niche, there is a fully extended personage adorned with a great headdress shaped like a fish, painted yellow and outlined with red (Pl. XXV). The caudal fin shows as though viewed laterally, and dorsal fins appear on each side.

Fig. 4   Fig. 5   Fig. 3

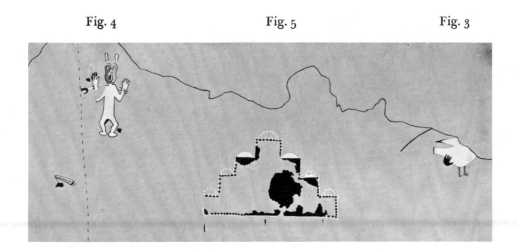

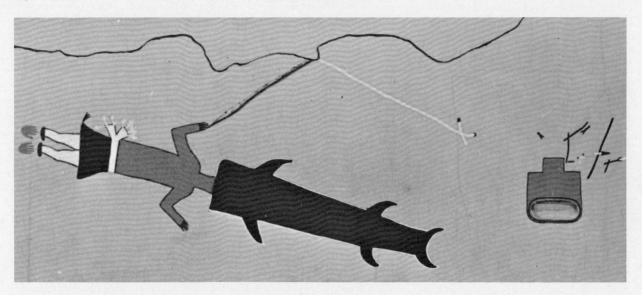

Fig. 1. Younger son of the Sun, Kwelele, god of Heat. *Layer A-8.*

The head of the fish is severed (like Layer D-14:25) and unites with, or encompasses, the head of the personage; thus the two coalesce (fig. 2). Short, parallel red marks "drip" toward the personage on either side of his neck.

The personage has white body and arms akimbo outlined with red; the extended hands are red. Near the upper hand, a red, feather-shaped element, with pointed end toward the hand, extends on a diagonal upward; this may bespeak a torch. Because the being is probably facing toward the niche, the "upper hand" would be the right one. About the waist is a white sash with the ends outlined in red and with black fringes, tied on the upper side. There is a black kilt with red border and red fringes on the upper corner. The legs and feet are yellow, outlined with red. The total extent of this depiction is about 60 inches, with the headdress 34 inches in extent. The lowermost fin is about 22 inches above the floor.

Below the feet is an irregular splotch of red color, from which four fringe-like projections extend, directed toward Figure 4. Below and to the north, reaching to the corner, is a fragmentary element. The rather rectangular black unit, to which a feather-shaped element

is tied, suggests the usual "pollen pouch" or sacred bundle of a priest. The feather (?) is black with white central area; across the posterior end are black, red, white, and red bands.

To the right of the niche, a similar personage is shown recumbent (fig. 1; *cf.* Pl. B-13). The fish headdress is painted black and is outlined with white. Where the severed portion of the fish unites with the neck of the personage, black parallel marks "drip" toward the personage. The body and upraised arms are yellow with red outline. The hands are red. From the upper (left) one, an arc or bow extends to the upper limit of the wall. This is painted in a strong red color, above which a bleared red area is shown, as on Layer G-26 (fig. 106). Where this terminates, a long shaft with black tip crosses over a similar fragment, coming to within approximately six inches of the red point above the altar-niche.

The personage has a white sash like that of Figure 2. The black kilt has a red border, but shows black fringes; these and the sash ends extend upward. Legs are white with red outline, and the moccasins are red. Below, or back of, each foot, a yellow hand reaches toward it.

These two personages, said Zna'ote, are FIGURES OF MEN GODS (BOTH), MÓ-O-TASHA

["Long head"—E. J. L.]. NOBODY SEES THESE MEN IN THE DAY TIME, EXCEPT SOMETIMES WHEN THE SUN IS GOING DOWN OR PARTLY VISIBLE. THEY WATCH THE SUN. SOMETIMES ONE COLOR; SOMETIMES ALL COLORS. THEY WATCH THE PEOPLE. THEY WEAR MASKS (the tall head-dresses). THEY ARE PLACED THUS BECAUSE THEY BELONG THIS WAY, ONE ON EACH SIDE, THE SUN BETWEEN.

The symbols around the niche, here representing the sun, are SUN RAYS, TÉK A TSHLAN. Referring to the hands shown behind Figure 1, he said, HANDS ARE TO SHOW REFLECTED SUNLIGHT, ÁSIN. And then he added, CHÍMI KES, "O.K."[very good].

Around on the south wall there is a fragmentary depiction (Pl. XXV, fig. 15), perhaps the remains of another personage. Of this, a black area, 20.5 inches above the floor, may represent a kilt or skirt, and, below it, the white with red outline may indicate a leg bent in a dancing position.

In the first place, this painting relates to the history myth of the coming of the people into the present world from the undermost world,[524] searching for the light of day, or *Lu'kiu*. Thus the principal characters would include Pautiwa and his deputy, 'Kiaklo; the twin War gods (represented by the elder and younger brother Bow priests); the father of the ancestral gods, Father Koyemshi; the katsina director and his assistant; pekwin—deputy to the Sun Father; and there would be the fetishes for rain and fructification. These personages recite the drama in narrative, song, and prayer.[525]

In brief, the myth tells that the twin pair, working together in the Below, thought and talked of ways to aid their people. They wanted the light. They summoned the Rain priest of the North, of the West, of the South, and of the East, all of whom came bringing their "precious things" [sacred bundles] to bring rains and crops. All came through "the hole," all looking for the Middle place, the middle of the world.[526] The Koyemshi talked together, and came through the hole with their precious things. The elder brother came forth followed by many people from the watery Below. Later, the younger brother came forth, and the other people after him. All of the places to which the travelers came are enumerated; e.g., "They came to the gaming-stick spring . . . the gaming-ring spring . . . the Newekwe baton spring," etc.; all of their accomplishments are mentioned in the telling, and the natural features along the route; the names of their gods are given and their insignia and paraphernalia. 'Kiaklo is called and comes on the back of an ancient one to show the middle way, which is followed. He recites the route, naming all the places where the people traveled, always moving on.

Since then, when the drama is re-enacted, the directors and laymen assemble in the kivas to receive 'Kiaklo, who still comes on the back of a Koyemshi, and recites the narrative in full (*see* pages 44 and 106 herein) .

Dr. Benedict has recorded a Zuñi myth concerning a little boy and his younger sister of the Kianakwe people at Kamaka. Suffering great famine, the Kianakwe went to Acoma seeking food; they left the children behind.[527] At first the boy and his sister lived on woodrats, then he went hunting for deer and discovered two inhabited pueblos (Ketshipawa and Hawikuh) . He collected his few possessions, fastened his medicine bundle about his left wrist, and took his sister forth. Near the place called Ketshipawa they were seen by the priest's daughter who ran home to tell her father: "I

---

524. Ladd concurs in this identification, and recalls that "the children dropped by the frightened mothers into the water became all the sea (water) creatures, such as fish and water snakes."

525. *See* Stevenson, 1904:73 ff.

526. *See also* Stevenson, 1887:540. Ladd notes that, "according to myth, the Koyemshi were 'created' en route to the middle world."

527. *See also* Benedict, 1935-I:29.

saw two children at the spring. One side of their faces is white, the other red. They have snout-like mouths. Under their eyes there are curlicues. They are dressed in beautiful white ceremonial blankets." The priest reported this to the Bow priest, who went to the children and brought them into the plaza. There the boy gave his name as Kanithlana, and explained their plight. They and his medicine bundle of great power—which had been the Yellow Corn fetish, now turned to Black Corn —were welcomed and adopted among the people of Ketshipawa.[528]

This description of the children fits well with that of the Kuaua Figure 4, and the association with the deer appears significant.[529] The fact that the children are indicated here as twain—shown by the double outline along the right side of our personage—is not disturbing, although the depiction of the boy and a girl together seems not to have occurred before. Layer N-41 showed a merging of personages in Figure 95, Kanashkule; Figure 27 of Layer D-14 proved to have dual character in Neipatch, as did Figure 11 of Layer B-9, Anahoho; and each pertained to priest-clown-medicine men. It thus may be inferred that Figure 4, identified as Lúᵗkia, is likewise a personage of this class, and that his fetish was in possession of the Black Corn clan at Kuaua. It would seem that this further identifies Figure 4 with the twin War gods, as in the previous occurrences, and places them with the deities mentioned above as participants in the history myth.[530] This might, then, elucidate Figure 3 further, indicating (by the red hand) that the War gods were sending forth a message to Pautiwa, summoning him to give them aid.

At another time, Dr. Benedict recorded a

Zuñi tale about a little man called *Tsiposho* [doubtless Itsepasha, a Koyemshi], who killed the people as they went forth for wood. He killed them with a stone with a hole in its center, attached to a string. Then he dragged their bodies into his house, "where there was a passage going far in." The village people gathered around his "house hole," planning to kill Tsiposho. "Before sunrise he started from the bottom. When he came out he made a noise with the stones fastened around his legs. When the sun (yellow light) came out, his head came out too [fig. 2 ?]. When the sun was up, he came out. He looked around. He said, 'Look at the people hiding.' Then he ran into his hole."

The people tried again the next day, "They waited there for him before sunrise. Before sunrise his head came out. At sunrise his whole head came out. As the sun moved he moved out. When the sun was up he came out and he said, 'Look at the people hiding around.' Then he walked about his hole. This side the people were hiding, others on the other side, and some on this side, the people were hiding in every direction. 'Let me eat,' he said. So he ate off the bushes."

The contest continued in similar manner, Tsiposho always evading the people and going into his hole. Then the two Ahaiyuta or War gods came to aid the people. They fashioned stone masks which just fitted their heads, and made holes for the eyes [fig. 4 ?]. They made kick sticks to carry them rapidly to where Tsiposho was, in his mountain watching them approach. He outwitted them, and so they went to the Hopi for help. The next morning the little man came out of his hole and did as before. While he was out eating around, the Hopi put black blankets in the bottom of his hole. The tale continues:

On top they put the white blankets worn by the Koko, the buckskins and rabbit skins. They fixed it while the others chased Tsiposho. He went far with the men who chased

---

528. *From* Benedict, 1935-I:8.

529. Cushing, 1901:464-465, also sheds more light on the twin-deer (or antelope) relationship (*see* Pl. B-12).

530. Ladd suggests that Figure 4 might equate with the Zuni witch, *Ha'ti kwi'*, "who came up and was not killed because he brought up with him the 'staff of life,' corn!"

him. He turned back when he was tired and went to the same place where he had been. When he came close to his hole, the men near the hole chased him. Then he went up into the air. He looked straight down to his hole, then he came down. He went in, but his head got stuck in the rabbit skins. He was hanging in the hole. Then the Aihayuta caught him. Then the people tied up his arms and legs. They asked him, "Who is your father, and who is your mother? How did you grow up?" the Aihayuta asked him. "My father is Sun, and my mother is Moon, they brought me up. My father is Sun, that is the reason I keep coming up before the day light. I come out the same time my father comes up. That is the way we are," he told them.[531]

That there is very close association in the Indian mind between light and life is illustrated by the Zuñi word, *tekohanan·e,* which means "daylight."[532] The sun is daylight, and thus is recognized as the source of all life, as has been pointed out previously. Consequently, the Sun cult is of primordial importance. The greatest observances relating to the sun come during the solstices.

The tale concerning Tsipooho has to do with the movement of the sun from south to north, the days when the sun seems to stand directly over head, or in the Above, and its return from north to south. There is also a hint as to the practice of "binding the years."

The personages (figs. 1 and 2) guarding the sun-niche are doubtless representations of the twin sons of the Sun, for they were "in the days of creation, the benignant guardians of man; but when the world became filled with envy and war, they were changed by the eight gods of the storms into warriors more powerful than all monsters, gods, or men. The elder one was right-handed, the younger, left-handed . . ."[533]

Figure 2 is recognizable as the elder, who carries his weapon in the right hand, and Figure 1, as the younger, with his bow and "medicine-pointed arrows" in the left.

Having created the two sons, through the impregnation of a foam cap on the waters, the Sun imparted to them "control-thought and his own knowledge-wisdom," while yet retaining these. Thus he gave them of himself and of their mother, "the great cloud-bow, and for arrows the thunderbolts of the four quarters [two to each], and for buckler the fog-making shield, which (spun of the floating clouds and spray and woven, as of cotton we spin and weave) supports as on wind, yet hides (as a shadow hides) its bearer, defending also."[534]

Further consolidation of deific manifestations is permitted here. The white body of Figure 2 and the black body of Figure 1 indicate their identity as Shutsukya (or Shulawitsi), the white, or Fire god, and his brother, Kwelele, the black god, or god of heat, such as discussed on page 71. This suggests that this painting was made during the Winter solstice ceremony, at which time the new year is brought from the east.

Bunzel mentions that at Zuni, each morning, "as the sun sends his first level beams striking across the houses his people come out to meet him with prayers and offerings," and that men and women stand before their doors, facing the east, with their hands full of cornmeal, which is offered to the sun, with prayers for long life. This, doubtless, reflects a practice which obtained at Kuaua. Bunzel says that every priest or appointee to ceremonial office and every man during the time he is engaged in any ceremony must observe this morning ritual; and that many others never omit it, "even on the most bitterly cold winter mornings."[535]

Thus, Layer A-8 indicates that the cult of

---

531. Parsons, 1930:6-10.

532. Bunzel, 1932:511. Ladd amplifies this by giving: *tek'ohati,* "daylight"; *tek'ohanna,* "light, day"; and *tek'-ohonna,* "life."

533. Cushing, 1901:441.

534. Cushing, 1896:382.

535. Bunzel, 1932:512.

the Sun was of foremost importance at Kuaua. It may represent the final ceremonial which was held by the groups which used Kiva III. At any rate, it was the last plaster layer to have been painted. After the cycle of ceremonials which has been discussed had been enacted, seven layers of plaster were applied to the kiva walls, none of which showed any decoration.

The pictorial record of Kiva III at Kuaua thus comes to its end.

THE PAINTINGS OF KIVA VI

It has been noted that paintings had also occurred on the walls of the small kiva in the east plaza, but that these were in exceedingly poor state. Insofar as the author knows, the only survivals are five fragmentary reproductions which have no data other than that shown thereon.

From the east wall, Figure 1 depicts a personage wearing a black kilt, which is bordered at the bottom and up a short way on each side with red. The red legs extend awkwardly from the kilt as though the latter hung down behind them in part. The knees are flexed as in a position of dancing. There are black moccasins on the feet, and a white anklet shows above the right foot. At the left of the personage a pointed black streak extends in a diagonal. Near its lower portion a red dot occurs, and another spot of red is seen to the left of the kilt.

On the back of the reproduction there is the penciled information, "14½″ from 1st floor, 2′ 9½″ from north edge of ventilator opening."

The next representation was found at the northeast corner of the chamber, above the first floor. A notation on the back of the reproduction says, "7′ 4″ from NW corner of altar to 'navel,' and 8′ 8½″ from east wall to navel." This and the quoted information above is in the handwriting of Dorothy L. Luhrs, who

PL. XXVI. Fig. 1. Unidentified personage.

served as supervisor on the Kuaua project for some time. Fortunately, the scale of each drawing is alike.

This Figure 2 appears to represent a disproportionate personage, decked out in a gay blazer (*cf.* Layer N-41:96). The head is missing, as are the neck and upper left part of the shoulder. Body to the waist and both arms are painted in a grey-blue color, different from any used in Kiva III, judging from the reproduction, and indicating a close-fitting, long-sleeved garment. The arm holes are encircled with a two-color band, red on the outer side and yellow toward the body. About the upper right arm is a narrow band of red and yellow; and a wrist ornament is shown by two bordering bands of red, between which the blue color of the arm is interspersed by equal elements of yellow—these at right angles to the red borders.

The left arm appears to be only about half the ordinary length and slightly smaller than the right one. At approximately the expected elbow region, a yellow wrist band is secured, with three-part tie or notched element above. Outward from the wrist ornament is a fingered portion, as if a hand, showing but four digits. Tucked into the wristlet and extending body-ward is a small rectangular device of black with a yellow stripe through the mid-part, longitudinally. Near the upper end of this, and above it, is a tiny black, pointed feature with red interior, which points toward the wrist.

About the waist is a belt, apparently of woven type, with red border on each outer edge, and white central area with black mid-line, across which short black units extend. Below the belt, twelve short diagonal elements are pendant, thus overlying a kilt or skirt of dirty white or bluish color. Below the yellow decoration, six bands of fine, short black diagonal dashes cross the midsection of the skirt for about one-half of its extent, like symbols of falling rain. Above the belt on the left extreme of the body, a red "tear drop" occurs. Near it is an oval black dot; and at the right side of the body is a red dot like the first.

The "navel" mentioned on the reproduction appears as an emblem on the blazer. It is in the center of the body laterally, which indicates that what looked like an eroded segment from the left of the body, rather, adds to the deformity. It would seem that the entire upper left side of the personage is strangely formed. Longitudinally, the "navel" is about half-way between the right shoulder and the belt—an odd location for a heart symbol such as was common in Kiva III—but this *is* an odd character, and so it may represent the heart. It is shown as an inverted cone, the right side in red and the left, in yellow. Above this, one red dot is surrounded by four others which radiate from it, perhaps representing drops of blood.

On the wall above this being's left side, is a colorful feature, scarcely identifiable. A triangular fragment shows a right angle at the lowest point, this bordered on each side by a heavy outer line. On the longer projection, a

PL. XXVII. Fig. 2. Malformed personage.

white stripe occurs inside the black, and then another black stripe sets off a wider white band, above which, and reaching to the black border on the shorter projection, the figure is painted blue like the body of the personage. At the lower point of the blue section, a small red triangle is shown with two red dots above its apex. From the corner of the whole feature, two yellow feathers bordered with red—cut off squarely at the outer ends—and one black feather are tied. From behind the latter a red cord hangs down with two red and two yellow "plumes" at the lower extreme. A similar unit on a black cord extends downward about midway of the black and white border. A short red mark overlies this border slightly, near the corner.

On the west wall, the remains of a third personage were discernible, approximately 3′ 2″ above the second floor level. Its light blue colored body was outlined with white on each side; at the upper right of the figure a golden

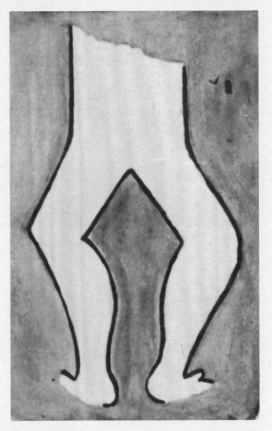

PL. XXVIII. Fig. 3. Unidentified personage.

PL. XXIX. Fig. 4. Unidentified personage (but similar to Luᵗkia).

colored stripe projects downward, obscuring the white for more than one-third of the way. Equidistant, in from each side are white elements, that on the right all the way from the upper limit of the depiction to midway of the blue expanse; it has about the same appearance as the black hair of many individuals portrayed in Kiva III. It and the fragment shown on the left breast of the personage are cut off squarely at the bottom. Between these two elements is another white stripe; it extends downward slightly farther than the other two.

The personage wears a black kilt, or apron, bordered with red on each side and across the bottom; on the right are three sets of red tassels or fringes, and on the left, two sets of red and white—at top and bottom. Around the waist is a white sash, tied on the right, with out-reaching tassel showing three elements. Four conch-like features hang down from the sash, painted

in white. Projecting from the kilt, as though thrust through slits in it, are white painted legs. These bow outward to bent knees and then inward for a few inches; both are eroded off a short distance below the knees. Each knee shows a decorative element painted in red, in the shape of an hourglass. Red also outlines the outer side of the legs from the kilt downward.

According to the scale given, the fragmentary figure measures about 12 inches in height. It is designated herein as Figure 3.

To the left, also on the west wall, 1' 4 6/8" from the left knee of Figure 3, and 6' 1/8" from its torso, was indication of another personage, Figure 4; it was otherwise located as being "1' 4" from SW corner, 3' 1" from 2d floor level; knee 1' 4" from SW corner. Same layer as" [Figure 3]. The fragment shows the lower part of a body which, like the legs and feet, is painted in white and outlined heavily with black. Both feet appear to be eroded off at the bottom. The left (if the being was facing to the fore) shows one large toe and part of another—or part of the foot. It would appear that this represents one of the priest-clown personages, similar to Lu^tkia (fig. 4) of Layer A-8 in Kiva III.

A final fragment, indicated as Figure 5, occurred on the south wall of the chamber. It was "40″ from west edge of doorway, 40″ from 1st floor." It would seem to portray one of the dual personages; half of the body, a leg, and a foot are shown in red, outlined to the latter with white; the other half is white, outlined with black. Between the feet is a small white X, and to the right of the red foot, another, each with black tips on the upper extremes. These may also bespeak the twain, or twin War god aspect of the personage. The figure measures but eight inches in present extent, and thus is a diminutive representation.

It is perhaps unfair to compare these small fragments with the many depictions from Kiva III, but one cannot help but feel that the paintings of Kiva VI lack the purity of those of the other portrayals, and that they are later in time, evidencing greater exuberance.

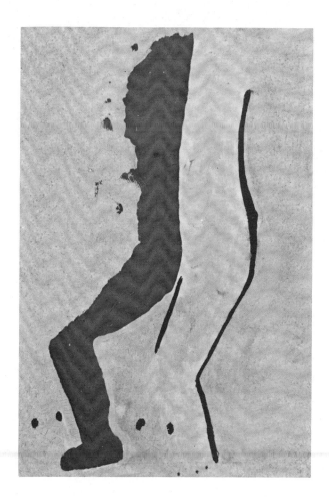

PL. XXX. Fig. 5. Unidentified twain personage.

REFLECTIONS

As stated in the beginning of this study, the Indians over a very wide expanse had the same basic concepts of religion, in which pre-eminence was accorded to the sun, generally as the Sun Father. Certain uniformity in development of religious practices and rites prevailed in many areas, while differences, degrees of evolution, and lags are observable in other localities.

Maize, or Indian corn (*Zea mays*), is known to have been in existence in the Mogollon area for about four thousand years, first, as one of the edible wild plants, and later cultivated.[536] Corn appears to have become increasingly appreciated; accompanying it were squash and beans. Added to the diet of uncultivated plants, these three are the ones which have played a major role in the life of the Indians, and they are the ones which have great ceremonial importance. In this work (page 126), the miracle of corn has been noted; the covert significance of the squash mentioned; and bean-growing magic is a feature of kiva legerdemain. Any or all of these plants, in the hands of a shaman, offered boundless opportunities for ritualistic development and cult evolution.[537]

The simple digging stick, which was the chief agricultural implement, is known to have been present in the Mogollon province between 5000 to 2000 B.C., and this is a point in evidence that a basic concept of religion prevailed generally over the anciently occupied regions of this country. It has been well stated that rudimentary farming knowledge and primitive farming tools and techniques possessed by the early, desert culture Mogollon people were traits shared "with all the other Indians from Oregon to Mexico City and from the Rocky Mountains to the Pacific Coast."[538] The territory may be further extended. Where elementary agriculture exists, magico-religious practices are present.

Apparently the cultural climate in the north was such that corn did not become significant there until much later. The earliest positive information which we have relating to corn in that area comes from a rock shelter site near Durango, Colorado, which has disclosed a tree-ring cutting date of A.D. 46, thus giving evidence of corn in that region in the first century of our era.[539] This may indicate an absence of communication between the Mogollon and Anasazi during the preceding centuries; and it points up a lack of data for the intervening area. It seems likely that corn became known in the north at a time for which no evidence has yet been found. Pumpkin was also cultivated by the early Anasazi; beans[540] and cotton arrived somewhat later.[541]

Another thing to be considered is that there may be marked discontinuity in the distribution of prehistoric crop seeds. Particular evidence of this is supported by maize, or corn, specimens derived recently from other sites on the northern periphery. In western Colorado and eastern Utah, it has been found that people of the Fremont culture province grew a type of corn believed to have come from the *Mesa Central* of Mexico. These specimens are reported to be "remarkably unlike most Basketmaker corn."[542] Still more recent findings show that a race of corn similar to that of these northern locations has been identified from the Isthmus of Tehuantepec in Mexico. This race demonstrates its capability of growing at

536. Martin, Rinaldo, et al., 1952; Jones and Fonner, 1954; Mangelsdorf and Smith, 1949; Mangelsdorf, et al., 1954.

537. For instance, *see* Ellis, 1952.

538. Martin, 1959:71.

539. Morris and Burgh, 1954:48; Jones and Fonner, 1954:93, 114.

540. *See* Wheat, 1955:207.

541. *See* Jones and Fonner, 1954, for discussion of plant materials; also Carter, 1945, who records that the species of corn, beans, and squash of the Anasazi are recognized as being different from those of the Mogollon.

542. Anderson in Wormington, 1955:139.

different latitudes "without acclimatizing gradually,"[543] a trait which would have permitted it to have adapted itself to different conditions of altitude and growing season very rapidly.[544] One thing is certain, corn must be carried by people. Therefore, the fact of discovering a pure Mexican type of corn in Utah and Colorado sites, which date within the 7th century, alerts one to the probability that contacts between the greater Southwest and Mexico were due to some movement of people from the south in that period.[545]

Dr. Wormington observes that, "There is no doubt that the Mexican Complex [the name given to the dented Mexican pyramidal type of corn with high row count] was well represented in the earliest Basketmaker maize which was found in the Durango area. . . ." Referring to corn specimens with high row numbers which were recovered from Tularosa Cave in southwestern New Mexico, where the lowest levels have been dated about 2300 years ago by radiocarbon methods, she adds: "If this corn should prove to be connected with the Mexican Complex, this type may have entered the Southwest at a very early date and moved north through the Mogollon country."[546]

Inasmuch as pottery plays an important part in the establishment of chronological sequences, it should be noted that pottery (plain brown and red slipped wares) was introduced, presumably from Mexico,[547] into the Mogollon province by 300 B.C. or earlier, where it continued to be made for more than 1500 years. Between A.D. 400 and 600 several new ceramic types were evolved—the first innovation in 800 or 900 years.[548]

As with corn, pottery was late in appearing in the north. Knowledge of it and the idea of pottery making became known to the Anasazi after A.D. 400.[549] Because of the clays from which the pottery was fashioned and of firing practices, the Anasazi wares were characteristically light grey to white.[550] A fugitive red wash was commonly applied after firing.[551] Some vessels were decorated with simple geometric designs and occasional life figures in black pigment.

Around A.D. 600, significant culture traits from Mexico appeared along the present day Arizona—New Mexico corridor and areas adjacent thereto, reaching as far north as northeastern Arizona, or beyond.[552]

That the Mogollones then had relatively advanced religious beliefs is evidenced by the finding of prayersticks, hoops, *tablitas*, mineral pigments and paint palettes, reed flutes and cigarettes, figurines, charms, and other items of a ceremonial nature in sites dating to that period.[553] In the north, Mexican traits—in part

---

543. Wormington, 1955:182.

544. *See* Wormington, 1955:183.

545. It is of note that this date follows closely the efflorescence of culture at Teotihuacan, in highland Mexico, which dominated the scene and extended its influence far and wide. Teotihuacan traits have become well known in southern Mexico and Guatemala. Are we now beginning to recognize some of them in the distant north?

Perhaps it is difficult to realize that people may have traveled from the Mexican plateau to these marginal highlands on the northern periphery, yet those who populated this entire hemisphere are credited with having walked from inner Asia across the Bering straits, to settle well over the New World. So it must be remembered that the indigenous peoples were experienced travelers . . . and they were ever moving from one place to another. Furthermore, they would not have been the first to have reversed the direction of the route traversed.

546. Wormington, 1955:183.

547. Martin, 1959:79. The reader is referred again to the book, *Potsherds,* by Dr. H. S. Colton, 1953:63 ff.

548. Martin, Rinaldo, et al., 1952; Martin, 1959:83.

549. *See* discussion in Wheat, 1955:215 ff.

550. Martin, 1959:85; Wheat, 1955:216-217; Shepard, 1953; Reed, 1949:5; Roberts, 1935:12-13; 1929:107-118.

551. Roberts, 1935:12; *see also* Brew, 1946:294, and Wheat, 1955:220.

552. *See* Wheat, 1955:218-219 (Mexican pottery forms); Gladwin, 1957:67-68 (polished red pottery and beans); Wormington, 1955 (corn, figurines, etc.); Jones and Fonner, 1954 (corn, etc.); Morss, 1954 (figurines); O'Bryan, 1950:91, 105; Reed, 1949:5-9 (discussion of Abajo red-on-orange ware); Brew, 1946:291-294; Morris, 1939:43.

553. Martin, Rinaldo, et al., 1952; Martin, Rinaldo, and Bluhm, 1954; Wheat, 1955; Martin, 1959; Rinaldo, 1959; Lehmer, 1948; Haury, 1936.

diffused through the Mogollon—were added to the early Anasazi features, resulting in a florescence which becomes increasingly apparent in the Four Corners region of the San Juan drainage, and of gradually widening scope.[554] Early Anasazi sites have yielded materials comparable to those of the Mogollon. Among items recovered are prayersticks, mineral pigments, medicine pouches and ceremonial bundles, head ornaments, feather boxes, rattles, bone whistles, wands, corncobs on sticks, charms, tubular pipes, clay figurines, etc.[555] Many of these are such as would not be divorced from a basically complete pattern of associated traits, and, therefore, indicate that certain complexes of cult or societal nature were accordingly introduced into the receiving culture.

Circular, subterranean dwellings were used in part for ceremonial purposes, signifying that ritual followed certain formalized procedures. The Anasazi were agriculturalists; they doubtless had calendrical observances and magical controls of the elements, and engaged in animism-curing practices.

It appears that contacts between the Anasazi and the Mogollon were sporadic and largely indirect up until about A.D. 700.[556] Therefore, the acceptance of Mexican traits should be viewed as individual (group) responses to cultural stimuli. As the author comprehends the evidence, it seems that, in the north, the introduced traits accelerated cultural development, but that before long the older patterns prevailed to such an extent that the foreign touches were primarily engulfed and became more or less incorporeal—or were, perhaps, pushed on into other localities, those peripheral to the then established centers. Certain decorated pieces of greyware pottery and many pictographs show anthropomorphic or mythical representations[557] which definitely relate to the culture history of the early inhabitants of the Anasazi region, and which may be associated harmoniously with the ceremonial accoutrement recovered from archaeologic sites. Later, however, such pictography—which appears strongest in the northern and western margins of the Anasazi terrain—seems to disappear in that region, not to occur again until at a relatively late time, if at all, implying that correlative ideas were likewise submerged, or rejected.

The area which was to be the heartland of the Chaco Canyon development of Anasazi culture was at that period little inhabited.[558] Likewise, the Rio Grande valley was but sparsely peopled.[559] The meager evidence in hand shows, however, that religious tenets were basic in the cultures there represented.

In the south, in contrast, the Mexican traits and influences seem to have been more effective and of enduring nature. Once introduced into the Mogollon province, these stimuli were grafted onto the basic patterns and continued to enrich the steadily developing culture of that area.

After A.D. 700, there was a marked expansion of peoples. Ideas which had developed in the Four Corners country became part of a very uniform culture which extended over the southern parts of Nevada, Utah and Colorado, and over the northern sections of Arizona and New Mexico. Black-on-white pottery

---

554. *See* Wheat, 1955:212; Kroeber, 1939:46, 221; *see also* footnote 552.

555. *See* Kidder and Guernsey, 1919; Guernsey and Kidder, 1921; Nusbaum, Kidder, and Guernsey, 1922; Morris and Burgh, 1954; and Wheat, 1955, who summarizes known facts thus: "We do not know the origin of the Anasazi, although it is not unlikely that they represent an eastern extension of early Great Basin hunters and gatherers. Since the Cochise [early Mogollon] appear also to have moved out of the Great Basin at a somewhat earlier date, certain generalized trait resemblances may reflect a very early relationship between these groups." *See also* Kroeber, 1939:45-48.

556. Reed, 1949:5.

557. For example, Martin, Lloyd, and Spoehr, 1938, pl. CLXVIII; Martin, 1939, fig. 134; Steward, 1936:59; Reagan, 1930.

558. Wendorf and Lehmer, 1956:190.

559. *See* Wendorf and Reed, 1955:138-140.

(actually black decorations on the character-istic grey-fired wares)[560] served as the "common denominator."[561]

Whereas the Anasazi culture spread widely across the northern limits of the Southwest, the Mogollon culture was equally prominent across the southern reaches, extending over southern Arizona—including the entire Salt-Gila-Verde drainage—and New Mexico to the Pecos, and from Chihuahua, Mexico, northward to the Little Colorado and a like latitude of the Rio Grande.[562] Brown and red-slipped pottery served as a prime diagnostic of the Mogollon.

After A.D. 700, it is also observable that the regional cultures become increasingly less distinct. Within the Mogollon province there is a conspicuous addition of wooden artifacts, and new pottery types occur. The hunting bow and arrow take predominance over the spear thrower; and miniature and ceremonial bows and arrows appear for the first time. Reed cigarettes increase; painted sticks and worked gourds come into use; and there are corncobs on sticks [563] for some esoteric purpose. These and related items reflect an increase in ceremonial activities. The adoption of the bow and arrow and related cult items may be taken as heralding the arrival of the warrior-hunt complex of traits and the associated katsina cult from Mexico.[564] During a span of about two hundred years, these and other southern traits were amalgamated with the older ones, resulting in a recognizable Mogollon assemblage which has been designated as the Three Circle period.[565]

At approximately this time, dwellers in the Anasazi domain—particularly those settling in the Chaco province—came into possession of many of the same traits as those prevalent among the Mogollon, and perhaps even certain ones which they adopted directly from Mexico, or other areas.[566] Traders and small parties of Southwestern Indians were frequently making trips into other regions, carrying news and gossip, ideas, and even some objects back and forth.[567] To name a few of the Anasazi items which denote increasing ceremonialism, there are: ceremonial bows as well as those for hunting—some stained red or black; prayersticks, prayer plumes, golden eagles kept captive for feathers; painted and carved sticks, crooks, juniper bark torches; bone dice and gaming pieces, whistles; *tcamahia* (ancient agricultural tool which came to have esoteric use); medicine cylinders; pigments and various forms of palettes; concretions and modeled figurines pertaining to a fertility cult; pipes, etc. These prove that the expanding cultures of the north were adding to their religious precepts and incorporating such compatible ideas as were feasible to a growing priesthood and the paralleling dramatic enactments.

Until around 900, peoples in both the Anasazi and Mogollon provinces dwelt in pithouses. Then the northerners moved above ground and began constructing dwellings of masonry[568] or coursed adobe; the Mogollones

560. Reed, 1949:5-9, gives information regarding the firing of Anasazi and Mogollon ceramics; *see also* Roberts, 1929.

561. *See* Stubbs, 1953:60-61.

562. *Cf.* Reed, 1950:126; *see* Lehmer, 1948.

563. Martin, Rinaldo, et al., 1952; Martin, 1959.

564. It may be added that hair binding was likewise introduced at this time (Martin, Rinaldo, et al., 1952:366). Hunters and warriors, particularly, bind their hair to avert restriction of vision when aiming for a kill.

565. Haury, 1936; Wheat, 1955. Martin, 1959:50, lists the Cochise-Mogollon periods or phases with their approximate dates thus: Sulphur Springs (a Cochise manifestation), c. 5000 to 2500 B.C.; Chiricahua period (a Cochise complex), c. 2500 to 300 B.C.; Pine Lawn period, 300 B.C. to A.D. 500; Georgetown period, 500 to 700; San Francisco period, 700 to 900; Three Circle period, 900 to 1000; Reserve period, 1000 to 1100; Tularosa period, 1100 to 1200; and Foote Canyon period, 1200 to 1350.

566. Contacts with peoples in all adjacent areas, and some far removed, were made from time to time, but these are not brought to attention in the present work.

567. *Cf.* Judd, 1954:265.

568. Kroeber, 1939:46, suggests that stone masonry may have been one of the traits radiating from Mexico. The same might be said of coursed adobe.

built surface structures slightly later.[569] There came to be small, unit type pueblos with circular, subterranean kivas which retained the features of the pithouses. This religious conservatism is indicative of long followed procedures of a ceremonial nature.[570] In time, the building assemblages grew into larger, multistoried pueblos with many small circular kivas and, commonly, one or two great kivas.[571]

It is believed that the Mogollones did not devise masonry, but rather that they borrowed this trait and the idea of house construction from the Anasazi, who rapidly developed into fine builders, once the idea of masonry came into their lives. On the other hand, it seems probable that the practice of building around a court or plaza may have derived from the Mogollon,[572] who received the idea, originally, from Mexico. The earliest evidence at the present time is that rectangular ceremonial chambers, the kiva so-called, first appeared in Mogollon sites in the first century before Christ, from which it is postulated for the Cochise homeland some two centuries earlier.[573] Thus it becomes evident that the expansion of peoples and the exchange of ideas throughout the greater Southwest were transmitting concepts from one area to another, responding to them in various ways, developing them, and passing them on to others. Currents were flowing in different directions, branching out, and even reversing themselves. At this time, the peoples dwelling in the Mogollon province abandoned their preference for brown and red wares and took over the Anasazi technique of making black-on-white pottery, although they continued to manufacture the traditional types in lessening quantities.

The small kivas are thought to have been associated with clans, or social divisions, which traced descent through the female line. The clans owned or had control of particular ceremonies, and held totemic regard for specific animals, plants, objects, or appropriate phenomena. The great kiva apparently served an entire pueblo or several lesser villages, or, in the north, one of the two major village divisions, or moieties.

As the population grew there were increased opportunities for ceremonial organizations and ceremonial leaders, and for new societal developments and dramatic representations. Culture history records the visits of individuals from one pueblo to another, or to even distant groups.[574] Doubtless, the leaders went forth to learn of practices suitable for introduction to their own people; they certainly elaborated upon the simpler beginnings of indigenous magic and religion; and visitors came bringing their contributions.

A notable increase in pueblos again occurred after A.D. 900.[575] Both temporally and spatially, the situation was ripe for development in all cultural categories in the Chaco province. New settlements spread eastward as far as the Canadian drainage, and beyond Taos in the north. In the upper Rio Grande region, the small vil-

---

569. Martin, Rinaldo, et al., 1956:202.

570. Although outside the consideration of the present work, it may be noted that the concept of circular, subterranean houses and religious structures is postulated to have been brought from the Old World to the New (*see* Reiter, 1946).

571. Roberts, 1929:82, records that in the north "the earliest kivas, under normal conditions, were circular, semisubterranean rooms detached from the main building," and that "later kivas were attached to the main building and eventually were brought above ground and incorporated into the pueblos." Martin et al., 1956:200, observe that the idea of the kiva was important to the Anasazi as early as A.D. 800.

572. Martin, 1959:104, 122.

573. Martin et al., 1956:200-201; but *see* Judd, 1954:30, 33-34.

574. *See* pages 85, 110-111 herein.

575. This is just after the collapse of culture occurred at Teotihuacan, the great Classic center not far northward from present day Mexico City, sending a large population into other areas. The fact that numerous traits apparently new to the northern regions become evident during the 10th and 11th centuries makes this event particularly significant.

lages had both pit and surface structures. There, the ceramics and ceremonial rooms display differences from the contemporary San Juan types. Earlier features persisted in the east, without relation to the developments which continued in the west. The kivas, while circular and subterranean, are closer akin to Basket Maker III-Pueblo I pithouses of the San Juan,[576] lacking the encircling bench, pilasters, recess, etc., which became part of the western Anasazi tradition, along with masonry construction of houses.

Inasmuch as it is commonly the conservative faction which removes itself in the event of cultural strife, this lack of change may indicate differences of opinion which arose over the introduction of religious practices distasteful to certain of those dwelling in the San Juan, and which motivated their move into the northern Rio Grande, under guidance of a shaman, or leader, who continued to engage in agricultural magic and related animistic rites according to his dictates.

Around A.D. 1000, there were further extensive movements of peoples throughout the Southwest, and the areas beyond. The culture history of the western Pueblos includes frequent allusion to earthquakes, and mentions times "when the land boiled." It is recognized that the lava flow of the Grants, New Mexico, area occurred no more than a thousand years ago, thus affecting the Acoma-Zuñi region.[577] It, therefore, approaches certainty that earthquakes and volcanic activity were experienced by peoples then inhabiting the Southwest. It follows that these catastrophic events and their aftermaths—which may well have included droughts, arroyo cutting, and related changes—were responsible for some population shifts from one locality to another.

This may have been the situation responsible for the flow of peoples into the Chaco region, which apparently had been practically unoccupied for some two hundred years. From 950 onward, the Chaco built up its classic culture, with many evidences of intense ceremonialism reflected in the architecture and artifacts. This religious evolution mirrors growing sacerdotal functions and the promotion of priesthoods, in turn, denoting an expanding economy, primarily in terms of agriculture. Agriculture flourished, as evidenced by remains of corn and by the prevalent use of grinding bins in small and large dwelling units alike. Significant to this work is a painted-root specimen in the likeness of a snake recovered at Pueblo Bonito and probably dating to the 1000's, which indicates that the phallic-marked serpent which occurs at Kuaua in paintings relating to the snake cult and katsina initiations was a ceremonial item in Chaco at that time.[578]

Innovations were generally accepted by the Mogollones and these, merged with older features and practices, paved the way for development of the classic cultures of that province, Several permanent pueblos were established;[579] the larger ones usually had a great kiva for community use.[580] Agriculture was expanded and farming techniques and tools were improved, making possible the food stuffs necessary to the building up of religious priesthoods. Slab metates were set in bins, tilted, and graduated as to grinding surface (coarse, medium, and fine), with pottery bowls arranged to catch the cornmeal as it was ground with a mano, or hand tool. Several kinds of corn were cultivated, as were two varieties of squash, bottle gourds, and kidney and tepary beans.[581] Wild foods and game added items which resulted in ample foods for all. By then,

576. Which date between A.D. 400 and 800, approximately.

577. See Hewett and Dutton, 1945:145-146.

578. See Judd, 1954, fig. 78, and page 128 herein.

579. For instance, see Peckham, 1958.

580. These were entered by means of a long ramp, sufficiently wide as to allow six men abreast to descend into the structure.

581. See Martin, 1959:109.

bows and arrows had completely replaced the older weapon, the spear thrower.

Doubtless, the upsurge of ceremonialism, in turn, stimulated the evolution of all arts and crafts. Among the things which were fashioned were excellently made and painted ceremonial objects of clay,[582] stone[583] and wood. Ceramic designs included masked beings, obviously pertaining to the venerated personages concerned with religious observances, for example, the priests and personators of the Sun, Moon, and the stars, in their various manifestations.[584]

Thus, during the latter part of the 1000's and the 1100's, there was conspicuous religious evolution and development in both the Chaco and Mogollon areas. Pueblos became still more numerous and increased in size. There were villages several stories in height. In the Rio Grande there were fewer pithouses,[585] but circular subterranean kivas of the eastern type continued; and there occurred the innovation of ceremonial rooms within the house blocks, as well as the plaza kivas.[586] Excavations reveal a steadily increasing number of artifacts and features relating to ceremonial advancement.

A site (LA 835) northwest of Santa Fe, probably dating to the 1000-1100's, has been found to consist of ten or more scattered small house units, these with from seven to more than fifteen contiguous dwelling and storage rooms built above ground. Two or three kivas pertain to each unit, encompassing round and rectangular—one of these within a house block—subterranean and above ground chambers, and also a great kiva. The latter is circular and below ground, with crude masonry walls. In the house units a variety of building media was employed, "but most had upright slab foundations, with the remainder of the wall of adobe or adobe with stone core."[587] Ceramics are chiefly of "Chacoan" varieties, the black-on-white pieces decorated with mineral pigment.[588] Mogollon brownware occurs, indicating contact between the north and south.

This was the period during which the Chaco canyon settlements, having reached their climax, were being abandoned gradually, one small group after another seeking new homesites.[589] If any of the Chaqueños moved into the Taos region they left the later architectural and ceramic developments behind. Coursed masonry was characteristic in the west, in the east coursed adobe was used primarily.[590] One wonders if the scattered houses, rectangular ceremonial chambers, and brownware may represent the presence of people in the upper Rio Grande from the Mogollon province during the 11th and 12th centuries,[591] as carriers of these traits. If so, the society of the upper Rio Grande conservatives was apparently sufficiently strong as to withstand most of the material traits which may

582. Cf. Martin, 1959:119; Martin, Rinaldo, et al., 1952.

583. Martin, 1959:121.

584. Bradfield, 1929, pl. LXXIX (364); Cosgrove and Cosgrove, 1932, pls. 225-227; see footnote 501, page 167 herein.

585. In a tributary, the Hondo valley, north of Taos, pithouses dating in the 1000's have been excavated which include circular and rectangular forms equipped with ventilator toward the east, and movable slab damper. Artifactual items include tubular pottery pipes, corn, rib bone rasp, bone ornaments and tools, in addition to the ceramics which are of "Chacoan" character (Blumenschein, 1958:107-111).

586. See Stubbs, 1953:61.

587. Wendorf and Reed, 1955:141.

588. See Wendorf and Lehmer, 1956:160-161.

589. See Kidder, 1958:128, for a reasonable explanation.

590. Although adobe was used to a certain extent in western sites, this medium was generally abandoned there before 1000 (see Wendorf and Reed, 1955:142).

591. Rinaldo, 1959:185, in speaking of the masonry of several Mogollon sites, says that these have been compared to Chaco Canyon Type 2 masonry, and reveal superficial resemblances which were due to the practice of placing large stones in courses, alternating with one or more thin layers of laminated stone or small slabs, and with the irregular ends chinked with small slabs. But, he states, "In the north, at Chaco Canyon, these were always laid horizontally. In the south these slabs were often set on edge, creating the impression of a frame of slabs around some of the larger stones."

have been introduced. Their simple round kiva form prevailed[592] and so did their pottery tradition.

During the late 1100's and the 1200's practically every occupied site in the Southwest became a defensive one, built as a fortification itself, or located in a cave or on a promontory which permitted the utmost in security from enemy peoples. We do not know who the marauders may have been. They may have been, at least in part, peoples within the area warring against one another. We do know that at this same period, the Toltec culture of central Mexico was breaking up and that peoples in great numbers were moving to new locations. There is adequate evidence that they moved southward from highland Mexico, and proof is now being assembled to show that movements to the north and west were greater than formerly recognized.[593]

It is entirely possible that Toltec peoples themselves migrated into northwestern Mexico (which may well have been their ancestral home), carrying with them a complex social organization with priestly officials and powerful societies, adept artisans and developed industries. Some of these people, and/or the succeeding generations of their offspring, doubtless went into one area while others sought locations elsewhere. Many moved from one place to another, over considerable periods of time. The very fact of their impact upon an already expanding population—either directly or as cultural stimuli—would have caused pressures upon areas formerly enjoying relatively scattered habitation, or would have brought new traits into their midst, and may have impinged upon the Southwestern peoples. At any rate, the Mogollon province, particularly, and

the Anasazi to a considerable degree, thenceforth demonstrate traits which certainly had their source in Mexico.

The Chaco sites were almost completely deserted by 1150, only a small aggregate of people remaining to dwell there for perhaps another fifty years. Thus the Chaqueños did not have an opportunity to participate, in situ, in the ceremonial efflorescence which was then on the horizon. Anasazi culture shifted to the Kayenta and Mesa Verde regions of the San Juan and grew to eminence there during the 12th and 13th centuries. The Kayenta displayed a preference for organic pigment in pottery decoration. After 1050 or 1100, use of this medium became marked in the growing Mesa Verde domain, where it replaced the earlier mineral pigment. Each group developed characteristic styles, especially in the black-on-white wares, employing predominantly geometric embellishments.

In the Kayenta-Hopi communities, polychrome wares were developed on red and buff backgrounds, with increasing popularity. The ultimate came in the so-called Sikyatki polychrome which appeared about 1400, and which utilized katsina beings, masked personages, and many ceremonial features in elaborate decorations.[594] The Mesa Verde potters maintained their preference for black-on-white until the end.

In the northern Rio Grande, excluding the Taos area and the Canadian drainage, between 1150 and 1200, many of the pottery makers began to use organic pigments in decorating their ceramics.[595] A type pueblo, Pindi—which was walled for protection—consisted of thirty to forty small rooms constructed of

---

592. Kidder, 1958:144, observes that the six kivas at Taos, and the six at nearby Picuris, "are the only round, subsurface examples that survive."

593. One of my colleagues, quite independent of my researches, has offered an interesting paper on Mexican-Southwestern parallels (Ferdon, 1955), and his work is reviewed and augmented by Schroeder, 1956:299-308.

594. In the late 1800's, a Tewa woman, Nampeyo, living in the pueblo of Hano, secured sherds of this ware from archaeological excavations and revived the old Sikyatki type of decoration, which is continued in our day by her descendants and other potters.

595. Wendorf and Reed, 1955:144, do not look upon this as reflecting the movement to this area of any significant numbers of new immigrants.

coursed adobe, and three underground circular kivas which were adobe walled. The kivas had ventilators toward the east or south, with movable slab dampers. Roofs rested directly on the walls, or upon a four-post support system. The decorated pottery was of a type called Santa Fe black-on-white, and this was accompanied by body-corrugated utility types. Several trade wares from the Mogollon province were present, as were others from the northwest and the northeast. [596]

Slightly later, still other ceramic introductions and new architectural features appeared along with a pronounced increase in population. Shortly before 1300, a new pottery type which is called Galisteo black-on-white appeared in the Rio Grande valley, especially in the region southeast of Santa Fe, now known as the Galisteo basin. It is significant because of characteristics shared with the ware called Mesa Verde black-on-white. Pueblos were built of masonry and floors were covered with rock slabs in preference to packed adobe. Contemporary with these structures were pithouses in clusters of ten or twelve, these being shallow, undercut chambers accompanied by circular subterranean kivas oriented toward the east. Partially incorporated in the house blocks of the masonry structures, at this time, were above ground, corner kivas.[597] Specialized rectangular rooms, with ventilators, deflectors, and fire pits also occur in the house blocks. Orientation of floor features was toward the south or east. Ceramics bespeak trade or influxes of people from the south and southwest and from the west and northwest.

In the Mogollon province, the endemic and the newly accepted traits were united into a cultural whole which reached its apogee during the 13th century, after much of the San Juan had been abandoned. As mentioned above, their red-brown pottery tradition was strongly overshadowed by styles from the north by people favoring mineral pigments. Particularly in the southern part of the region, among the Mimbres people, katsinas, ceremonial personages, and sacred subjects were added to ceramic decorations.[598] There is no doubt that some of the northern peoples moved into the southern region, contributing Anasazi attributes and sharing in the cultural advancement,[599] nor that influences from the south were welded into the social complex. By 1350-1400, the Mogollon region was, in turn, depopulated, meaning that thousands of people must have moved to other regions.[600]

In review of this brief summary, it is seen that by 1150-1200 the Chaco was entirely abandoned, indicating that many hundreds of people with an advanced degree of culture had sought new homes in other localities of the Southwest. This was before Kuaua was founded. By 1300, the Mesa Verde was mainly depopulated, again bespeaking the movement of large numbers of people into more desirable areas. Some of these might have come into the Rio Grande to establish themselves at the site of Kuaua, but that they did so is not evident from the architectural or artifactual material to any extent. The initial occupants of Kuaua portray a basic Rio Grande pueblo pattern, with small surface dwellings made up of rectangular blocks of rooms, and with circular

596. Wendorf and Reed, 1955:144-145; see Stubbs and Stallings, 1953.

597. Dutton, field notes, Pueblo Largo, Galisteo (one such structure excavated has a masonry ventilator shaft extending from floor to upper limit of the wall, with small, rectangular supra-floor air duct; the whole unit had been built inside the northeast corner of the chamber); see Kidder, 1958:35-42.

598. See Martin, 1959b:7-8.

599. Rather spectacular evidence has been established that a group of people from the Kayenta-Hopi region moved southward into Point of Pines (roughly midway between Reserve, New Mexico, and San Carlos, Arizona), in the closing decades of the 13th century (Haury, 1958:4). Many other sites display Anasazi traits in Mogollon villages; and others display Mogollon features in Anasazi settlements—frequently indicating peaceful coexistence (Dittert, 1959; Rinaldo, 1959:134; Danson, 1957:110; Martin et al., 1956:201; Wendorf and Reed, 1955:147).

600. See Danson, 1957:120.

kivas, orientated toward the east, located in the plaza. The kivas had no bench, pilasters, or recesses, and no evidence of painting was found in them. Ceramics were of the northern, greyware varieties, with a small amount of black-on-white decorated with organic pigment. The latter was overwhelmingly replaced by red, glaze paint decorated wares.

At other locations there is evidence that fully developed cultural manifestations from the Kayenta-Hopi region—showing strong southern influence, e.g., the Sikyatki pottery[601]—were carried eastward and southeastward. They occur abundantly at sites on tributaries of the Rio Grande, particularly the Rio Puerco and Cuchillo river, and in the intervening area. This movement appears to have gone almost entirely to the south of Kuaua, and its appearance in the east seems not to have influenced to any degree the developments at this pueblo. The typical Hopi wares of 1200 and 1300 are absent from Kuaua.

Consequently, it would seem that the most likely source for the influx of cultural stimuli at Kuaua, shortly following its establishment, must have been the Mogollon. In the first place, the time at which the new influences arrived in the Rio Grande coincides with the migrations of peoples from the Mogollon province, from the Quemado-Reserve-Mimbres areas. It is evident that they went northward by various routes, some working eastward toward the Rio Grande and thence northward, settling here and there as opportunity afforded. Their influence is recognized in the middle Rio Grande, in the general Acoma-Zuñi areas,[602] and to some extent as far north as Taos.

These people, like the Anasazi, were agriculturalists who followed matrilineal practices. They were traditionally the brown or red pottery makers,[603] who had adopted black-on-white techniques from their northern neighbors, around A.D. 1000, and who had assimilated numerous traits from Mexico. They were acquainted also with the fine new wares being produced in the Pinedale-Showlow region . . . having made use of some of them before they left their former homesites. Along with their pottery, they fashioned animal effigies of clay which they baked. They used other fetishes of stone, medicine stones, ceremonial concoctions, and conical and tubular pipes. That curing was performed is indicated by medicine bag remains. They had acquired shells from neighbors closer to the ocean, and used them to a considerable degree as beads and other ornaments, some of them carved; they also had stone and bone jewelry. Their clothing included cotton cloth, woven sashes, leather moccasins and leggings. With them, the hunting bow and arrows with leather quiver were accompanied by miniature bows and arrows, certainly for esoteric uses.[604] They built square or rectangular chambers for ceremonial purposes, large and small, within the plaza.[605] Pigments in red, yellow, and blue (hematite, limonite, and malachite, respectively) were significant possessions. We know that certain articles were painted with them for ceremonial uses, such as wooden tablitas (headdresses) and shafts of feathered prayersticks, and probably bottle gourds. The Mogollones were skillful decorators of pottery, with a wide range of artistic designs.[606]

For whatever reason the southwestern area was forsaken, with the people gradually moving to the north and east, it has been shown that the abandonment was orderly. The migrants took along everything that could be carried easily. This may be taken to indicate

---

601. Dating about A.D. 1400-1625. *Note* Beals, 1944:246, and Brew, 1944:242-244.

602. Rinaldo, 1959; Dittert, 1959; Woodbury, 1955 and 1956 a and b. *Cf.* Hawley, 1950:291 ff.

603. Wheat, 1955:72 ff.

604. *Cf.* Hough, 1914:97-101.

605. *See* Martin, Rinaldo, and Barter, 1957:128.

606. These included extensive use of fishes, among other subjects.

that they knew where they were going and moved in accordance with well laid plans. Those objects which were left behind were carefully arranged.[607]

It is the author's belief that some of the people from the Mogollon culture province arrived, then, at Kuaua, bringing their concepts which included a well developed warrior cult and veneration of the Moon Mother,[608] as wife of the Sun—especially significant in their agricultural and hunting rites.

At Kuaua, in the Lummis section, where the original dwellings were built along an east-west axis, the ceremonials were carried on in subterranean, circular kivas, detached from the houses. They were concerned, in all likelihood, with rites and magic relating to agriculture, fertility, and weather control, with the Corn Mother concept and rain making primary features. The newcomers introduced the war cult with its hunting, katsina, and curing societies, and ultimately built the rectangular ceremonial chambers which they decorated with paintings of folk history—these featuring the katsina niche on occasion. They lived in houses which tended toward a north-south direction. As the esoteric practices developed, society or council chambers in the house blocks were used for ceremonial functions, in addition to the subterranean rooms.

I am aware that paintings of this nature have not been reported from Mogollon sites, but insofar as I can determine no wall plaster remained in the ruins excavated, so there is as much chance that paintings may have existed, as that they did not. People capable of portraying folk personages and mythical representations, as well as complex geometric designs, which the Mogollones did execute, could have painted murals with equal knowledge and skill.

Inasmuch as the traits new at Kuaua were ones which had evolved from the universal concept of deity, they were such as could have been accepted and, perhaps after an interval of time, joined harmoniously onto a culture which had not previously attained a corresponding degree of advancement.[609] Coexistence of one group with another was nothing new in the Southwest. Several instances have already been noted, and many more could be cited.

Although a complete inventory of the Kuaua artifactual material is not available, I am told that the following things were recovered during the excavations:[610] large quantities of bone items, including whistles and fragments of flutes, notched-rib rasps, awls, beads and pendants; shell ornaments (*Olivella* and discoidal beads); large numbers of stone items, such as milling implements (manos and metates—on occasion, several together on the floor, suggesting that they may have been in series, supported on rocks), fire dogs, gaming balls, notched and full-grooved axes and mauls; concretions, two of which were in the likeness of female humans, reminiscent of the legendary people who were turned to stone, and which certainly were significant in fertility rites; an abundance of worked potsherds, many of which were probably used as gaming

---

607. As an example, this situation prevailed at the Foote Canyon pueblo, where there was no sign of burning or of warfare (Rinaldo, 1959:284).

608. Lummis, 1910:71, has recorded that with the Tiwa (Isleta), the Moon was considered "the first and loveliest woman in all the world," who was made to be the wife of the Sun. "From them began the world and all that is in it." He adds that the Moon "is honored in almost every detail of the Pueblo ceremonials. The most important charm or implement of the medicine-men, the holiest fetish of all, is typical of her. It is called Mah-pah-roó, the Mother, and is the most beautiful article a Pueblo ever fashioned. A flawless ear of corn (a type of fertility or motherhood) is tricked out with a downy mass of snow-white feathers, and hung with ornaments of silver, coral, and the precious turquoise." It is the author's observation that the Moon was particularly venerated by hunt societies, and thus must have been important in Mogollon life.

609. *Cf.* Wheat, 1955:205, and Anderson, 1955:410.

610. Mrs. Lambert, who was for a time supervisor of the Kuaua excavation project. For information on the human skeletal remains, *see* Luhrs and Ely, 1939.

discs; ceramic pipes of the tubular, cloud blower variety, and one of polished redware which had an expanded bowl that was decorated with a cross painted on each of the opposing sides . . . an item which fits into the warrior cult accoutrement.

Other pipes showed incised and punctate decorations, including terraced designs. There were some specimens which had flattened mouthpieces. There were a great many miniature vessels in the form of bowls, ladles, canteens, and paint dishes. The pottery deer has been described on page 25. Turquois was not found to any extent, but there was a notable amount of malachite (pigment for painting ceremonial items; and the colors of the murals prove that several other pigments were in use). There were pieces of textiles and fragments of coiled and wicker basketry. In addition to the corn which has been discussed previously, there were various kinds of seeds. There was evidence of a great many turkeys having been kept at Kuaua. Their pens, eggs, and bones were found. There were animal teeth and claws—the latter believed to include bear—and "finger stones" or medicine cylinders which are common to priests' pouches or bundles. Other than small quantities of black-on-white pottery dating to the late 1200's, the ceramics were of the glaze-paint decorated varieties.[611] That the economy of Kuaua was based primarily on agriculture seems evident in that there were but few hunting implements, projectile points, and arrow shaft smoothers, and from the fact that relatively few animal bones and no fish bones[612] were recovered.

It would seem that the above assemblage of items and information shows that Kuaua shared sufficient traits with the Mogollon as to make reasonable the assumption that emigrants from the Mogollon province settled at the Rio Grande site and contributed their more advanced attainments to the endemic culture, resulting in the florescence which is reflected in the kiva paintings—which provide a pictorial record of the religious life at Kuaua thenceforth. That there were adept artists among the Mogollones, capable of producing paintings of human beings and mythical personages, animals, birds, fish, and reptiles, and an array of symbolic representations, is demonstrable through their ceramic portrayals and pictography.

In Kiva III at Kuaua, the earliest painting recognizable (Layer Q-59), shows an initiation into the katsina society, with the horned serpent, Kolowisi, as foremost character. The fill in the large circular kiva indicates its contemporaneity with the square Kiva III, as well as with the large rectangular kiva in the north plaza. This would indicate that the "Squares" and the "Rounds" had arrived at mutually compatible ideas ceremonially. Perhaps it was then that the "Rounds" were first initiated into the katsina organization.

If the plaster layers may be taken, at this stage, as indicators of annual renewal or the portrayal of set ceremonies, it appears that twelve years elapsed before Kiva III observed another occasion with mural painting, Layer P-46, which is unidentifiable. Apparently, however, four years later, a ceremonial was performed in which Layer O-43 depicts the activities of the warrior priests, introducing the character, 'Chakwena okya, and other katsinas who participate in a Rabbit Hunt of the gods. This was painted over with a single wash, after which Layer N-41 portrayed an initiation into the Newekwe society (mighty medicine men, warriors and priests) , which may be taken to indicate that the warrior organization was increasing its membership. Following this immediately is Layer M-40 with a hunting ceremony, introducing the Scalp dance and the Shumaikoli warriors, with initiation into the Bow priesthood. Rain is important to success-

611. Among the designs employed was the realistic figure of a horned lizard, on a polychrome bowl.

612. Insofar as Mrs. Lambert is aware.

ful hunting, and so the Rain priests have vital rites to perform also.

Three washes indicate another lapse of years, with Layer K-36 occurring on the fourth year, this portraying another quadrennial warrior cult observance, with arrow swallowing activities (*see* Pl. B-3), which were accompanied by ceremonies for cold rains and snow. This painting was covered with one wash, after which the Scalp dance bespeaks further warrior functions, with initiation, and rain making rites.

With Layer I-33 which follows immediately, there is again initiation into the katsina society. Plasterwise, it appears that this may be the 28th year since the application of Layer Q-59.

Layer H^1-32 introduces the game of Sholiwe, which is a warrior contest, with initiation into the Arrow division, along with which the Rain priests practice their rain making rites, implying an increasing unification of the societal components into a cultural entity.

With Layer H-31—which may include the portrayals of Layer H^1-32—there appears to be indication of dominance by the Rain priesthood. This, too, is a very sacred portrayal. In the Corn drama, women have a major part, suggesting that veneration of the Corn Mother, with close affinity of growing things with weather control and the moon, may have come to receive due attention, after the apparent warrior cult domination. There is also the suggestion of a war curing ceremony with the Bear people in prominence.

Four plain washes follow, then Layer G-26 brings the warrior priesthood and the Rain priests together in a great, sacred drama involving the Corn dance, the katsinas, kick-stick race, curing (?), and rain making. The fact that only two washes were then applied may indicate the prevalence of a drought, in light of the previous rainmaking events and the shorter interval between ceremonies. Layer F-23 celebrates the Summer solstice with emphases on rain making, and seeking the aid of the tortoises, "our other selves." Again, one wash indicates that the painting was simply covered over.

The uncertainty about Layer E breaks the continuity somewhat, but a rain ceremony is indicated by Layer E^2-21, and Layer E-19 gives another initiation of the katsina society, showing it as increasing its strength. Further integration of the warrior and the rain priesthoods is apparent in this celebration, for the Salimopiya, or seed gatherers, have parts commensurate with those of the deific representatives. This painting is covered with a single wash.

Depiction of an ancient ceremony follows on Layer D^1-17, suggesting a retreat in the interest of weather control during a period of drought. Perhaps the rain making rites were efficacious, for another interval of regular duration is indicated—three washes before Layer D-14 was painted. This opens the hunting season and combines sacred observances of all organizations, including corn grinding. It may be of significance that the informant Zna'ote for the first time used the term *Chiani,* in referring to the head of the medicine society involved in this curing.

After this there were two sterile washes, and then Layer C^1-12 deals with rain making again.

At this point it would appear that an event of consequence took place. Whether structural features received attention in Kiva III, or whether a new society or order was installed, something transpired giving rise to a Blessing ceremony, as depicted by the painting of Layer C-11, which ordinarily would have been made when a kiva was first put into use, or reconstructed—an entreaty for the favor of the gods. An uncertain layer follows, which may reflect repairs that had taken place.

Layer B-9, the next painting, gives still another initiation into the katsina society, with retreat of the Rain priests, again showing the union of participating organizations. And this is immediately followed by the final painted layer, A-8, which portrays the history myth, from the time of the emergence from the undermost world . . . which telling must have been sufficiently uniform as to be basic to each of the merged groups. Seven layers of plaster were applied after this, and the kiva was abandoned before another ceremonial could be recorded.

It is thus suggested that Kiva III was put into use by a people who came to Kuaua from former residence in the Mogollon culture province. Perhaps the increase of warlike conditions, which prevailed as outside peoples pushed into the Rio Grande and harassed the Pueblo settlements, made welcome a friendly group with organized war cult. Kuaua, like many another village of the period, found it necessary to take protective measures. It was not expedient to move to a mesa top far removed from the farms, and so a wall was built around the pueblo.[613] Here, doubtless, the aggregate population was subject to increasing influences coming out of the greater Southwestern areas.

It is possible that people coming from the Mogollon area (A.D. 1300-1400) and used to rectangular ceremonial chambers may have been too few at Kuaua to necessitate a kiva. Perhaps their initial need was met by a specialized intramural chamber, such as was arranged in the house block. The unsettled conditions of the period would have made subsequent construction of a kiva within the pueblo confines feasible, rather than an outlying one. When their strength was sufficient, they sank their rectangular chamber below the plaza level and carried on their covert religious rites within it, perhaps at first without embellishments on the walls.

Within about twenty-five years there were enough males to hold an initiation ceremony and induct them into the katsina society, with appropriate kiva rites and paintings. Some

fifteen years later, there was strength sufficient in the warrior priesthood and associated societies to recount a Rabbit Hunt of the gods, with the 'Chakwena okya, Koyemshi, War gods, and others impersonated by members of the katsina and clown organizations at Kuaua. From then on, increasing activities of the warrior cult in the ceremonies are manifest, for perhaps twelve years. This may have been due to peace and plenty with natural increase in population; and/or traits may have been received from the south. Then the rain priesthood seems to assert its authority. Henceforth, an increasing blend of activities appears to be indicated. The warrior cult has its prerogatives and the rain makers their formula of procedures. The former probably operated through a Bow priesthood, interlocking with the Newekwe, while the katsinas became more and more a part of the religious enactments of the Rain priests. For approximately twenty-five years this situation prevailed, or as long as Kiva III continued in use.

If the foregoing analysis be correct, the evidence of paintings in Kiva III, then, shows its construction, or reconstruction, by a group of immigrants, who used it for some twenty-five years without recording their folk history through mural depictions. It is possible that the latter came as a somewhat later stimulus from the southwest. It seems probable that the original inhabitants may have been accepting gradually all or part of such new traits as were introduced, and incorporating them into their rites and traditional practices, imposing, at the same time, certain of their precepts upon the newcomers. Corn was the most important item in the culture of each, with close affiliation with the earth in which it grew and with the moon which betold the seasons. Consequently, even if there may have been somewhat distinct ideas prevalent in the minds of these peoples, they were not of such import as to hinder their coalescing into one all embracing concept, in which the Corn-Earth-Moon Mother became

613. *Cf.* Kidder, 1958:128 (Pecos).

their major fetish. About this core, rain making, fertilization, growth, and thanksgiving ceremonies were centered, all of which provided limitless scope for the development of the katsinas—the earthly personators of the superhuman religious hierarchy and of the manifestations of the Sun in his various guises.

Inasmuch as these activities related primarily to the summer season, a certain body of religious officials seemingly came to have charge of those ceremonies that fell between the vernal and autumnal equinoxes. The winter season was favorable to the warriors and hunters, and it appears that the remainder of the year came under their charge. Under the guidance of their priestly leaders, they affected control of the winter rites which were concerned chiefly with hunts, guarding the people, and occasional warfare. Insofar as their rites pertained to agriculture, compatible enactments doubtless added embellishment to the ceremonies of the Rain priests.

With increased male population and sanctioned practices, the warrior cult and its correlative organizations came to dominate the scene, and readied itself for a ceremonial in which initiation into the katsina society included recitation of the folk history and painting cult personages and symbols on the kiva walls. This undoubtedly added to the strength and influence of the warrior cult, and to the increasing significance of the katsinas.

This situation continued and developed through another quarter-century. Then, perhaps due to increasing drought and difficulty of producing sufficient food for an expanding population, the rain priesthood grew stronger until the warrior cult and all correlative societies were working together, on a par, for the well-being and protection of their people. This symbiotic arrangement must have been general in the region, though not understood by Benavides, who, in 1598, referred to the peoples among whom his missionary efforts were effected (Keres, Tiwa, Piro, and Tano)

as all being divided into two factions, warriors and sorcerers (see page 15 herein).[614] Closely associated with the warriors were the hunters who had a society of their own, and the Newekwe clowns, whose leader was Paiyatuma—the personification of all three: great hunter, jester-musician, and medicine man preeminent.

After about one hundred years, with some seventy-five evidencing folk history painted on the walls, Kiva III was abandoned. From the ceramic record, this chamber was filled with refuse during the 1500's, which indicates that it was abandoned while other portions of the pueblo were still occupied. If my suggestion that the site was abandoned between 1573 and 1593 is correct, Kiva III must relate to a period around the turn of the 16th century, which would denote that the paintings that we have from Kiva III refer chiefly to the 1400's, extending into the 1500's.

From historical accounts of the attire of the peoples in the Rio Grande pueblos, with particular reference to their painted and colorfully embroidered garments, it is apparent that the individuals portrayed in the paintings in Kiva III were earlier and more simply clad than those who were seen by the earliest Spaniards, and thus before 1540. The practice of elaborately decking out the deific ones is ancient, and it is beyond doubt that the artists who depicted their folk history at Kuaua would have shown the finest garments and ornaments with their representations of the Divine. The Kuaua paintings are clear portrayals of folk history without exuberance. They would seem to represent a relatively unadorned concept, earlier than the Awatovi paintings and those at Pottery Mound. There

614. And he says further: "The warriors attempted to reduce all the people to their dominion and authority; and the sorcerers, by emulation and argument, persuaded them all that they were the ones who made the rain fall and the earth yield good crops, that they formed the clouds in the heavens . . . and such other things, at which the warriors jeered greatly. This gave rise to civil wars among them . . ."

is no evidence at Kuaua of any ceremonial "killings." From these observations, it would seem that the Kiva III representations at Kuaua fit best into the 1400's, and reflect cultural practices of that period.

There was evidence that an older set of paintings, even thicker in their entirety than those which we are discussing, formerly existed in Kiva III.[615] These may have pertained to the original construction. At any rate, they indicate that perhaps an equal or longer period of mural painting preceded the period herein described. On this basis, it seems plausible to add another seventy-five or one hundred years to the age of the kiva's use. This, then, would place the initiation of the square chamber and mural decoration within the late 1300's.

The paintings of Kiva VI seem somewhat later.

Toward the end of Kuaua's occupancy, if conditions were getting progressively harder, it is possible that family groups may have left from time to time. Some may have joined the Sandia Indians, and some the people of Santa Ana. Doubtless, others sought a better life elsewhere.

At Zuñi it is believed that their first esoteric fraternities were organized by the Divine Ones, or warrior sons of the Sun Father. These were four in number and were the priesthood of the priests (Shiwannakwe); its closely associated "little brothers," the Newekwe; the hunters (Saniyakikwe); and the Achiyakwe (Great Knife people—sword swallowers). It has been shown herein that each of these organizations existed at Kuaua, where they were highly developed, with formalized portrayals and ritualistic accompaniments indicative of a long pre-Kuaua history.

Perhaps it was more than fortuitous that we were able to take our quest for information regarding the murals to Zuñi. Not only is the Indian way of life better preserved and more adequately documented there than in the Rio Grande pueblos, where Spanish contacts were much more intense, but the folk history cites occurrences which merit consideration.

Cushing recounts the journeying of the ancient Zuñi as having included the building of homes along the Rio Grande. Prior to that they dwelt in the north, where some of their dwellings were "high among the cliffs, others in the plains."[616] This could well account for our original settlers at Kuaua. He also cites good evidence in support of certain of the Zuñi having come from southern and/or southwestern locations, some from the Piman territory. This and other known facts make it plain that the historic Zuñi are a composite resulting from past mingling of various sanguine and cultural groups.

Recent studies, such as that of A. Kimball Romney, suggest that the Zuñi are relatively late comers to their Southwestern location. His glottochronology studies[617] indicate that they may have reached here about eight hundred years ago, or about A.D. 1150. By that date, they could have been the bearers of highly advanced cultural concepts such as prevailed in the southern regions, as well as in the southern Anasazi (Chaco) domain, which was being abandoned at that time.

Whatever routes they followed and how long they may have tarried in the intervening expanses is as yet unknown, but a significant

615. Bliss, 1948:222. When the excavations were advanced it was found that the floor of the kiva "had been blackened with each new wall decoration." At a point near the floor level, a remnant of an older set of laminated layers of plaster was found which was slightly thicker than the accumulation of layers which was preserved. Mr. Bliss considered it possible that older layers of decorated plaster may thus have been destroyed, accounting for the fact that inner layers were not better preserved than the outer ones; rather, they had only occasional fragments of paintings on them.

616. Cushing, 1896:426; *see* Stevenson, 1904:278, 407; Roberts, 1931:8.

617. Reported in a paper read at the Salt Lake meeting of the Society for American Archaeology, 1 May 1959.

number reached and built pueblos in the region of modern Zuñi. Therefore, it appears wholly possible that people, upon leaving Kuaua, traveled to the west. Perhaps they initiated their orders among those whom they found dwelling along the way, thus passing their esoteric practices to the Keresans.[618] Surely they settled themselves in the Zuñi province, where their ceremonial inheritance persists to the present, following the primary concept: recognition of the sun as representing the omnipotent, with a comprehensible vehicle for dispensing the dogma of its leaders effected through the biological family group— the Sun Father and other celestial or temporal phenomena, Moon-Earth-Corn Mother, and twain offspring, the Morning and Evening stars, initially.

Mrs. Stevenson records that the Zuñi believe that one of their former locations was a place called Chipia, situated in or near Sandia mountain (east of Albuquerque, New Mexico), where the War gods dwelt (these bearing the same names among the Zuñi as among the Keresan peoples). She states that the Zuñi believe that the entrance to their Place of Mist (Shipapolima) [619] is located on a mountain near the pueblo of Cochiti, where the well known pair of Stone Lions guard the sacred spot, a long recognized shrine of the hunters.

Mr. Ladd gives the term, *Chipia yalanna,* as meaning "Sandia mountain." He states that the Shumakwe society is the only organization which has its place of origin there. He says, "Folklore of the Shumaakwe tells of a large hole, or cave, in the mountain, which is considered to be the home of Shumaikoli and

Siyapakwe, the two gods associated with the society. However, at Zuñi, there is a division within the society, separating it into two groups. Each performs distinct ceremonies and has different initiation rites."

In regard to Shipapulima, Ladd cites a Zuñi myth which tells of great healer-warriors of a place so called, but not as the place of origin. According to his information, the "place of origin for Zuñi is *Ha tli piakya,* which is considered to be in the vicinity of Witch Wells, Arizona."

We know that close contacts have been maintained between the Zuñi and present day Keresans, in that esoteric knowledge is interchanged, and that those of the west and those of the east participate in initiations, each of the other.[620] For another thing, the Zuñi culture hero, Poshaiyanki, is supposedly of eastern origin. The fact that all which we have revealed for Kuaua lived on at Zuñi, to some degree at least, gives testimony that here, then, in a peripheral culture area, we have ethnological evidence of a great and universal concept which prevailed among the indigenous peoples of the western hemisphere. This basic idea permitted of harmonious interrelationships, borrowings and exchanges, through the centuries, as one group advanced in certain respects, while others progressed along somewhat different lines.

After 1300, the influences from the south, from Mexico proper, were increasingly strong. They must have wrought significant changes in the simpler societies which until then obtained along the Rio Grande. To this day, evidences of these pre-Spanish influxes are manifold among the Tiwa, Tewa, and Towa, the Keresans, the Zuñi, and the Hopi.

618. *See* Dozier, 1958:23.

619. Cushing records it *(Shipapulima)* as being in Colorado; the concept was probably moved into the new area, as it is at Zuñi today. *Cf.* Eggan, 1950:214.

620. Ladd says that this practice is frowned on today.

CONCORDANCE OF PLASTER LAYERS

Note: In discussing the murals recovered from Kiva III at Kuaua, it will be remembered that the earliest layers of plaster had no paintings (*see* page 49). The left-hand column, below, indicates the consecutive order of the plaster layers from the original layer through the last. The 1st through the 26th layers were unpainted; thereafter, the numbers in the left column refer to the 27th layer, the 28th, and so on. The second column, following designations given in the laboratory, shows the corresponding order of the recorded layers of plaster from the first appearance of paintings through the final depictions. The third column gives page reference in the text to the respective layers.

Order	Laboratory Description	Page
	1st through 26th layers—no paintings found.	
27.	*Layer Q-59,* north wall, fig. 104 (copper layer); initiation into katsina society; Kolowisi; rain making, fertility.	49
28.	*Layer 58*—no paintings found.	50
29.	*Layer 57*—no paintings found.	50
30.	*Layer 56,* south wall (copper layer).	50
31	*Layer 55*—no paintings found	50
32.	*Layer 54,* north wall, heavily smoked.	50
33.	*Layer 53,* south wall, mica in black paint.	50
34.	*Layer 52*—no paintings found.	50
35.	*Layer 51,* south wall, evidence of red paint.	50
36.	*Layer 50*—no paintings found.	50
37.	*Layer 49*—no paintings found.	50
38.	*Layer 48,* north and south walls, evidence of yellow and black paint (copper layer).	50
39.	*Layer 47,* south wall, evidence of red paint.	50
40.	*Layer P-46,* north wall, figs. 102, 103; unidentifiable.	50
41.	*Layer 45,* south wall, evidence of black paint.	50
42.	*Layer 44,* south wall, evidence of red paint.	50
43.	*Layer O¹-44,* north wall, fig. 105 (red splotch).	50

Order	Laboratory Description	Page
44.	*Plate IX: Layer O-43,* north wall, figs. 100, 101; south wall, fig. 61—Rabbit Hunt with the Gods; ᵗChakwena'okya, Koyemshi, and other katsinas; ceremonial hunt, rain making, fertility.	50
45.	*Layer 42*—no paintings found.	55
46.	*Plate X: Layer N-41,* north wall, figs. 90-95; west wall, figs. 95-99—initiation into Newekwe society; return of lost Corn maidens, katsinas, ceremonies for winter moisture, etc.	55
47.	*Plate XI: Layer M-40,* north wall, figs. 89, 90; west wall, figs. 86-89—Shumaikoli, Scalp dance, hunting ceremony, rain making.	73
48.	*Layer 39*—no paintings found.	85
49.	*Layer L-38,* west wall, fig. 85 (a grey-black band on upper part of wall; lower part has no paintings).	85
50.	*Layer 37*—no paintings found.	86
51.	*Layer K-36,* north wall, fig. 85; west wall, fig. 83—winter ceremony, arrow-swallowing, rain making.	86
52.	*Layer J¹-35,* west wall, fig. 58 (splotch of green paint).	88
53.	*Plate XII: Layer J-34,* north wall, figs. 78, 79; west wall, figs. 80-82; south wall, figs. 56, 67—Kupishtaya, Squaw or Scalp dance and initiation into Scalp society, rain making.	88

* Laboratory note: "From all appearances this painting was put on over the top of another, as spots of
another color which have no connection with this painting show up over the entire figure." This may also account for the green splotch near Figure 66.

TEXT FIGURES

(Referring to personages and accoutrements in mural layers.)

APPENDIX PLATES

(*A* Plates illus. on pages 214, 216, 217.)

(*B* Plates illus. on pages 218, 219, 220.)

Plate No.

A-1. Early man with horns and tail, as shown on Galisteo dyke, near the pueblo ruin of Galisteo (*see* Layer D-14, p. 166).

A-2. Horned serpents at Pueblo Blanco, Galisteo (*see* Layer Q-59, p. 49; *cf.* Layer I-33, figs. 72-73, 75-76, 77, pp. 98-99).

A-3a. ᵗChakwena at Bocas de Senetu (*see* Layer O-43, fig. 61, p. 54).

A-3b. Komokatsi on Galisteo dyke (*cf.* Layer O-43, fig. 101, p. 51).

A-4. Shulawitsi or Fire god, Comanche Gap (*cf.* Layer G-26, fig. 49, p. 127).

A-5. Goose or Owa, San Cristobal ruin, Galisteo (*cf.* Layer N-41, fig. 94, p. 58).

A-6a. Mythical deer?, showing heart line, Galisteo dyke (*cf.* Layer G-26, fig. 63, p. 123).

A-6b. Mythical rabbit, San Cristobal (*cf.* Layer E-19, fig. 34, p. 158).

A-7. Newekwe Youth up tree, looking for lost Corn maidens, San Cristobal (*cf.* Layer N-41, fig. 92, pp. 56-57).

A-8a. Shiwanokia or Yellow Corn maiden, Cienaguilla.

A-8b. Ne'paiyatam'a exhibiting desire for the Corn maiden, Cienaguilla (*cf.* Layer D-14, fig. 23, p. 165).

A-9. Paiyatuma depiction at Comanche Gap (*cf.* Layer N-41, fig. 93, p. 56).

A-10. Caterpillars eating corn, San Cristobal (*see* pp. 68-69).

A-11. Kwelele or Kokokwin·e, Black god or god of Heat, San Cristobal (*see* Layer N-41, fig. 95, p. 58).

A-12. Growing corn, San Cristobal (*cf.* Layer N-41, fig. 99 and Layer H-31, pp. 56, 61).

A-13. Black Corn person, San Cristobal (*see* Layer N-41, fig. 99, pp. 56, 61).

Plate No.

B-1. Bison or "ground cow" (big lying star) as shown at San Cristobal and on Galisteo dyke (*cf.* Layer M-40, fig. 89, pp. 74-75).

B-2. Shumakoli or dragon flies above a rain altar, with clown above, Comanche Gap (*cf.* Layer M-40, fig. 86, pp. 74, 77).

B-3. Depictions of arrow-swallowing, Galisteo dyke and at Comanche Gap (*see* Layer K-36, figs. 83, 84, p. 86).

B-4. Bats, Bat people, Comanche Gap (*see* Layer H¹-32, fig. 69, p. 104).

B-5. Shulawitsi, Fire god, Comanche Gap (*cf.* Layers G-26, fig. 49 and H-31, fig. 66, pp. 113, 127).

B-6. Kupishtaya or Lightning Man, with feather tears, Comanche Gap (*cf.* Layer G-26, fig. 52, p. 137).

B-7. Pautiwa as Duck, Black Mesa, San Marcial (*see* Layer N-41, figs. 92, 93, p. 56).

B-8. Hehe'a masks, San Cristobal (*see* Layer D-14, pp. 160, 166).

B-9. Shumaikoli, Black Mesa, San Marcial (*cf.* Layer B-9, figs. 8, 10, pp. 173, 175).

B-10. Anthropomorphic personages (Shumaikoli?) at San Lazaro, Galisteo, and at Comanche Gap (*cf.* Layer B-9, figs. 8, 10, p. 173, 175).

B-11. Blue Horn or Sayaᵗhlia at San Cristobal and Comanche Gap (*cf.* Layer B-9, fig. 19, p. 171).

B-12. Pautiwa as Deer, Comanche Gap (*cf.* Layer G-26, fig. 63, p. 123).

B-13. Fish men at Comanche Gap (*cf.* Layer A-8, figs. 1, 2, pp. 181, 182).

APPENDIX

214

1   3a   3b   4

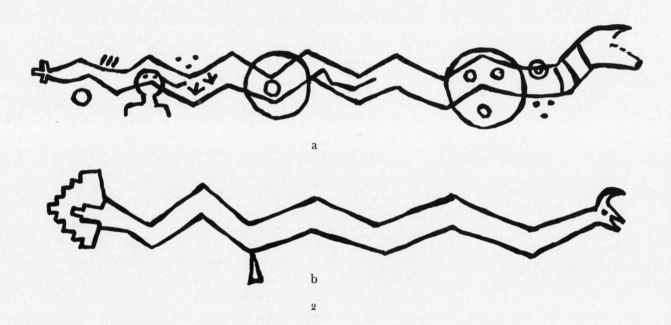

a

b

2

PLATE A. 1) Early man with horns and tail, as shown on Galisteo dyke, near the pueblo ruin of Galisteo (*see* Layer D-14, p. 166) . 2) Horned serpents at Pueblo Blanco, Galisteo (*see* Layer Q-59, p. 49; *cf.* I-33, Figs. 72-73, 75-76, 77) . 3a) ᵗChakwena at Bocas de Senetu [where Rio Santa Fe leaves the mesa, near La Bajada] (*see* Layer O-43, Fig. 61) . 3b) Komokatsi, Old Dance Woman—mother of the gods, at Galisteo dyke (*cf.* Layer O-43, Fig. 101) . 4) Shulawitsi or Fire god at Comanche Gap, south of Galisteo, N.M. (*cf.* Layer G-26, Fig. 49) .

ROCK CARVINGS, A RECORD OF FOLK HISTORY

by Agnes C. Sims

Petroglyphs are figures and symbols carved upon rocks.* They are commonly prehistoric, and are found in most parts of the world. They are particularly abundant in the Southwest.

Among the three thousand petroglyphs recorded by this writer within a forty mile radius of Santa Fe, New Mexico, a surprising number relate to the personages, ceremonies, and symbols found on the Kuaua murals. From this group, a few have been selected for reproduction because of their relationship to the kiva paintings. Most of these are from sites in the Galisteo basin. A few were found near Cienaga and Cienaguilla on the trail up La Bajada, used by the Rio Grande people over the centuries. Also shown are a few comparable carvings recorded from Mesa Canoa (Mesa Prieta), in the Rio Grande canyon, west of Velarde, New Mexico. Two are included from a site in Socorro county, from the middle Rio Grande area. Since there are undoubtedly many more to be discovered, it is hoped that this short appendix will serve as an incentive for further research in the comparison of carvings and murals.

In comparing the crude petroglyphs with the detailed figures painted in the murals, it must be borne in mind that the former are of necessity much simplified. A petroglyph is carved or pecked on the face of a rock by the tedious process of striking the surface repeatedly with a small hard stone held in the hand. Consequently, all but the most necessary detail is usually omitted, and the carving becomes a sort of shorthand symbol of the object represented. Perspective as we know it is not used at all, neither in the petroglyphs nor in the murals. Protuberant eyes or snouts become no more than circles or dots when a mask is shown full face. Feathers on headdresses often become simple straight lines, or are omitted altogether.

Nevertheless, the symbolism is exact enough for the trained eye to identify the same personage over and over again in sites many miles apart. We know that the Galisteo basin people, living in close proximity to the Rio Grande pueblos, must have been in almost daily contact with these and other neighbors. A busy exchange of trade and cultural features undoubtedly took place, including an interchange of customs and rituals.

The rock depictions show that the same ceremonial forms existed over wide expanses of the Southwest. Since many of the individual pictures denote certain recognizable complexes of traits— and in some instances detailed portrayals—it becomes clear that the rock carvings are important factors in the recording of folk history.

Petroglyphs and pictographs† are usually located near a habitation site, where they were made by the residents, for the most part; or they are found on places of vantage where guards were posted, or where group activities were performed. Their relation to such sites may be determined, frequently. Thus, the pictorial record affords a means of illustrating that the various Indian cultures included kindred practices and ceremonies, ritualistic paraphernalia and symbolism, important personages and deific beings.

Twenty-eight sizable ruins scattered through-

---

* *Petro* = stone, or rock; *glyph* = a carved figure.

† Mental images of people, lower life, celestial bodies, and things, represented by painting, drawing, carving, or other media.

out the Galisteo basin have been counted. In 1912, Nels C. Nelson, of the American Museum of Natural History, excavated eight of the pueblo sites, among them San Cristóbal, which was established around A.D. 1250, and persisted into historic times. More than two hundred petroglyphs have been recorded from the rocks above this ruin, alone, and in addition traces of many painted figures remain under the protection of overhanging cliffs.

San Cristóbal was abandoned some time between 1680 and 1692, possibly because of raids by Comanche and Teya Apache Indians, possibly as a result of the smallpox epidemic that ravaged neighboring pueblos at that time. Whatever the cause, in the latter year the Spanish General de Vargas found the inhabitants in a new homesite in Santa Cruz, north of Santa Fe, from which location they fled in 1696, after the killing of the Catholic priest who was assigned to that village.

It is after this that we hear of the arrival of these Tewa-speaking Indians in northeastern Arizona, where they settled among the Hopi. In 1716 they were made welcome by the Indians of Walpi, and became what we know as the Hano (Tano) people. Today, over two centuries later, some of the deities found carved at San Cristóbal and other Rio Grande sites, and painted at Kuaua, are still a part of the Hopi pantheon. The Hopi themselves say that these gods were brought from the east by the people from the Rio Grande region.

5   6a   6b

PL. A, cont'd. 5) Goose or Owa at San Cristobal ruin, Galisteo basin (*cf.* Layer N-41, Fig. 94). 6a) Mythical deer (?), showing heart line, on Galisteo dyke. 6b) Mythical rabbit at San Cristobal (*cf.* Layer E-19, Fig. 34).

PL. A, cont'd. 7) Newekwe Youth up tree, looking for lost Corn maidens who were hiding under the wings of Duck, San Cristobal (*cf.* Layer N-41, Fig. 92) . 8a) Shiwanokia or Yellow Corn maiden, Cienaguilla. 8b) Ne'paiyatama exhibiting desire for the Corn maiden, Cienaguilla (*cf.* Layer D-11, Fig. 23) . 9) Paiyatuma depiction at Comanche Gap (*cf.* Layer N-41, Fig. 93) . 10) Caterpillars eating corn, San Cristobal (*see* p. 68) . 11) Kwelele or Koko kwin·e, Black god or god of Heat, San Cristobal (*see* Layer N-41, Fig. 95) . 12) Growing corn, San Cristobal (*cf.* Layer N-41, Fig. 99 and Layer H-31) . 13) Black Corn person, San Cristobal (*see* Layer N-41, Fig. 99) .

PLATE B. 1) Bison or "ground cow," big lying star as shown at San Cristobal and on Galisteo dyke (*cf.* Layer M-40, Fig. 89) . 2) Shumaikoli or dragon flies above a rain altar, with clown above, Comanche Gap (*cf.* Layer M-40, Fig. 86) . 3) Depictions of arrow-swallowing on Galisteo dyke and at Comanche Gap (*see* Layer K-36, Figs. 83, 84) . 4) Bats, bat people, Comanche Gap (*see* Layer H¹-32, Fig. 69) .

PL. B, cont'd. 5) Shulawitsi, Fire god, Comanche Gap (*cf*. Layers G-26, Fig. 49 and H-31, Fig. 66). 6) Kupishtaya or Lightning man, with feather tears, Comanche Gap (*cf*. Layer G-26, Fig. 52). 7) Pautiwa as Duck, Black Mesa, San Marcial (*see* Layer N-41, Figs. 92, 93). 8) Hehe'a masks, San Cristobal (*see* Layer D-14, p. 166). 9) Shumaikoli, Black Mesa, San Marcial (*cf*. Layer B 9, Figs. 8, 10).

PL. B, cont'd. 10) Anthropomorphic personages (Shumaikoli?) at San Lazaro, Galisteo, and at Comanche Gap. 11) Blue Horn or Saya^thlia at San Cristobal and Comanche Gap (*cf*. Layer B-9, Fig. 19) . 12) Pautiwa as Deer, Comanche Gap (*cf*. Layer G-26, Fig. 63) . 13) Fish men at Comanche Gap (*cf*. Layer A-8, Figs. 1, 2).

REFERENCES CITED

Anderson, Frank G.
1955 "The Pueblo Kachina cult: a historical reconstruction," S.W. JOURN. ANTHRO., vol. 11, no. 4, pp. 404-418. Albuquerque.

Auttos tocantes; al Alsamiento de los Yndios de la Provincia de la Nueba Mexico. 123 folios. In Mexican archives. Complete transcripts and later documents were obtained by Herbert E. Bolton. *See* Guide to materials for the history of the United States in the principal archives of Mexico (Washington, 1913).

Ayer, Mrs. Edward Everett (Transl.)
1916 THE MEMORIAL OF FRAY ALONSO DE BENAVIDES, 1630. Chicago. Private printing. Annotated by F. W. Hodge and Charles F. Lummis.

Bandelier, Adolf F.
1890 "Final report of investigations among the
-92 Indians of the southwestern United States, carried on mainly in the years 1880-1885," 2 vols. PAPERS, Arch. Inst. of America. Amer. Series, IV. Cambridge.

Bartlett, Florence
1914 "The creation of the Zuñis," OLD SANTA FE, vol. II, no. 5, July, pp. 79-87. Santa Fe.

Beals, Ralph L.
1944 "Relations between Meso America and the Southwest," *El norte de Mexico y el sur de Estados Unidos,* 3ª REUNIÓN DE MESA REDONDA, pp. 245-252. Mexico.

Benavides, Fray Alonso de
1945 REVISED MEMORIAL OF 1634. With supplementary documents and annotations by F. W. Hodge, G. P. Hammond, and Agapito Rey. Albuquerque.

Benedict, Ruth
1930 "Eight stories from Acoma," JOURN. AMER. FOLK-LORE, vol. 43, p. 59.
1934 PATTERNS OF CULTURE. New York.
1935 ZUÑI MYTHOLOGY. 2 vols. New York.

Bliss, Wesley L.
1935 "Preservation of the murals of Kiva III, Kuaua pueblo ruins," Master's thesis, Univ. of New Mexico (unpublished). Albuquerque.
1936 "Problems of the Kuaua mural paintings," EL PALACIO, vol. XL, nos. 16-18, pp. 81-86. Santa Fe.
1948 "Preservation of the Kuaua mural paintings," AMER. ANTIQUITY, vol. XIII, no. 3, Jan., pp. 218-222. Menasha.

Bloom, Lansing B.
1940 "Who discovered New Mexico?" N. M. HIST. REVIEW, vol. XV, no. 2, April, pp. 101-132. Albuquerque.

Blumenschein, Helen G.
1958 "Further excavations and surveys in the Taos area," EL PALACIO, vol. 65, no. 3, pp. 107-111. Santa Fe.

Bolton, Herbert Eugene
1916 SPANISH EXPLORATION IN THE SOUTHWEST, 1542-1706. New York.

Bradfield, Wesley
1929 CAMERON CREEK VILLAGE (a site in the Mimbres area in Grant County, New Mexico). Santa Fe.

Brew, John O.
1944 "On the Pueblo IV and on the Katchina-Tlaloc relations," *El norte de Mexico y el sur de Estados Unidos,* 3ª REUNIÓN DE MESA REDONDA, pp. 241-245. Mexico.

1946 "Archaeology of Alkali Ridge, south-eastern Utah," PAPERS, Peabody Mus. of Amer. Arch. and Ethnol., Harvard Univ., vol. XXI. Cambridge.

Bunzel, Ruth L.
1932 "Introduction to Zuñi ceremonialism," 47th Ann. Rept., BUR. AMER. ETHNOLOGY, SMITHSONIAN INST., pp. 473-609; "Zuñi ritual poetry," pp. 615-835; "Zuñi katcinas: an analytical study," pp. 843-1086. Washington.

Carter, George F.
1945 "Plant geography and culture history in the American Southwest," VIKING FUND PUBS. IN ANTHRO., No. 5. New York.

Chapman, Kenneth M.
1927 "A feather symbol of the ancient Pueblos," EL PALACIO, vol. XXXIII, no. 21, Nov. 26, pp. 525-540. Santa Fe.

Chavez, Fray Angelico
1959 "Nuestra Señora de la Macana," N. M. HIST. REVIEW, vol. XXXIV, no. 2, April, pp. 81-91. Albuquerque.

Colton, Harold S.
1953 POTSHERDS: an introduction to the study of prehistoric Southwestern ceramics and their use in historical reconstruction. No. Ariz. Soc. of Sci. and Art, Mus. Northern Ariz. Bull. 25. Flagstaff.

Cosgrove, H. S., and C. B.
1932 "The Swarts ruin: a typical Mimbres site in southwestern New Mexico," PAPERS, Peabody Mus. of Amer. Arch. and Ethnol., Harvard Univ., vol. XV, no. 1. Report of the Mimbres valley exped., seasons of 1924-1927. Cambridge.

Cushing, Frank H.
1896 "Outlines of Zuñi creation myths," 13th Ann. Rept., BUR. AMER. ETHNOLOGY, SMITHSONIAN INST., pp. 325-447. Wash.
1901 ZUÑI FOLK TALES. G. P. Putnam's Sons. New York and London.
1920 "Zuñi breadstuff," INDIAN NOTES AND MONOGRAPHS, vol. VIII. Museum of the Amer. Indian, Heye Found. New York.

1941 MY ADVENTURES IN ZUÑI. Santa Fe. Republished from THE CENTURY MAGAZINE (1882-1883).

Cutler, Hugh, and L. Kaplan
1956 "Some plant remains from Montezuma Castle and nearby caves," PLATEAU, vol. 28, no. 4, April, pp. 98-100. Flagstaff.

Danson, Edward B.
1957 "An archeological survey of west central New Mexico and east central Arizona," PAPERS, Peabody Museum of Arch. and Ethnol., Harvard Univ., vol. XLIV, no. 1. Cambridge.

Dittert, Alfred E., Jr.
1959 "Culture change in the Cebolleta Mesa region, central western New Mexico," Doctoral dissertation, Univ. of Arizona (unpublished).

Douglass, A. E.
1935 "Dating Pueblo Bonito and other ruins of the Southwest," CONTRIBUTED TECHNICAL PAPERS, Pueblo Bonito series, no. 1. Wash. Natl. Geog. Soc., 56 pp. Washington.

Dozier, Edward P.
1954 "The Hopi-Tewa of Arizona," PUBS. IN AMER. ARCH. AND ETHNOL., vol. 44, no. 3, pp. 259-376. Univ. of Calif. Berkeley and Los Angeles.
1957 "Rio Grande Pueblo ceremonial patterns," N.M. QUARTERLY, vol. XXVII, nos. 1-2, Spring, Summer, pp. 27-34. Albuquerque.
1958 "Ethnological clues for the sources of Rio Grande Pueblo population," MIGRATIONS ... Soc. Sci. Bull. No. 27, pp. 21-29. Univ. of Arizona. Tucson.

Dutton, Bertha P. (Ed.)
1963 INDIANS OF THE SOUTHWEST. A pocket handbook. S.W. Assn. on Ind. Affairs. Santa Fe.

Eggan, Fred
1950 SOCIAL ORGANIZATION OF THE WESTERN PUEBLOS. Chicago.

Ellis, Florence Hawley

1952 "Jemez kiva magic and its relation to features of prehistoric kivas," S.W. JOURN. OF ANTHRO., vol. 8, no. 2, pp. 147-163. Albuquerque.

Espejo, Antonio de

1916 ACCOUNT OF THE JOURNEY TO THE PROVINCES AND SETTLEMENTS OF NEW MEXICO, 1583. English transl. by Herbert E. Bolton, 1916.

Espinosa, Gilberto (Transl.)

1933 HISTORY OF NEW MEXICO BY GASPAR PEREZ DE VILLAGRÁ. The Quivira Soc., IV. Los Angeles.

Ferdon, Edwin N., Jr.

1955 "A trial survey of Mexican-Southwestern architectural parallels," MONOG. NO. 21, School of Amer. Res. 31 pp. Santa Fe.

Fewkes, J. Walter

1891 "A few summer ceremonials at Zuñi pueblo," JOURN. AMER. ETHNOL. AND ARCH., vol. I. Boston and New York.

1892 "A few summer ceremonials at the Tusayan pueblos," JOURN. AMER. ETHNOL. AND ARCH., vol. II. Cambridge.

Fisher, Reginald G.

1931 "Santa Fe sub-quadrangle A," 2d report of the archaeological survey of the Pueblo plateau. BULL., UNIV. OF N.M., vol. 1, no. 1, July 1 (Survey series). Albuquerque.

Gladwin, Harold S.

1957 A HISTORY OF THE ANCIENT SOUTHWEST. Portland, Me.

Goldfrank, Esther S.

1927 "The social and ceremonial organization of Cochiti." MEM. AMER. ANTHRO. ASSN., No. 33. Lancaster.

Guernsey, Samuel J., and A. V. Kidder.

1921 "Basket-Maker caves of northeastern Arizona," PAPERS, Peabody Mus. of Amer. Arch. and Ethnol., Harvard Univ., vol. VIII, no. 2. Cambridge.

Gunn, John M.

1904 "History of the Queres pueblos of Laguna and Acoma," RECORDS OF THE PAST, vol. III, pt. X, Oct., pt. I, pp. 291-310; vol. III, pt. XI, Nov., pt. II, pp. 323-344.

Hackett, Charles Wilson

1911 "The Revolt of the Pueblo Indians of New Mexico in 1680," THE QUARTERLY, XV, Texas State Hist. Assn., Oct., pp. 93-147.

1915 "The location of the Tigua pueblos of Alameda, Puaray, and Sandia in 1680," OLD SANTA FE, vol. 2, no. 4, pp. 381-391. Santa Fe.

1937 HISTORICAL DOCUMENTS RELATING TO NEW MEXICO, NUEVA VIZCAYA, AND APPROACHES THERETO, TO 1773. 3 vols. Washington.

Hammond, George P., and Agapito Rey

1927 "The Gallegos relacion of the Rodriguez expedition to New Mexico" (1581-1582), N.M. HIST. REVIEW, vol. IV, Dec., pp. 1-58. Albuquerque.

1929 EXPEDITION INTO NEW MEXICO MADE BY ANTONIO DE ESPEJO, 1582-1583, as revealed in the journal of Diego Pérez de Luxán, a member of the party. The Quivira Soc., I. Los Angeles.

1940 NARRATIVES OF THE CORONADO EXPEDITION, 1540-1542. Coronado Cuarto Centennial Pubs., 1540-1940, vol. II. Albuquerque.

Haury, Emil W.

1936 "The Mogollon culture of southwestern New Mexico," MEDALLION PAPERS NO. XX. Gila Pueblo, Globe, Ariz.

1945 "The excavation of Los Muertos and neighboring ruins in the Salt river valley, southern Arizona," PAPERS, Peabody Mus. of Amer. Arch. and Ethnol., Harvard Univ., vol. XXIV, no. 1. Cambridge.

1958 "Evidence at Point of Pines for a prehistoric migration from northern Arizona," SOC. SCI. BULL. NO. 27, Univ. of Ariz., Migrations in New World culture history, July, pp. 1-6. Tucson.

Hawley, Florence

1950 "Big kivas, little kivas, and moiety houses," S.W. JOUR. OF ANTHRO., vol. 6, no. 3, pp. 286-300. Albuquerque.

Hewett, Edgar L., and Bertha P. Dutton
1945 THE PUEBLO INDIAN WORLD. Albuquerque.

Hibben, Frank C.
1955 "Excavations at Pottery Mound, New Mexico," AMER. ANTIQUITY, vol. XXI, no. 2, Oct., pp. 179-180. Salt Lake City.
1960 "Prehistoric paintings, Pottery Mound," ARCHAEOLOGY, vol. 13, no. 4, Winter, pp. 267-275. New York.

Hodge, Frederick W. (Ed.)
1907 "The narrative of the expedition of Coronado by Pedro de Castañeda," *in* ORIGINAL NARRATIVES OF EARLY AMERICAN HISTORY: SPANISH EXPLORATIONS IN THE SOUTHERN UNITED STATES, 1528-1543. New York.

Hodge, F. W., G. P. Hammond, and Agapito Rey
1945 REVISED MEMORIAL OF 1634 [Benavides]. Albuquerque.

Hough, Walter
1914 "Culture of the ancient Pueblos of the upper Gila river region, New Mexico and Arizona, 2d Museum-Gates expedition," U.S. NATL. MUS. BULL. 87. Washington.

Hull, Dorothy
1916 "Castaño de Sosa's expedition to New Mexico in 1590," OLD SANTA FE, vol. III no. 12, Oct., pp. 307-332. Santa Fe.

Jones, Volney H., and Robert L. Fonner
1954 Appendix C (Plant Materials) *in* Morris and Burgh, 1954.

Judd, Neil M.
1926 "Archaeological observations north of the Rio Colorado," Bull. 82, BUR. AMER. ETHNOL., SMITHSONIAN INST. Washington.
1954 "The material culture of Pueblo Bonito," SMITHSONIAN MISC. COLLS., vol. 24. Washington.

Kidder, Alfred V.
1958 "Pecos, New Mexico: archaeological notes," PAPERS, Robt. S. Peabody Foundation for arch. Andover.

Kidder, Alfred V., and S. J. Guernsey
1919 "Archaeological explorations in northeastern Arizona," Bull. 65, BUR. AMER. ETHNOL., SMITHSONIAN INST. Washington.

Kidder, Alfred V., and Anna Shepard
1936 THE POTTERY OF PECOS, vol. II. New Haven.

Kirk, Ruth F.
1943 "Introduction to Zuñi fetishism," PAPERS, School Amer. Res. Santa Fe. Reprinted from EL PALACIO, vol. L, nos. 6-10, June-Oct. 64 pp.
1950 "Buffalo hunting fetish jar," EL PALACIO, vol. 57, no. 5, May, pp. 131-141.

Kroeber, A. L.
1916 "Thoughts on Zuñi religion," HOLMES ANNIV. VOL. Washington.
1939 "Cultural and natural areas of native North America," PUBS. IN AMER. ARCH. AND ETHNOL., vol. 38, Univ. of Calif. Berkeley.

Lehmer, Donald J.
1948 "The Jornada branch of the Mogollon," BULL., vol. XIX, no. 2, Univ. of Ariz. April. 90 pp.

LeViness, W. Thetford
1959 "Pottery Mound murals," NEW MEXICO MAGAZINE, March, pp. 22-23, 52. Albuquerque.

Luhrs, D. L., and A. G. Ely
1939 "Burial customs at Kuaua," EL PALACIO, vol. XLVI, no. 2, Feb., pp. 27-32.

Lummis, Charles F.
1910 PUEBLO INDIAN FOLK STORIES. New York.
1916 *In* Ayer, 1916 (note 41 on fishes, p. 261).

Lynch, Cyprian J.
1954 BENAVIDES' MEMORIAL OF 1630 (Transl. by Peter P. Forrestal with hist. introd. by Lynch). Washington.

Mangelsdorf, P. C., E. S. Barghoorn, W. C. Galinat, and M. Wolfe
1954 News release of 28 Feb., Harvard Univ. News Office. Cambridge.

Mangelsdorf, P. C., and C. E. Smith, Jr.
1949 "New archaeological evidence on evolution in maize," BOTANICAL MUS. LEAFLETS, Harvard Univ., vol. 18, no. 8, pp. 213-247. Cambridge.

Martin, Paul S.

1939 "Modified Basket Maker sites in the Ack-men-Lowry area, southwestern Colorado, 1938," ANTHRO. SER., vol. 23, no. 3, Field Mus. Natural Hist. 27 June. Chicago.

1959a DIGGING INTO HISTORY: A brief account of fifteen years of archaeological work in New Mexico. POPULAR SER., Chicago Natural Hist. Mus. (Anthropology, No. 38). 150 pp. Chicago.

1959b "Katchina cult traced back to A.D. 1250," BULL., Chicago Natural Hist. Mus. vol. 30, no. 9, Sept., pp. 7-8. Chicago.

Martin, Paul S., C. Lloyd, and A. Spoehr

1938 "Archaeological work in the Ackmen-Lowry area, southwestern Colorado, 1937," ANTHRO. SER., vol. 23, no. 2, Field Mus. Natural Hist. Chicago.

Martin, Paul, and John B. Rinaldo

1950 "Sites of the Reserve phase, Pine Lawn valley, western New Mexico," FIELDIANA: ANTHRO., vol. 38, no. 3, Oct. 18. Chicago.

Martin, Paul S., John B. Rinaldo, and Eloise R. Barter

1957 "Late Mogollon communities. Four sites of the Tularosa phase, western New Mexico," FIELDIANA: ANTHRO., vol. 49, no. 1. Chicago.

Martin, Paul S., John B. Rinaldo, and Elaine Bluhm

1954 "Caves of the Reserve area," FIELDIANA: ANTHRO., vol. 42, June 11. Chicago.

Martin, Paul S., John B. Rinaldo, Elaine A. Bluhm, and H. C. Cutler

1956 "Higgins Flat pueblo, western New Mexico," FIELDIANA: ANTHRO., vol. 45, April 16. Chicago.

Martin, Paul S., and J. B. Rinaldo, Elaine Bluhm, H. C. Cutler and Roger Grange, Jr.

1952 "Mogollon cultural continuity and change. The stratigraphic analysis of Tularosa and Cordova caves," FIELDIANA: ANTHRO., vol. 40, Nov. 17. Chicago.

Mecham, J. Lloyd

1926 "The second Spanish expedition to New Mexico," N.M. HIST. REVIEW, I, July, pp. 265-291. Albuquerque.

Mera, Harry P.

1933 "A proposed revision of the Rio Grande glaze paint sequence," LAB. OF ANTHRO., Arch. Survey, Tech. Ser., Bull. no. 5. Santa Fe.

Morris, Earl H.

1939 "Archaeological studies in the La Plata district, southwestern Colorado and northwestern New Mexico," PUB. NO. 519, CARNEGIE INST. WASH.

Morris, Earl H., and Robert F. Burgh

1954 "Basket Maker II sites near Durango, Colorado," PUB. 604, CARNEGIE INST. WASH.

Morss, Noel

1954 "Clay figurines of the American Southwest," PAPERS, Peabody Mus. of Amer. Arch. and Ethnol., Harvard Univ., vol. XLIX, no. 1. Cambridge.

Nesbitt, Paul H.

1931 "The ancient Mimbreños," based on investigations at the Mattocks ruin, Mimbres valley, New Mexico. LOGAN MUS. BULL., no. 4. Beloit College, Beloit, Wis. 102 pp.

Nusbaum, Jesse L., A. V. Kidder, and S. J. Guernsey

1922 "Basket-Maker cave in Kane county, Utah," INDIAN NOTES AND MONOG., No. 29, Mus. of Amer. Indian. Heye Found. New York.

O'Bryan, Deric

1950 "Excavations in Mesa Verde National Park, 1947-1948," MEDALLION PAPERS No. XXXIX, June. 111 pp. Gila Pueblo. Globe, Ariz.

Parsons, Elsie C.

1916 "The Zuñi Mólawia," JOUR. AMER. FOLK-LORE, vol. XXIX, no. CXIII, July-Sept., pp. 392-399.

1920 "Notes on ceremonialism at Laguna," ANTHRO. PAPERS, AMER. MUS. NATURAL HIST., vol. XIX, pt. IV, pp. 87-129.

1922 "Winter and summer dance series in Zuñi in 1918," Univ. of Calif. PUBLICATIONS IN AMER. ARCH. AND ETHNOL., vol. 17, no. 3, pp. 171-216.

1924 "The scalp ceremonial of Zuñi," Mem. Amer. Anthro. Assn., vol. XXXI. Menasha.

1930 "Zuñi tales," Journ. Amer. Folk-Lore, vol. 43, no. 167, Jan.-Mar., pp. 1-51.

1939 Pueblo Indian Religion. 2 vols. Chicago.

Peckham, Stewart

1958 "Hillside pueblo: early masonry architecture in the Reserve area, New Mexico," El Palacio, vol. 65, no. 3, June, pp. 81-94.

Reagan, Albert B.

1930 "Some notes on the archaeology of Ashley and Dry Fork valleys in northeastern Utah," ms. with illus. on file at Museum of New Mexico. Santa Fe.

Reed, Erik K.

1949 "The possible origins of San Juan orange-ware," Region III Anthro. Interpretation Circular No. Two. May, pp. 5-7.

1950 "Eastern-central Arizona archaeology in relation to the Western Pueblos," S.W. Journ. of Anthro., vol. 6, no. 2, Summer, pp. 120-136.

Reiter, Paul

1946 "Form and function in some prehistoric ceremonial structures in the Southwest," Doctoral dissertation, Harvard Univ. (unpublished).

Rinaldo, John B.

1959 "Foote Canyon Pueblo, eastern Arizona," Fieldiana: Anthro., vol. 49, no. 2, Feb. 20, pp. 149-285. Chicago.

Roberts, Frank H. H., Jr.

1929 "Shabik'eshchee village, a late Basket Maker site in the Chaco Canyon, New Mexico," Bull. 92, Bur. Amer. Ethnol., Smithsonian Inst. Washington.

1931 "The ruins at Kiatuthlanna, eastern Arizona," Bull. 100, Bur. Amer. Ethnol., Smithsonian Inst. Washington.

1932 "The village of the great kivas on the Zuñi reservation, New Mexico," Bull. 111, Bur. Amer. Ethnol., Smithsonian Inst. Washington.

1935 "A survey of Southwestern archaeology," Amer. Anthro., vol. 37, no. 1, Jan.-March. Reprint. 33 pp.

Rodeck, Hugo G.

1954 Appendix D in Morris and Burgh, 1954.

Sauer, Carl O.

1937 "The discovery of New Mexico reconsidered," N.M. Hist. Review, vol. XII, no. 3, July, pp. 270-287. Albuquerque.

Scholes, France V.

1935 "The first decade of the inquisition in New Mexico," in Hackett, 1937:4.

1937a "Notes on Sandia and Puaray," El Palacio, vol. XLII, nos. 10-12, Mar., pp. 57-59.

1937b "Troublous times in New Mexico, 1659-1670," N.M. Hist. Review, vol. XII, no. 4, Oct. pp. 380-451. Albuquerque.

Schroeder, Albert H.

1956 "Comments on 'A trial survey of Mexican-Southwestern architectural parallels,'" El Palacio, vol. 63, nos. 9-10, Sept-Oct., pp. 299-308.

Shepard, Anna O.

1942 "Rio Grande glaze paint ware," Contribs. to Amer. Anthro. and Hist., Carnegie Inst. Wash., No. 39, March. Preprinted from C. I. W. Pub. 528, pp. 129-262.

1953 Appendix I (Notes on color and paste composition) in Wendorf, Fred: Archaeological Studies in the Petrified Forest National Monument, Arizona. Mus. Northern Arizona, Bull. 27. Flagstaff.

Sims, Agnes C.

1949 San Cristobal Petroglyphs. Santa Fe.

Sinclair, John L.

1951 "The story of the pueblo of Kuaua," El Palacio, vol. 58, no. 7. Reprinted as Paper No. 45, School of Amer. Research. 11 pp.

Smiley, Terah L.

1952 "Four late prehistoric kivas at Point of Pines, Arizona," Bull. vol. 23, no. 3, Univ. of Ariz. (Soc. Sci. Bull. no. 21).

Smiley, Terah L., S. A. Stubbs, and Bryant Bannister

1953 "A foundation for the dating of some late archaeological sites in the Rio Grande area, New Mexico: based on studies in tree-ring methods and pottery analyses," BULL. Univ. of Ariz., Lab. of tree-ring research bull., no. 6 (vol. XXIV, no. 3), July. Tucson.

Smith, Watson
  1952 "Kiva mural decorations at Awatovi and Kawaika-a, with a survey of other wall paintings in the Pueblo Southwest," PAPERS, Peabody Mus. of Amer. Arch. and Ethnol., Harvard Univ., vol. XXXVII. Reports of the Awatovi exped. Report No. 5. Cambridge.

Stevenson, Matilda Coxe (or Tilly E.)
  1887 "The religious life of the Zuñi child," 5th Ann. Rept., BUR. AMER. ETHNOL., SMITHSONIAN INST., pp. 539-555. Wash.
  1894 "The Sia," 11th Ann. Rept., BUR. AMER. ETHNOL., SMITHSONIAN INST. Washington.
  1904 "The Zuñi Indians," 23d Ann. Rept., BUR. AMER. ETHNOL., SMITHSONIAN INST., 608 pp. Washington.
  1915 "Ethnobotany of the Zuñi Indians," 13th Ann. Rept., BUR. AMER. ETHNOL., SMITHSONIAN INST., pp. 35-100. Washington.

Steward, Julian H.
  1936 "Pueblo material culture in western Utah," BULL., UNIV. OF N.M., vol. 1, no. 3 (Anthro. series), June, 63 pp.

Stirling, Matthew W.
  1942 "Origin myth of Acoma and other records," Bull. 135, BUR. AMER. ETHNOL., SMITHSONIAN INST. 114 pp. Washington.

Stubbs, Stanley A.
  1953 "A brief summary of northern Rio Grande archaeology," *in* Smiley, Stubbs, and Bannister.

Stubbs, Stanley A., and W. S. Stallings, Jr.
  1953 "The excavation of Pindi pueblo, New Mexico," MONOG. No. 18, School Amer. Res. and Lab. of Anthro. Santa Fe.

Thompson, J. Eric S.
  1939 "The moon goddess in Middle America," CONTRIBS. TO AMER. ANTHRO. AND HIST., CARNEGIE INST., WASH., No. 29, June, pp. 121-173.

Tichy, Marjorie Ferguson
  1938 "The kivas of Paako and Kuaua," N.M. ANTHROPOLOGIST, vol. II, nos. 4-5, Mar.-June, pp. 71-80. Albuquerque.

Villagrá, Gaspar Pérez de
  1933 HISTORY OF NEW MEXICO (1st pub. in 1610). Transl. by Gilberto Espinosa. The Quivira Soc. Los Angeles.

Vivian, Gordon
  1932 "A re-study of the province of Tiguex," Master's thesis, Univ. of N.M. (unpublished). Albuquerque.
  1934 "The excavation of Bandelier's Puaray," EL PALACIO, vol. XXXVII, nos. 19-20, Nov. 7-14, pp. 153-159.

Wendorf, Fred, and D. J. Lehmer
  1956 "Archaeology of the Wingate products line," *in* PIPELINE ARCHAEOLOGY, pp. 158-195. Santa Fe and Flagstaff.

Wendorf, Fred, and Erik K. Reed
  1955 "An alternative reconstruction of northern Rio Grande prehistory," EL PALACIO, vol. 62, nos. 5-6, May-June, pp. 131-165.

Wheat, Joe Ben
  1955 "Mogollon culture prior to A.D. 1000," AMER. ANTIQUITY, vol. XX, no. 4, pt. 2, April. 233 pp.

White, Leslie A.
  1930 "A comparative study of Keresan medicine societies," PROCEEDINGS, 23d Internatl. Cong. Americanists, pp. 604-619, New York.
  1932 "The Acoma Indians," 47th Ann. Rept., BUR. AMER. ETHNOL., SMITHSONIAN INST., pp. 23-190. Washington.
  1942 "The pueblo of Santa Ana," AMER. ANTHRO., vol. 44, no. 4, pt. 2, Oct.-Dec. No. 60 of the titles in the MEMOIR series of the Amer. Anthro. Assn. 353 pp. Menasha.
  1944 "A ceremonial vocabulary among the Pueblos," INTERNATL. JOURN. OF LINGUISTICS, vol. 10, no. 4, Oct., pp. 161-167.

Winship, George Parker
  1896 "The Coronado expedition, 1540-1542," 14th Ann. Rept., BUR. AMER. ETHNOL., SMITHSONIAN INST. Washington.

Woodbury, Richard B.
  1955 "Preliminary report on archaeological investigations at El Morro National Monument, New Mexico, during the summer of 1955," Mimeographed report. 2 pp.
  1956a "Zuñi prehistory and El Morro National Monument," SOUTHWESTERN LORE, vol. XXI, no. 4, pp. 56-60, March. Boulder.
  1956b "The antecedents of Zuñi culture," TRANSACTIONS, N.Y. Academy of Sci., Ser. II, vol. 18, no. 6, April, pp. 557-563.

Wormington, H. M.
  1955 "A reappraisal of the Fremont culture," PROCEEDINGS, No. One, Denver Mus. of Natural Hist. Denver.

Yarnell, Richard A.
  1959 " Prehistoric Pueblo use of Datura," EL PALACIO, vol. 66, no. 5, Oct., pp. 176-179.

INDEX AND GLOSSARY